⊲ COYOTE VALLEY ⊳

COYOTE VALLEY

Deep History in the High Rockies

Thomas G. Andrews

Harvard University Press

Cambridge, Massachusetts
London, England
2015

Second printing

Library of Congress Cataloging-in-Publication Data is available
from the Library of Congress.

ISBN 978-0-674-08857-3 (hardcover)

For Santiago and Fiona,
To the moon and back—and then some

And to Amy,
For her fearless love

⊲ CONTENTS ⊳

List of Illustrations .... *ix*

Map: Rocky Mountain National Park and the North American West .... *xi*

INTRODUCTION: Coyote Creek *1*

PART ONE: NATIVE PEOPLES

1. EMERGENCE *19*
2. ENDURANCE *34*
3. DISPOSSESSION *63*

PART TWO: SETTLERS

4. MINERS *97*
5. FARMERS *117*
6. CONSERVATIONISTS *138*

PART THREE: FEDS

7. COMMON GROUND *161*
8. RESTORING THE VALLEY PRIMEVAL.................... *185*
9. THE TRAGEDY OF THE WILLOWS...................... *216*

CONCLUSION: Seeing the Forest *and* the Trees *249*

Notes *259*
Acknowledgments *321*
Index *325*

◁ ILLUSTRATIONS ▷

FIGURES

The Toll Expedition 5

Winter scene 9

A glacial valley. 21

"Scenes in the Life of a Trapper". 48

"Colorado—the Late Ute Outbreak and Massacre
at the White River Agency". 64

Wanzits, or Antelope. 74

A Nuche delegation to Denver. 80

"Reducing the U.S. Army Again" 90

Lulu City 108

The Grand Ditch. 123

"Harbison Ranch: Plowing in the Meadow" 131

The Harbison family 135

Enos Mills 143

Dedication of Rocky Mountain National Park 155

Early tourists at Lake Irene 165

"Planting Fish in Glacier Creek" 169

"Fall River Road at Big Drift" 174

"Fall River Road: Clearing for New Road" 176

The Grand Ditch "scar" 191

Dude ranch visions 196

Holzwarth Living History Museum 207

"Fishing in the Beaver Dams of the Colorado River" 219

Bull elk, Kawuneeche Valley *238*
Bull moose, Kawuneeche Valley *241*
Mountain pine beetle and elk herd. *246*

MAPS

The Ice Age Valley *24*
Settlement landscapes. *120*
Park expansion, 1930–2013. . . . . *202*

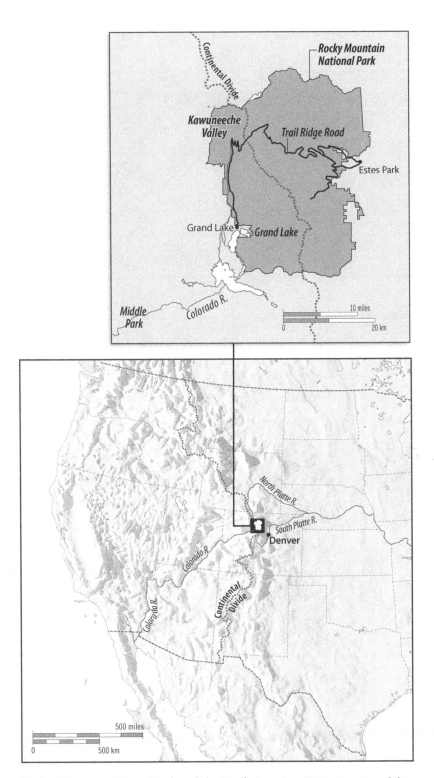

Rocky Mountain National Park and the North American West. Courtesy of the National Park Service.

INTRODUCTION

COYOTE CREEK

WHAT IF you were to take one small stretch of soil and explore the story of people and nature there over as long a span of time as the scientific and historical evidence would allow? What could you learn about that place—and what, in turn, could that tiny corner of the earth reveal about broader patterns of human-environment interaction across time and space? From Henry David Thoreau and Aldo Leopold to William Cronon and Terry Tempest Williams, this exercise of attending closely to little pieces of the planet has propelled nature writers, environmental historians, and kindred spirits to produce microhistories of place that fulfill William Blake's injunction "to see a world in a grain of sand."[1]

In recent decades, though, scholars have increasingly treated small-scale investigations as passé, implicitly rebuking them as too parochial to shed much light on the urgent global predicaments confronting humanity. Historians in particular have dramatically expanded the scales on which their analyses unfold. Big history, transnational history, global history, and planetary history: since the 1980s, these buzzwords and the trends they signify have reshaped our understanding of the past by exposing the ligatures and interconnections that bind seemingly disparate peoples, places, and processes into larger patterns of change. Given the stunning insights that these broader-scale approaches are generating, it may seem quaint to devote an entire book to a tiny, seemingly insignificant speck of the globe. I want to convince you, however, that attending to small places remains not just worthwhile, but more important than ever as we contemplate the vexed relationships between humanity and the natural systems on which our lives continue to depend in this age of escalating environmental anxiety.[2]

Coyote Valley relates the story of people, nature, and history in one little-known place from its emergence in the last Ice Age—an epoch geologists have long known as the Pleistocene—through the Anthropocene—the current era in which skyrocketing concentrations of greenhouse gases in the earth's atmosphere are posing potentially catastrophic threats to our planet's climate, ecology, and human populations. The central character throughout these pages is not a person or group of people, nor is it an institution, an idea, or a process. Instead, this book tells the tale of the Kawuneeche Valley, a small, high trough perched just below the source of the Colorado River on the western side of Rocky Mountain National Park, about a hundred-mile drive northwest of Denver.[3]

For millennia, this wondrous but formidable stretch of the Colorado high country has figured as a place of vital importance to small and mostly transitory groups of people who have left few archaeological or historical vestiges. But there is more to this place than meets the eye, as the stories behind two of the many names this part of the Rockies has borne over the eons suggest. In 1921, the U.S. Congress bestowed a new moniker on the magisterial stream that coalesces at the valley's head: the Colorado River. When American explorers and settlers first penetrated the Rocky Mountains in the early 1800s, they borrowed place names from the French-speaking fur trappers who preceded them. The newcomers called the lake at the Kawuneeche's southern edge Grand Lake, after the French *grand* or "big." Thereafter, the stream that flowed out of the lake and beat a swooping path toward the Gulf of California became known as the Grand River. When miners and homesteaders first began to push northward from Grand Lake into the valley above, they christened the stream that snaked along its floor the North Fork of the Grand.[4]

Colorado representative Edward Taylor revolutionized the way his fellow Americans thought about how water coursed—and thus how power flowed—in the arid interior of the western United States by convincing his colleagues in Washington to forever banish the Grand River from the American map and extend the Colorado River all the way to the head of the Kawuneeche Valley. For many decades, American cartographers had insisted that the Colorado River started in eastern Utah, where the waters of the Green and Grand Rivers joined forces. Taylor's legislative triumph, though, suddenly extended the Colorado River several hundred miles eastward. Much to the dismay of many Utahns and Wyomingites, the lifeline of the Southwest thereafter originated not in the canyon country of the Colorado Plateau, but instead at the head of the stream hitherto known as the North Fork of the Grand. Today, you can still trace the source of the mighty, mightily troubled Colorado River to its burbling headwaters by driving and hiking into Colorado's Rocky Mountain National Park, which was established in 1915 when President Woodrow Wilson signed into law a bill cosponsored by Edward Taylor.[5]

At the dawn of the twenty-first century, the Colorado's descent from the Kawuneeche through the canyons of the Colorado Plateau and across the southwestern deserts to the Gulf of California might seem to offer a perfect metaphor for the ecological fall from grace resulting from the American conquest of the arid West. Environmentalists, scientists, rafters, writers, and many others have spent more than half a century lamenting the once-wild Colorado's domestication and defilement. At first glance, this narrative of environmental decline appears to map remarkably well on to the river's actual course. At its source, the Colorado rages strong and unchecked through the Kawuneeche, a valley that strikes most visitors as a timeless wilderness: a place unsullied by human hands and maintained in its primeval state by the U.S. National Park Service. After reaching Grand Lake, though, the Colorado begins to veer downhill rapidly—figuratively as well as literally. The river, many critics contend, has been reduced to a mere instrument of human will. Dammed up, siphoned off, and frittered into oblivion, this wellspring of the runaway development that has enveloped so much of the western landscape seems to embody a tragic story in which we squandered the land's Edenic promise.[6]

Likening the course of American environmental history to the Colorado's descent from the Rockies to the sea, though, is neither accurate nor helpful. Even at its headwaters, the Colorado River is no paragon of the pristine. The Kawuneeche may strike present-day visitors as a redoubt of wild nature, but for at least the last thirteen millennia, the valley has been an inextricably peopled landscape. Instead of retelling a just-so tale of ecological ruination, then, *Coyote Valley* instead tells the story of a place that has more contradictory—and also more useful and mysterious—lessons to teach us about wilderness, civilization, and the course of American environmental history.[7]

⊠ ⊠ ⊠

Seven years before Edward Taylor succeeded at turning the North Fork of the Grand into the Colorado River headwaters, another project to rename the Kawuneeche was coming to fruition. In 1914, Oliver Toll of the Colorado Mountain Club (CMC), a recently formed organization that combined the social pursuit of mountaineering with active lobbying to preserve the West's high-country landscapes, sought to gather Arapaho place names from three residents of Wyoming's Wind River Reservation: Gun Griswold, a seventy-three-year-old tribal judge; Sherman Sage, a sixty-two-year-old chief of the reservation's police force; and Tom Crispin, the thirty-eight-year-old métis interpreter for the group. Toll and his fellow club members were intent on convincing the federal government to use Arapaho names to grace the proposed national park that the CMC, Edward Taylor, and their allies were working to create along the Continental Divide in north-central Colorado. The club's co-founder and president, James Grafton Rogers, despised the prosaic names American settlers had slapped on these scenic landscapes. And so Rogers, Toll, and other CMC leaders took it upon themselves to supplant unimaginative designations—Green Mountain, Grand River—with euphonious Native American toponyms—Onahu, Tonahutu—that would better "reflect the romance and adventure" of Colorado's past. Soon after the national park campaign prevailed in 1915, the U.S. Geological Survey sanctioned the club's suggestion that dozens of mountains, creeks, lakes, and valleys in and around Rocky Mountain National Park be renamed with Arapaho toponyms that Oliver Toll had collected from Griswold, Sage, and Crispin.[8]

Kawuneeche, a simplified transliteration of the Arapaho *Kooh'ohwuuniicii-hehe*, was just the kind of name to send Toll, Rogers, and other scenic preservationists into paroxysms of delight. Meaning "Coyote Creek," it remains an especially apt name for this corner of the high Rockies. Coyotes have inhabited the valley for millennia, but Kawuneeche also holds more metaphorical meanings. In Arapaho oral literature, after all, it was Coyote who lit the people's fires, shepherded them safely home when they got lost, and fed them when they were

Sherman Sage and Gun Griswold, Arapaho participants in the Toll Expedition, pose with the Cairns family of Grand Lake, Colorado, 1914. MSF Neg. 3691, Ramaley Collection, NPS photo, courtesy of the National Park Service.

hungry. As two authorities on Arapaho language and culture explain, the Coyote of Arapaho tradition was an inextricably "helpful figure."[9]

The leaders of the Colorado Mountain Club cared little that the valley they successfully renamed the Kawuneeche lay beyond the westernmost fringe of the Arapaho homelands. From 1400 CE at the very latest (and quite possibly centuries or even millennia before) until the late 1870s, that stretch of the Colorado Rockies was seasonally inhabited by band-based groups known to the Spanish as Yutas; to most Americans as Utahs, Eutaws, or Utes; and to themselves simply as the Nuche, which translates as "the People." It is worth pondering whether the Arapaho might have borrowed the name Coyote Creek from the Nuche, longtime rivals with whom they had battled several times on that very ground. The Arapahos are known to have captured more than a few Nuche as tensions between the two peoples escalated in the mid-nineteenth century, so perhaps Oliver Toll's informants were following Nuche usage when they described the stream running north of Grand Lake as Coyote Creek.[10]

Whether the Arapahos borrowed and translated the Nuche name for this place or coined their own designation, the Coyote of Nuche lore does share at least one crucial quality with his doppelganger in Arapaho tradition: a determination to aid human beings. Coyote gave the People the all-important gift of fire. Even today, the Northern Utes remember him as the one "who gave life to the Indians." Perhaps the Nuche associated Coyote with the stream that gathers where the Front Range meets the Never Summer Mountains (another Arapaho place name collected by Toll) because its waters "gave life" to every place they touched. Or perhaps the People associated the valley that the stream's waters had etched into the high Rockies with the toothsome game animals that the inveterate scamp Coyote had bequeathed to them. Long, long ago, after all, Coyote and his older brother Wolf had squared off in an epic war of wills. By the time the feud had abated, Coyote's escapades had unwittingly populated the primordially barren mountains with all of the wild creatures the People needed to survive. Coyote's irrepressible curiosity leapt into action when he learned that Wolf had secreted away a veritable menagerie of animals that were good to eat in some distant cave. With ears perked, Coyote resolved to sniff out the cave and seize his brother's stash. After searching far and wide, Coyote finally found the cave. With a mighty shove he dislodged the boulder Wolf had used to seal the cave shut. Then "the animals poured out," Nuche storytellers recounted in the 1970s—"so many that it took several days for all of them to come out." Coyote expected that he would have no trouble hunting down food after he liberated Wolf's cache of elk, bison, deer, rabbit, and other nutritious beasts. But much to Coyote's chagrin, "the animals had all run into the mountains." Ever since, game had propagated and thrived in the high country, including the rich ranges that rose several thousand feet from the banks of Coyote Creek to the alpine tundra of the Never Summers and the Front Range. Coyote's meddling made the Kawuneeche a rich and reliable hunting ground—a realm that the People would fight long and hard to maintain and defend against incursions from Arapahos, Spaniards, Americans, and other invaders.[11]

The story of how Coyote liberated wild game from Wolf's grasp and loosed them on the People's mountain homelands comprises but one of many skirmishes in a long and often bitter sibling rivalry. The Kawuneeche may have earned its name, then, not simply because it was a welcoming place alive with coyotes and all manner of other animals, but also because of its location in the shadows of the Continental Divide, which marked the boundary between Nuche and

Arapaho domains throughout the first two-thirds of the nineteenth century.[12]

We do not have to find literal truth in Nuche stories about Coyote to appreciate this oral literature's allegorical insights. Powerful, perverse (one of Coyote's many nicknames was "Big-Penis" because his member was so long that "he used to carry it," as Bertha Groves of the Southern Ute tribe recounts, "slung over his shoulder"), and never predictable, Coyote lopes tirelessly through Nuche cosmology, fleshing out the extremities and ambiguities of the physical world and moral universe as Creator, Trickster, and Wolf's inevitable adversary.[13]

Whether the Arapahos imposed the name Coyote Creek on today's Upper Colorado of their own accord or borrowed the name from their Nuche adversaries, I like to think that the name could have reflected a common recognition by both peoples that this stream meandered through a wondrously tricky landscape. *Coyote Valley* explores this place and its deep history, focusing on the often unexpected stories forged by a wide range of human beings and the still more diverse and dynamic constituents of the natural world. The book reveals how the Kawuneeche has endured by adopting one guise, then another, shifting shape and sometimes even becoming many things at the same time. From the Pleistocene to the Anthropocene, the Coyote Valley has mimicked the generative potential of its namesake, rivaled Coyote's virtuosity at playing the misfit, and embodied this famous trickster's unmistakable penchant for working himself into many a strange and revealing tale.

🗵 🗵 🗵

The questions that animate *Coyote Valley* are easy to frame but hard to answer. How have the valley's landscapes and ecosystems changed over time, and what continuities have endured? How have the physical and biological processes at work in the high Rockies shaped the lives and labors of the region's human inhabitants from the dawn of its human history some 13,000 years ago to the present day? What ideas, worldviews, perceptions, and value systems have a succession of peoples ranging from Clovis hunter-gatherers to present-day national park visitors used in their struggles to understand, control, and prosper within this ever-changing place? To what extent has the "nature" that people have imagined in their heads aligned with the material realities that have confronted them in the Kawuneeche—and how have different groups responded to the realization that the real place has often proven trickier and more complicated than their ideas about it have led them to expect? How have different ways of imagining and interacting with non-human nature generated or aggravated cultural, social, and political conflict in and around the Coyote Valley? And perhaps most important of all, what can we learn about the past, present, and future of humanity's place on earth by paying close attention to the changes that have made and remade the ecology of this irrepressibly wild corner of North America?

Before we can tackle such questions, though, it helps to have a better sense of the Coyote Valley and the present-day arrangement of its landscapes and ecosystems. From its northern limit at a saddle running between the Front Range and the Never Summer Mountains at upwards of 10,200 feet above sea level, the Kawuneeche extends almost fifteen miles nearly due south to the northern outskirts of Grand Lake, a resort village on the shores of Colorado's largest natural lake. From the heights of the Never Summers to the west at elevations up to 12,940 feet above sea level to the summits of the Front Range on the east, which tower more than 13,000 feet above sea level, the valley's profile resembles a giant U—a telltale sign that great glaciers plowed out the valley floor during the last Ice Age. At the base of the U courses the North Fork of the Colorado River, the valley's vibrant, meandering lifeline. The remarkably flat bottomlands of the valley floor gently rise from about 8,700 feet outside of Grand Lake to above 9,000 feet at the Kawuneeche's northern end.

The Coyote Valley is at once stunning and commonplace—beautiful, to be sure, but not appreciably superior in its scenic endowments to dozens of other places in this exceptionally glorious stretch of the world. Like Coyote, the valley knows how to blend into its surroundings. The Kawuneeche's ecosystems are typical of the southern Rockies more broadly, and they are arrayed in more or less the same patterns that prevail elsewhere in this physiographic province. Most ecologists who study the Rocky Mountains organize its complex ecosystems into vegetative communities. Though many factors—including soil, exposure, and human land use—help to determine where various plants can grow, altitude generally exerts a controlling influence in mountain landscapes. The Kawuneeche's ecosystems thus occupy distinct elevational bands. A hike of just five or six miles from the valley floor to the peaks of the Front Range or Never Summers above can entail a vertical gain of almost

Future Rocky Mountain National Park superintendent Roger Contor captured this idyllic winter scene at Baker Gulch in December 1956. Meadowland and willows occupy the foreground, bordered by lodgepole pine. The Never Summer Mountains loom above. MSF Neg. 3757, courtesy of the National Park Service.

a mile. More important, such a hike replicates in greatly compressed form a journey across an ecological transect that would require several thousand miles of hard travel if you were to remain at sea level, from the northern mainland of the United States all the way to the high Arctic.[14]

The Colorado River stands at the heart of the Coyote Valley's lowest-lying ecosystems. After emerging from the noisy chorus of rushing brooks that commingle at the Kawuneeche's head, the Colorado slows precipitously, tracing lazy, swooping curves along much of its course through the valley. Here at the headwaters, the Colorado offers rich and complex aquatic habitats. The river's abundant macroinvertebrates sustain a range of larger creatures, including native, exotic, and hybridized trout varieties.[15]

The bounty of mineral and organic matter laid down by the Colorado River makes the riparian zone along its banks one of the most productive ecosystems in the entire Coyote Valley. Moist stretches of bottomland sustain water-loving species like sedges and rushes, as well as several species of willow, the shoots and leaves of which rank among the very favorite foods of beaver, elk, and moose. On slightly higher and drier ground, grasses and forbs flourish in rich meadowlands. Some of the Kawuneeche's meadows consist largely of native plants, but others are now dominated by timothy, clover, and other species brought to the high country by American settlers in the late nineteenth and early twentieth centuries. Clusters of lodgepole pine and an occasional colony of aspen round out the most common vegetation types on the valley floor.

While the ecosystems of the Coyote Valley's lower reaches are heterogeneous and humming with life, the upper montane forests that cloak the lower slopes of the valley's steep flanks appear monotonous and austere. Up to roughly 9,500 feet above sea level, lodgepole pines blanket most of the available ground. These spindly conifers often huddle so closely together that they block most sunlight from reaching the forest floor. As naturalist Audrey DeLella Benedict explains, "even-aged and single-storied" forests of lodgepole pine exhibit a "density and homogeneity" reminiscent "of a tree farm." Though American pioneers once associated thick tree cover with fertile soils and fecund environments, the "depauperate understory" typical of lodgepole forests offers "a limited larder to all but a few species of mammals and birds," making these the least productive of the Coyote Valley's major vegetative communities.[16]

The Coyote Valley's subalpine forests are ecologically richer than the upper montane zone below—and thus more useful to human beings. Between 9,500 and 11,000 feet above sea level, patches of limber pine, aspen, blue spruce, and diminutive meadows tucked into forest clearings all occupy specialized niches. Most of the subalpine zone, though, consists of mixed stands of Engelmann spruce and subalpine fir. In the ecotone, or transition zone, between the subalpine and alpine biomes, just a few hundred vertical feet away from sheltered sites where ancient firs and spruces reach heights of 120 feet or more, mature Engelmann spruces survive only as gnarled, dwarfish tangles of krummholz huddling low against the icy blasts of wind that savage the mountain tops year-round.[17]

Between about 11,400 feet above sea level (lower on north-facing slopes or exposed promontories) and the top of the Never Summers and Front Range, trees give way to hardy plants that have evolved remarkable strategies to survive amid rock, snow, blazing sun, and ferocious storms. Abrupt variations in microclimates and soils across the tundra biome lead plants and lichens to grow in intricate patchworks. Small creatures such as pikas, marmots, and ptarmigans inhabit the heights of the Coyote Valley throughout the year. But the warm season that stretches from summer through autumn is when the alpine tundra and the subalpine-alpine ecotone really seem to come alive, as thriving plants draw elk, bighorn sheep, mule deer, and other large mammals up from lower elevations.

The aquatic habitats of the Colorado River, the willow thickets and meadows of the riparian zone, the lodgepole and subalpine forests above, and the tundra on the valley rim: these are the ecosystems that people from Paleo-Indians to modern-day tourists, and from gold miners to National Park rangers have encountered, interacted with, and altered over the course of the Kawuneeche's surprisingly long human history. Though different parts of the Coyote Valley have been adorned by much the same guises during the last several millennia, an assortment of factors—including regional climate change, forest fires, and the dietary proclivities of organisms ranging from minuscule mountain pine beetles to hungry human inhabitants—have constantly pushed and pulled at the Kawuneeche's vegetative communities, altering both their location and their composition.

⊠ ⊠ ⊠

If the Coyote Valley has always figured as a shape-shifting kind of place, recent developments are leading some scientists and land managers to conclude that changes of unprecedented duration and severity are under way. An array of complex and interconnected problems—an outbreak of mountain pine beetles, falling water tables on the valley floor, a decline in the vigor of the willow thickets along the Colorado River, the depopulation of the valley's once-teeming beaver colonies, and climatic shifts that threaten the subalpine and tundra ecosystems of the Mountain West with imminent extinction—are presently unfolding on scales ranging from the microscopic to the global. These transformations, some already well advanced, others still incipient, demonstrate that all is not well in the Kawuneeche. No less important, they reveal the foolishness of treating history and ecology, people and nature, as if they inhabit distinct categories or domains instead of a single inextricably interconnected planet.[18]

In the Colorado River headwaters, as in so many other parts of the North American West, voracious bark beetles—especially the mountain pine beetle—have killed immense swaths of timber. Dying lodgepole and limber pines undoubtedly strike most visitors to the Coyote Valley as ugly. Just a few weeks after swarms of beetles bore their way into a tree's flesh, it begins to turn a rusty red; a year or two later, the same tree will have gone a ghostly purplish gray. For a combination of economic and ecological reasons, the National Park Service has decided to leave most beetle-killed trees in Rocky Mountain National Park alone. But along Trail Ridge Road and some of the park's hiking trails, as well as around many park facilities, the agency has decided to cut down especially dangerous trees (so-called widow makers) before they can fall on and crush unsuspecting visitors and employees. The agency has even conducted a number of small-scale clear-cuts, piling up the resulting debris when weather and fuel conditions are right and setting it aflame to kill pine beetles and return nutrients from dead trees to the soil. Far and away the most obvious such clear-cut in the Kawuneeche, ironically enough, is just off Trail Ridge Road at Timber Creek, stripping the only federally operated campground in the Kawuneeche of virtually all of its trees.[19]

Dead pine forests are hardly the only cause for alarm about the direction of environmental change in the Coyote Valley. Elk and moose—the former reintroduced to northern Colorado in the 1910s, the latter a nonnative creature brought in by state wildlife officials in the 1970s—have become so populous in the Kawuneeche that their prodigious metabolisms are wreaking havoc on willows and beavers—a worrisome trend indeed, since the mutualistic relationships between these two organisms have inextricably shaped the valley's ecology and landscape for many thousands of years. Beavers survived the onslaught of American fur traders, it seems, only to die out under National Park Service management. Some 600 of the creatures inhabited the Coyote Valley around 1940, but today not a single beaver colony remains, mostly because of dramatic declines in the vitality of the willow thickets that cover large stretches of the Colorado River bottomlands. The collapse of beaver populations means tough going ahead for willows, which need the high water tables and mineral-rich soils that vibrant beaver colonies are uniquely capable of fostering. No one knows for certain whether willow communities—the heart and soul of the Coyote Valley bottomlands for at least ten millennia—can recover, and it is anyone's guess whether beavers will ever recolonize the Colorado River headwaters.[20]

The valley's waters face other problems, too. The Grand Ditch, a diversion canal cut into the sides of the Never Summer range between the 1890s and 1930s, continues to carry away perhaps 60 percent of the precipitation that falls on the Upper Colorado watershed across La Poudre Pass and down the Rockies' eastern slope. A breach in the ditch's banks in 2003 caused a massive debris flow to choke a stretch of the Kawuneeche bottomlands with gravel, mud, and rocks. And despite collaborative efforts by ecologists and fisheries scientists from several state and federal agencies to bring back native Colorado River cutthroat trout, the erstwhile apex predator of the Upper Colorado still struggles to hold on in its native waters in the face of stout competition from brook trout, rainbow trout, Yellowstone cutthroat trout, and hybrids thereof.[21]

Looming over these and other ecological shifts in the valley is the granddaddy of them all: climate change. Most scientists attribute the severity of the recent mountain pine beetle outbreak to drought, which weakens trees' ability to defend themselves against insects, as well as a string of warm winters that lacked the long, deep cold snaps that regularly checked mountain pine beetle populations in the past. While no one knows for certain why the Rocky Mountains experienced so little cold weather between the 1990s and the early 2010s, most scientists attribute these warmer temperatures to rising concentrations of greenhouse gases thrust into the atmosphere by human activities. Climate models predict that temperatures will continue to increase, while year-to-year variations will grow still more pronounced and erratic. Organisms that have evolved to survive in the high-altitude biomes of the Front Range and the Never Summer Mountains now face the grim prospect of local extinction, pushed off the mountaintops and into oblivion by global climate change.[22]

Alone or in concert, these challenges threaten to turn the Coyote Valley into an altogether different place—one unmoored from its past and drifting through an uncertain and perilous future. Efforts by Park Service managers, policy makers, environmental advocacy groups, researchers from an array of disciplines, and others to respond to the perils the Kawuneeche is facing will best serve the valley's ecosystems and human stakeholders if they rest on a sound understanding of this place and its deep history. *Coyote Valley* reminds us that despite much hullabaloo celebrating "the national park idea," places like Rocky Mountain National Park are actually legal and cultural constructions imposed on the physical world. The ideas that have shaped and reshaped these federal preserves have not always rested comfortably on the land. No small part of the drama that permeates the environmental history of the Kawuneeche during its first century under Park Service governance stems from the tensions and uncertainties that emerged when agency officials could no longer ignore the fact that nature in the valley was neither as pristine nor as malleable as they had previously believed. The incorporation of the Coyote Valley into the National Park System has brought mixed blessings. By establishing protected areas like Rocky Mountain and attempting to maintain them as static remnants of a vanishing primitive America, preservation has actually precipitated sweeping changes to the very natural systems that Congress charged the Park Service with protecting.[23]

This book differs from most existing histories of the U.S. national parks in two key respects. First, my approach is unabashedly ecological, materialist, and interdisciplinary. The stories I recount and the arguments I make are premised on the conviction that history represents the product of intense and ever-unfolding interactions between an array of human and nonhuman entities. Much as the Nuche tried to better understand their world by tracking Coyote's many semblances, we need to try to make sense of the Coyote Valley's past in all of its manifestations by integrating questions, arguments, and evidence from fields such as ecology, archaeology, ethnography, hydrology, geology, and wildlife biology. The book's second defining feature is chronological. Understanding even the most recent environmental changes in the Kawuneeche requires that we adopt a long-term perspective. The story told in these pages thus unfolds over a much longer timescale than previous studies of U.S. national parks. Because Rocky Mountain was not just a political construction, but also a material landscape, more than half of *Coyote Valley* explores the centuries and millennia *before* the national park's creation.

Like many Coyote tales, mine is a story that intends to humble as well as to instruct and entertain. Large-scale approaches have made monumental contributions to our understandings of the past, but they are incapable of revealing everything we need to know about the interconnected workings of nature and history. The pages that follow chart what might best be considered a deep microenvironmental history of place. Themes of colonization, resistance, fragmentation, resilience, and unintended consequences suffuse and unite the book's three parts, which tell the stories of native peoples, American settlers, and federal land managers, respectively. Taken as a whole, this book aims to show why attending closely to small and seemingly unimportant places still matters. If we are to make responsible decisions about the future of the places we inhabit, we need histories that complement broad truths with the depth, complexity, and richness that microscale studies are uniquely suited to offer.[24]

As we grapple with the conundrums of thinking about nature and history across a range of interconnected scales ranging from the local to the global, we must not forsake our commitment to the particularities of time, place, and culture. Like the helpful cad whose name it bears, the Coyote Valley has always evinced a preternatural capacity for confounding human expectations—mine included. I expected that the Nuche would have used fire to manage the valley's ecosystems, but I was wrong. I searched for evidence that epidemic diseases such as smallpox and measles must have devastated the native peoples of the Colorado high country during the early decades of European imperial expansion, but to no avail. I thought that the Nuche would have been laid low by trade dependency and a declining subsistence base in the years leading up to their forced dispossession by American settlers and troops in the 1870s, yet the historical record failed to support this assumption. Everything I had read about the American preservation movement in the late 1800s and early 1900s led me to believe that the men and women who had homesteaded the Kawuneeche would have grappled against the oppression of federal conservation authorities, when in fact the valley's settlers quickly discovered that accommodating national park visitors afforded them more security and prosperity than subsistence agriculture ever could. These are just a few examples of just how much we all still have to learn about the ongoing saga of people, nature, and place in America.

I

NATIVE PEOPLES

⟪ 1 ⟫

EMERGENCE

NO ONE KNOWS for certain when or how human beings first came to the Coyote Valley, but archaeological and ecological evidence suggests that the story of people and nature there may have begun like this:[1]

A crisp July morning perhaps 13,000 years ago . . .

After having spent the previous day walking from the open expanses of Middle Park into the tightening high country above, you awake in a camp pitched the night before along the far upper reaches of a river that Americans would later know as the Colorado. You load up spear shafts, spearheads, scrapers, and your few other possessions, then set off. A few hours later, the morning chill still bites at your face as you skirt around a deep, cold lake, its waters gleaming bright aqua in the brilliant noonday sun. From Grand Lake, you trudge up a small hill—the terminal moraine marking the farthest advance of an immense tongue of ice and debris that had long covered the entire valley above you. You have entered a landscape indelibly shaped by the growth and retreat of glaciers. Even as you move out from camp, scattered remnants of ice sparkle beneath the Rocky Mountain pinnacles above.[2]

The footprints marking your passage represent the first signs of human life in the Coyote Valley. And yet you are hardly alone here. Your kin, faces brightened by the strong mountain sun, walk behind you. Empty stomachs—theirs and yours—have brought your people deep into the Rocky Mountains. But what is it that pulls you deeper into this raw land pressed hard between looming peaks?

A lifetime spent tracking gigantic beasts has made you a keen interpreter of the tracks and signs they leave. After several hours of following their scat from heap to heap, the piles grow noticeably fresher. Your spirits lift: they cannot be far now.

Moving again—always moving—you leave the creatures' trail and climb from the boggy valley floor to higher ground. Diminutive spruces and firs dot the jagged slopes. Together with periodic outcrops of rocks, this vegetation conceals your approach.

Fear tempers your excitement. You and your companions have walked too far, penetrated too deep into uncharted territory, to come away empty-handed. If the mammoths and giant bison you are stalking detect your approach, they will thunder off. Worse, the beasts may turn and fight. The quarry you stalk can fend off predators far larger and stronger than you and your kind. The giant bison wields horns six feet long and as thick as your thigh, while the mammoth's arcing tusks are so immense that a single blow from them can turn your skull to jelly. You and your people know you must strike first and in concert to wound one of these giants. And even then, the hunt will be far from finished. The injured beast will try to run away and hide, forcing you to trail it patiently, doggedly, until the moment is right to unleash a final flurry of stone-tipped spears.[3]

Late afternoon brings you to a milky blue lake perched beneath high peaks. There at the water's edge you spy them: shadowy hulks drinking and feasting on the flourishing tundra. You and your companions huddle and plot. The fate of your venture never rests entirely in your own hands. Are ferocious predators such as saber-toothed cats and short-faced bears lurking just out of view? Will your quarries wheel around to defend themselves with horns and tusks? And what of all the beings and forces you can neither see nor understand—will they help or hinder?

Staying downwind and disguising your movements as best you can, you turn your attention back to the present moment, taking a deep breath and sharing a steely glance with your kinfolk. Hands clenching your weapon, you sidle down to the lake shore.

Raising the Rockies, Carving the Kawuneeche

The Coyote Valley was never just a stage on which people acted out the dramas we call history, nor was it a blank book on whose pages people could inscribe whatever story they wished to live out. Instead, the natural world has always organized the contours of human possi-

Mountain building, the Great Exhumation, Pleistocene glaciation, and postglacial biological migrations together shaped the Coyote Valley landscape. Norman A. Bishop photo, MSF Neg. 3755, courtesy of the National Park Service.

bility in the Colorado River headwaters. This was as true at the dawn of the Kawuneeche's indigenous history as it is today.

Whoever the first people to inhabit the valley were and whatever their destiny, this much is clear: They had entered a landscape at once ancient and new—a place where continuity and change traded blows in a never-ending struggle for supremacy. Any attempt to grapple with the Coyote Valley's deep past must move from the ground up, starting with the ancient natural processes and events responsible for molding both the valley's form and much of its content. A succession of four dramatic episodes in the region's deep history—the rise of the Rocky Mountains around 70 million years ago, the eruption of the Never Summer Mountains starting about 29 million years ago, the carving of the Kawuneeche by glaciers and rivers during the ice ages of the last two million years, and the colonization of the valley by plants and animals after the ice receded roughly 15,000 years ago—together forged the topography and ecology that First Peoples encountered in the Colorado River headwaters.

The Rocky Mountains are a surprisingly recent addition to the North American landscape. Near the end of the Cretaceous period, in the most recent 2 percent of the earth's history, poorly understood forces began to propel the range upward in what the peerless nature writer John McPhee has aptly called "one of the oddest occurrences in the tectonic history of the world." By the time the earth ceased its squeezing and thrusting about 45 million years ago, the formerly low-lying heart of North America had risen some three miles above the seas. This phase of mountain building (known to geologists as the Laramide Orogeny or Revolution) exposed long-buried rocks of almost imponderable antiquity. Many outcrops on the flanks of the Coyote Valley date from 1.4 to 1.7 billion years ago, long before multicellular life forms first evolved.[4]

Millions of years of tectonic tumult pressed and pulled previously flat expanses into one of the greatest cordilleras on the planet. Yet the transformative powers of the Laramide Revolution also ramified deep into the earth's surface. Cretaceous mountain building endowed the floor of the Kawuneeche Valley with its defining structural feature: a pair of parallel, north-south faults separated by a mile or less.[5]

Even as the Front Range of the Rockies was being "jacked up more than four miles from its basement origins," erosive forces were already grinding these highlands back down. The twin cracks underlying the Kawuneeche offered lower terrain than adjoining blocks of the earth's crust, so water inevitably flowed toward the valley's faults. Starting tens of millions of years ago, a stream began to course from north to south, following the same general trajectory as today's Upper Colorado River, only on a course perched several thousand feet higher in elevation. Yet unlike today's Colorado, which famously slices and dices its way through canyons and valleys on its long route to the Pacific Ocean, this primordial ancestor loafed lethargically across a landscape choked by ashfall from the inland West's many active volcanoes.[6]

Some 15 million years of dormancy ensued before the forces responsible for making the Rockies reemerged and powered another phase of mountain building. Just west of the twin fault lines marking the floor of the Coyote Valley, volcanic eruptions and magmatic intrusions gave rise to a new range: the Never Summer Mountains. By the time the commotion calmed down perhaps 27 million years ago, the volcanic peaks of this north–south mountain chain loomed some 16,000 to 17,000 feet above sea level.[7]

The Laramide Revolution made the Front Range; Tertiary volcanism then built the Never Summers. The most spectacular quality of the present-day Rocky Mountain National Park landscape, though, is not its lofty elevation, but instead its dramatic relief. Tectonic forces molded mountain masses, but it took the erosive powers of water and ice to carve out the spaces in which most of the region's human history has taken place. Geologist Keith Meldahl explains that for tens of millions of years, the Rockies remained so "deeply buried" by "thick blankets of sand, gravel, and volcanic ash" that Colorado and Wyoming "looked like somewhat lumpy versions of Iowa or Indiana." Even the loftiest mountaintops peaked just one to four thousand feet above their sediment-choked surroundings. The jaw-dropping topography of the present-day high country resulted from intensified erosion during the last 5 to 10 million years. Water, ice, and other forces scoured, dissolved, and carried off immense quantities of material, excising basins, cirques, valleys, and other voids from the Rockies in the monumental and still ongoing process known as the Great Exhumation.[8]

Rivers newly energized by another bout of tectonic uplift dominated the Great Exhumation's early phases. During the course of millions of years, the South Platte and its tributaries scooped out a massive basin beneath the Rockies' eastern slope. Known as the piedmont—a geographic term meaning "foot of the mountains"—this "vast, riverine bowl" today lies almost a thousand feet *below* the highest parts of the High Plains. In this fertile trough pressed between mountains and plains, plants and animals—including the West's First Peoples—could generally find better shelter, more plentiful and reliable supplies of water, and a milder climate than prevailed in either the flatlands to the east or the mountains to the west. As the South Platte was carving out the piedmont, the ancestral stream that had long flowed atop the Coyote Valley's faulted floor linked up with the newly emergent Colorado River system. By the onset of the Pleistocene some 2.6 million years ago, the great rivers of the West had "bulldozed away the debris that had covered the mountains, and brought the Rockies back to the world."[9]

During the repeated cycles of glaciation and deglaciation that defined the Pleistocene epoch, flowing ice joined running water as a major

Native Peoples

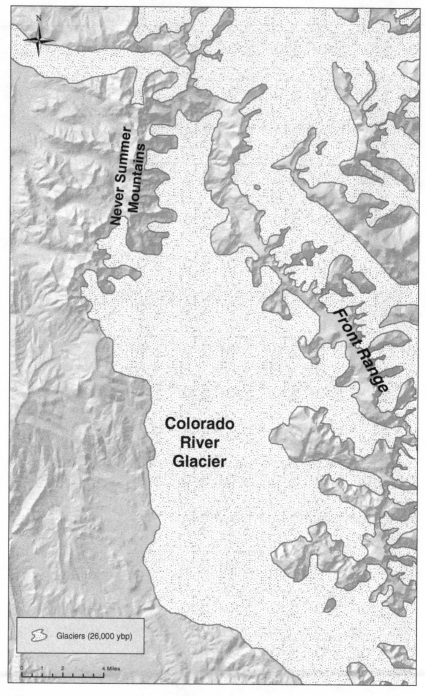

The Ice Age Valley. Courtesy of the National Park Service.

erosive force. The preglacial landscape of Rocky Mountain National Park, a recent guidebook to Colorado geology points out, "was undoubtedly scenic, but it lacked the grandeur that today draws millions of annual visitors." During cold climatic phases, ice accumulated at the heads of the valleys of the Never Summers and the Front Range. Gravity then set these bodies of ice in motion. Streams of ice coursed down from the high country into the valley scraped out by the ancestral Colorado River, producing an immense glacier 1,500 feet thick and twenty miles long. Each episode of glacial scouring lowered the floor of the Coyote Valley a little farther; each whittled away at the cirques that indent the peaks and ridges of the Front Range and Never Summers. By the peak of the last Ice Age about 20,000 years ago, the colossal Colorado River Glacier had submerged virtually every stretch of ground from present-day Grand Lake up to between 11,000 and 12,000 feet above sea level.[10]

Roughly 14,500 years ago, renewed warming forced the glaciers of the Rocky Mountains to beat a rapid retreat. As the ice melted, hundreds of ponds and lakes formed in the region's cirques, bejeweling the upper elevations of the Greater Rocky Mountain National Park Ecosystem like so many sapphires and emeralds. When the climate entered a short but severe cold phase known as the Younger Dryas between about 12,800 and 11,500 years ago, ice began to advance once again. By the time this last gasp of extensive glaciation drew to an abrupt halt, ice and water had together refashioned the physiography of the Coyote Valley into pretty much the same basic U-shaped form that visitors to Rocky Mountain National Park encounter today, with the flat bottomlands along the Colorado River rising abruptly to form the slopes of the newer Never Summers and the older Front Range.[11]

The ecology of the place that emerged from beneath the glaciers remained utterly unrecognizable, however, until plants began to take root. Downward flows of water in both solid and liquid forms drove the Great Exhumation. The postglacial colonization of the Colorado River headwaters by the forebears of today's vegetative communities, by contrast, proceeded mostly from lower to higher ground—and hence in a northerly direction from the Kawuneeche's southern margins around Grand Lake. The hardy denizens of tundra ecosystems presented the major exception to this general rule; having taken refuge above the glaciers, many of these plants began to migrate downward to fresh ground as the climate warmed. Almost all of the area's other major plants and vegetative communities—hardy sedges and grasses; shrubby, water-loving willows; the aspens and lodgepoles of today's upper montane zone; and the firs and spruces that would eventually dominate the subalpine—migrated upward in successive waves, shifting their range steadily with each generation in response to climatic shifts, bark beetle outbreaks, and other processes and events.[12]

Throughout the ice ages, a scant but hardy fauna had clung to mountain refugia above the glaciers. The greening of a world long dominated by ice and rock, though, soon drew larger creatures back to the Coyote Valley. In the wake of the Ice Age, the so-called Pleistocene megafauna (mammoths, giant bison, saber-toothed cats, giant beavers, and so forth) pursued newly available plant foods—and each other—into the Colorado River headwaters. By perhaps 11,400 years ago, however, almost all of North America's largest mammals had died out. The cause of this epochal extinction event remains hotly disputed, with suspicion falling on rapid climatic change, overhunting by First Peoples, epizootic disease, and even asteroid impacts. No one knows how long it took, but the Kawuneeche's bestiary eventually stabilized. By roughly 10,000 years ago, the valley was sustaining a panoply of birds, insects, fish, amphibians, invertebrates, and small mammals; a bevy of the hoofed herbivores collectively known as ungulates, including elk, mule deer, bighorn sheep, and perhaps pronghorn antelope and bison; and a predator guild whose larger members included martens, bobcats, lynx, wolves, mountain lions, black bears, grizzly bears, and, of course, coyotes.[13]

Complex and dynamic ecological relationships linked the organisms actively colonizing the Coyote Valley to each other and the physical world. The emergence of the so-called beaver-meadow complex in the Colorado River headwaters offers an especially vivid illustration of the systems of interdependence that First Peoples encountered when they pushed into the Kawuneeche. As the Colorado River Glacier retreated, beavers pursued aspen and willow, two favored sources of food and building material, up into the Colorado River headwaters and began to construct lodges and dams. Wherever beavers labored and thrived, rich riparian ecosystems gained a foothold. Willows, which had evolved to spread onto soil that is fresh, rich in minerals, and moist, readily colonized the sediments beaver dams impounded. The rodents even unwittingly abetted the spread of some willow species by chomping off their stems and carrying them to new sites, where they soon took root if left undisturbed. Healthy willow thickets, in turn, stabilized stream banks, created excellent habitats for a range of birds and mammals, and even provided the shade and cover that fish such as the Colorado River cut-throat trout preferred. Beavers and willows, in short, performed vital ecological, hydrological, and geomorphological work by trapping sediments, splitting large streams into multiple channels, raising the water table, and enabling many other organisms to flourish in the Kawuneeche's riparian zones.[14]

First Peoples and the Kawuneeche Environment

When Europeans first arrived in western North America in the sixteenth century CE, the Coyote Valley lay on the northeastern edge of the Nuche homelands. By that point, First Peoples had inhabited the Kawuneeche for more than twelve millennia. Though the valley's precontact history left behind few artifacts and no written records, the scarce but suggestive archaeological research on the Colorado high country documents how a diverse and shifting assortment of nomadic Native American individuals and groups inhabited the Greater Rocky Mountain National Park Ecosystem and made it a crucial warm-season site for procuring material resources and encountering sacred power. From the initial peopling of the Rockies in the Clovis period through the American conquest of the late nineteenth century, an intricate interplay of change and continuity defined how indigenous peoples interacted with their homelands. In the face of unstinting and often severe climatic, cultural, and political changes, the Nuche and their predecessors sought—and usually found—refuge in a remarkable set of adaptions to mountain ecosystems. The resulting ways of living at high altitude underpinned several hundred generations of Native American inhabitation in the Colorado Rockies without transforming refractory mountain ecologies.

Examining the deep history of the Coyote Valley shows that even this remote and inhospitable region was hardly "wilderness" in the peculiar sense of the term that has dominated American usage since World War II. It has been thousands of years since the region met Congress's 1964 definition of wilderness as a place "untrammeled by man." The precontact Kawuneeche was neither unpeopled nor pristine. But the valley's early environmental history also contradicts a new scholarly orthodoxy that casts the pre-Columbian Americas as fundamentally altered and intensively managed by indigenous peoples. Over the millennia, the First Peoples of the Rockies influenced game populations while producing subtler effects on the area's vegetation. Yet from their arrival in the high country more than 13,000 years ago through Nuche times, indigenous peoples neither sought nor achieved dominion over Rocky Mountain nature. Across time, space, and culture, indigenous populations remained too small, their wants too bounded, and their ventures into the Colorado River headwaters too circumscribed in duration, extent, and purpose to revolutionize the region's ecology.[15]

The peopling of the Coyote Valley began during a phase that archaeologists call the Clovis period, as rising temperatures beat back the mountain glaciers that had blanketed the Colorado high country for thousands of years. As plants, animals, and other organisms migrated into the Kawuneeche to colonize ground exposed by melting ice, First Peoples followed suit, pushing into the valley in bands that probably numbered fifty or fewer members. All Clovis-era artifacts found in Rocky Mountain National Park were fashioned from rock quarried in Middle Park. This suggests that already at the dawn of the region's human history, indigenous peoples moved seasonally into the Colorado River headwaters from winter camps located in lower-lying, better-sheltered terrain to the south and west. If the traditional archaeological view of Clovis peoples as prototypical big game hunters is correct, then these people's understandings of the Kawuneeche's ecosystems would have centered on the know-how required to track, kill, and process mammoth, giant bison, and the other "ambulatory meat lockers" that trundled through postglacial landscapes. More recent interpretations, by contrast, portray Clovis peoples as generalized foragers who supplemented occasional kills of big game by harvesting fish, plants, and smaller mammals.[16]

Evidence of human inhabitation suddenly vanishes from the Greater Rocky Mountain National Park Ecosystem about 11,000 years ago, probably because of the onset of cooler climatic conditions and a renewed pulse of glaciation. With ice and snow again gripping the high mountains, people would have had trouble finding enough food to survive in the Coyote Valley. For the next two millennia First Peoples seem to have avoided the Colorado River headwaters in favor of lower-lying and more congenial dwelling places.[17]

The return of warmer, moister conditions around 9,300 years ago renewed the appeal of the Coyote Valley to native North Americans by reinvigorating its vegetative communities. Though the immense creatures that had dominated the Rockies throughout the Pleistocene had died out thousands of years earlier, improved grazing and browsing conditions nonetheless led hungry game species including mule deer, bighorn sheep, and elk to migrate back into the Kawuneeche. As ungulate populations burgeoned, First Peoples began to reinhabit the Colorado River headwaters during the warmer months.[18]

Many centuries of experimentation and innovation ensued. By roughly 7,000 years ago, the Greater Rocky Mountain National Park Ecosystem emerged as an integral venue for the Mountain Tradition—a stunningly robust set of practices for surviving and even thriving in the high Rockies that would endure with only slight modifications into the late nineteenth century CE. The First Peoples who developed and perfected this array of ingenious, hard-won "adaptations to high-altitude environments" calibrated their seasonal movements and resource-procurement strategies to take advantage of the intricate topography, diverse ecology, and ever-shifting climate of the Mountain West. Archaeologist Robert Brunswig, the foremost authority on Rocky Mountain National Park's ancient human history, hypothesizes that the Mountain Tradition peoples who inhabited the Kawuneeche and adjacent watersheds "developed the region's earliest sustained, seasonally transhumant, high altitude hunting systems." These "closely related, mountain-adapted groups," he argues, inhabited lower valleys outside the national park's present boundaries during the colder months, and then moved to the high country as the weather warmed. Mountain Tradition peoples seem to have focused their efforts on mule deer, but they also stalked other creatures. New spear point patterns combined with novel techniques to make these First Peoples formidable hunters. Mountain Tradition practitioners skillfully designed and built game drive structures that employed "topographic depressions, saddles and ridgelines" to funnel their quarry toward natural and man-made "ambush points where hunters could conceal themselves." Evidence from game drive sites in the Big Horn Flats region of the Kawuneeche Valley indicates that ungulates killed above tree line were roughly butchered at adjacent temporary camps; the resulting cuts were then packed hundreds of feet down the mountainside to staging camps in the alpine-subalpine ecotone for further processing.[19]

With the emergence of the Mountain Tradition, the Kawuneeche probably supported more people than ever before. Artifacts from the valley indicate that the Mountain Tradition matured into a "long-term, relatively stable, and very effective and adaptable way for people to live." The Mountain Tradition peoples of the Greater Rocky Mountain National Park Ecosystem almost certainly boasted more extensive and intimate knowledge of the natural world than their Clovis predecessors. Yet they could do little to prevent this relatively prosperous phase in the human history of the Rockies from drawing to a close about 4,500 years ago.[20]

For some two thousand years thereafter, cooler, wetter weather lashed the high country. Severe snowstorms blew upslope from the Great Plains much more frequently than in previous millennia, hampering travel and foreshortening the already fleeting mountain summers. Ungulates retreated to lower ground as their habitat deteriorated. Throughout these bleak millennia, First Peoples nonetheless continued to inhabit Coyote Valley, but they shied away from the increasingly inhospitable higher elevations and spent much more of their time in the Colorado River bottomlands. Harsh conditions persisted into the Late Archaic period, running from 3,000 to 1,900 years ago, but this era also witnessed several important cultural innovations to the Greater Rocky Mountain National Park Ecosystem. The Kawuneeche's inhabitants began to make heavier use of lithic materials drawn from more distant quarries, including quartzite from south-central Wyoming, petrified wood from eastern Colorado, and chert from South Park. Mountain Tradition peoples lashed points knapped from these new sources to newly introduced bow-and-arrow systems, which offered a significant improvement in range, precision, and power compared to their existing arsenal of spears and atlatls.[21]

In the final reckoning, however, the profound continuities in human-environment interactions across the Mountain Tradition's long reign seem even more striking than the changes the Late Archaic inaugurated. First Peoples in and around the Kawuneeche had to adapt to constant and often erratic environmental shifts. Ungulate populations rose and fell. Wildfires erupted to destroy vast swaths of subalpine forest. Potent storms beat against the high country, sometimes bringing heavy flooding to the valleys below. Insects such as mountain pine beetle periodically infested the woodlands of the Colorado River headwaters. And "periodic and probably abrupt changes" in climate repeatedly "whipsawed the cultures of the region." In the face of these and other turbulent forces, the core practices of the Mountain Tradition nonetheless persisted across many thousands of years.[22]

Anthropologists hypothesize that throughout the Mountain Tradition's long zenith—a period stretching from about 7,000 years ago through the dispossession of the Nuche by American settlers and troops—First Peoples inhabited the Coyote Valley in the course of seasonal migrations known as transhumance rounds. Though the precise configuration of these cyclical movements remain poorly understood, two general scenarios seem most likely: an "Up-Down" pattern, in which First Peoples moved back and forth within a relatively narrow latitudinal band between lower-elevation winter camps and summer hunting grounds atop the Continental Divide; and a "Grand Rotor" circuit that led from winter camps in the eastern Colorado foothills to spring hunting grounds in present-day northern Colorado and southern Wyoming, then to a warm-season stint in the high country before a late-fall descent to lower elevations. Inhabiting the Rocky Mountains required considerable flexibility and incessant adaptation. The extended kin groups that probably constituted the basic unit of social and political life for Mountain Tradition folk must have improvised incessantly, drawing on both the Up-Down and Grand Rotor patterns. Throughout their migrations, Mountain Tradition practitioners oriented themselves using the sun, moon, and various constellations. But signs immediately perceptible in the earthly environment that enveloped them, especially changing weather, the maturation of different plants, and animal migrations, offered more immediate signals that it was time to shift from one segment of their annual rounds to the next. The extended family groups who made heaviest use of the Coyote Valley may well have spent the coldest months of the year not on the piedmont or foothills on the Rockies' eastern slope, but instead in Middle Park or the lower, drier valleys of northwestern Colorado.[23]

Though little archaeological evidence remains to document the plant foods that Mountain Tradition peoples gathered in the Colorado River headwaters, native foragers probably harvested dwarf blueberry, squawbush, wax currant, and buffalo berry. These fruits could be eaten raw, but they also could be dried in the arid mountain air and pulverized on grinding stones hefted up from the eastern foothills. Native peoples almost certainly supplemented meat and fruit with a variety of starchy, carbohydrate-rich roots, including bitterroot, yarrow, bistort, and Indian potato. Dried and pounded tubers yielded a year-round supply of flour-like powders that practitioners of the Mountain Tradition could incorporate into breads, stews, and other dishes. The summer and fall weeks when native peoples harvested the ample and varied supplies of fresh, tasty, and healthful plant and animal foods that flourished in the Coyote Valley marked a season of unusual plenty—a respite of prosperity that contrasted conspicuously with the rigors that characterized most other phases of their annual transhumance rounds.[24]

Throughout the Mountain Tradition's heyday, human hunting inflected relationships between game species, predators, and plants. From Clovis times onward, First Peoples figured prominently among the Kawuneeche's guild of apex predators. Mountain Tradition practitioners pursued large ungulates with great gusto. Indigenous hunting almost certainly played a significant role in limiting populations of favored quarry; it also probably changed how ungulates behaved, with important ecological consequences. Over time, animals would have learned to defend themselves against Mountain Tradition pursuers by dispersing throughout the Greater Rocky Mountain National Park Ecosystem instead of congregating in large, geographically restricted herds. Facing near-constant danger from people and other predators, elk, deer, and other ungulates would have had to graze and browse surreptitiously, moving frequently to avoid detection. Most ecologists surmise that over the long run, the impact of human hunting on ungulate behavior and demography would have facilitated a loose equilibrium between carnivores, herbivores, and plant communities. First People hunters and other predators presumably kept populations of hoofed herbivores sufficiently low for willows and aspens to thrive—and thus for beaver, Colorado River cutthroat trout, and a wide range of other organisms to flourish in the rich habitats nurtured by these vigorous plant communities.[25]

By hunting, gathering, moving across the land, making homes, having children, telling stories, and engaging in all the other activities on which their ability to inhabit the high country hinged, the First Peoples of the Mountain Tradition carved out niches for human beings in the Coyote Valley. The numerous sacred sites identified in and around the Kawuneeche remind us that even as the practitioners of the Mountain Tradition labored to incorporate energy and nutrients from the valley's ecosystems into their own bodies, they also took pains to honor, enlist, and assuage the sacred powers that governed human interactions with other entities. Western philosophical traditions that cast "culture" and "nature" as distinct and disconnected realms would have made little sense to people who had become inextricably enmeshed in the landscapes and ecosystems of the Colorado high country.[26]

⊠ ⊠ ⊠

From the time Clovis foragers first set foot in the Greater Rocky Mountain National Park Ecosystem through the enduring heyday of the Mountain Tradition, First Peoples clearly acted on and changed their environments by killing animals, harvesting plant foods, procuring firewood, building camps, blazing and following trails, engaging in trade with other peoples, and engaging sacred powers. At the same time, however, none of these native groups ever intensively manipulated the valley's ecology through agriculture, fire setting, or other intensive land-management strategies commonly practiced by other Native American societies. First Peoples' impact on the Greater Rocky Mountain National Park Ecosystem thus remained localized, transitory, and diffuse from Clovis times onward. The Kawuneeche's indigenous inhabitants occupied the valley for only part of the year and in limited numbers, and they focused almost all their energies on meeting the basic needs of small, kinship-based bands. Accumulation and exchange remained sharply limited among these pedestrian nomads. During a seasonal pattern of inhabiting the Kawuneeche that remained vibrant even as other civilizations across the globe rose and fell, Mountain Tradition peoples deployed a set of tools and practices that changed only slightly over many thousands of years.[27]

Indeed, the Mountain Tradition endured with only modest adaptations long after Europeans arrived on American shores. In the refractory landscapes and ecosystems bequeathed by the Laramide Revolution, Tertiary volcanism, the Great Exhumation, and the postglacial colonization of the Kawuneeche by a succession of human and nonhuman organisms, there remained no more reliable way to forge a living in the Colorado River headwaters. Whether subsequent centuries have yielded any wiser ways to inhabit the Coyote Valley remains an open question.

◀ 2 ▶

ENDURANCE

IN FEBRUARY 1822, just weeks after New Mexicans alternately celebrated and lamented Mexico's independence from Spain, the American
trader Thomas James witnessed an unforgettable sight: "a deputation
of fifty Indians from the Utah tribe on the west side of the mountains"
riding into Santa Fé. The First Peoples who comprised this "deputation"
almost certainly considered themselves Nuche. Two decades later, James
could still recount how they "came into the city, and paraded on the
public square, all well mounted on the most elegant horses I had ever
seen." James, who had seen plenty of horseflesh in the course of the
adventure that had taken him from his native Maryland to New Mexico
via St. Louis, the Mandan country astride the Upper Missouri River, and
the Osage and Comanche homelands of the southern plains, ranked the
Nuche ponies among the finest he had ever beheld. "Of a very superior
breed," they possessed "slender tapering legs and short, fine hair, like
our best blooded racers."[1]

James was no less impressed by the delegation's leader, "a young man
of about thirty and of a right Princely port and bearing," whom James,
presumably following the lead of the French-speaking traders and trappers who had preceded him to Santa Fé, called "Lechat" ("The Cat"). At
Lechat's suggestion, James met with the Nuche leader later that day at
the Council House, in the presence of curious "Spanish officers and
gentlemen." The trader's parley with Lechat began with a handshake.
Speaking in Spanish, "which he spoke fluently," the Nuche headman
informed James that "he had come expressly to see me and have a talk
with me. 'You are Americans, we are told,'" Lechat began. "'And you

have come from your country afar off to trade with the Spaniards.'"
Then the Nuche leader got to his point: "We want your trade."[2]

The ensuing conversation revealed the remarkable success with
which Lechat and his fellow Nuche had weathered the tumults first
unleashed nearly three centuries earlier, when Spanish conquistadores
invaded the Rio Grande Valley. Lechat portrayed the People, whose
homelands stretched from New Mexico's northern borderlands to around
the southern boundary of present-day Wyoming, as prosperous, practical,
and eager to do business. "Come to our country with your goods," he
beseeched James. "Come and trade with the Utahs. We have horses,
mules and sheep, more than we want." Lechat expressed pride in his
people's herds, but he knew that James had not ventured all the way to
New Mexico simply to buy livestock. "We heard you wanted beaver
skins," the headman bluntly declared. "All our rivers are full of them. . . .
Come over among us and you shall have as many beaver skins as you
want."[3]

Having portrayed the Nuche domains as flush with furbearers, Lechat proceeded to depict the *Nuevo Mexicanos* as too impoverished to merit
the Americans' trade. The Nuche leader pointed to the "officers and gentlemen" who had gathered to eavesdrop on his conversation with James
and scoffed, "What can you get from these?" The erstwhile Spanish colonists, he continued, "have nothing to trade with you . . . but a few poor
horses and mules, a little *puncha,* and a little *tola* (tobacco and corn meal
porridge) not fit for any body to use." The New Mexicans, Lechat sneered,
"are poor—too poor for you to trade with. Come among the Utahs if you
wish to trade with profit."[4]

Lechat then turned James's attention to the Nuche deputation's ponies, which told James everything he needed to know about Nuche prosperity and New Mexican poverty. "Look at our horses here," the Nuche
leader implored. "Have the Spaniards any such horses? No, they are too
poor. Such as these we have in our country by the thousand, and also
cattle, sheep and mules." Then Lechat pointed a disdainful finger back
toward the Spaniards and demanded: "What are they? What have
they?" The *Nuevo Mexicanos,* Lechat concluded, "have nothing that you
want. We have every thing that they have, and many things that they
have not."[5]

One of the New Mexicans attempted to turn the tables on Lechat.
"You have no money," he shouted. "And you," the Nuche roared back,

"have very little. You are *depicca*." James helpfully translated this insult as: "You are poor miserable devils and we are the true capitalists of the country," an assertion Lechat clearly intended to impress James and his fellow Americans, whose reputations as master traders preceded them to Santa Fé. After Lechat "concluded his harangue," the Nuche leader "mounted his noble steed" and rode off "without the least show of respect for the Spaniards"—indeed, with what James described as "a strong demonstration . . . of contempt for them."[6]

This account of an encounter between an American trader and a southeastern Nuche headman reveals three important insights about power, nature, and history in and around the Greater Rocky Mountain National Park Ecosystem as U.S. commercial expansion into the American West quickened. First, southeastern Nuche bands such as Lechat's were thriving in the early 1820s—and there is every reason to believe that conditions were at least as salutary for their northeastern Nuche kinfolk who seasonally inhabited the Coyote Valley. Second, the People's exceptional ponies were both cause and consequence of their success. The particular variation of equestrianism perfected by the Nuche simultaneously embodied the People's prodigious adaptability *and* the fundamentally conservative manner in which they assimilated these powerful and potentially disruptive creatures into the tried-and-true practices of the Mountain Tradition. And third, Lechat and his fellow Utes responded to the arrival of American traders from a position of considerable strength. Nearly three centuries after Spanish invaders set their sights upon the Nuche homelands, the People remained sovereign, not dependent—thriving, not impoverished.

Lechat and his fellow Nuche seemed, in short, to have mastered the subtle arts of endurance. How they did so might just figure as one of the most compelling untold stories in North America's deep history. It is a tale, moreover, that can teach us a great deal about how the Coyote Valley changed—and how it stayed much the same—across the tumultuous borderlands that have long presumed to sever "prehistory" and "history" into separate realms.[7]

The People

No one knows for certain when or whence descendants of the Nuche first arrived in the Greater Rocky Mountain National Park Ecosystem.

Anthropologists have long asserted that the Nuche migration to Colorado formed one salient in the broader expansion of Uto-Aztecan speakers across the North American interior. According to this view, the People pushed into the Rocky Mountains from the Great Basin relatively recently, between 1000 and 1400 CE. By the time of the Spanish conquests, the Nuche domains stretched from the eastern foothills of the Front Range to the western slopes of the Wasatch Front, and from the Green River valley to the Upper Rio Grande basin.[8]

Though many historians have mirrored this interpretation of Nuche origins, the case for casting the Utes as Johnny-come-latelies to the Rockies rests mostly on inference and assumption. Instead of relative newcomers who barely preceded Coronado and Oñate to the Rockies, the People may well have been long-established denizens of the high country. It is nearly impossible to attribute archaeological artifacts manufactured in the Mountain West prior to the early centuries of the second millennium CE to modern tribal groups with any certainty or precision, so physical evidence cannot discredit the possibility that the Nuche emerged in situ—true Colorado natives biologically descended from the region's earlier inhabitants. The most likely scenario of all, though, is that the Nuche emerged as a distinct people through the combined effects of in situ development and migration. Whenever and however the People became the stewards and sovereigns of most of the present-day Colorado Rockies, members of the northeastern Nuche bands had become indigenous to the Coyote Valley by 1400 CE *at the very latest,* and they would continue to inhabit the Kawuneeche until Americans dispossessed them in the 1870s.[9]

The ongoing debate over Nuche origins hints at the enduring continuities that characterized material culture, social structures, and Native American interactions with nonhuman nature in the Greater Rocky Mountain National Park Ecosystem across the great divide between "prehistory" and "history." It is difficult to distinguish artifacts created by the Nuche from those discarded by earlier high-country peoples precisely because the People perpetuated the same repertoire of basic strategies that had sustained the region's human inhabitants in earlier epochs. To understand how the Nuche managed to carry forth the Mountain Tradition in the face of the profound disruptions that European and American intrusions unleashed, we first need to grasp some key dimensions of Nuche society, politics, and culture.[10]

The extended family group constituted the fundamental unit of Nuche society and the only level of political organization that cohered to any significant degree prior to the mid-nineteenth century. Each kin group identified with a band. Most scholars and contemporary Ute peoples concur that the Nuche were divided into more than a dozen loosely organized bands. It is helpful to subdivide these bands based on cultural, historical, and environmental criteria into three clusters: western, southeastern, and northeastern. The western Nuche—whose lifeways closely resembled those of their Paiute, Goshute, and Shoshone neighbors—possessed rich homelands in central Utah and rarely ventured into what is present-day Colorado. The influx of Mormons to the Great Salt Lake region in the 1840s would further differentiate the western Nuche from their eastern kin. The southeastern Nuche bands, most commonly known in English as the Capote, Muache, and Weminuche, ranged throughout the southern Colorado Rockies and northern New Mexico, where they began to encounter Spanish conquistadors in the late sixteenth century. The northeastern bands of the People, generally referred to as the Parianuche or Grand Rivers and the Yampas, Yamparikas, or White Rivers, inhabited northwestern Colorado, northeastern Utah, and parts of southern Wyoming. Their domains, unlike those of their western and southeastern relatives, remained largely isolated from direct European and American incursions until the 1860s. A final band—initially known as the Tabeguaches, but later called the Uncompahgres—occupied an intermediate geographic and cultural position between their southeastern and northeastern relatives.[11]

The People's mountainous homelands could never support even a brief encampment of all the family groups composing the northeastern Nuche. In fact, it is highly unlikely that any band of the People had ever assembled in one place until the U.S. government started forcing some Nuche onto reservations in the early 1860s. Nor did family groups or bands exercise clearly defined, exclusive rights to separate territories. In fact, the ability of Nuche groups to exploit lands customarily used by other bands without generating conflict comprised a critical marker of their common Nuche identity, together with a shared language, extensive kinships ties across bands, and shared religious beliefs and practices.[12]

The Nuche, like most other First Peoples of the Far West, never possessed an overarching political structure to unite multiple bands into a chieftaincy, empire, or nation. Social organization and leadership among the Nuche, always fluid and constrained to particular functions, remained firmly rooted in family groups and bands. The exigencies of collective life—ceremonial obligations, trading expeditions, raiding parties, peace negotiations, and so forth—temporarily brought different headmen and leading women into positions of responsibility within individual bands. Nuche leaders never exerted coercive authority. Instead, the People decided on weighty matters of collective interest through painstaking consensus building, and dissenters felt no obligation to abide by any decision that others had made over their objection. This flexible, ever-shifting power structure valorized the persuasive arts needed to coax fellow band members into pursuing a given course of action. Any leader who failed to deliver, though, was bound to lose authority to his or her rivals.[13]

The intrigues of Nuche political life unfolded as the People pursued the same transhumance cycles their Mountain Tradition forebears had pioneered, especially an Up-Down pattern that brought some family groups from the northeastern bands (and possibly some Tabeguaches) from winter camps in lower-elevation valleys into the Coyote Valley and other parts of the high country during the warmer months. As we discover in greater detail later in this chapter, Nuche family groups moved frequently, harvesting a wide range of food and fiber. They even adopted many of the game drives their Mountain Tradition precursors had used in earlier centuries.[14]

Long before Europeans arrived on American shores, the People evinced a notable knack for adapting to novel possibilities while safeguarding themselves against new dangers. Their move to become what Thomas James called "the true capitalists of the country" began centuries before Spaniards arrived on their doorstep. By the middle centuries of the second millennium CE, the northeastern Nuche bands were embracing new objects and technologies from an array of native trading partners. Artifacts from the Greater Rocky Mountain National Park Ecosystem document the accelerating pace of Nuche interactions with other native societies during these tumultuous centuries. The People now obtained more of the stone they used to make tools from quarries well beyond Coyote Valley instead of from local sources. The appearance of new kinds of ceramics also suggests that Nuche exchange networks were growing in their intensity and extent. Shards of pottery manufactured by Ancestral Puebloan, Fremont, Upper Republican, Dismal River, and Intermountain cultures demonstrate that goods were flowing into the Colorado high country from the Great Plains, Great Basin, and Four Corners.[15]

The exchange networks connecting the Nuche to other native peoples brought risk alongside opportunity. Centuries prior to the European "discovery" of the Americas, the People learned how to keep volatile forces of change at bay by taking refuge within their mountainous homelands. Consider, for instance, the spread of maize-based agriculture, which initiated sweeping transformations in land use, religiosity, identity, and political life among some of the Nuche's neighbors and trading partners. Distant linguistic cousins of the Nuche first introduced corn from Mesoamerica to the present-day U.S. Southwest before 2100 BCE, and to the Wasatch Plateau by the dawn of the Common Era. By 900 CE or so, other First Peoples had begun to grow maize on the central plains. As corn became king in many parts of the West, native peoples fashioned heady but ultimately unstable arrangements with each other and the land. Larger, more sedentary human populations exhausted timber and game from ever more of the Four Corners area. The vicissitudes of the West's erratic climate, meanwhile, bedeviled native farming societies. Agricultural crises caused by prolonged droughts (including the infamous "Great Drought" of 1276–1299 CE and a lesser-known but even longer arid phase between 1118 and 1179 CE) metastasized into ecological, political, and spiritual cataclysms. Some western and southeastern Nuche may have tried their hand at farming, but the short growing seasons throughout the northeastern Nuche homelands effectively shielded them from the turmoil, instability, and violence that erupted throughout the Ancestral Puebloan domains of the Southwest as maize agriculture faltered.[16]

Winds of Change

By the time new and even more daunting threats materialized on the Nuche borderlands, the People had a long history of seeking safety by continuing to practice the Mountain Tradition on their ancestral domains. Between the 1540s and the early 1800s, the People astutely navigated the forces unleashed by a trio of far-reaching developments that together remade the North American West: Spanish colonialism; the unsettling of the western plains as Apaches, Comanches, Kiowas,

Cheyennes, Arapahos, and other newcomers jostled for primacy; and the invasion of the North American interior in the early 1800s by trappers and traders employed by American and British fur companies. Unlike those native peoples who suffered the misfortune of occupying home-lands hard by the beachheads of Euro-American imperialism, however, the northeastern Nuche inhabitants of the Coyote Valley encountered the consequences of intercontinental contact gradually and in greatly attenuated form. Over the course of three peril-strewn centuries, these bands steadfastly preserved their sovereignty and security by incorpo-rating horses, cultivating trade with new neighbors, and—above all—holding fast to familiar ways and time-honored places.

The remarkable continuity in Nuche lifeways before and after the conquest of New Mexico depended in part on the Spaniards' persistent failure to extend their sphere of influence northward into the Rockies. After Don Juan de Oñate colonized New Mexico in the spring of 1598, a host of new trade goods, technologies, organisms, and ideas began to surge toward the Nuche domains. But the forbidding nature of the Rocky Mountains combined with tenacious and often ferocious resistance from the Nuche and other native peoples to block further Spanish expansion. These explanations alone, however, fail to fully explain why a colonial colossus that had pushed rapidly into the Andes, the Sierra Madre Oc-cidental, and other formidable mountain ranges while subjugating some of the most populous and powerful native empires in the Western Hemisphere stalled out in the North American interior.

Three differences help to explain why the Nuche homelands went unvanquished and almost entirely uncharted in the centuries after the Spanish conquests of Mexico and Peru. First, northern New Spain was connected to the Spanish Atlantic by lines of communication that were significantly longer and more tenuous than in Mesoamerica or South America. Second, the wealth assembled during the 1400s by the Aztecs and Incas offered a powerful motivation for Spanish conquest; it also gave rise to the physical, political, and ideological infrastructure on which the subjugation of Mexico and Peru hinged. Persistent rumors held that fabled cities of gold loomed beyond New Mexico's northern limits. Yet neither the Nuche nor their neighbors possessed any apparent mineral riches. The North American West struck Spanish newcomers as chaotic as well as poor. Language, politics, culture, geography, and history had fragmented the region's peoples into dozens of fiercely independent societies. The resulting atomization hampered Spanish designs by making it exceedingly difficult for would-be imperialists to obtain accurate information about the lands or peoples to their north. Last but not least, epidemic diseases such as those that had cleared the way for Spanish victories at the Aztec capital of Tenochtitlàn in 1520 and the Inca capital at Cajamarca in 1532 took decades—and possibly even centuries—to penetrate the northeastern Nuche homelands.[17]

We know all too little about the timing and intensity of virgin soil epidemics in and around the Greater Rocky Mountain National Park Ecosystem because of the area's isolation from centers of colonial power and the underdeveloped state of archaeological and ethnological scholarship on the northeastern Nuche. In more southerly lands, disease served as what the eminent borderlands historian David J. Weber has rightly called "Spain's most important weapon in the conquest of America." Smallpox, influenza, measles, and other virulent ailments originating in the Eastern Hemisphere enabled vastly outnumbered Spanish forces to overthrow Mesoamerican and South American superpowers, as well as the Puebloan peoples whose lands bordered the southeastern Nuche domains. There is no direct evidence, however, that any of these microbes afflicted the northeastern Nuche prior to the 1840s. If the family groups of the White River and Grand River bands indeed managed to avoid the worst of the virgin soil epidemics that decimated so many other First Peoples, their good fortune stemmed from the Spaniards' failure to venture north of the Upper Arkansas Valley, as well as these bands' long-standing practice of channeling exchange with New Mexico through southeastern Nuche intermediaries such as the delegation Thomas James met in Santa Fé in 1822.[18]

The slow diffusion of disease toward the Coyote Valley seems all the more remarkable given the rapidity with which horses, another vital component of the Columbian Exchange, reached the northeastern Nuche bands. The first clear evidence of the People obtaining horses dates to 1640, when southeastern Nuche prisoners of war in Santa Fé jumped onto their captors' mounts and made off for the Rockies. For decades thereafter, the People probably acquired most of their horses through raiding. In the wake of the Pueblo Revolt of 1680, though, a massive native uprising during which an alliance of native peoples seized hundreds of horses in the course of expelling the Spanish from New Mexico for more than a decade, the People expanded their herds. By the dawn of the eighteenth century, if not before, the Nuche inhabitants of the Kawuneeche were breeding ponies of their own, thus beginning their metamorphosis into some of the greatest horse people North America has ever seen.[19]

Throughout the American West, the introduction of horses catalyzed groundbreaking changes in indigenous societies. "For the first time in the region's long history," historian Elliott West explains, "men and women were not limited by their own speed and endurance. Hunters on horseback could range more widely for game and could kill it more often; they could cover more ground in search of water and useful plants." Trade networks "greatly expanded." Thanks to horses, native peoples "could also carry around more possessions, including larger lodges to contain them." Equestrianism also "revolutionized warfare. Mounted warriors not only dominated those on foot, but far-ranging horsemen also could raid villages almost at will while remaining out of retaliation's reach." Horses, West concludes, enabled First Peoples to make an unprecedented "leap of power," inspiring "a heady feeling of suddenly widening potential" and even "a sense of grand destiny." By adopting an old-world animal and making it their own, Native Americans liberated themselves from age-old constraints of time, distance, and imagination. In the process, they began to reimagine themselves as what Kiowa writer N. Scott Momaday memorably calls "centaurs in their spirit."[20]

The Nuche almost certainly responded to the equestrian revolution with much the same feelings of emancipation and communion as other native peoples. The People's growing admiration for their horses showed in their rock art, for instance, which began to incorporate equines and equestrian figures in the seventeenth century. No mere objects of affection, horses were creatures of history who literally and figuratively drove consequential shifts in Nuche life.[21]

Horses, as scholar David Rich Lewis explains, "facilitated the accumulation of more material goods and sparked an elaboration of Ute material culture." Almost as soon as the Nuche began to acquire ponies from New Mexico, they learned that neighboring peoples would pay good prices to obtain animals of their own. As horses became trade goods in their own right, the Nuche established themselves as "important middlemen in the intertribal horse trade and noted raiders." While the southeastern Nuche also became important players in the western slave trade, their northeastern kinfolk seem to have played little part in the markets for human flesh that flourished in many of the places where horses changed hands. Instead of using the beasts to ride down and capture rival peoples, the White River and Grand River Nuche instead employed horses to refashion transhumance rounds rooted in the Mountain Tradition. The most notable short-term effect of equestrianism involved the Great Plains buffalo hunting grounds, which the People could now access from their eastern borderlands in a few days' ride.[22]

Horses helped the People to range more widely and hunt with more certain success. Nuche family groups, long constrained by the limited local resources accessible by foot, could now camp with other kin for more of the year. New forms of leadership arose alongside larger social agglomerations, with band heads assuming more power over a broader range of functions. Horses transformed trade as well as politics. Ponies helped the Nuche to transport two key commodities to New Mexican markets: buffalo meat taken on fall hunting expeditions to the plains, and impeccably tanned deer and elk hides produced within the People's own domains by Nuche women. Ethnographer Anne Smith's Northern Ute informants could still recall in the 1930s how nineteenth-century White Rivers traded skins to the Apaches for clay, pots, and bridles, and to the *Nuevo Mexicanos* for "steel fishhooks and brass bracelets." Northeastern Nuche bands were even known to barter ponies to habitual enemies; from the Arapahos, for instance they obtained "leggings and blankets decorated with beads or bands of porcupine quills." Horses loomed so large in Nuche exchange and production that the creatures themselves "became symbols of wealth, success, and social status"—a role that rarely escaped the notice of American interlopers like Thomas James.[23]

Even as horses quickened Nuche economies, they also kindled conflict between the People and their neighbors. From the 1600s onward, the Nuche vied with expansive native rivals over hunting territories and access to guns, ammunition, and other trade goods. Horses and the sheltered pastures they needed to survive harsh midcontinental winters became key prizes in struggles pitting the northeastern Nuche bands against foes such as the Lakotas, Cheyennes, and Arapahos. The resulting violence almost certainly increased the power of band heads, who were better positioned than the leaders of family groups to defend the People and their homelands against raiders from the Plains.[24]

By indigenizing a domesticated animal first introduced to the Americas by Europeans, the Nuche unloosed far-reaching changes. In the Rocky Mountains, though, the equestrian "revolution" followed a decidedly conservative course. Horse-based pastoralism melded remarkably well with the Mountain Tradition. Initially, husbanding horses confronted the Nuche with novel logistical challenges. Access to grass, for instance, had previously mattered only during seasonal seed-gathering forays. As the People's herds expanded, though, the availability of pasture increasingly determined where the Nuche traveled and camped, as well as how long they could stay in one place before moving on. And yet the Nuche possessed a crucial asset in the struggle to integrate horses into their established ways of life: centuries' worth of experience with the Rocky Mountain region's mercurial climate and ecology. The needs and preferences of horses were so similar to those of the larger game species long pursued by the People that the Nuche could feed and shelter their ponies throughout the year by making only slight changes to transhumance patterns honed over the Mountain Tradition's long zenith.[25]

By harnessing the horse—a powerful creature flush with unruly possibilities—to old designs, the Nuche eluded the temptation to abandon their mountain homelands. Unlike the many other First Peoples who migrated onto the Great Plains and became specialized bison hunters, the Nuche instead redoubled their hold on the mountains and adapted to changing circumstances by continuing to survive as generalists. Long after most of their native neighbors and enemies had become cripplingly dependent on European trade goods, the Nuche could still meet virtually all of their own needs through skillful seasonal movements within their traditional homelands.[26]

As Thomas James recognized, the fleet ponies of Lechat's "deputation" held the key to the People's prosperity. And though the Americans' brash interlocutor almost certainly hailed from a southeastern band, the story was much the same among his northeastern Nuche cousins. In the Colorado River headwaters, as in the Río Grande basin, the Nuche boasted immense herds of fine horses and a country rich in furs. Almost three centuries after Coronado inflicted rapine and ruin on the Southwest and Great Plains, and more than two centuries after the Spanish began to colonize New Mexico, the Nuche remained masters and mistresses of their own destinies.

Fur Trades

The arrival of James and other American traders and trappers at the dawn of the nineteenth century posed the greatest threat yet to the People's independence and well-being. The northeastern Nuche had always managed to keep the Spanish safely distant. In the early 1800s, though, the quest for beaver pelts and bison robes drew motley crews of French Canadians and Spanish Missourians, Scots-Irish Kentuckians and Ohioans of Puritan stock, Delaware Indians, African Americans, and others deep into the Colorado Rockies. The integration of Native American homelands into national and international markets for animal pelts and hides usually wrought devastation on furbearers and Indian peoples alike. But the northeastern Nuche managed to escape the worst consequences of the fur and hide trade by using horses to pursue time-tested lifeways within a mountainous homeland that offered formidable defensive advantages. Members of the White River and Grand River bands, however, also benefited from two fortuitous accidents of timing: First, the development in the early 1820s of the so-called Rocky Mountain Fur Trade System, which largely prevented the People from trapping beaver to exchange with American newcomers; and second, the sudden crash of the international market for beaver pelts around 1840, before invading trappers could exterminate them from the Upper Colorado.

Starting in the early seventeenth century, the Nuche found a ready market for skins, hides, and furs in Spanish New Mexico. *Nuevo Mexicanos* even grew to rely on deerskins produced by Nuche women. In 1754, for instance, Governor Tomás Vélez Gachupín lamented that residents of his colony "have no other commerce than these skins." At a juncture when rising tensions threatened to disrupt the flow of deer hides from the Nuche domains into New Mexico, Gachupín bemoaned that his people were "without the possibility of clothing themselves and existing."[27]

By the time Gachupín recorded this complaint, the People were also profiting from a vigorous trade in beaver pelts with New Mexico. Imperial authorities had tried as early as 1712 to prohibit New Mexicans from venturing into the Nuche country from Abiquiú, Taos, and other northern settlements. But the *vecinos* (citizens) of New Spain's far northern borderlands stubbornly flouted imperial efforts to eliminate the trading ties they had forged with Nuche family groups. In 1805, Governor Joaquín del Real Alencaster offered a revealing description of the exploits of Mestas, a "longtime Ute interpreter and trader" from Abiquiú. After half a century of dodging Spanish authorities to obtain horses, Paiute slaves, and beaver pelts from southeastern Nuche bands, Mestas was imprisoned on Real Alencaster's orders. Other officials, though, sometimes sought out traders familiar with the Nuche country and hired them to guide expeditions such as the unsuccessful 1776 quest by Dominguez and Escalante to blaze a land route from New Mexico to California.[28]

The Nuche had traditionally valued dead animals for the immediate usefulness of the food and fiber their bodies provided. Slowly but surely, though, the hides and furs of some creatures were becoming commodities—objects of exchange that the People slaughtered and processed in order to obtain other goods. Significant as this shift was, however, the northeastern Nuche bands remained relatively small and widely dispersed. New Mexican demand for deerskins and beaver pelts, moreover, remained sharply limited under Spanish rule. People in other parts of New Spain had little need for the beaver pelts the Nuche harvested or the deerskins they manufactured. The long, slow, and uncertain routes leading from the northern outposts of New Mexico to the ports of Mexico, meanwhile, made it impossible for skins and furs from the Rockies to compete in global markets. It should come as little surprise, then, that the People's growing involvement in exchanging hides and furs with New Mexicans prompted neither fundamental changes in Nuche material culture and daily life, nor any discernible downturn in wildlife populations anywhere in the Rockies. When Lechat boasted to Thomas James that his people possessed "every thing that [the New Mexicans] have, and many things that they have not," he sought to impress on his potential American trading partners that his people retained the upper hand in the New Mexico trade.[29]

James's venture to Santa Fé helped to inaugurate a new era in the western fur trade. In the decades that followed, two interrelated developments—the advent of the Rocky Mountain System of beaver trapping and the rapid acceleration of commerce in buffalo hides and robes—hastened the incorporation of the Rockies and Plains into the U.S. economy. Before the 1820s, European colonists and their American descendants throughout North America had almost invariably obtained beaver pelts as the New Mexicans did: by trading with Native American

Engraver William de la Montagne Cary looked back nostalgically on the heyday of the Rocky Mountain fur trade in this drama-laden tear sheet for *Harper's Weekly,* October 17, 1868. Denver Public Library, Western History Collection, Z-3829.

trappers. In the wake of James's journey, though, American fur companies led by the entrepreneurial St. Louis trader William Ashley resolved to break from this firmly entrenched precedent. Ashley realized that he could obtain more furs at lower costs by forcing indigenous peoples out of the western beaver trade. To streamline the flow of pelts from Rocky Mountain hinterlands to American and European markets, Ashley engaged a polyglot force of trappers who possessed little to no experience in the Far West, outfitted them at mercantile outposts on the Missouri River, and dispatched them across the plains in armed brigades with orders to kill beaver up and down the waterways of the western cordilleras.[30]

This new system motivated by the greed of American fur barons unwittingly spared the Nuche the grim fate suffered by many of the First Peoples ensnared by the fur trade. Epidemic disease and alcohol gained little ground, while very few northeastern Nuche women intermarried with outside trappers in the early nineteenth century. In stark contrast to the pattern prevailing on North America's other fur trade frontiers, nineteenth-century Nuche archaeological sites contain an unusually small number of trade goods manufactured by Europeans and Americans.[31]

The Rocky Mountain System may have afforded the Nuche an unintended mercy, but it almost spelled disaster for the West's beaver colonies. American trappers methodically eradicated the rodents from one watercourse after another, leaving so-called "fur deserts" in their wake. It took only a few years for the depletion of lower-lying colonies to propel the newcomers into the upper reaches of the Grand River. In 1831, American brigades started to work North Park and Middle Park, open expanses within an easy day's ride of the Coyote Valley. The Upper Colorado River basin soon became what historical geographer David Wishart calls "an important hunting ground." Nuche bands contributed to the slaughter, too, through continued trade with New Mexicans. In the early 1840s, for instance, trader Rufus Sage discovered that the Nuche "living in the neighborhood" of Fort Robidoux, a post in the Uintah Basin of present-day Utah operated by a New Mexico–based trader, obtained "ammunition, fire-arms, knives, tobacco, beads, awls, &c." by bringing in "beaver, otter, deer, sheep, and elk skins."[32]

Despite the onslaught from outside trappers and the smaller, steadier harvest by the Nuche, beaver nonetheless endured in some parts of the

high country. Early fur trade historian Hiram Chittenden contended that
the Upper Colorado, though "not so much frequented by the traders as
were the streams farther north," was widely seen as "good trapping territory." But the Nuche did not take kindly to strangers trespassing on their
homelands in search of peltry. Fears of Indian attack combined with the
Greater Rocky Mountain National Park Ecosystem's difficult terrain and
long winters to convince even the hardiest of the self-professed "mountain" men that the Coyote Valley was no place to linger.[33]

The Kawuneeche's beaver colonies owed their salvation, though,
more to the whims of fashion than to Nuche resistance or the Rockies'
arduous topography. By the time outsiders began to set traps along
higher-elevation streams in the Colorado River headwaters, the centuries-
old preference of American and European hatmakers for felt made from
beaver fur was faltering. When silk hats became all the rage in the late
1830s, the market for Rocky Mountain beaver pelts disintegrated. This
shift reflected not just the caprices of trendsetters but also the beaver's
growing scarcity, which forced the prices hatmakers paid for raw materials sharply upward. Not long after American trappers converged for one
final ruckus at the infamous Green River rendezvous in southwestern
Wyoming in 1840, the western fur trade collapsed. At least a few colonies of the rodents remained in or near the Coyote Valley, enabling beavers to stage a dramatic recovery during the early 1900s.[34]

On the Great Plains, meanwhile, not even William Ashley imagined
that nonindigenous hunters could kill enough bison to supply skyrocketing U.S. demand for robes and hides. The adventurers who established
Bent's Fort and other Great Plains trading posts during the 1820s
and 1830s cynically encouraged their Indian customers to grow ever
more dependent on guns, ammunition, beads, alcohol, wool blankets,
copper kettles, metal tools, and other trade goods. Many Plains Indian
peoples satisfied their burgeoning consumer habits by becoming special-
ists in hunting bison and processing their skins for American markets—a
move that left them progressively less time and energy for maintaining
and passing on the skills required to tap into other sources of subsistence
and commerce.[35]

Even as the diabolical dynamics of the buffalo trade were inexorably
grinding down their plains counterparts, though, the Nuche continued
to pursue a different path. Rather than permanently migrating onto the
plains, the People preferred to launch seasonal buffalo hunts from their

old mountain homelands. And instead of becoming full-fledged buffalo people, the Nuche preferred to retain the flexible, diversified strategies that had always underpinned the Mountain Tradition. While other native peoples placed all bets for their future on the bison trade, the Nuche elected to sustain the elaborate economic and ecological safety nets that had served them so well for so long. Relying too much on a single resource, after all, flew in the face of everything the People had learned throughout their long history of carving out a livelihood from their unpredictable, far-flung, and often scanty homelands.[36]

Though the northeastern Nuche bands never got swept away by the swirling currents of the commerce in furs and hides, they could not entirely avoid its caustic effects. The People suffered from mounting violence during the early 1800s as enmities rooted in the buffalo hunting grounds of the flatlands reverberated deep in the high country. Declining bison populations along the foot of the Rockies and in the Platte and Arkansas River valleys brought redoubled assaults against the People and their horse herds up and down the eastern frontiers of the Nuche domains. As Colonel Richard Dodge of the U.S. Army explained, "all the powerful plains tribes, though holding [the Nuche] in contempt on the plains, have an absolute terror of them in the mountains." That "terror" made the Nuche worthy targets, particularly for young men on the make. In the mid-1840s, for instance, American explorer John C. Frémont looked on as Arapaho raiders struck a Nuche camp in South Park, well inside the Nuche perimeters. A local legend of uncertain origin recounted another instance in which Arapaho warriors attacked a Nuche camp on Grand Lake. Glory alone, however, fails to explain the upswing in raiding. The good pasture, excellent hunting, and prodigious horse wealth found in the Nuche's eastern borderlands together made them a favored target for the People's plains enemies.[37]

What Wolf Decreed

Between the 1500s and the mid-1800s, the spread of epidemic diseases, the introduction of horses, the extension of global exchange networks, and the decimation of bison and beaver caused sweeping reconfigurations in political power and military force throughout the American West. The People faced especially grave challenges, however, in the quarter century after Thomas James's memorable encounter with Lechat.

Mexico and the United States would jostle against each other to claim the People's territories; fresh epidemics would ravage many Nuche families; Hispano herders and colonists would push into the homelands of the southeastern Nuche; and Mormon exiles would seek to found godly communities on lands the western Nuche had populated since time immemorial. The Treaty of Guadalupe Hidalgo then heaped insult upon injury for southeastern and western Nuche bands struggling to cope with the erosion of their land base and the diminution of game animals and other crucial resources, consolidating Washington's paper claim to the entirety of the People's domains. Yet for all this, the northeastern Nuche inhabitants of the Coyote Valley witnessed only negligible and temporary incursions into their territory. Even as colonialism and its consequences remade the region, the Nuche endured and prospered, cautiously embracing equestrianism, trade with outsiders, and other innovations while holding fast to the Mountain Tradition.[38]

Throughout the mid-nineteenth-century decades that preceded the People's forcible dispossession from Coyote Valley, the land remained the bulwark of their continuing autonomy. Present-day Coloradans sometimes celebrate the Nuche as "The People of the Shining Mountains." This moniker shrouds the native inhabitants of the Rockies in a romantic glow, distracting us from the military and material ramifications of the ties that bound the Nuche to the high country. The People's masterful understanding of the Rockies' intricate topography continued to lend them a decisive home field advantage against raiding parties, trapping expeditions, and other invaders.[39]

And yet the high country offered much more than protection. An oft-told tale recounted to the American explorer John Wesley Powell in the late 1860s offers revealing insights into how the People conceived of and interacted with the Greater Rocky Mountain National Park Ecosystem after the trade in beaver pelts fizzled. Before Powell could embark on his famous descent of the Colorado River, he first had to traverse the northeastern Nuche domains, where the one-armed Civil War veteran, scientist, and ethnographer eagerly recorded the stories the People told him. Around a campfire one night, the explorer's Nuche hosts regaled him with a tale of two brothers—Coyote and Wolf, mythical culture heroes who still loom large in Nuche oral tradition.

Coyote proposed that "as long as [the Nuche] live[d]," their means of subsistence "shall never fail, and thus they will be supplied with abundance of food without toil." But Wolf, the older and more powerful of the siblings, demurred. If the Nuche could obtain their livelihood without working, he forewarned, "then will the people, idle and worthless and having no labor to perform, engage in quarrels, and fighting will ensue and they will destroy each other, and the people will be lost to the earth." And so the People, Wolf commanded, "must work for all they receive."[40]

Due to Wolf's decree, the Nuche could never survive by sitting idly by. Compelled to labor for their living, the People knew full well that their homelands were no pristine wilderness. By acting on their surroundings, the Nuche carved out niches for themselves in ecosystems that spanned the entire length and breadth of their homelands. The People's lives and labors certainly transformed the ecosystems they inhabited. But the localized, moderate, and generally short-lived changes the Nuche imposed on their lands did little to blunt the obstacles and constraints that capricious high-country environments imposed on the Coyote Valley's human inhabitants. For all their skill at fulfilling Wolf's decree, the People of the Shining Mountains could never forget that in the fickle and often ferocious uplands, they were powerful but hardly omnipotent beings.[41]

During the mid-nineteenth century, the northeastern Nuche attuned the seasonal movements of people and horses to the maturation of foodstuffs scattered across a mosaic of ecosystems rising from the high plains to the high Rockies. The People celebrated spring's arrival with the Bear Dance, the most important ceremony of the year. Soon thereafter, family groups of White River and Grand River Nuche prepared to decamp from sheltered valleys on the Rockies' western slope. In late spring or early summer, they followed the Colorado and its tributaries up into the Coyote Valley and other parts of the high country. Between summer and early fall, perhaps two to four dozen Nuche populated the riparian bottomlands of the Kawuneeche and favored hunting grounds in the subalpine-alpine ecotone (the People, like their Mountain Tradition forebears, had little use for the valley's coniferous forests). Signs of impending winter led most large ungulates to migrate down the mountains and into either the eastern foothills of the Front Range or the large, relatively low-lying expanses fur trappers called "parks," which boasted pasture, browse, and shelter during all but the worst winters. As elk, mule deer, bighorn sheep, and other creatures left the Kawuneeche, the

People followed suit, retreating to favored winter camping grounds in Middle Park or the valleys of the White, Yampa, and Bear Rivers.[42]

On their annual migrations up and down the continental crest, the People and their ponies pursued an intricate network of trails and paths. The travel routes that bound the Nuche world together bore scant resemblance to the clearly marked, carefully engineered trails that traverse present-day Rocky Mountain National Park. Even the most important pathways consisted of faint tracks arrayed in braided courses through wider "corridors" offering what one archaeologist describes as "the path of least resistance" between two places. Mountain Tradition forerunners had blazed some of the trails the Nuche traveled. Others, though, had been worn into the land by the People's own moccasins, their dogs' paws, and their horses' hoofs. Nuche trail networks eased the People's seasonal migrations, but they also carried more dangerous possibilities. Nuche trails transmogrified into warpaths when enemy peoples embarked upon them. Take, for instance, one of the more important routes in the Greater Rocky Mountain National Park Ecosystem, which led from Middle Park through Colorado River headwaters to intersect with three separate routes across the Front Range. Arapahos like those who described part of this route to Oliver Toll in 1913 as *Kooh'ohwuuniicii-hehe* or Coyote Creek followed this system of trails to attack the Nuche borderlands.[43]

Once a Nuche family group arrived at its destination on one of these trails, its members began making camp. The Northern Utes interviewed by ethnographer Anne Smith in the 1930s remembered that during their childhoods, the People's mobile villages normally included "5 to 10" lodges—enough to house between twenty-five and fifty Nuche. On occasion, though, Nuche encampments might encompass as many as twenty shelters, placing the maximum warm-season population of the Colorado River headwaters during the mid-1800s at roughly one hundred people.[44]

The People of Coyote Valley used two main kinds of dwellings to protect themselves against the forceful elements of the high mountains. Wickiups, conical structures originating in the Great Basin, were made by using willow saplings to bind together trunks of lodgepole pine or other locally accessible trees. The Nuche then covered these vertical supports with hides, boughs, or brush. Doors of woven rushes harvested from rivers or lakes facilitated access; open hearths provided heat; and a floor made of locally harvested tree boughs or juniper bark hauled up from lower-lying woodlands insulated the People from the bare earth beneath. After adopting horses, the Nuche began to build tepees as well as wickiups. Each tepee cover required about ten buffalo hides (or a larger number of elk skins) stitched together with sinew. Twelve to twenty poles (taken from the eponymous lodgepole pine when possible, but from aspen when necessary) supported the animal-skin sheaths of these comfortable, versatile lodges. In Great Basin–style wickiups and Great Plains–style tepees alike, the People made their beds by laying skins and furs atop several layers of flexible willow branches. Even in summer, the People probably nestled beneath thick, cozy buffalo robes, since overnight temperatures in Coyote Valley frequently dropped below freezing.[45]

The Nuche's moving villages housed a somewhat larger, more varied range of possessions than the camps of their foot-bound predecessors. Northern Utes told Smith that "a typical Colorado Ute family" of the mid-nineteenth century "owned a painted parfleche [a folded rawhide bag] and a buckskin bag for clothing, a buffalo hide parfleche for meat, two basket water jugs, a berry basket, parching tray, wood and horn cups and ladles," as well as "baskets (or pots) for boiling." The Nuche crafted baskets from squawbush gathered in spring at the peak of its pliability. "For coarse work"—heavier-duty basketry serving utilitarian purposes—the People favored willow, which was plentiful throughout the Colorado River bottomlands. Pine pitch served to waterproof the basketry jugs used to haul water into camp. For cooking and storing food, the Nuche preferred the distinctive pottery known as Uncompahgre Brown Ware, most often in the form of unembellished eight- to twelve-inch tall "jars with slightly flaring, wide necks, poorly to well-defined shoulders, and pointed to gently rounded bases."[46]

As they pitched camp, northeastern Nuche kin groups unpacked weapons and tools alongside household utensils. Enduring components of the Mountain Tradition arsenal included bows (traditionally fashioned from the horns of bighorn sheep, but later made from curved wood), arrows, clubs, spears, and buffalo hide shields. The Nuche tool kit, like that of earlier inhabitants of the high country, comprised fishing gear, grinding stones, digging sticks, drills for starting fires, and scrapers and other implements for preparing hides and furs. Last but hardly least, the Nuche unloaded at least some goods obtained through trade with other native peoples, New Mexicans, and Americans, including firearms, pots, knives, and other metal tools.[47]

After setting up camp, Nuche women ventured out to gather a range of plants for food, medicine, and other purposes. With an expert stroke of their digging sticks, they unearthed roots of violet, puccoon, miner's candle, arrowleaf balsamroot, and alum root, as well as the bulbs and bulblets of mariposa lily, bistort, and other plants. The People especially favored yampa, a wild member of the carrot family that lent its name to one northeastern Nuche band, the Yamparika or "yampa eaters." The Nuche, like their Mountain Tradition ancestors, supplemented starchy roots, tubers, and bulbs with leaves, seeds, and fruits. Women not only gathered most or all of these plant foods but also toiled to dry, grind, boil, parch, or otherwise preserve and prepare the fruits of the harvest.[48]

Though most plants gathered by Nuche foragers had probably sustained Mountain Tradition practitioners during previous millennia, the People likely harvested some foods unknown to earlier inhabitants of the high country. Archaeological sites in Rocky Mountain National Park associated with Nuche inhabitation appear to contain more grinding stones than older sites, suggesting that the People probably relied more heavily than their predecessors on grass seeds. The Nuche also seem to have introduced new ways of using the Kawuneeche's tree species. The People not only stripped the outer bark from pines to access the nutritious cambium beneath but also honored cultural taboos against gathering wild honey by tapping aspen trees and collecting their sweet sap in bark containers.[49]

In the People's gendered vision of labor, plant foods were considered women's special responsibility. Hunting, by contrast, figured as men's work. The Nuche prized venison above all other meat. They also considered bear a great delicacy, though the People believed it was only safe to hunt these formidable creatures in spring, after months of hibernation had depleted the creatures' energy reserves. In addition to mule deer, black bears, and grizzlies, Nuche hunters targeted the Kawuneeche's bighorn sheep and elk. The White River and Uncompahgre Utes told Smith that they hunted the latter species chiefly during the winter, when deep snows made it harder for elk to elude them. But the Nuche also used rock blinds and game drives first built by Mountain Tradition forgoers to kill elk after the beasts reached their high-altitude summer ranges.[50]

Nuche men figured among the greatest hunters ever to stalk the Rockies. Their skill seemed to mesmerize John Wesley Powell on his explorations of the People's homelands. Powell described how an experienced Nuche hunter "exhibits great patience and his success is due chiefly to this characteristic." A Nuche huntsman, Powell explained, "never discharges his gun or shoots an arrow from a distance," preferring instead to "crawl upon the deer so as not to frighten him." With a "practiced eye," Nuche men could discern the tracks of their quarry "at a great distance." Having "walk[ed] around for a long distance to get in such a position that the deer will be to the windward," the man then edged closer to his quarry "in a crouching attitude through the woods or over the plains with almost noiseless step," always "cover[ing] his approach" by hiding himself behind "little trees and bushes even, or the inequalities of the ground."[51]

Through patience and prowess, Nuche huntsmen endeavored to replenish the People's meat bags. They readily took sustenance from the Kawuneeche's smaller animals, too. The Nuche attacked beaver colonies as if they were enemy villages, falling on the rodents' lodges and clubbing the inmates as they scurried for cover. Nuche men (and, less frequently, Nuche women) also killed snowshoe hares, cottontail rabbits, jackrabbits, marmots, and other mammals with spears, arrows, snares, and traps. Last but not least, the People pulled Colorado River cutthroat trout from the valley's lakes and streams with horsehair lines and hooks made of bone or steel. On occasion, the People even waded into shallow water and shot fish with arrows.[52]

The Nuche sometimes ate their prey immediately, either raw or hastily cooked. More often, they chose to preserve meat and fiber from the animals they killed. The People skinned and gutted beaver, removed the rodents' toothsome tails for roasting in smoldering ashes, and boiled the rest of the carcasses. Muscular cuts of venison were dried, pounded, and stored for later consumption. The fattiest parts of deer were then rendered and mixed with red clay to form a paste that safeguarded the People's skin against the fierce Rocky Mountain wind and sun. Powell extolled the extraordinary thoroughness and efficiency with which the People tapped into practically every store of vital energy hidden within the bodies of the animals they slaughtered. The Nuche, the awestruck American related, took "great pains . . . to break open the bones containing marrow which is highly esteemed" and "carefully preserved" the blood of "all" the animals they hunted. The People even ate the hide "when it [wa]s not deemed desirable to preserve the skin for other purposes."[53]

Skins provided the Nuche with much more than food, of course. The same hides and coats that enabled the Rockies' wild creatures to survive the region's treacherous climate afforded the Nuche with bedding, trade goods, clothing, and other necessities. Smith's Northern Ute informants told her with unmistakable pride that Nuche buckskins were acknowledged far and wide as "exceptionally well done and were frequently used as trade articles with other tribes, and with the Spanish colonists of New Mexico"—a clear testimonial to the skill and dedication of Nuche women. It took half a day to stretch a deer hide, after all, and several hours' additional labor to tan it properly.[54]

The Nuche believed that they were bound to the natural world by sacred forces as well as material exchanges. *Puwa,* a concept that scholars variously translate as "medicine power," "the life force of the universe," or "supernatural power-and-energy," shaped most every aspect of the People's interactions with their surroundings. *Puwa* never stopped flowing. Instead, anthropologist Jay Miller explains, it was "kinetic"—a force "underlying all aspects and activities of the native universe, conveying notions closer to those of modern physics than to other folk beliefs." This "causal and dynamic" power constantly made and remade the People's world. Like the watercourses with which the Nuche often associated it, *puwa* flowed, moving "through a web-like structure that connects all things and beings, human or otherwise."[55]

Puwa had especially pressing implications for the relationships between the People and nonhuman animals. The White River band, to cite just one example, honored prohibitions against eating snakes and most insects—a luxury unthinkable to their western Nuche kinsmen, who depended on protein from horned toads, grasshoppers, crickets, earthworms, lizards, and other animals that crept and crawled through the Great Basin. *Puwa* attracted the People to some creatures even as it repelled them from others. "Various animals and birds," the Northern Utes told Smith, "could be sources of power. Buffalo, grizzly bear and mountain lion were particularly strong sources." Decades earlier, Powell's informants had elaborated on the conduits between *puwa,* the People, and the land. The Nuche and their relatives, Powell explained, "believe in an ancient race of people who were the progenitors of all human beings and also of animals, trees and even of the rocks." The Nuche claimed that every element of the physical world traced its lineage back to these common "progenitors." And so the Nuche, Powell reported, "speak of an ancient people, and a species of animals, or plants in the same manner as if they were co-ordinate. So they have the nation of Nu-mas, the nation of Tai-vus, the nation of bears, the nation of rabbits, and rattlesnakes, the spiders, the pines, the sunflowers, the nation of black flints and many others." Twenty-first-century Northern Ute elder Clifford Duncan expressed much the same idea: "When we say animals, we are actually talking about people also."[56]

The Nuche perceived and experienced their surroundings as suffused with *puwa's* vital agencies. This worldview lent the People's interactions with nonhuman entities an inextricably social character. The People never acted on inferior beings and inert matter as if the world were subject to their dominion. Instead, the Nuche saw themselves as important but hardly all-powerful players within a unitary and broadly egalitarian world populated by many different types of persons.[57]

This value system invested the act of killing nonhuman beings with grave perils. Nuche hunters, for instance, always took care to remove a deer's eyes before bringing its carcass into camp, thus sparing the creature's spirit the offense of having to watch as the People dismembered and ingested its worldly remains. The Nuche and their kin, Powell discovered, also conceived of "a great number of beings whom we call demons. The air above, the earth beneath, the waters, the recesses in the rocks, the trees, everything is peopled by strange, weird beings." The Nuche took particular care not to offend mighty entities known as *"Kai-ni-suva"* who dwelled "in the highest mountains." These beings would "usually remain in deep chambers or underground compartments in the mountains by day, but when the storms gather over the mountains they come out under cover of the clouds and ride at breakneck speed over the peaks and crags." The *Kai-ni-suva* harnessed the thunderheads and blizzards that raged against the Shining Mountains, exercising "special control over mountain-sheep, elk and deer." Whenever a Nuche hunter killed one of these ungulates, he took pains to leave a "portion of the carcass where the animal has fallen to propitiate the good will of the *Kai-ni-suva.*"[58]

By the mid-nineteenth century, the extension of Spanish, Mexican, and American frontiers was exposing both the northeastern Nuche bands and their domains to new pressures and possibilities. The indigenous inhabitants of the Greater Rocky Mountain National Park Ecosystem had embraced horses; forged vigorous exchange economies with a variety of native and nonnative partners; and become conversant in the languages and ambitions of a succession of European and North American powers. The vicious violence spurred by Euro-American imperialism had taken several centuries to reach the northern Colorado high country, but the 1800s witnessed the invasion of the Upper Colorado River watershed by American trapping brigades, escalating aggression between the People and several Plains Indian enemies, and the first recorded outbreaks of epidemic disease among the northeastern Nuche.

And yet several decades after Lechat captured the attention of American newcomers to New Mexico, the People maintained a staunch hold over the Coyote Valley. As in the decades and centuries that had passed since the Nuche emerged, the People remained strong because of the protection their Rocky Mountain homelands provided against all comers and the vast wealth of knowledge, power, and humility they and their Mountain Tradition forebears had accumulated over many millennia of eking out a living in some of the most foreboding environments on the planet.[59]

A Peopled Wilderness

The Coyote Valley was neither unpeopled nor pristine when Americans discovered gold at the foot of the Rockies in 1858. Instead of passively standing outside the balance of nature, the Nuche and their predecessors had always behaved as Wolf had decreed: by working to live. The labors that sustained the People and their Mountain Tradition predecessors had always unfolded within, upon, and against the natural world. The Colorado River headwaters—far from the timeless refuge of pure nature unsullied by human hands that incoming American settlers imagined it to be—was an inextricably humanized place that had already sustained many hundreds of generations of indigenous inhabitation.

Nearly three decades ago, historian Richard White assailed U.S. environmentalists for suggesting "that Indians had moved over the face of

the land and when they left you couldn't tell they'd ever been there."
White argued that this view "demeans Indians" by caricaturing them
as ecological saints. "It makes them seem simply like an animal species,"
he contended, "and thus deprives them of culture. It also demeans the
environment," White concluded, "by so simplifying it that all changes
come to seem negative—as if somehow the ideal is never to have been
here at all. It's a crude view of the environment, and it's a crude view
of Indians."[60]

In the decades since White articulated this influential critique, environmental historians have joined archaeologists, anthropologists,
ecologists, and others in assailing the so-called pristine myth. As
journalist Charles Mann explains in his best seller *1491: New Revelations
of the Americas before Columbus* (2005), the iconoclastic body of scholarship
produced in the 1990s and early 2000s "radically challenged conventional
notions." A growing chorus of scholars drawn from many disciplines,
Mann declares, disavow the long-held notion that pre-Columbian North
America was an "almost untouched, even Edenic land" in favor of a new
synthesis portraying the continent to have been "thoroughly marked
by humankind."[61]

It would be foolish to deny that the Nuche, too, had "marked" the
Greater Rocky Mountain National Park Ecosystem in countless ways
throughout their long-running reign. And yet it would be just as un-
wise to exaggerate the People's impact on the Coyote Valley and the rest
of the high country. If it is demeaning to view the Nuche as ecological
nonentities, is it somehow more flattering to allow interpolations drawn
from research on other places and peoples to cloud our understanding
of human-environment interactions in North America's mountain
heart?

Family groups from the northeastern Nuche bands inhabited the
Kawuneeche in relatively small numbers and only during the warmer
months. Unlike the densely settled agricultural societies that proliferated in many other parts of North America on the eve of European
contact, the lives and labors of the Nuche hinged on interactions with
nonhuman nature that were sharply limited in time and space: pasturing horses, blazing trails, procuring lodgepoles, harvesting willow
shoots, taking sufficient fish and game to feed a few dozen people for
several weeks or months, gathering berries, drying roots and meat
for the long winter ahead, manufacturing trade goods from skins and

fur, placating powerful nonhuman persons, and so on. Each intervention undoubtedly affected the Kawuneeche's ecology, and yet each
also unfolded within narrow, relatively stable ranges of variability.

The case of wildfire in the subalpine zone nicely illustrates the light
touch that characterized northeastern Nuche land-use practices. An
emerging consensus among environmental historians holds that Native
Americans almost universally employed fire to manage the ecosystems
they inhabited. Mann's *1491* and other popular works have drawn on
scholarly research to cast native peoples as skilled land managers who
deployed fire to transform and control North American environments.
"From the Atlantic to the Pacific," Mann confidently asserts, and "from
Hudson's Bay to the Río Grande," native peoples "shaped their environment, at least in part, by fire."[62]

The Nuche were not averse to setting some parts of their homelands
ablaze. But they also recognized that fire, like all tools, was useful for
some tasks but inappropriate for others. Subalpine forests such as those
that flank the slopes of the Coyote Valley played virtually no role in
Nuche subsistence, while the cool, wet climate of these upper-elevation
woodlands made them almost impossible to ignite except during prolonged droughts. Researchers have conclusively demonstrated that presettlement fire regimes in the subalpine forests of the Greater Rocky
Mountain National Park Ecosystem were driven not by Native American
land managers, but instead by the El Niño-Southern Oscillation and
other distant processes that cause extended phases of drier climate in
the Colorado high country.[63]

Throughout the American West, Euro-American colonialism caused
widespread and often calamitous ecological, social, and political changes.
In the Coyote Valley, by contrast, the name of the game remained
much the same from the dawn of the Mountain Tradition through the
mid-nineteenth century: Get in, fit in, and get out before winter's descent. The influx of American gold seekers to the Colorado piedmont in
the late 1850s, though, set the stage for the eventual dispossession of
the northeastern Nuche from their homelands—but not before the
People applied lessons learned throughout three centuries of adaptation and endurance to wage an astonishing stand against the jugger-
naut of American imperial expansion.

◄| 3 |►

DISPOSSESSION

IN SUMMER 1878, serious trouble was brewing between the northeastern Nuche bands and American settlers. The first sign of the impending collision occurred just outside the Coyote Valley, in Middle Park, where a group of White River Nuche allegedly sought refuge after tussling with Americans on Colorado's eastern plains. A few dozen miles downstream from Grand Lake at the Junction Ranch, the Nuche slashed the harnesses on several horses, tore down fences, and laid out a racetrack for their ponies. As the Nuche contingent's male members galloped around at breakneck speed, its women and children made camp.[1]

Some of the Americans who had only recently established homesteads and ranching operations in the area accused the Nuche of stealing horses and arms. A posse deputized to inspect the People's camp found only women and children there. With no warriors to stop them, the posse rifled through Nuche lodges in search of contraband. On their return to camp, Nuche men found that settlers who had recently filed claims to the People's ancestral lands were rummaging through their homes and personal possessions. Heated words were exchanged, leading to a scuffle between a former fur trapper named Frank Addison and a White River Nuche headman known as Tabernash. After Addison pulled a gun and fired several shots into Tabernash, the Nuche beat a hasty retreat toward their northwestern Colorado agency. En route, they vented their outrage at Tabernash's killing by murdering an American rancher on the Blue River.[2]

Nuche leaders subsequently returned to Hot Sulphur Springs and gave back every horse the Middle Park settlers had accused them of

This etching, based on a sketch by Lieutenant C. A. H. McCauley of the Third U.S. Cavalry, depicted the White River Agency as a scene of devastation. *Frank Leslie's Newspaper,* December 6, 1879, Denver Public Library, Western History Collection, X-30699.

taking. American settlers reciprocated by handing over firearms seized from the People's lodges at the Junction Ranch back in August. These conciliatory gestures temporarily restored the tense and tenuous peace that had previously prevailed in the Colorado high country.

A little more than a year later, however, open warfare erupted between some members of the northeastern Nuche bands, U.S. troops, and federal officials at the White River Agency in northwestern Colorado. The resulting struggle—Colorado settlers called it the Ute War—unfolded more than a hundred miles west of the Coyote Valley. Yet it nonetheless brought momentous changes to the Greater Rocky Mountain National Park Ecosystem by completing the dispossession of the northeastern Nuche from their Colorado homelands.[3]

American settlers had first cast covetous eyes on the Nuche domains after the 1858 discovery of gold along the base of the Rockies. The northeastern Nuche bands responded to the social, political, and ecological upheavals catalyzed by the Pike's Peak Gold Rush with the same flexibility and resourcefulness they had deployed to fend off threats ranging from the collapse of Ancestral Puebloan polities in the Four Corners in the fourteenth century to the invasion of American fur trappers in the early nineteenth century. By the late 1870s, though, the People's startling success at forestalling American incursions would impel Colorado settlers and the politicians who curried their favor into pressuring the federal government to remove all Nuche from the newly established state. Distraught at the continuing refusal of the Nuche to sign over title to their homelands, or, better still, to vanish altogether, a rising chorus of American newcomers bluntly demanded that "the Utes must go!" The Ute War gave U.S. leaders the pretext they needed to permanently remove the northeastern Nuche from Colorado. In turn, Nuche dispossession initiated far-reaching changes for ecosystems and landscapes that had been shaped over many centuries by the People's lives and labors.

Gold!

The Pike's Peak Gold Rush has always served as the founding myth of American Colorado—and for good reason. Before the late 1850s, Anglos migrated into the area only in faint, sporadic trickles. After William Green Russell's party of Georgians and Cherokees struck pay dirt, though, Americans surged across the Great Plains toward the foot of the Rockies in a mass migration that would have disastrous consequences for the Nuche and other native peoples. By the time the summer of 1859 faded into fall, more than 100,000 gold seekers had embarked on the arduous, hazard-filled journey. Though at least half turned back before they even reached the diggings, and many others moved on after a few weeks or months, the Pike's Peak excitement nonetheless set in motion a chain of events that soon led hopeful prospectors to scour every nook and cranny of the Rocky Mountains. By stimulating road construction, ranching, town building, and other pursuits, the gold rush accelerated the pace and intensified the ruthlessness of American imperial expansion and native dispossession.[4]

Gold strikes along the eastern base of the Colorado Rockies—the so-called northern piedmont,"—almost immediately inspired speculators to lay out Auraria, Denver, and other town sites near the confluence of Cherry Creek and the South Platte River. But argonauts soon discovered that in comparison to the rich placers of California's Sierra Nevada foothills, the stream deposits of the Rockies offered slim pickings. All but the most skillful and fortunate miners struggled to recoup enough gold to pay back the debts they accrued to outfit themselves for their westward journey. Miners soon deduced that the tiny flecks and occasional nuggets of gold they pulled from the frigid streams spilling down from the Rockies comprised just the pulverized traces of larger, more concentrated deposits. Even the dimmest sourdough understood that the gold found in the beds of piedmont streams must have originated in some "mother lode" hidden away in the mountains above.[5]

And so even as tens of thousands of gold seekers returned home from Colorado empty-handed, thousands of their more ambitious brethren pushed into the high country. Prospectors had made several promising finds by late 1859, including Gold Hill, Breckenridge, California Gulch, and, most promising of all, the rich diggings at Gregory Gulch and Russell Gulch in the Clear Creek watershed. Most prospectors, of course, never found paying deposits. Even unsuccessful forays, though, could impinge on the People's prerogatives. Miners who pushed into Middle Park in 1859, for example, found neither silver nor gold, but they did happen upon Hot Sulphur Springs—a favorite Nuche camping and watering spot previously unknown to Americans that William Byers, the entrepreneurial editor of Denver's *Rocky Mountain News*, soon began to tout as a health resort.[6]

Wherever miners ventured, they projected a set of deeply held ideologies about nature, native peoples, and nationalist mission. The newcomers believed that a beneficent Providence had generously seen fit to bury precious minerals beneath the Rockies. These treasure troves had lain untouched by human hands for eons, awaiting the arrival of Americans—God's chosen people—whose industry, intelligence, and virtue would transmute Colorado's hidden placers, veins, and lodes into personal wealth and national power.[7]

The Americans' God, as befitted a figure of incomprehensible potency, moved in mysterious ways. The Rockies' gold and silver deposits proved difficult to locate, extract, and refine. Instead of the fabled "mother lode," prospectors and miners struggled to unlock the mysteries of Colorado's irregular "mineral belt." The Rockies' precious metals lay ensconced in complex subterranean features and refractory chemical compounds. "The minerals of Colorado," as historian Hubert Howe Bancroft explained in 1890, "were not easy to come at. . . . Nor was there any rule of nature known to mineralogists which applied to the situation of mines in Colorado." Only in the late 1870s and early 1880s would metallurgists begin to devise new techniques to supplant the faulty "old traditions" Bancroft invoked to explain the disappointing performance of Colorado's mining industry in the decades after the Pike's Peak rush began.[8]

Throughout these years of uncertain prospects, American wealth seekers also struggled against more immediate obstacles: the First Peoples who claimed, inhabited, and defended all of the lands coveted by miners and their fellow settlers. Most new arrivals to Colorado came predisposed to despise Native Americans. Citizen-settlers considered it both their duty and their right to spread U.S. rule to western lands. They expected the federal government, in turn, to act on their seething hatreds by pacifying, concentrating, and removing the West's First Peoples. Many frontier folk wanted the government not just to marginalize Indians or force them out, but to eradicate them altogether. As a federal official from Utah explained in 1865, "the emigrants who traverse these plains, the settlers in these mountains, and the officers and soldiers who are here for their protection, are almost entirely in favor of the extermination of all Indians." Coloradans and Utahns disagreed on many counts, but they shared a deep desire to eliminate the Nuche and other native peoples from a region they believed it was their special destiny to possess.[9]

American settlers viewed the continuing presence of independent Indian peoples as a threat to their personal and collective quest for wealth, status, and security. Edward McCook, Colorado Territory's governor and ex officio superintendent of Indian Affairs, forthrightly articulated this widely shared conviction in an 1870 report to the U.S. commissioner of Indian Affairs. "I believe," McCook revealingly intoned, "that God gave to us the earth, and the fullness thereof, in order that we might utilize and enjoy His gifts. I do not believe in donating to these indolent savages the best portion of my Territory." The Almighty, McCook reasoned, had entrusted him and his fellow Americans with the mission of redeeming western lands from their barbaric Indian occupants. If the federal government attempted to stand in the way—if it held fast to the policy of "donating . . . the best portion" of the lands under McCook's supervision to the Nuche through overly generous treaties—then Colorado's settlers and the officials entrusted with executing their will would not hesitate to take matters into their own hands, as Frank Addison's shooting of Tabernash at Middle Park would demonstrate eight years later.[10]

Unaccompanied by Cruelty

By the time McCook voiced the assumptions and anxieties underlying the long-standing push by settlers to dispossess the Nuche, the Americans had all but eliminated Cheyennes, Arapahos, and other Plains Indians from eastern Colorado. The 1860s also witnessed large cessions of land from the Nuche, whose homelands had originally sprawled across the western two-thirds of Colorado into New Mexico and Utah. Despite these successes, though, McCook still fumed with frustration. More than a decade after William Green Russell had noticed gold glinting in his pan at the mouth of Little Dry Creek, the Nuche were showing no inclination to abandon Colorado without a fight.

The governor, like Colorado's other citizens, blamed the federal government for this predicament. The most recent treaty between the United States and the Nuche, McCook griped, had recognized the People's claims to "one-third of the whole area of Colorado for the use and occupation of the Ute nation." This parcel of "over 40,000 square miles" included what McCook called "the best agricultural, pastural [sic], and mining land on the continent." By validating Nuche sovereignty over this rich domain, McCook bristled, the federal government had shown that it was more interested in coddling "aboriginal vagrants" than in satisfying the American people's voracious hunger for land and wealth.[11]

Driven to distraction by a treaty system that he berated as "wrong, because it is unjust to the white, and of no real benefit to the red man," McCook proposed "a simple solution." He urged the government to break up the Nuche's communal lands into parcels of 160 acres; assign "every individual man, woman, and child" a parcel of their own; and "allow every American man to go freely, and without hindrance, wherever the American flag covers American soil." Such a policy, McCook contended, would confront the Nuche with a clear choice: Die out, quit Colorado, or conform to the new order by embracing the settled lifeways that Americans upheld as the foundation of their moral superiority as well as the bedrock of their republic.[12]

McCook expressed the greed and arrogance that fueled increasingly strident campaigns by American settlers and the U.S. government to remove or exterminate First Peoples. But the governor's vitriol toward the Nuche also betrayed fear and frustration. As the governor was writing his report in 1870, after all, gloom shrouded Colorado's future. The territory's once-bright prospects seemed to dim as its economy faltered. The transcontinental railroad had bypassed Colorado in favor of Wyoming, while the mining industry was wracked by irresponsible financial speculation and refractory ores that stubbornly refused to give up their silver and gold.[13]

Given the already uncertain enterprise of settler colonialism, the persistence of the Nuche struck McCook and many other Coloradans as an intolerable threat. The governor and his people were incensed that the Nuche refused to act according to the script that settlers and policy makers had expected them to follow. In 1866, McCook's gubernatorial predecessor, Alexander Cummings, had articulated the core story line in the drama many Americans desperately hoped would unfold in the mineral-rich Colorado high country: "It would not be difficult," Cummings predicted, "for the government to adopt measures which, while liberal to the Indians, would actually be economical as well as humane, so that if, as is now evident, they are destined to vanish from the earth, their extinction may be *unaccompanied by cruelty*."[14]

Four years later, McCook fretted that the government's "measures" had become too "liberal" and "humane." The Nuche, the governor and many settlers now worried, were improvising with such aplomb that they just might hold their ground. The possibility that the People might forestall their destiny and remain on their Rocky Mountain homelands struck dread into the restless, acquisitive Americans who were massing along the borders of the Ute reservation. The dispossession of the Nuche, McCook and his people were increasingly convinced, would require the federal government to adopt a harder line in its dealings with the People.

Enmity and Opportunity

The northeastern Nuche owed their surprising persistence in the face of American invasions to the interplay of three main factors: the People's opportunistic response to U.S. assaults against their common enemies; their successful adaptation of time-tested transhumance migrations in response to new constraints and possibilities; and the federal government's gradualist approach to securing Nuche lands for American settlers.

The Nuche inhabitants of the Coyote Valley benefited from the declining fortunes of some of their traditional foes. Just as southeastern Nuche bands intensified their raids against the Navajo, Hopi, and other once-mighty rivals, the northeastern Nuche and the Tabeguache reaped material and political rewards from the American conquest of the Cheyennes and Arapahos. Throughout the first half of the 1800s, these two allied nations had dominated the high plains. Even before the gold rush, though, declining bison populations, overdependence on trade with outsiders, and U.S. imperialism were beginning to sap the People's longtime adversaries.[15]

A bad situation grew even worse when gold seekers trailed through the Plains Indians' homelands en route to Colorado. To the mounting distress of Arapahos and Cheyennes, outsiders traveling on the overland trails across the plains shot game, cut timber, and pastured hungry livestock; they also started dozens of so-called road ranches—trailside outposts that sold food, drink, and shelter to American emigrants. Before long, settlers were even taking possession of the fertile, well-watered, and temperate valleys along the base of the Rocky Mountains, where they established farms, cattle ranches, and towns on lands that had long figured centrally in the seasonal migrations of Arapahos, Cheyennes, and other peoples.[16]

Mounting tensions between American settlers, on the one hand, and the Arapahos and Cheyennes on the other, exploded in the 1864 Sand Creek Massacre. This unconscionably immoral attack showed just how far the newcomers would go to fulfill their exterminationist fantasies. For the sin of standing between the Americans and their self-declared destiny, Native American men, women, and children paid dearly. Colonel John Chivington's force, drawn almost entirely from the settlements of Colorado Territory, slaughtered some 150 Cheyennes and Arapahos while wounding hundreds more. Soldiers proceeded to mutilate dozens of indigenous corpses, slicing off scalps and genitalia as loathsome trophies for display or sale. Federal officials responded to allegations that the Indian encampment at Sand Creek was inhabited by "friendlies" who bore no responsibility for the misdeeds the Arapahos and Cheyennes were accused of perpetrating by censuring Chivington and his men. But this rebuke did nothing to slow the U.S. Army's relentless push to drive the Arapahos and Cheyennes out of Colorado.[17]

The Nuche played no part in the atrocities at Sand Creek, yet the U.S. conquest of the piedmont and plains nonetheless enhanced the People's reputation and enlarged their economic reach. Americans brought to the Rocky Mountain West a firmly entrenched habit of divvying First Peoples into "noble" and "savage" types. Even as Colorado governor John Evans demonized the Cheyennes and Arapahos, he thus praised the Nuche. Of all "the wild Indians of this superintendency," Evans intoned, "there are none whose general character and intelligence give so much promise of future improvement as this band." Evans went on to commend the Nuche as "cheerful, full of conviviality and good humor, and enjoy a joke with great zest." The Colorado governor interpreted the People's unwillingness to come to the aid of their plains neighbors as a clear demonstration of their loyalty to the Americans. "During the past year," one Ute agent reported in 1865, "when all the prairie Indians have been at war and bidding open defiance to our troops and to our citizens, the Utah Indians have remained at peace with our people."[18]

Friendly relations with the Americans in the wake of Sand Creek enabled the Nuche to exploit new opportunities. In summer 1868, Colorado's governor reported that the People's long-standing enemies were "nearly all voluntarily withdraw[ing] from our boundaries, only showing themselves in the form of marauding parties." That same year, another official claimed that some one hundred lodges of northeastern Nuche "under the Chief We-va-ra, having heard that the Cheyennes were away to the eastward, moved their camp down into the buffalo country." In response to the forced displacement of the Cheyennes and their Arapaho allies, the Nuche reconfigured their seasonal movements and began to devote several late-summer weeks to hunting bison on their enemies' former homelands. By the time the last Nuche hunting party to venture into the plains buffalo grounds returned to the Rockies in 1875, the Nuche had profited from many seasons of plenty.[19]

The People's Game

The People's skill at reaping dividends from the American conquest of competing native nations, however, offers only a partial explanation for their persistence. To understand Governor Edward McCook's exasperation with the Nuche, we need to consider a second pillar of the People's ongoing strength: their adeptness at reconfiguring their subsistence practices and transhumance rounds in response to the destabilizing forces the Americans' quest for mineral riches had loosed upon the land. We know regrettably few details about how the Coyote Valley figured into this larger pattern of improvisation, but warm-season stops in the Colorado River headwaters almost certainly played a critical role in sustaining the northeastern bands' struggle against settler colonialism.

For a decade or more after the gold rush began, Americans confidently predicted that the wild animals of the mountains and plains would soon be exterminated. Some newcomers lamented the imminent decline of bison, elk, deer, bears, and other large mammals, but most greeted the prospect of these creatures' extermination with resignation and even delight. Benjamin Davies, Utah's superintendent of Indian Affairs, summed up the connections settlers drew between animals, Indians, and western conquest during the 1850s and 1860s. "Civilization," Davies asserted, "seems to have had the same effect here as has been noticed elsewhere in this country since the first settlement by our forefathers, in driving before it the game natural to a wilderness, and the Indians complain bitterly that since the white man has come among them their game has almost entirely disappeared from their former hunting-grounds, and they are now obliged either to beg food from the white settlers or starve." Casting the past as prologue, Davies and other newcomers viewed the eradication of western wildlife as both inevitable and highly desirable, since it would force hungry native peoples into submission.[20]

Davies was hardly the only observer who believed that the game animals of the Nuche domains were dying off right on schedule. In 1861, a group of northeastern Nuche complained to federal Indian agent Henry Vaile that "their game [was] becoming very scarce." Some Nuche had been so famished that one confessed: " 'Nute [sic] have to eat ponies. Don't like it.' " Though the horse-loving People found it deeply distasteful to kill and eat their animal companions, these Nuche could no longer find any wild game. In 1866, Alexander Cummings portrayed still greater suffering among the Tabeguaches of central Colorado, admitting that he "was much surprised" at "the destitute condition of these Indians," the "mass of" whom had descended into "squalid wretchedness, many of them being nearly naked." The most alarming thing about this state of affairs, Cummings noted, was its timing: "during the hunting season," when the People's hide clothing should have been new (or at least freshly repaired) and their meat bags bursting at the seams. Two years later, Cummings's successor offered an even grimmer portrait: "Game, except in certain locations remote, is now almost extinct," Alexander Hunt declared of the Nuche. "A few black-tail deer, high up against the snow peaks, occasionally small herds of antelopes ranging over . . . [the] plains, and a very limited number of bears in the most distant recess of the mountains, form the supply on which these poor people with very indifferent guns and uncertain supplies of ammunition, are compelled to draw for their subsistence, which under such circumstances must be very scanty and unreliable; indeed it is entirely inadequate." The next year, Edward McCook himself portrayed the Nuche as teetering toward an abyss. Bison, "their main dependence in past years," had "almost entirely disappeared from the old hunting grounds on the plains," while the wild creatures of the mountains proved "fast vanishing before the steady march of advancing civilization."[21]

Other evidence, however, paints a more complicated picture. The same Nuche bands who complained to Vaile about having to eat their ponies also informed him that a "great many elk, wild turkey, mountain sheep, &c." still roamed northwestern Colorado's Flattop Range. Because the Nuche had never abandoned the skills and environmental knowledge needed to harvest a wide variety of creatures, they could still redirect their efforts to other quarry when favored food animals became locally scarce. When April arrived, the Nuche told Vaile, they would "leave the Elk mountains [the Flattops] . . . and slowly make their way to the north." Different family groups would follow old trails along various watercourses to the Laramie Plains or even the Snake River basin, where they "generally remain . . . through the months of July and August, catching buffalo, deer, fish &c." By early September, "the cold nights start them back to their country again." Nuche family groups returned to "the parks . . . about the months of November and December" before launching "midwinter" hunting forays into the Flattops. Some northeastern Nuche may also have intensified their involvement in borderlands exchange economies. Even the northeastern bands, Vaile learned, sent occasional deputations "into the Navajo country to trade with those Indians and the Mexicans; they get most of their guns and ammunition down there." As they had for centuries, the northeastern Nuche astutely recalibrated their time-honored resource migrations to

The northeastern Nuche leader known alternately as Antelope, Wanzits, or
Wanzitz—a frequent visitor to Denver, Colorado City, and other American
settlements—struck a defiant pose in this undated studio portrait. One owner of
this photograph took care to note that Wanzits was alleged to have killed agent
Nathan Meeker. Denver Public Library, Western History Collection, X-30427.

navigate the shifting currents of American colonialism. Wielding a peerless grasp of the region's ecosystems, travel routes, and exchange networks, the People harnessed their horses, loaded their guns, and lit off across what Vaile rightly described as their "extensive range."[22]

The Nuche understood that possibility still beckoned in many corners of the West: the plains bison hunting grounds opened up by American expansion; the no-man's-land of the Nuche borders, a conflict zone where game had presumably flourished in the decades leading up to the Colorado Gold Rush; and, not least, the new American settlements, from which the Nuche obtained food, livestock, and other goods. In 1865, for instance, a party of Tabeguaches, reduced to privation by an "unprecedented hard winter" that prevented "them from visiting their usual hunting grounds," descended on Colorado City and stole "ten sacks of flour to relieve their pressing wants and necessities." Usually, though, the Nuche preferred buying and begging to stealing. Some American farmers, ranchers, and townsfolk would later pat themselves on the back when they recalled their generosity toward the hungry Nuche supplicants who appeared on their cabin thresholds; other settlers, meanwhile, begrudged the People every crumb. For their part, the territory's merchants eagerly cultivated the People's trade at posts ringing the Nuche domains, as well as in Denver and other settlements. Colorado's capital of hustle and bustle exerted particular magnetism. In the 1860s and early 1870s, Nuche groups often visited Denver on their circuit to "the glorious annual buffalo-hunt, the *ne plus ultra* of excitement and profit to all semi-civilized Indians." To the delight of tourists, the People frequently camped outside of the city because it offered "the best market in the Territory for what they have to sell"—chiefly meat, hides, furs, and ponies—"and the most complete assortment of goods from which to select the articles they need"—especially guns, ammunition, and novelties such as the sodas one party of Nuche sipped in 1874 as they strolled through the city's streets.[23]

Throughout the 1860s, settlers and government officials alike had forecast the speedy eradication of Colorado's game and the imminent conquest of the First Peoples who depended on them. By 1871, though, James Thompson, a U.S. Indian agent stationed in Denver, expressed alarm that the Nuche were not performing as settlers and government officials expected. Thompson complained that about 450 Nuche "who habitually frequent Denver and vicinity" were rebuffing his pleas to

move to the White River Agency some 200 miles northwest of the capital. "If the Government did not see fit to provide for their wants," these
Nuche gave Thompson to understand, "they would try to provide for
themselves, which means nothing more nor less than this: that they will
roam where they please, hunt where they happen to find game, beg in
the towns, and steal from the ranchmen." A dozen years after the gold
rush, the People remained highly mobile, fully capable of drawing on a
broad and shifting assortment of resources, and firmly committed to
maintaining their independence on and around their ancestral lands.[24]

No wonder Governor McCook could no longer assume that the Nuche
would simply disappear into the Rocky Mountain sunset.

Federal Frustrations

Compounding the worries kindled by the unexpected survival of the
Rockies' wildlife and the northeastern Nuche's impressive skill at
modifying their age-old transhumance patterns was a third and final
factor: the government's reluctance to impose its authority on the People.
Federal foot-dragging reflected the Nuche's well-deserved reputation
as formidable opponents ensconced in high-country redoubts posing
daunting logistical and tactical challenges to the U.S. Army. American
and southeastern Nuche forces had sometimes clashed in the 1850s and
1860s. Though the newcomers had fared well enough in these outbreaks
of violence, the People's ample ponies, plentiful rifles and ammunition,
and unmatched talent for turning the nearly impregnable topography
of the Rockies to their own advantage continued to strike fear into American hearts well into the 1870s.[25]

An 1863 incident hinted at the uneasy calculations American and
Nuche leaders made as they grappled for primacy. The trouble started
when a group of Nuche fell upon a ranch near Fort Halleck on the Overland Mail's transcontinental route through southern Wyoming. After
the Nuche made off with "a lot of horses," cavalrymen poured from the
fort in hot pursuit. Overtaking the raiders, the troopers "demanded" that
they surrender "the stolen horses." But "this the Indians refused to do,
claiming them as legitimate booty from the Sioux Indians." A gunfight
erupted and "the soldiers were repulsed, with the loss of one killed and
four wounded." The Nuche attackers then "made their escape with their

stolen property," prompting cavalrymen led by Edward Wynkoop to ride out from Denver with orders to "chastise the Indians." The Nuche and their ponies swiftly disappeared, having "made such rapid flight over their rugged mountain trail," Governor Evans explained, that Wynkoop and his troopers were "obliged, after a hard campaign, to give up the pursuit."[26]

Though this group of Nuche got away, the running confrontation generated festering anger at the Americans' impudence. Soon after, Tabeguache warriors, "complain[ing] bitterly of the interference of the soldiers," reportedly sought to broker "a combination with other bands of Utah Indians for the purpose of going to war with the whites." This nascent resistance movement fell apart, however, because of "the urgent protestations of the chiefs and headmen who had but recently returned" from an official visit to Washington, where, Evans claimed, they had "become conversant with the power of the government." Led by Ouray, the most powerful Tabeguache leader, these leaders counseled "their brethren" that the Americans possessed "enough soldiers to surround their whole immense mountain country, and, closing in upon them, to wipe them from the face of the earth." War with the Americans, the "chiefs and headmen" of the Nuche recognized, posed an existential threat.[27]

When peace prevailed, Evans shared Ouray's relief, remarking that the United States had narrowly avoided "one of the most troublesome and expensive Indian wars in which we could be engaged." The cautious approach Evans advocated made perfect sense with U.S. military forces mired in the Civil War. Yet long after Appomattox, American officials continued to share Evans's apprehension that the Nuche could only be forcibly dislodged from their rugged homelands at immense cost. "These Indians," an 1866 report from Colorado declared, "occupy a mountainous country inaccessible at present, except in the summer season, and then only with pack animals; a war with them," it predicted with palpable trepidation, "would consume several years of time and a frightful amount of treasure." Even in 1877, as settlers clamored against the boundaries of the Ute reservation, the Nuche still impressed one of their agents as fearsome adversaries. "Every day it becomes of higher importance," he advised, "that friendly relations should be maintained with the Utes, for it is in their power to stop, for a time at least, the development of the great San Juan mining-district, which borders on the reservation."[28]

Fearful that open hostilities with the Nuche would embroil U.S. forces in protracted, bloody fighting on the People's home turf, federal officials instead maneuvered to subdue the Nuche through treaties, reservations, and assimilationist policies dedicated to remaking the Indians in the Americans' own image. For their part, most Nuche leaders continued to favor negotiation over confrontation, since any act of armed resistance would give settlers a pretext for demanding federal military intervention. The shared desire of Nuche peace advocates and U.S. officials in the executive branch to forestall violence spawned a series of treaties, agreements, and unwritten understandings. The big question, though, was whether either group of leaders could persuade or cajole the peoples they ostensibly represented to abide by the hotly contested, deeply unpopular compacts that resulted.

In 1863, American officials responded to the Fort Halleck incident and Nuche efforts to expel prospectors from Middle Park by pressing the People for additional land cessions. Federal agents attempted to bring chiefs and headmen from the northeastern bands to a treaty council. Having failed to track down any White River or Grand River Nuche, however, U.S. commissioners decided to enter into unilateral negotiations with Ouray and other Tabeguache headmen. In the resulting Conejos Treaty of 1863, the Tabeguaches relinquished the northern and western edges of their customary territories, while the United States recognized Tabeguache hunting rights in the southern Rockies and promised to provide Ouray's band with "goods," "provisions," and livestock. John Nicolay, Abraham Lincoln's private secretary and an influential member of the commission that negotiated the Conejos Treaty, detailed how sheep, "stallions for breeding stock," and cattle would serve as vital tools for transforming the Tabeguaches into settled, self-supporting husbandmen. Just "a very few years will elapse," the American prognosticated, "before all the available and desirable spots in the mountain regions, where they now subsist by hunting, will be invaded and occupied by white emigration and settlement." With settlers poised to "destroy or drive away the game, thus completely cutting off [the People's] present means of living," Nicolay believed that the Nuche could only survive if they forsook hunting and gathering for a new life dedicated to raising domesticated animals on tiny remnants of their once-expansive homelands.[29]

Congress, however, prioritized the prosecution of the Civil War over Nuche treaty obligations. Without the money needed to fulfill the promises Nicolay and his colleagues had made, the Conejos Treaty became at once a dead letter and a flashpoint in the worsening divisions among the various peoples contending for control of the Colorado high country. "The Great Father had received lands from them," Tabeguache leaders complained to Colorado's governor in 1866, "and was rich enough to pay them all that was agreed upon." Other Nuche bands, meanwhile, had even bigger grievances with the 1863 treaty. Though the document made no mention of the lands traditionally inhabited by the northeastern Nuche bands, settlers wrongly presumed that the treaty had extinguished aboriginal title to Middle Park and other parts of north-central Colorado to which the Tabeguaches had only rarely ventured.[30]

Federal policy makers sought further concessions when they called northeastern Nuche leaders to another council in summer 1866. In the resulting Treaty of Middle Park, headmen from the Yamparika, White River, and Grand River bands allowed Americans to build a stage road through Middle Park. Yet they steadfastly refused to cede any of their lands. After the Senate failed to ratify the treaty, American officials planned another round of negotiations for 1868, with representatives from all of Colorado's Nuche bands in attendance. Senate ratification of the 1868 Ute Treaty extinguished once and for all the People's legal claims to a large strip of central Colorado, including Middle Park and the Coyote Valley. To Governor Edward McCook's later consternation, though, the Nuche nonetheless retained a massive reservation covering tens of thousands of square miles in western Colorado. Even more alarming for Colorado's settlers, the 1868 covenant did nothing to prevent the People from leaving their reservation to hunt buffalo on the plains, travel to Denver and other American settlements to trade and take in the sights, and continue their age-old subsistence migrations throughout the territory they had formally relinquished to the United States.[31]

The treaties of the 1860s pledged the United States to compensate the Nuche for the loss of large chunks of their ancestral homelands with food, money, schools, seeds, livestock, and instruction in agricultural techniques. But the government rarely delivered on its promises.

The tension, complexity, and intimacy of relationships between the northeastern Nuche and American newcomers to Colorado suffuse this portrait taken by William Gunnison Chamberlain in his Denver studio around 1872. Chamberlain identified the figures as: "Standing: J. S. Littlefield, agent, White River; Tab-u-cha-kat; Pah-ant; Catz; Uriah M. Curtis, interpreter. Sitting: Wanzitz (Antelope); Maj. J. B. Thompson, special Indian agent; and Han-ko." Denver Public Library, Western History Collection, X-19258.

Lawmakers dragged their feet on appropriations; corruption and incompetence plagued the Office of Indian Affairs; and high freight costs and precarious travel routes delayed and damaged most of the supplies the government sent the People's way. Despite all of these problems, however, annuities, rations, and government-sponsored cattle herds nonetheless played increasingly important roles in the Nuche economy. Beef butchered from agency steers not only filled the People's bellies but also alleviated some of the toll Nuche hunting might otherwise have levied on the West's wild game. Though federal treaty making offered the Nuche bands no panacea, it nonetheless reinforced their ability to withstand the incursions of American settlers and survive as independent and sovereign peoples.[32]

"The Utes Must Go!"

In 1866, Alexander Cummings still could fantasize that the American conquest of the People might come to pass "unaccompanied by cruelty." By the 1870s, however, more and more settlers were coming to share the conviction that the only way to rid Colorado of the Nuche was through force. The People's equestrian expertise and their knowledge of the West's ever-shifting ecological and economic niches had prevented them from overexploiting the resources on which their independence had always pivoted, while federal treaties recognized Nuche claims to an extensive and valuable swath encompassing most of western Colorado.

An uprising waged by some members of the White River band in 1879—a conflict the Americans immediately labeled the Ute War—obliterated federal reluctance to dispossess the People and convinced even high-minded eastern moralists that Nuche removal was a righteous cause. This eruption of violent resistance resulted, in turn, from the escalating pressure settlers were placing on Nuche lands and resources, the government's failure to fulfill its treaty obligations, and Agent Nathan Meeker's efforts to destroy the People's time-honored equestrian lifeways. As more than two decades of tension between the Nuche and the Americans neared a tragic denouement, Colorado settlers attempted to legitimate removal by spreading falsehoods demonizing the People as unfit stewards of their ancestral homelands.

The thrust by American prospectors, herdsmen, and settlers into the Upper Colorado basin unfolded as part and parcel of a broader assault on Nuche land tenure. The Coyote Valley and its environs remained peripheral to the Colorado Gold Rush, largely because of ongoing resistance from the northeastern Nuche. In 1863, for instance, "some Utah Indians" confronted a "party of prospecters [*sic*]" in Middle Park—probably not far from the Junction Ranch where Tabernash was shot in 1878—then "robbed [them] of their horses and provisions," and "warned them to leave the country." Not a single settler filed a legal claim to public lands within the boundaries of Grand County until 1865. Americans began to push into the area in force, however, in response to the 1866 Treaty of Middle Park and especially the 1868 Ute Treaty. The northeastern Nuche repeatedly tried to expel outsiders, attacking a party of miners near Hahn's Peak in 1866, assaulting prospectors in North Park, and setting fire to a blacksmith shop at Hot Sulphur Springs in 1870, and threatening campers and employees at the same site in 1872. These and other confrontational acts signaled to settlers that many northeastern Nuche were committed to retaining their patrimony, even if this meant defying treaties signed by some of their chiefs and headmen.[33]

In the face of Nuche antagonism, American settlers kept their eyes focused on the prize: land, which was to say gold and grass, water and coal, opportunity and escape, and, above all, the promise of a place to call one's own. The Cozens family started their Junction Ranch near present-day Fraser in the early 1870s, by which point Hot Sulphur Springs and Grand Lake were starting to grow into small resorts. Homesteading in the Middle Park area accelerated in 1874. That same year, the new-comers organized Grand County, which encompassed all of the Coyote Valley. Meanwhile, entrepreneurs and work crews completed toll roads over Berthoud and Rollins Passes, thereby hastening the integration of the Greater Rocky Mountain National Park Ecosystem into American transportation and exchange networks.[34]

Once roads connected Middle Park and adjacent high mountain val-leys to Colorado's foothill mining camps and piedmont supply towns, Grand County's appeal to American land seekers soared. Ranchers proved especially bullish. By the early 1880s, Grand County's cattle herds boasted more than 13,000 head divided among 175 brands; a few ranchers had presumably begun to pasture their cattle on the Kawun-eeche's riparian meadows. By that point, hundreds of settlers had wedged even further west into the Yampa Valley and other choice spots long cherished by the northeastern Nuche.[35]

As the Americanization of Middle Park and its environs suggested, Colorado's previously unstable settler society solidified during the 1870s. As the decade began, railroads reached Denver, loosing the fetters that isolation had long placed on the region's growth. Mining flourished as never before. The discovery of rich deposits by prospectors trespassing on the Ute Reservation in the San Juan Mountains of southwestern Col-orado compelled the United States to force the Nuche into ceding 3.7 million acres in the infamously corrupt Brunot Agreement of 1874. Surging migration combined with rising prosperity to propel Colorado to statehood in 1876. Denver, a stagnant backwater of 4,759 residents in 1870, boasted more than 35,000 inhabitants by decade's end; Colorado's total population swelled nearly 500 percent during the decade, reaching nearly 195,000. Ever more numerous, confident, and fearful that other newcomers might beat them to the main chance, Colorado's settlers now looked on Nuche lands as *their* American birthright. Miners, ranchers, town builders, entrepreneurs, resort promoters, railroad entrepreneurs, and even farmers hastened to realize Edward McCook's vision of a future in which "every American man" could "go freely, and without hindrance, wherever the American flag covers American soil."[36]

The End of the End

The ceaseless hue and cry of American settlers for more land, on the one hand, and the unexpected persistence of the northeastern Nuche, on the other, generated an irrepressible tension. For many years, acts of diplomacy ranging from the meals ranchers dispensed to the Indians who materialized on their doorsteps to the treaties signed by Nuche leaders and federal commissioners successfully contained these tensions. By September 1879, however, the conciliatory arrangements forged with varying degrees of sincerity and expediency by the People, American settlers, and the federal government lay in tatters. Tabernash's murder in Middle Park and the revenge killing of a white rancher by kinsmen of the slain Nuche leader marked the first clear signs of the breach ahead. Congress heeded the pleas of Coloradans by dispatching a commission in May 1878 to seek further land cessions and consolidate Colorado's Nuche bands at a single agency.[37]

Nuche chiefs and headmen, though, remained steadfast in their refusal to sign over any additional territory to the Americans. They complained, moreover, about the government's failure to honor pledges made in previous treaties and agreements. "The Utes have been treated badly," White River agent Nathan Meeker conceded to Colorado senator Henry Teller in 1878, "and they know it as well as you and I." By that time, the northeastern Nuche bands of the White River Agency were drawing perhaps half of their subsistence from the compensation the federal government agreed to provide in exchange for the lands ceded by the treaties of 1863 and 1868. The provisions on which the Nuche had come to depend customarily arrived late or in poor condition, yet the delays encountered in 1878 were so extreme as to strain the People's patience to the breaking point. "So long as the present system of the government obtains in regard to the rations of the Indians," one U.S. treaty commissioner conceded that September, "they will have to hunt."[38]

By that point, though, Agent Meeker had already resolved to eliminate hunting and the equestrian migrations that continued to undergird the People's independence. Meeker arrived in northwestern Colorado possessing a lengthy résumé as an agricultural and social reformer. After graduating from Oberlin College, which was then rife with abolitionism, vegetarianism, and other antebellum enthusiasms, Meeker threw himself heart and soul into a commune devoted to realizing the utopian ideas of French socialist François Fourier. The failure of this idealistic effort led Meeker to Horace Greeley's *New York Tribune*, where he became agricultural editor. Meeker's most consequential venture, though, was his posting by Greeley to superintend the Union Colony in Colorado's northern piedmont. Though the colony was prospering when Greeley, heartbroken by the combined effects of his wife's recent death, a disastrous presidential bid against Ulysses Grant, and his dismissal from the *Tribune*'s editorship, suddenly died in 1872, Meeker was deeply indebted to his late champion's estate. Greeley's daughters asked Meeker to pay up, leaving him no choice but to seek out a salaried position. The economic crisis known as the Panic of 1873, though, upset Meeker's plans. Only after six years of desperately casting about did Meeker convince Senator Teller to finagle a commission for him as U.S. Indian agent to the White River Utes.[39]

From his May 1878 arrival in the Nuche country until his death at the hands of White River rebels sixteen months later, Meeker devoted nearly all his energy to turning the People into farmers. In the process, he earned the enmity of many White River Nuche. "Hunting is a leading and chief pursuit," he grumbled to the Indian Office that July. " 'Buckskin' is sold to the traders in heavy aggregate amounts, and is hauled to the railroad by the ton, a ton being worth $1,000. When to this resource are added annuity goods and weekly issues of beef, flour, sugar, coffee, soap, &c., it is seen that these Indians are placed in a comfortable position." The following year, Meeker huffed that the White River Nuche were "rambling hither and thither over a vast extent of country, half as large as their reservation, living by hunting, trading horses (perhaps horse stealing), racing, gambling, and begging." As long as "this state of affairs lasts,"

Meeker despaired that it would be impossible to "bring influences to bear upon" the Nuche and convince them to cultivate the soil.[40]

Meeker astutely recognized the centrality of equestrianism to the highly migratory, endlessly improvisational way of life the Nuche had mastered over the preceding decades and centuries. "They have large bands of horses," he noted, "which they carefully increase; and, to find fresh and wide pastures, they are induced, perhaps compelled, to roam. While they possess horses, the care of them prevents their working, and it calls for the help of all the children who can be of service." Meeker blamed the People's sizable horse herds—a member of the federal commission dispatched to White River in 1878 claimed that "hardly an Indian has less than twenty-five ponies"—for "crowd[ing] out the cattle and mak[ing] their care more expensive and difficult."[41]

Meeker ardently believed that he could compel the Nuche to forsake their equestrian ways if the government would simply "take away all the horses except such as could be useful" for ranching, farming, and hauling goods. The Nuche rightly recognized Meeker's campaign against their ponies as a direct assault on the tried-and-true strategies that had underpinned their persistence in the face of constant challenges—the ways of "work[ing] for all they receive" that Wolf had obligated them to pursue back at the dawn of their history. As Meeker understood, horses had almost certainly become more significant to the northeastern Nuche during the 1860s and 1870s than ever before. "The Indians possess a large number of horses," Meeker's counterpart at the Southern Ute Agency lamented, "and strive to increase this kind of stock, too much of which they already have." The agent to the Tabeguaches likewise griped that members of that Nuche band possessed "probably ten times as many ponies as they can make useful or profitable." By lashing out against Nuche equestrianism and the 4,000 ponies he estimated the White Rivers to possess, Meeker sought to undermine the People's independence and destroy a key foundation of their individual and collective identity. "The Indian is wealthy, and he has standing," Meeker had learned, "precisely because he owns horses." Meeker recognized that ponies and persons were so entangled in Nuche culture that "the Indian who has not a horse to run is nobody." Meeker's campaign to eliminate horses from the reservation kindled such fervent opposition precisely because it threatened to reduce every White River to a mere "nobody."[42]

Soon after arriving at White River, Meeker resolved "to remove the agency to a more suitable location, for the reason that there was no land that could be cultivated in the vicinity." Thereafter, Powell Park, a 3,500-acre stretch of "excellent land" some eleven miles west and downstream of the original White River Agency, became ground zero in the collision between Meeker's evangelical reformism and the northeastern Nuche's desperate quest to retain their horses and homelands. "The Indians," Meeker discovered, "were decidedly opposed to the occupancy of Powell Valley for the Agency because they had always used it for their winter encampment, particularly for pasturing their horses, since snow seldom lies there more than a few days." The Nuche had been accustomed not only to pasturing horses at the new agency site but also to racing them there. When Meeker began to plow up the Powell Park sod in fall 1878, he encountered further "opposition of the Indians to the occupancy of this valley," with some Nuche "threaten[ing]" him and "declar[ing] they would not live there, & not one of them would have any thing to do with farming." Undaunted, Meeker continued to push ahead, convincing some White River Nuche led by a headman the Americans called Douglas to dig a ditch to irrigate some of the fields near the new agency.[43]

A tense winter and a dry, scorching summer ensued. As Meeker began to step up his campaign against Nuche horses and the off-reservation hunting and trading expeditions the creatures made possible, the U.S. agent fatefully added a third complaint to his arsenal of grievances against the Nuche: Meeker accused the People of fiendishly destroying timber and game throughout the northern Colorado lands their leaders had ceded in 1868. For years, settlers in Middle Park, the Yampa Valley, and other areas had accused the northeastern Nuche of scheming to destroy the Rockies' flora and fauna. By derogating the White Rivers as game wasters hell-bent on exterminating deer, elk, and other creatures, settlers sought to recast a people John Evans and his contemporaries had lauded as friendly, intelligent, and loyal as dangerous neighbors and unworthy stewards of the land.[44]

An 1877 petition from Grand County settlers summarized these complaints. "We are living on the frontier," Middle Park's new American residents declared, "on the confines of civilization, as it were, miles away from any military post, and without adequate protection." The Nuche, the petition continued, "spend more than two-thirds of the year

off their reservation in our country, purposely slaughtering our game indis-
criminately and driving it into remote districts as far as possible from
the white settlements—slaughtering this game at all seasons on the
white man's territory." The petitioners also reproached the Nuche for
"set[ting] fire to the forests in this park, thereby causing immense destruction of the finest pine timber in the State, which is of incalculable
value to all, and should be preserved." The Indians' intentions were all
too clear: "They repeatedly threaten to kill our settlers here if they do
not *go out over the range and stay out of Middle Park,* and frighten tourists
and others who peaceably visit this section for health and recreation,
retarding, by their presence and menaces, the settlement and development of Northwestern Colorado."[45]

Historical, ethnographic, and scientific evidence on Nuche hunting
practices and fire use, however, contradicts the settlers' accusations that
the People were perpetrating a vindictive, scorched-earth campaign on
lands the Americans had recently seized from them. "They appear to be
less destructive of their game than other Indians," Henry Vaile had remarked of the northeastern bands back in 1861. "They abandon their
elk and antelope country while those animals are breeding their young,
and go into the buffalo country." In the mid-1870s, Meeker's predecessor
at White River astutely noted that "Generally the most complaint is made
by persons who have the least cause for it," especially "irresponsible"
settlers "who have cruelly selfish and dishonest purposes to serve." The
frequency and earnestness with which American commentators hailed
the Rocky Mountains as a sportsmen's paradise raises further questions
about the settlers' complaints against the Nuche. "Game of all kinds is
plenty," Grand County commissioner Wilson Waldron crowed in 1880,
just three years after Americans there had drafted their angry petition,
"and more numerous than it has been for years."[46]

Settler accusations depicting the Nuche as arsonists seem equally far-
fetched. Meeker's precursor explained that settlers typically accused the
Nuche of arson for two main reasons: to divert blame for fires they had
set themselves, and "to create a sentiment unfavorable to the Indians,
and precipitate a trouble which may be made the occasion of depriving
the Indians of some of their rights." Investigations by other U.S. Indian
agents also absolved the Nuche of responsibility for the large wildfires that burned in western Colorado in the late 1870s. Fire ecologist
William Baker has reinforced this perspective by pointing out that

Americans almost never presented eyewitness evidence of Ute fire setting. The newcomers also lacked any appreciation of lightning's role as
the primary ignition source in high-country forests (an insight that only
gained acceptance in the 1920s). The widespread fires that broke out in
Middle Park and other stretches of the Colorado high country in summer
1879 likely resulted not from Nuche fire bugs, but from the unprecedented confluence of tinder-dry conditions (prompted, in turn, by an
intense region-wide drought) with an upswing in man-made ignitions
caused by the inrush of American prospectors, miners, stockmen, loggers, and railroads.[47]

By July of that incendiary summer, Nathan Meeker was turning a
blind eye to contrary evidence and instead crediting his fellow Americans on faith. State officials and local people flooded Meeker and his superiors with complaints. On July 5, Colorado governor Frederick Pitkin
notified the commissioner of Indian Affairs: "Reports reach me daily
that a band of White Rivers Utes are off their reservation, destroying forests and game, near North and Middle Parks. . . . Immense forests are
burning throughout Western Colorado," Pitkin continued, "supposed to
have been fired by Indians." Then the governor cut to the chase: "These
savages should be removed to the Indian Territory, where they can no
longer destroy the finest forests in this state." Two days later, Meeker
informed the commissioner that he had "received authentic information
that my Indians are committing trespass on Snake and Bear Rivers, and
in Middle Park, burning timber and wantonly destroying game." The
agent quickly followed up with a second dispatch in which he excoriated
the White Rivers' "burning of timber and their wanton destruction
of game . . . simply to get the skins. . . . This lack of ordinary economy,"
Meeker fumed, "this total disrespect for values in the natural resources and wealth of the country, are disheartening to contemplate."[48]

Two months later, a few hundred White River Nuche rose up, their
ire fueled by Meeker's efforts to tar them as profligate ingrates as well
as his stiffening resolve to decimate their horse herds and prevent them
from leaving the reservation. That month, Meeker told the Nuche "that
they must not go into Middle and South Parks, because they scared the
whites," and then made himself even less popular by permitting Grand
County's sheriff to arrest and take away two White River Nuche,
Chinaman and Bennett, for burning the house of settler and former
Nuche agent James Thompson.[49]

To the most discontented faction among the White Rivers, however, Meeker's greatest sin was his obsession with eradicating Nuche equestrianism, which he rightly perceived as the linchpin of their culture and the foundation of their sovereignty. The Ute War involved a chaotic and confusing outbreak of violence. Only a minority of White Rivers participated directly in the fighting, and their chiefs and headmen later managed to stonewall federal commissioners seeking to determine the causes of the uprising—and thus to punish the rebellion's leaders. Ouray, the Tabeguache chief whom some White Rivers had accused of unjustly assuming authority over their band, too, repeatedly came to his kinsmen's defense. In response to one commissioner's complaint that "none of them want to speak the truth," Ouray expressed both his own limited power ("I cannot force them to say what they do not wish to") and his keen understanding of American legal culture ("Show me any act of law by which a man is compelled to criminate himself"). Though mystery continues to shroud the events of September 1879, it is nonetheless clear that disagreements over horses, horse pastures, and horse racing—the same factors that had incited Tabernash's murder a year earlier at the Junction Ranch in Middle Park—figured centrally in the White River uprising.[50]

Meeker had been grumbling about the People's ponies ever since he first arrived at White River. When he began to target Nuche equestrianism in earnest, however, the agent began to push some White Rivers to their breaking point. This string of events began innocently enough, when a headman named Canalla or Johnson ("they have several names, you know," Meeker's daughter Josephine later testified) asked the agent in February 1879 to break a pair of his horses. Meeker initially greeted Johnson's request as a promising sign; Johnson, who had already lent considerable help to the agent's efforts to irrigate the new agency's fields, gave Meeker to believe that "he wants to do teaming." Meeker's pleasure turned to rage, though, when he began to suspect that Johnson was actually tricking him into training his horses not because he wanted to use them to haul freight, but instead because he wanted to race them on the track at Powell Park. Johnson's "object" all along, Meeker thundered, "had been to get them in good heart so that he could beat his brethren of the turf, and I told him to take away his horses. . . . [T]his 'horse business,'" Meeker concluded, represented "a powerful obstacle to progress."[51]

HARPER'S WEEKLY.

JOURNAL OF CIVILIZATION

Vol. XXIII.—No. 1191.]   NEW YORK, SATURDAY, OCTOBER 25, 1879.   [WITH A SUPPLEMENT. PRICE TEN CENTS.

Entered according to Act of Congress, in the Year 1879, by Harper & Brothers, in the Office of the Librarian of Congress, at Washington.

REDUCING THE U. S. ARMY AGAIN—LET ALL SAVAGES REJOICE.

Thomas Nast depicted the Nuche as ferocious, rifle-toting hybrids of wolf and man in a cover illustration that juxtaposed the *Harper's Weekly* masthead, emblazoned with the symbols of "Civilization," with the savagery some 200 White Rivers allegedly unleashed against Nathan Meeker and his employees. "Reducing the U.S. Army Again—Let All Savages Rejoice," *Harper's Weekly,* October 25, 1879, Denver Public Library, Western History Collection, Z-4027.

Meeker's anger festered for a few weeks. Then the agent announced his intention to resume plowing on the fine grasslands where the Nuche had pastured their horses since time immemorial. Meeker's Nuche housekeeper, whom he called Jane, told the agent that she and her extended family possessed rights to the lands he intended to plow. Jane warned that she and her people would not allow Meeker to transform these meadows into farmland. Rather than heeding Jane's caution, Meeker pushed ahead and ordered his employees to plow up Jane's pasture. Several Nuche responded by firing warning shots at the agent, his employees, and their teams. Johnson then implored Meeker to leave the pasture alone, telling the agent " 'that he had plowed enough land,' and that the Utes 'must have feed for their horses.' " Meeker's stubborn rejoinder signed his death warrant: "You have got too many horses," the agent screamed. "You had better kill them." Meeker had gone too far, and Johnson let the American know it by shoving him down into the dirt.[52]

Meeker, fearing for his life, begged Colorado's governor to call in federal troops. Days later, U.S. cavalrymen dispatched from Fort Steele, Wyoming, were besieged by 200–300 White River Nuche led by two headmen known as Jack and Colorow at the intersection of the Milk River and the Ute Reservation boundary. Less than twenty miles away, at Meeker's new Powell Park agency, dozens of other Nuche rose up and killed Meeker, nine other government employees, and an unfortunate peddler; the agency's attackers also took five captives—three women and two children, including Meeker's wife and daughter. As the U.S. Army and Colorado militiamen mobilized to put down the insurgency, nearly every member of the White River Nuche dissolved into the countryside. By melting into the mountainous homelands they knew so well, the People avoided the ferocious vengeance American troops had unleashed at Sand Creek and other blood-soaked killing grounds along the jagged edge of America's expanding continental empire. As the northeastern Nuche hid out and bided their time, and as the Southern Utes and Ouray's Uncompahgres—the name by which the Tabeguaches were now generally known—anxiously attempted to restore peace, the First Peoples of the Colorado Rockies rightly agonized over their fate. As they understood all too well, a rebellion waged by a small group of their kinsfolk had the potential to unify the U.S. government and Colorado's settlers behind the common cause of removing all Nuche from Colorado.[53]

Widowed Land

The dispossession of the northeastern Nuche from their Rocky Mountain homelands was sealed in March 1880, when nine Nuche leaders signed an agreement with U.S. officials consigning the White River Utes to Utah's Uintah Reservation. The same compact also assured the Uncompahgres a reservation, which federal negotiators intimated would be located near the present-day site of Grand Junction in far western Colorado. Indian Office bureaucrats, though, later deemed that location unsuitable because it would be prohibitively expensive to irrigate—and thus impossible to farm. When U.S. troops rounded up the northeastern and Uncompahgre Nuche in the late summer and forced them to march to Utah Territory, the last tenuous ties connecting the People to the Greater Rocky Mountain National Park Ecosystem had been broken. American settlers, whom the agent to the Uncompahgres derided as "hungry land pirates of the frontier, who have encroached and trespassed upon the rights of the Indian so long," had finally bent both the federal government and the Nuche to their will.[54]

From the start, life was hard on the Uintah and Ouray Reservations to which the federal government had consigned the northeastern and Uncompahgre Nuche. Americans and Colorado Nuche alike regarded these Utah lands as inferior to the People's former domains in the Rockies. In 1875, a U.S. Indian agent pronounced the Uintah reserve "about one-hundredth part tillable, one-thousandth wooded, one-half grazing, and the balance worthless." More than a century later, Northern Ute tribal member Francis McKinley recalled conversations with "older people" who told him about the Uintah Basin "as it originally was." According to these northeastern Nuche elders, the Utah reservations possessed "a fragile ecology . . . that they did not use heavily" prior to their dispossession from Colorado. The elders impressed on McKinley that it "wasn't a happy occasion when you're being evicted and going to a strange place . . . consisting mostly of a pile of rocks and desert[, u]nlike the green valleys and the pines and the forests that they were vacating in Colorado." To make matters worse, the Uintah Reservation had been occupied since the 1860s by Nuche bands from central Utah. Mutual resentment soon developed between the reservation's old-timers and newcomers; the former blamed their Colorado cousins for exacerbating the travails of reservation life, while the latter mocked their Utah kin for embracing the very same American agricultural practices that Nathan Meeker had attempted to implement at White River with such distressing results.[55]

It should come as little surprise, then, that McKinley's elders still recalled that "many of them didn't want to come" to Utah. Most White River Utes spent just a few weeks or months on the Uintah Reservation in 1881 before galloping back to Colorado "with their families," enticed by what an incredulous official called "their attachment to their old homes" and driven away by "the government's failure to supply them with annuity goods." Though many northeastern Nuche would eventually take up farming and ranching on the Uintah and Ouray Reservation (consolidated in 1886), some continued to return to northwestern Colorado on fall hunting expeditions. As these unauthorized subsistence migrations demonstrate, the People's ponies continued to sustain Nuche life decades after Meeker set his sights on eradicating the long-standing relationships linking the People, their horses, and Colorado's wild game. Northern Ute Tommy Appah recalled that his people retained their "horse property" well into the twentieth century. Clifford Duncan recalled that during his childhood in the 1930s and 1940s, "We did a lot of horseback riding—in fact, that was the main thing—horseback riding. That was it." By the early 1900s, when state game wardens and local sheriffs expelled the last northeastern Nuche hunting party from Colorado, most Northern Utes did most of their hunting in the Uintahs and other mountain ranges closer to their reservation. "I'm a mountain person myself," Ruby (Antwine) Black of the Northern Ute reservation declared in the late twentieth century. "I love mountains, I love to be there." Even as the People confronted new obstacles and opportunities, equestrianism remained the flexible mainstay of Nuche resilience. To this day, Northern Utes continue to perpetuate aspects of the ancient Mountain Tradition in the Utah high country several hundred miles west of the Coyote Valley. But they also uphold the People's ancient practice of continually integrating new innovations into their existing ways in response to ever-changing constraints and prospects. "Indian people," as Tommy Appah told an interviewer, "are always ones that become adapted because that's their old instinct[,] . . . something that is almost what you would call automatic."[56]

⊠ ⊠ ⊠

Just as the Coyote Valley's long history as a Nuche homeland was nearing its bitter end, prospectors began to push into the valley. Nuche dispossession had cleared the way for a mineral rush by American settlers.

Nearly two decades after the gold strikes near Denver, mining—a pursuit that had already reconfigured social, environmental, and political relationships throughout the Colorado Rockies—reached the Colorado River headwaters. The hundreds of prospectors, miners, and townsfolk who poured into the Kawuneeche Valley starting in the late 1870s were all intent on remaking a landscape forever cleansed of its indigenous past into the prosperous embodiment of America's glittering desting.

In this trickster place, though, the natural world's obduracy would combine with global capitalism's iron laws to doom any dream of easy riches. The collapse of the Coyote Valley's short-lived mineral rush set the stage, in turn, for homesteaders to file in. Nipping at their heels came tourists, federal conservationists, and aesthetic preservationists, who together would initiate still more pervasive and problematic transformations in the Greater Rocky Mountain National Park Ecosystem.

II

SETTLERS

◁ 4 ▷

MINERS

EVEN BEFORE inrushing Americans succeeded at removing the northeastern Nuche from their Colorado homelands, prospectors seeking silver, gold, and other precious metals had begun trickling into the Colorado River headwaters. By the time federal troops forced the People into Utah in 1881, American settlers had already established two mining districts in the Coyote Valley: the Campbell Mining District, created in 1875 in Bowen Gulch, and the Lead Mountain Mining District, organized in 1880 near the head of the Kawuneeche.[1]

Despite vigorous boosting by promoters and residents, neither mining district ever amounted to much. Gaskill, the humble metropolis of the Campbell District, lasted just six years and never housed more than one hundred inhabitants. Lulu City, which was reported to have boasted as many as 500 citizens, was abandoned just five years after it was founded. By 1885, the mining rush's failure was plain for all to see. Though a few hardy souls stuck around, the mining camps of the Coyote Valley began to dissolve into ghost landscapes nearly as swiftly as they had materialized because of the Kawuneeche's geographic isolation and the meager extent and quality of its ore deposits.[2]

The story of mining in the nineteenth-century U.S. West has often been told as a tale of conquest in which gold and silver booms inaugurated full-blown American assaults on the region's lands. Digging more deeply into the Coyote Valley mineral rush, though, belies the notion that American settlers acted as omnipotent agents of environmental devastation. Prospectors, miners, capitalists, and the many fellow travelers lured to the Campbell and Lead Mountain mining districts by dreams of easy riches soon learned that they could do little to alter those material realities that mattered most. More surprising, some of the newcomers interacted with the Kawuneeche landscape not simply as environmental despoilers, but also as ardent nature lovers. Indeed, mineral rush participants were the very first American observers to conceive of the Coyote Valley as beautiful and sublime. When miners, townspeople, and other migrants to the Kawuneeche sensed that the valley's once-hopeful prospects were evaporating into the thin mountain air, they rationalized their failure by bemoaning the vagaries of nature alongside the vicissitudes of capital. Today, the decaying ruins of Lulu City and Gaskill embody the ambivalent legacies of a tumultuous, faintly recorded, and fleeting period when the Coyote Valley seemed filled with both wonder and doom—at once a blank canvas on which Americans could project any and all ambitions, *and* a harsh, remote redoubt that stubbornly refused to bend to the will of the hardy but overmatched settlers who pushed up the Colorado River even as the Nuche removal crisis was reaching its culmination.[3]

The Rush Begins

The rush to the Kawuneeche began in the late 1870s, with the leakage of rumors from the Greater Rocky Mountain National Park Ecosystem to the outside world. Investors and newspaper editors from Fort Collins, Georgetown, Denver, and other Colorado towns locked in a rough-and-tumble struggle for economic survival hastened to enter the fray. Together, entrepreneurs, boosters, and common miners conspired to spin dreams of a gilded future for a little-known valley rising above a stream then known as the North Fork of the Grand River.

Benjamin Burnett, the driving force behind Lulu City, first heard of promising discoveries along the upper reaches of that stream from Joseph Shipler, a fellow Fort Collins resident who started to probe the mineral deposits of the Colorado River headwaters in the mid- to late 1870s. Enticed by favorable reports from Shipler, Burnett dispatched another prospector to examine the area. Burnett's son later recalled that after this prospector "found some good-looking float"—fine particles of gold—in the Colorado River headwaters, his father hastily set out from the flatlands of Larimer County and crossed the Continental Divide.[4]

Burnett relocated his family from Fort Collins to "a beautiful park" on the stream's east bank in summer 1879. That same year, Burnett and William Baker, a fellow Fort Collins resident, formed the Middle Park and Grand River Mining and Land Improvement Company. Soon thereafter, the two partners "got busy and laid out" Lulu City on the same ground where Burnett and his family had pitched their first camp in the Coyote Valley. Having surveyed and platted a rectilinear town grid of one hundred blocks on nearly 160 acres of prime riparian meadow, Burnett began to promote the camp in summer 1880. An adept salesman, Burnett swiftly drummed up considerable interest in the Kawuneeche's mineral deposits at a time when mining bonanzas in Leadville, Aspen, and other parts of Colorado were drawing considerable attention.[5]

Edward Weber, a representative of Illinois capitalists, was one of hundreds swept up in the resulting boosterism. Unlike the rest, though, Weber soon founded a settlement and mining operation to rival those of Burnett and Baker. Having incorporated the Grand Lake Mining and Smelting Company, Weber and his absentee investors acquired the Wolverine Mine, several miles downriver from Lulu City in the Campbell District. Weber's firm then laid out a town site of 161 blocks to house and service miners. Mine foreman Lewis Gaskill named the little burg Auburn after his hometown in upstate New York, but the Postal Service instead christened the new settlement Gaskill, and the name stuck.[6]

Burnett, Weber, and other boosters wasted few opportunities to puff the potential of the Coyote Valley's mines. Frank Fossett's 1876 guidebook for Colorado gold seekers crowed: "The fame of the Rabbit Ear range [the name by which nineteenth-century Americans generally knew the Never Summer Mountains] is spreading abroad, and the rich silver deposits there will soon be producing largely." Impartial observers, however, remained skeptical. After touring the Grand Lake area in 1876, Rossiter Raymond, the influential United States commissioner of mining statistics, blithely downplayed the area's potential: "Little can be said," he huffed, "except that the prospects are fair."[7]

Despite Raymond's tepid forecast, a steady force of miners pushed into the Coyote Valley and began to work its subsurface deposits. Merchants, sawyers, teamsters, saloon girls, and others followed, all seeking in their own fashion to "mine the miners." Because both Gaskill and Lulu expended nearly all of their short lives after the federal census of 1880 but before the state census of 1885, we can surmise only that the

two settlements' demographic makeup probably resembled that of other
Rocky Mountain gold and silver camps, with a populace comprised
largely of white men, most of them born in the United States.[8]

Together, the workmen and entrepreneurs who pushed up the North
Fork endeavored to do something the Nuche had never contemplated:
extract rich ores from veins and bodies of ore (rocks that held precious
metals in impure form) thrust up from the earth's depths tens of millions of years earlier, during the formation of the Front Range and Never
Summer Mountains. After prospectors burrowed into the earth's surface and assayers vouchsafed the richness of samples extracted from
these excavations, the real work of mining began. In the Lead Mountain and Campbell Mining Districts, as in most other reaches of Colorado, two essential steps were required to turn scattered subterranean
possibilities into the glittering actuality of gold or silver ingots. Miners
first had to sink shafts and tunnels to access irregular mineral deposits.
The ore thus extracted then had to be processed in mills and smelters,
which used a combination of mechanical and chemical processes to turn
raw rock into pure silver and gold.[9]

In the cool calculations of the capitalist system, the matter of profit
would ultimately determine the fate of the Coyote Valley mineral rush.
If the total expense required to turn latent mineral wealth into bullion
exceeded the cost of extraction, transportation, and refining, then the
Campbell and Lead Mountain Districts were destined to go bust. A pair
of vexing questions thus haunted boosters, prospectors, and hangers-on
alike: How much gold, silver, and other paying minerals did the earth
beneath the Coyote Valley contain? And what would it cost to turn these
latent prospects into the gold and silver that inrushing Americans so feverishly sought?

Newspapers used ample statistics to document the progress of mining
at Lulu City and Gaskill, as if the surety of numbers could compensate
for the maddening uncertainties that harried these makeshift camps.
"The work of developing the Wolverine lode is steadily pushed ahead,"
Georgetown's *Colorado Miner* reported in 1880, "and with excellent success. They have at present, a force of 20 men at work. The width of the
crevice, between walls, is from 4 1/2 to 5 feet and they have 18 inches of
a pay streak. A chunk of ore, weighing some 60 pounds, was brought
over and tested, which averaged 125 ounces of silver." A month later,
another *Miner* item told of how "a tunnel about seventy feet" deep had

"struck the crevice of the Hidden Treasure lode, Rabbit Ear range, which shows fourteen inches of gray copper ore which assays upwards of 200-ounces of silver per ton." To convince readers that the Coyote Valley's mines were destined for greatness, these and other reports deployed a barrage of numerical details. Though some undoubtedly reported actual matters of fact, others rested on nothing but hype.[10]

Boosters, miners, and other participants in the mining rush shared other assumptions beyond a shared susceptibility to puffery and a common faith in the power of numbers. They believed that nature's highest purpose was to provide things people (especially people like them) needed or wanted. Furthermore, they trusted that the application of human labor and capital would inevitably improve upon nature's crude virtues. In the minds of American settlers, work and industry would not sully the Colorado wilderness. Instead, they would redeem it by fulfilling the Coyote Valley's immense but hitherto wasted promise.[11]

Turning the Valley to Account

In both the Lead Mountain and Campbell Districts, surveyors hastened to mark off mining claims and town sites in compliance with federal laws and local customs. Stakes, benchmarks, and other markers helped the newcomers to bound the land and signify their possession of it. Property boundaries meted out and described with reference to the U.S. land survey grid literally mapped the U.S. private property system onto the Coyote Valley, thereby finalizing the incorporation of the northeastern Nuche's ancestral homelands into the American nation. Once settlers established title to claims and town sites, these tracts left the public domain and became commodities subject to exchange in the West's tumultuous real estate markets.

Ear-thumping blasts of powder and dynamite sounded especially sweet to newcomers bent on squeezing profits from the land. "Every miner and laborer now ha[s] employment," the *Colorado Miner* approvingly noted. Men "who heretofore have been lounging around undecided what to do, for their winters' grub stake, now can be found at work in the Wolverine, Silent Friend, or Grand Lake lodes, and the reports that can be heard here that sound like distant thunder although 12 miles away tell that they are not idlers." The next year, blasts from Lulu City joined the refrain emanating from Gaskill. The *Miner* claimed that powder and dynamite explosions from the Lead Mountain District could thereafter "be heard at any hour of the day" as far away as Grand Lake. Even in 1884, with mining in rapid decline, a letter to the *Fort Collins Courier* interpreted each detonation as a signal that Lulu City was down but not yet out: "There are but six of us here at present, but we make the woods ring, as we get off from 15 to 18 blasts per day." What most nineteenth-century Americans hailed as the tocsin of progress—the same cacophony that latter-day critics of mining would denounce as "noise pollution"—was becoming second nature in the Kawuneeche.[12]

Boosters desperately wanted to believe that each detonation of powder in the valley's subterranean workscapes represented a victory for the improving virtues of American labor and technology. They were just as keen, though, to portray the Colorado River headwaters as intrinsically healthful and blessed with an abundance of everything miners and townsfolk required. A *Fort Collins Courier* correspondent intoned from Lulu: "There can be no healthier place or climate than in this Grand river gulch. The weather is warm and pleasant, altho' we have heavy snow storms. Yet the air is not cold." The writer noted that he and his fellow townspeople were "protected from the hard wind storms by the heavy timber and the mountains which surround us." All in all, Lulu City was "truly the most beautifully situated mining camp I have ever seen or heard of." The same town, another report gushed, possessed "many advantages . . . that many other mining camps are deprived of; first, the beautiful, fertile valley lying so near, where thousands of tons of native hay grows that can be delivered to the mines for a mere trifle . . . ; next is the saw timber, the finest the Colorado produces, right where it will be needed without freight" charges that elsewhere reached $10 to $20 per thousand board feet; and "3rd, timber for cord wood and charcoal is without end." A final boast gilded the lily: "The weather is beautiful, the nights are somewhat frosty, [and] the days could not be more pleasant in any land." By singing the Coyote Valley's praises with nary a hint of equivocation, the authors of these and similar dispatches hoped to sell others on the Kawuneeche's advantages. If they could spark a full-blown boom there, after all, then investors and entrepreneurs might answer their prayers by building the railroads and smelters on which the mines' success hinged.[13]

Boosters charted a geography of desire for the valley by minimizing its demerits ("the air is not cold") and depicting its environs as flush not

only with rich ores but also with hay, timber, sunshine, and healthful-
ness. Yet newcomers drawn by these alluring visions would nonetheless
have to change the land to capitalize on the valley's unrefined promise.
An article boosting Gaskill succinctly described what American settlers
looked for in a potential town site: "Proximity to the mines" mattered,
of course. But so did a location "surrounded by hundreds of acres of good
meadow land, good water and timber." As the invocation of grasslands,
forests, and streams all suggested, the hunger for mineral wealth rippled
outward from Lulu City and Gaskill into the surrounding ecosystems.[14]

Consider the domesticated creatures American settlers rode, drove,
and herded into the Coyote Valley during the mineral rush. Animals
powered the boom at Gaskill and Lulu City in two main ways. First, participants in the rush harnessed energy from horses, mules, and oxen to
haul ore, timber, hay, and other goods. Draft animals carried riders and
packs; they also pulled wagons, carriages, sleds, and implements. Some
domesticated animals also performed another, more elemental function.
Killed, butchered, and eaten, they fueled the metabolisms of miners and
townsfolk alike. Whether destined to provide food or motive power,
the domesticated animals that Americans introduced into the Colorado
River headwaters served to place the solar energy captured by the area's
plants at the settlers' disposal.[15]

Americans generally conceived of their animals much as they thought
of mining claims and town lots: as species of private property. Cattle and
horses were too valuable and useful, predators and thieves too formidable and numerous, and the valley environment too unfamiliar and
inhospitable for settlers to risk allowing their animals to roam freely.
Settlers used fences, hobbles, and other contrivances to safeguard the
animals they claimed as their own. Keeping livestock close at hand,
however, unwittingly concentrated the environmental impact of animal
appetites. Importing feed to the North Fork proved costly, so settlers pastured their animals on the meadowlands adjoining Gaskill and Lulu
City. Grazing almost certainly contributed to the introduction of inva-
sive species and hastened their spread by stressing native grasses and
shrubs. The hooves of the settlers' stock also compacted the valley's
soils, especially in soggy riparian areas.[16]

The Americans' tendency to keep their animals in the Coyote Valley
throughout the year—a strategy the Nuche had sensibly avoided—soon
yielded still more consequential ecological changes. The newcomers'

dependence on hay to get their herds through the lean months of winter explained why boosters spilled so much ink extolling the North Fork's grass. A typical passage praised "the beautiful, fertile valley lying so near, where thousands of tons of native hay grows that can be delivered to the mines for a mere trifle compared to [other] camps." "We have a great advantage," another writer smugly contended, "over some of our best mining camps, in the way of making hay." The same source ventured a prediction: "Without exaggerating, from two thousand to five thousand tons of hay [could be] put up through the summer season between Lulu and Hot Sulphur Springs." By the early 1880s, the newcomers were probably stocking the Kawuneeche with many more domesticated animals than the People ever had. As settlers turned native meadows into neatly baled hay, they effectively siphoned off calories and nutrients from the Kawuneeche's riparian ecosystems and used them to fuel the mining boom's bodily and industrial metabolisms.[17]

The Americans, of course, had no intention of subsisting solely on the flesh and fat of their herds. Miners in the North Fork, like their counterparts in other western mining camps, consumed vast quantities of processed fare. Cans, sacks, boxes, and barrels of food imported from the outside world must have accounted for much of the freight that draft animals hauled into the valley from Georgetown, Boulder, Fort Collins, and other railheads. By supping on Wisconsin wheat, Iowa pork, California salmon, and Chesapeake oysters, mining rush participants eluded the great ecological bottleneck that had sharply limited the Coyote Valley's human populations since Clovis peoples first inhabited the high country. Only by drawing on energy and nutrients from the outside world could settlers withstand the long high country winters. Yet the utter reliance of miners and townsfolk on provisions freighted into the Kawuneeche also rendered them susceptible to a profound vulnerability. If the mines of the Campbell and Lead Mountain Districts proved as profitable as boosters such as Burnett and Weber had predicted, then residents of the mining camps could stand the steep charges that packers and freighters levied on every pound of food freighted over the Continental Divide. But if paying quantities of gold and silver failed to materialize, then the Americans could hold out for only so long before abandoning the Colorado River headwaters.[18]

High food prices stimulated stock raising in and around the North Fork; it also led a few settlers to see dollar signs in gardening. Lulu and

Gaskill offered lucrative markets for J. H. Hedrick, one of the first men to claim land in the Kawuneeche under the Homestead Act of 1862. An 1886 story in the *Grand Lake Prospector* described Hedrick as "making a success of vegetable growing on his ranch between here and Gaskill." Miners and townspeople also consumed wild plants, particularly the berries and currants that flourished wherever the large wildfires of the 1870s and 1880s opened up forest canopies and fertilized the soils below.[19]

The game and fish of the Coyote Valley made still more important dietary contributions. Most mineral rush participants undoubtedly shared George Crofutt's astonishment at the valley's richness: "The mountains are alive with game of all kinds, and the streams with fine trout." Contradicting widespread complaints by Colorado settlers to Nathan Meeker that Nuche hunters were decimating the region's wild game, an 1879 item in the *Colorado Miner* exalted the North Fork as a "paradise of sportsmen and fishermen." The throng of prospectors pushing into the Colorado River headwaters threatened to spoil this "paradise." In the years to come, hungry miners joined market hunters and sport anglers in declaring open season on the creatures of forest, stream, and tundra.[20]

The fishing stories settlers told celebrated the North Fork and its tributaries as paragons of plenitude. J. E. Shipler, already described as "an old miner" in one 1880 booster tract, claimed that in a single day, he had pulled 583 fish out of the waters of Middle Park and North Park. For his part, Frank Burnett claimed that the Colorado River cutthroats of the Coyote Valley were so innocent to the newcomers' wiles that they could be caught "with red flannel on the hook." An 1880 newspaper dispatch from the valley crowed that "there are any quantity of trout here" before offhandedly mentioning that "Frank Stover ate 32 at one meal, and yet says he was a little off his appetite."[21]

Stover was hardly the only recent arrival to unleash an extravagant hunger on the Kawuneeche's native wildlife. "Pioneers in golden Colorado," as Mrs. Macfarland-Hightower, granddaughter of Lulu founder Benjamin Burnett, recalled, "were in a veritable Garden of Eden when it came to stocking the cuisine." Lulu City's lone hotel, Macfarland-Hightower remembered, served "pheasant, deer, [and] sage hen . . . in abundance. Hot cakes and bear steaks for breakfast" and "trout for lunch." A contemporary item from the *Fort Collins Courier* corroborates

Macfarland-Hightower's memory of settlers pulling up to sumptuous re-
pasts chockablock with local game and fish. A Lulu City correspondent
detailed a "splendid dinner, to which forty-three hungry miners sat
down and filled up, from the following; Bill of Fare: SOUP—A la elk
track (with bean in it); FISH—Mountain trout; MEATS—Mountain
sheep steak, Quail on toast, Shoulder of blacktail deer with onion
dressing, Mud lark fried, boiled and fricasseed, Hind quarter of Missouri
chicken, boiled." Of the menu items that no doubt had *Courier* readers
licking their lips, only the beans, flour, and perhaps the "Missouri
chicken" (which was most likely prairie chicken) had to be freighted in.
Everything else—bear and deer, elk and bighorn sheep, quail and trout
and onion—could have been procured from the forests, streams, and
truck gardens of the Greater Rocky Mountain National Park Ecosystem.
Lavish feasting helped to temper the hardships of life on this remote
fringe of America's empire, but it also subjected the Coyote Valley's wild
creatures to unprecedented pressures. By the 1890s, the area's wildlife
populations had suffered drastic declines, with apex predators and elk
especially hard hit.[22]

The mining boom's impact on the Kawuneeche extended from the
valley's animals to its plant communities. Though the Nuche had always
harvested firewood and tepee poles from the upper montane and subalpine forests of the Colorado River headwaters, American settlers cast
altogether more covetous eyes on these woodlands. Benjamin Burnett,
Edward Weber, and their collaborators deliberately located both Gaskill
and Lulu at forest's edge. Settlers drawn to the high country by the
boosters' puffery used wood to build and heat homes, stores, boarding-
houses, mine works, hotels, saloons, fences, sheds, and other structures.
Even larger quantities of timber were used underground to prevent the
mines from caving in. The wood-burning steam engines settlers brought
in to power mining operations and lumber mills further taxed the North
Fork's forests.[23]

While wood destined for use as cordwood or mine props had only to
be chopped down, cut to size, and roughly hewn, structural lumber required sawing. To meet heavy demand for boards and planks, entrepreneurs built four sawmills in the valley during the early 1880s (two near
Lulu City, a third above Gaskill, and a fourth located on the future site
of Green Mountain Ranch). The valley's pioneer mill whirred into operation in summer 1880. A year later, though, this venture and its first

competitor still could not supply "half supply the demand for lumber," though both were reportedly "running night and day." Sawed lumber remained scarce in summer 1882, when the *Rocky Mountain News* lamented that the failure of local mills to "supply enough lumber . . . [wa]s slowing construction" at Lulu. The construction of a pair of higher-capacity mills finally ended the lumber shortage in 1883. The valley's full complement of four mills reportedly had no trouble "getting in the finest lot of logs . . . ever seen at any mill in the State," leading the *Colorado Miner* to boast that at long last, there would be no "scarcity of building material this year" in the North Fork mining camps.[24]

Settlers proved just as heedless of the North Fork's forests as they were of its wildlife. Logging operations and sawmills wasted prodigious quantities of wood. The mineral rush also coincided with—and almost certainly contributed to—an upswing in forest fires. Well over 1,500 acres of the Coyote Valley's forests were consumed by fire in 1879, the year in which the Lead Mountain Mining District was founded. Most Americans, as we learned in Chapter 3, wrongly blamed that year's epic fire season on the Nuche. In actuality, wildfires became more frequent that year and throughout the early 1880s because of the combination of an unusually dry climatic phase and the arrival in the North Fork of hundreds of American settlers. Some of these gold seekers used fire as a tool, fire ecologist William Baker explains, torching mountainsides "to expose rocks." But the newcomers' carelessness with fire also played a role in igniting the Kawuneeche's woodlands.[25]

By killing standing timber, logging and wildfire together set in motion a cascade of complex, poorly recorded environmental shifts. Without the shade that living trees provided, winter snows would almost certainly have melted more quickly. This, in turn, would have made stream flow more erratic, erosion more intense, and the edge habitats in which deer and other browsers flourished more expansive.[26]

We should be careful, however, not to overstate the mining boom's impact on the Coyote Valley's forests. A photograph taken at the abandoned site of Lulu City in summer of 1889 shows the mixed, generally moderate consequences of the short-lived North Fork mining boom. Dead, evidently burned standing timber cloaks the lower slopes of the mountainside across from the derelict mining camp. Yet the image reveals no obvious evidence of logging, in sharp contrast to the nearly total denudation so apparent in contemporaneous photographs of successful

Lulu City already lay in ruins just years after its abandonment. Note the contrast between the dead timber behind the ghost town's cabins (killed either by wildfire or mountain pine beetle) and the young conifers and willows pushing upward from the epicenter of the Kawuneeche mineral rush. "Lulu, Grand River Valley," July 20, 1889, Denver Public Library, Western History Collection, X-12238.

mining centers such as Leadville and Central City. Indeed, the young pines rising up from the charred stumps of their ancestors near the left edge of the Lulu City photograph offer mute testimony to the Kawuneeche's ecological resilience.[27]

Nature Strikes Back

By burning and cutting, shooting and fishing, harnessing and planting, digging and blasting, American settlers brought far-reaching changes to the Greater Rocky Mountain National Park Ecosystem. Yet no matter how hard they tried, miners and townsfolk remained beholden to the harsh constraints of the high country environment. Though the mineral rush precipitated a concerted campaign to subordinate and control nature, the boom crashed almost as swiftly as it began because of the natural world's enduring power to constrain human possibilities in the Coyote Valley.[28]

The influx of settlers could neither blunt nor shorten the Coyote Valley's long, ferocious winters. Both the Campbell and Lead Mountain Districts also continued to suffer from geographic isolation. Newcomers exploited local ecosystems to satisfy their wants and needs for lumber, fuel, food, fur, and much else. But unlike their counterparts in competing mining districts served by railroads, the people of the Kawuneeche remained utterly dependent on goods freighted in from the world beyond at great expense. Transportation difficulties contributed directly to the mineral rush's demise by increasing the cost of living, working, and doing business in Lulu City and Gaskill.[29]

Newcomers of all ages, occupations, and inclinations shared a desperate need for roads. "The Grand County mining fever," local historian Robert Black reminds us, "inspired more than towns." The boom "required . . . a system of routes that proposed to cope with the most improbable conditions of terrain and climate." The North Fork's towns and mines utterly depended on roads to transport people, food, machines, minerals, animals, money, and information. In 1877, a group of "Citizens of Grand County" complained to the county commissioners that "the rapidly increasing interest and travel towards the extensive (Lode) Silver Mines in the Rabbit Ear Range" had been "greatly retarded in consequence of the inferiority of the road to & from the mines." Proclaiming that they held "equal claims" to good roads "in common with others," the petitioners asked the county to fund a new road to the Campbell District. Two years later, a Fort Collins editor made a similar plea for building roads to the Lead Mountain District. If the area "was opened up to the public" by better travel routes, he predicted that "in twelve months a number of prosperous mining camps would be established, thus greatly adding to the business and prosperity [of] our county."[30]

The road network that eventually took shape in the Coyote Valley was a hodgepodge of old and new. Some routes, such as the one linking Lulu City to Gaskill, were blazed by settlers. Others, though, were constructed along or even on top of old Indian trails. By the height of the mining rush, the Kawuneeche's road network connected the Lead Mountain and Campbell Districts to Teller City (a small mining camp on the other side of the Never Summers), Fort Collins, and Grand Lake, where two important toll roads intersected: the Rollins Pass route to Boulder, and the Berthoud Pass route to the Clear Creek mining camps of Empire, Georgetown, and Idaho Springs.[31]

Building roads in high country ecosystems entailed extensive clearing, digging, grading, and leveling. Some segments, though, required even more elaborate work. Most every route used bridges to ford the Grand River's North Fork and other streams, while one stretch of the wagon road between Grand Lake and Lulu City was surfaced with "corduroy"—split logs laid side by side to provide a firm roadbed through marshy terrain. Roads ultimately placed a double burden on the lands they traversed: construction crews not only cleared vegetation from the right-of-way but also harvested bridge timbers and split logs from the adjoining forests.[32]

Once completed, roadways often became paths of least resistance for running water, especially during the spring snowmelt. Local historian Nell Pauly colorfully evoked a horrid road north of Grand Lake as nothing more than a "pair of deep ruts" leading "over permanent mudholes, through swamps, around or through beaver ponds, over rough corduroy patches of uneven poles because the so-called road was near the river." As the road "crooked around steep banks of washed-out earth," its surface "was usually muddy, with black sticky mud knee-deep to horses and hub-deep to the high-wheeled wagons." Though rough and rugged, the North Fork's road network nonetheless played a key role in hastening the integration of the remote Colorado River headwaters into regional, national, and even international exchange networks.[33]

Settlers desperately wanted roads, but they also recognized that train tracks would serve the North Fork mineral rush in ways that waterlogged wagon traces never could. The newcomers recognized from the outset that the mining camps' future hinged on railroads. Only the iron horse, it seemed, could break the fetters of isolation. Several schemes for extending rail lines to Grand Lake—including a few that might have brought tracks into the North Fork itself—seemed poised to unshackle the valley's mines, but all of them came to naught.[34]

Without a railroad, not even the boldest capitalist would venture to locate an up-to-date mill or smelter in the valley. The high cost of freighting in coal, coke, and bulky equipment by wagon made it prohibitively expensive to refine North Fork ores within the Kawuneeche. The mineral output of the Lead Mountain and Campbell Districts instead had to be hauled out of the valley by pack team or wagon train for processing in the Clear Creek Valley or Denver. Miners, townsfolk, and boosters blamed corporate scheming and malfeasance for the railroads' refusal to extend their tracks into the Colorado River headwaters. In truth, capitalist conspiracies had nothing to do with the settlers' woes. The mineral deposits around Lulu City and Gaskill were simply too poor to justify the immense expenditures required to build a railroad into the Coyote Valley.[35]

The endurance of wagon roads and the mining boom's collapse thus stemmed from the same root cause: The North Fork's ores could never repay the time, money, and energy that miners and capitalists had to expend in order to extract and refine them under prevailing technological, economic, and political conditions. Perhaps a few of the mines in the Lead Mountain or Campbell Districts might have become profitable if railroads and smelters had reached the valley. Colorado's railroad builders, though, showed remarkable acumen in sniffing out opportunity in the mining hinterlands of the Rocky Mountains. They inclined toward excessive exuberance, not unwarranted restraint; if anything, they built too much track too quickly. Every single mining district in Colorado to yield substantial and sustained riches eventually attracted at least one railroad line. The people of the North Fork mining camps were even more delusionary where smelting was concerned. Ore refining was undergoing tumultuous changes during the late 1870s and early 1880s. Even in Leadville, one of the richest silver mining centers anywhere in North American, smelters were closing down because they faced much higher costs than competing operations in Denver and Pueblo.[36]

Prospectors, miners, and townsfolk set about transforming the Coyote Valley in a range of ways. Yet nothing they did—and nothing that they failed to do, either—could liberate them from the legacies of the ancient tectonic processes that had shaped and reshaped the earth beneath their feet. The failure of the North Fork mineral boom thus reminds us of the continuing power of geology—as well as climate, geography, and other aspects of the natural world—to shape what human beings find possible, desirable, and profitable. Financial factors, particularly high transportation costs and a shortage of capital for developing mines and refining facilities in the North Fork camps, undoubtedly played a part in the mineral rush's undoing. Most every promising mining district in the West, however, grappled with analogous challenges. The fundamental difference between the Campbell and Lead Mountain Districts and other mining centers where the boom times lasted for several

decades instead of collapsing after just a few years was not an arti-
fact of culture, but instead a consequence of nature. Had the Kawuneeche's mineral deposits proven more ample, the valley could well have
realized the glistening dreams settlers had invested in its prospects.

Ferocious winters, unpredictable growing seasons, isolation from the
outside world—all of these served to demonstrate that in the Coyote
Valley, at least, the triumph over the wilderness that nineteenth-century
American settlers celebrated as part and parcel of their manifest destiny
would remain incomplete and uncertain.

Ghost Town Stories

The collapse of the short-lived mining boom revealed that there was
nothing foreordained about the American conquest of the Coyote Valley.
Settlers succeeded in removing the Nuche from the Rockies, and the
Americans' subsequent efforts to make the North Fork productive re-
worked the valley's ecosystems in significant, often long-lasting ways.
Hundreds of men and a handful of women labored for a succession of
years with a range of tools, technologies, and work animals in their
thrall—all in a vain attempt to close the yawning gap between the golden
dreams they had conjured up in their heads and the harsh realities that
hemmed in their lives and labors in the Kawuneeche.[37]

Within just a few years, the North Fork's miners and townspeople
alike realized that they could not force the material world to yield to
their mental visions. With just a few exceptions, the newcomers abandoned the struggle. They left behind burned hillsides, exotic plants, and
an array of other testaments to the intense but brief quest for silver
and gold. The boom's effects were hardest to miss near mine tunnels and
mining camps, where settlers littered the ground with piles of empty
tin cans, heaps of mine cars and rails, dumps of ore and waste rock, and
decaying structures ranging from mine tunnels to log cabins. The intensity of the would-be settlers' resolve to forsake the Colorado River
headwaters could be measured by the suddenness with which they
pulled up stakes. In their haste to leave Lulu City, some had even left
clothes hanging in their cabin closets.[38]

The mining rush left behind roads, too. Though some of the routes
settlers had built in the Kawuneeche during the late 1870s and early
1880s fell into disuse, others continued to connect the North Fork to the

world beyond. Even as these pathways were carrying away the outbound traffic wrought by mining's failure, they were already beginning to spirit homesteaders into the Colorado River headwaters. The people and technologies borne by these roads together fostered a more ethereal but equally important set of legacies: the circulation, interpretation, and preservation of stories about a stretch of high country that otherwise might have remained little known to Americans. Together, these stories mapped discordant meanings onto the Coyote Valley.

Many of the stories the mining rush left in its wake pivoted on relationships between people and other predatory creatures. In one way or another, all of these animal tales dwelled on questions of power, death, and abandonment. Through these leitmotifs, late nineteenth-century Americans tried to reckon with both the successes and failures of their ongoing struggles against the natural world.

In Lulu City's decaying remains, the ruins of an odd wooden structure—an 1880s bear trap—hint at the history of conflict between settlers and bears. Back during the height of the mining rush, stories glorifying the exploits of bear killers had filtered out of the North Fork and into newsprint. A brooding account of a reporter's visit to a cabin near Lulu, for instance, told of a man "who lives the life of an anchorite in the pleasurable occupation of bear catching." This correspondent was especially struck by the hermit's single-mindedness: "On every hand were unmistakable evidences that the objects of his pastime were numerous and vigorous. Bear tracks, bear wallows and bear scratches were painfully prevalent." Like many of his fellow settlers, this hunter was quite literally loaded for bear.[39]

Nineteenth-century Americans considered the elimination of bears and other predators as much more than a "pleasurable occupation." It was also an essential step in "civilizing" the West. Consider the story of what we might call the Great Gaskill Marten Massacre. According to the memoirs of Charles Hedrick, son of truck gardener J. H. Hedrick and a longtime inhabitant of the Coyote Valley, this strange and almost certainly apocryphal tale began one snowy January in Gaskill when "someone gave the alarm that the town was full of marten"—*Martes Americana*, a house cat–sized, carnivorous member of the weasel family that frequented the area's subalpine forests. "Everyone got excited," Hedrick recalled. The townsfolk "ran to see what was going on. In a snowbound little town like that," Hedrick pointed out, "anything that promised some excitement was welcome." The settler remembered how "you could see martens running in all directions"—200 or 300 in all. Shooting at the long, skinny, and impossibly quick little predators seemed pointless. So most settlers instead grabbed the nearest blunt object and "attacked the marten while they were running across the streets and over the cabins and jumping from tree to tree." Hedrick never specified how long the resulting killing spree lasted, nor did he offer any clues about what caused it. He did note, however, that Gaskill's citizenry eventually succeeded in killing about twenty of the elusive animals.[40]

There are many reasons to doubt the veracity of Hedrick's story. Marten are solitary animals that need large ranges to survive. Recorded densities of marten populations "are remarkably low," two leading researchers note, "even by comparison with other mammalian carnivores, which tend to occur at low densities." The estimated range required by the 200 to 300 marten Hedrick mentioned would have encompassed 100 to 300 km^2 of prime forested habitat (maybe even more given the habitat loss that the marten presumably suffered as settlers and their livestock transformed the high country). If Hedrick was telling the truth, then, every marten in the entire North Fork, reinforced by compatriots from the other side of the Never Summers or the Front Range, would have had to stage a coordinated assault on Gaskill. Why so many of the animals would have converged in lockstep on a hardscrabble mining camp is even more puzzling. Martens generally avoid people, and Gaskill had little to offer the carnivores.[41]

Hedrick, in short, was either exaggerating or lying. Perhaps ten or even twenty marten had happened upon the center of the Campbell mining district, and townsfolk may have succeeded in clubbing a few of the animals to death. At this remove, it is impossible to determine whether Hedrick was blowing an actual event out of proportion, or inventing an incident out of whole cloth. Though not literally true, the story of the Great Gaskill Marten Massacre nonetheless raises intriguing questions about people and predators on the Kawuneeche's mining frontier: Did the settler-protagonists of Hedrick's story attack marten as an unconscious outlet for the boredom, frustration, and worry that characterized life and work in a remote, winter-bound mining camp? Might Hedrick's account of townsfolk running amok to bludgeon martens have expressed the primal dread that newcomers to the North Fork felt in the face of the natural world's enduring might?

Though Hedrick's memoir offers few clear answers, a range of other stories about settlers and other animals confronted the mining camps' demise more directly. Several newspaper accounts hinted that the ongoing presence of large predators in the North Fork was jeopardizing the settlers' tenuous control over the valley. "Bears, of the most approved ferocity," an 1881 item in the *Fort Collins Express* noted, "are at all times within call." While this account evoked the proximity of savagery to illustrate the ruggedness of life in the Colorado high country, an 1884 article in the *Miner* veiled concern over the mining boom's impending failure with a peculiar jest about resurgent predators. "Much anxiety is felt for the safety of the mines at Lulu," it quipped. "Since the departure from there of Judge Godsmark and some more of the old timers, the bears and mountain lions have taken possession of the boys' houses and old gumboots, and are running a municipal government of their own . . . using all their efforts to restore Lulu to its primeval status." The paper anthropomorphized bears and mountain lions to make a serious joke about the tenuous nature of white settlement in the valley. With many of Lulu's long-standing citizens abandoning the camp and bears and cougars rewilding the domestic spaces that settlers had labored so hard to carve from the wilderness, the town seemed vulnerable to a coup d'état in which nonhuman predators reclaimed political control from their erstwhile conquerors.[42]

Another genre of stories about Coyote Valley, meanwhile, presented the North Fork environment in a complementary but much more flattering light. While predator tales cast the natural world as quite literally red in tooth and claw, paeans to the valley's scenery portrayed the high country as sublime and full of wonder. Even as residents and travelers were enumerating the North Fork's advantages to would-be miners and homemakers, they also waxed eloquent about the wonders of God's creation. A correspondent to the *Fort Collins Courier* portrayed the Coyote Valley as suffused with fearsome, glorious might. The writer rapturously described "the grand sight of a thunder and snow storm combined, on the continental divide" as "sublime beyond the poor ability of your correspondent to describe." The spectacle presented by "the continuous flashes of lightning and the constant roar of God's artillery, together with the majestic grandeur and forbidding aspect of the dark clouds as they gathered over and swept past the phantom looking spires and imaginary belfrys [*sic*] of the volcanic regions," the correspondent proclaimed, had "left an impression on my mind that will not soon be eradicated." No wonder a *Rocky Mountain News* account described the people of Lulu City as "enthusiastic in their admiration for the mountain scenery." The North Fork landscape, in short, struck many newcomers as sublimity incarnate—a mountain stronghold where the Creator's raw omnipotence was uniquely perceptible to mortal souls. Neither the craggy mountains nor the tempestuous weather seemed susceptible to improvement or vulnerable to destruction. Instead, these unsullied and incorruptible embodiments of nature's majesty evoked God's power and glory.[43]

Participants in the North Fork mining rush failed to discover gold or silver in paying quantities, but they did introduce the romantic ideals that would go on to shape the Coyote Valley's eventual inclusion in Rocky Mountain National Park and its emergence as a destination for recreational tourists. Mining's collapse prompted Charles Hedrick and others to spin yarns that revealed settlers and nonhuman predators as bitter rivals locked in a violent struggle for survival and supremacy. The adversarial view of nature that suffused these animal stories, however, lost ground in the decades ahead. By the early twentieth century, the perception of the Colorado River headwaters as a place suffused with sublimity was ascendant. Whether aesthetic preservation under federal management would benefit the valley's ecosystems, though, remained to be seen. American nature appreciation, after all, rested on foundations that were aesthetic, philosophical, nationalistic, and often self-serving—but hardly ecological in any modern sense of the term.

◁ 5 ▷

FARMERS

FOR THE TENS of thousands of farming folk who migrated to Colorado in the wake of the Pike's Peak Gold Rush, the Rocky Mountains conjured pragmatic designs as well as romantic flights of fancy. In fair weather, the high country loomed in plain sight from most of the piedmont and much of the plains beyond. From early fall through early summer, the mountains were clad in a downy coat of white. Even on blazing, lip-blistering August afternoons, the vestigial streaks of snow and ice that dappled the Rockies' slopes seemed to taunt farmers laboring on Colorado's semiarid flatlands. These cultivators realized, after all, that if they could just channel the melting snows of the mountains onto their fields instead of permitting this water to flow away toward the sea, then they could squeeze bountiful harvests from lands that rarely received enough natural precipitation to sustain thirsty and profitable crops such as wheat, corn, and sugar beets.[1]

And so in the early 1880s, at the height of the North Fork mining boom and just a few years after Nuche removal, entrepreneurs from Larimer and Weld Counties dispatched surveyors to the Greater Rocky Mountain National Park Ecosystem. These crews began to reconnoiter reservoir sites "at the head of the Cache la Poudre," then crossed over the Continental Divide to examine the Colorado River headwaters and Grand Lake. By summer's end, surveyors had staked out a route for an irrigation ditch that would intercept several streams on the eastern flanks of the Never Summer Mountains and divert their waters into the Poudre River, which would then carry them down the Rockies' eastern

slopes to the burgeoning agricultural hinterlands around Greeley and
Fort Collins.[2]

A succession of irrigation companies touted plans to build a diversion canal along the route that survey crews had staked out. For many
years, though, these firms focused on capturing what water they could
from surer and cheaper water sources in the Platte River watershed. It
took until the early 1890s for a firm called the Water Supply and Storage
Company—Water Supply, for short—to unveil its sweeping scheme for
the Grand Ditch, the first major project to divert water from Colorado's
Western Slope to the eastern side of the Continental Divide. Carving out
a functional ditch from the heights of the Rockies, however, proved more
difficult than anyone anticipated. Water Supply would not complete the
Grand Ditch until the 1930s.[3]

Entrepreneurial farmers from the northern Colorado piedmont were
hardly the only agriculturists to set their sights on the Coyote Valley
after the mineral rush crashed. During the same years in which Water
Supply began to carry water out of the Colorado River basin, other settlers were establishing farms and ranches on the floor of the Kawuneeche. The men and women who turned the valley into a peripheral but
active salient of the U.S. homesteading frontier between the 1880s and
early 1900s held few illusions about the area's agricultural potential.
They realized that farming scant soils at elevations ranging from 8,700
feet to 9,000 feet above sea level would yield them neither wealth nor
power. Instead, these homesteaders came in hopes of carving out places
of their own where the pursuit of mixed husbandry on a limited scale
might afford them some refuge from the pervasive economic uncertainty
and social turmoil that bedeviled industrializing America.

Together, homesteaders and irrigators brought many changes to the
North Fork's landscape and ecology. As construction crews inscribed the
Grand Ditch onto the flanks of the Never Summer Mountains, water diversion began to reroute the valley's hydrological systems. More than a
thousand feet below, meanwhile, homesteaders on the valley floor
cleared willows, put up fences, sawed timber, introduced livestock,
and otherwise unsettled the headwaters environment. Roughly half of
those who filed claims to valley lands under the Homestead Act of 1862
failed—a percentage roughly equivalent to the nationwide average. Those
who managed to prove up their claims and convert tracts of public
domain land into private holdings owed their success not just to the

fickleness of fate, but also to their own hard work and adaptability. By drawing on family labor, leaving the valley to find wage work, and exploiting a wide range of resources and markets, some two dozen homesteading households managed to maintain a foothold on tracts of Colorado River bottomland.

Yet, as the northeastern Nuche and the miners who took their place both discovered, the Coyote Valley was a tough place to live. Because the natural world generally retained the upper hand in human-environment interactions there, conservationists and preservationists in the early 1900s could still perceive the North Fork as a primeval refuge and potential playground—but only if they overlooked the widespread marks left on the Greater Rocky Mountain National Park Ecosystem by many millennia of Native American inhabitation, a half decade of mining activity, and several decades of ditch building and agricultural settlement.

Imagining and Building the Grand Ditch

Construction on the Grand Ditch began in late summer 1891. Crews had barely completed the first mile of the conduit, from Poudre Pass southwesterly across the face of the Never Summers, when winter descended. The ditch carried no water, though, until three years later, when the *Fort Collins Courier* exulted: "The waters of the Poudre river are now mingled with the waters of the Grand and the Laramie rivers." Workers widened the canal in 1895, and extended its right-of-way the next year. Shaky financing, though, brought construction to a premature halt until fall 1900.[4]

News coverage followed a familiar rhythm in the years thereafter. The advent of spring brought bold predictions. Optimistic reports endured through mid-summer. Autumn, though, inevitably witnessed downcast dispatches and half-hearted apologies for the project's slow progress. A characteristic 1902 account, for instance, explained that a force of more than 200 ditch diggers had made little headway because "timber two feet in diameter and 75 feet tall" had blocked the ditch's progress through virgin stands of subalpine forest.[5]

Neither obstacles nor delays, though, could shake the irrigators' faith. Water Supply resembled a cooperative enterprise, with all or nearly all of its 600 shares held by the farmers who depended on the company for

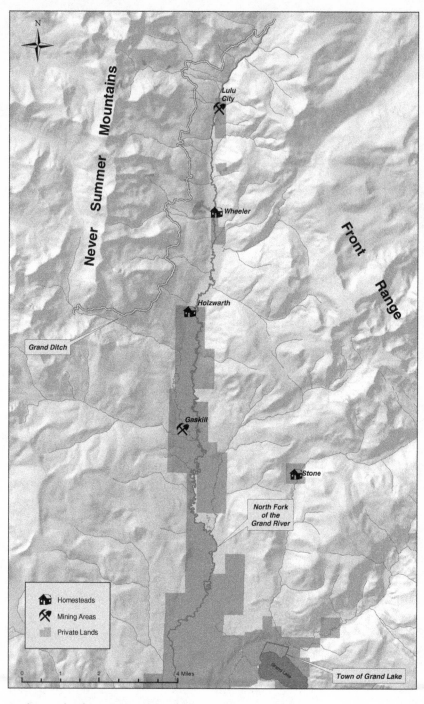

Settlement landscapes. Courtesy of the National Park Service.

irrigation water. Most Water Supply shareholders lived near Fort Collins, in Larimer County, but some farmed downstream in Weld County. The ditch company's perennial optimism was fueled in no small part by its shareholders' collective desire to transubstantiate the Rocky Mountain snowpack into luxuriant crops, prolific herds, prosperous households, and thriving communities.[6]

Boosters in the areas served by Water Supply saw diversions of water from the Colorado River watershed as the key to unlocking the northern piedmont's immense agricultural potential. The *Fort Collins Courier* explained that the river that began in the Coyote Valley boasted "the largest volume of any stream in Colorado, larger perhaps than both the Platte and the Arkansas combined"—a "supply of water" so immense as to seem "practically inexhaustible." The trouble was that the Colorado's natural course led through country where the only "arable land" was "confined to a narrow valley" around Grand Junction. On the Rockies' eastern slope, by contrast, the "conditions prevailing" were "reversed." The northern piedmont boasted plenty of land suitable for farming, but it suffered from inadequate precipitation and stream flow. By redirecting water from the Colorado River headwaters to the Poudre watershed, and thence to the fertile farmlands that fanned out from the base of the Rockies to the high plains beyond, the Grand Ditch would remedy nature's vagaries.[7]

Paeans to the Grand Ditch depicted water as an alchemical substance: add it to the rich piedmont soil and abundant harvests were bound to follow. An 1893 article hailed the project as "the direct means of adding millions of dollars to the wealth of Larimer and Weld Counties." But the ditch's true value was moral as well as financial. The project, a *Fort Collins Courier* reporter conceded, "will cost considerable money but the value of the water" that the completed system "will bring to the Poudre valley cannot be estimated in dollars and cents. The Water Supply and Storage Company is a pioneer in the effort to make water from the western slope do duty on the farms of the eastern slope."[8]

"Do duty": the muscular verb phrase spoke volumes about the assumptions undergirding the broader effort to divert the West's waterways in the late 1800s and 1900s. Reclaiming the region's lands and waters, a growing chorus of farmers, engineers, politicians, town builders, and boosters believed, would empower progressive Americans to overcome the vicissitudes of a fickle and wasteful nature. In the process, irrigation would, in historian William Cronon's insightful analysis, supplant "natural scarcity" with "artificial abundance." The Colorado River and its tributaries, the *Courier* reporter implied, had shirked their responsibilities for eons. The Grand Ditch would end nature's profligacy and advance the collective good by making water that would otherwise have flowed down the Coyote Valley "do duty" on the Rockies' eastern slope.[9]

Irrigation boosters cleverly spun the slow and halting pace of construction in the Never Summers as a sign of the Grand Ditch's heroic dimensions. A 1903 *Courier* story, for instance, celebrated the diversion as a triumph of human industry and ingenuity "constructed upon a most scientific and thorough plan." Though perched "for most of its length . . . on the slope of a mountain side whose incline is at least of an angle of 45 degrees," the Grand Ditch, the article explained, was nonetheless "built upon what is known as regular railroad curves." Because the canal and the embankment that held it in place were "carved out of the hill side as a complete and continuous excavation," they formed "such a solid structure" that they could support "heavily loaded freight teams" without "the slightest damage." The *Courier* reassured readers that skillful construction "obviat[ed]" any "danger of the ditch's breaking." What made the canal "of greater value still" was its ability to "afford both early and late water" to piedmont farmers; the Grand Ditch, the paper pointed out, intercepted creeks supplied by slopes that faced north, south, and east, so it received snowmelt from the start of the piedmont growing season through midsummer.[10]

Designed and built to tease out the latent potentialities of Colorado's terrain and climate, Colorado's first major transmontane water diversion canal thus embodied a time-honored American creed. Irrigation boosters contended that the application of human intelligence and labor to the landscape would perfect what the Creator had wrought. The Grand Ditch, like other improvements, would reap both individual wealth and collective betterment, as Water Supply president A. A. Anderson argued in a 1903 op-ed, "Does Irrigation Pay?" Anderson claimed that the price of his company's stock had increased from $500 to $2,250 a share since 1895 because "of the construction of the mountain ditches and reservoirs and the perfection and enlargement of the plains system of reservoirs." Anderson contended that before the Grand Ditch was built, "almost every farm under our canal" had been "poorly supplied with

The Grand Ditch twisted and turned across the flanks of the Never Summer Mountains, diverting water from the basin of the Colorado River toward the irrigated farms of Colorado's northern piedmont. Undated photograph, MSF Neg. 1735, courtesy of the National Park Service.

buildings and mortgaged for all it would stand." Thanks to water diverted from the upper reaches of the Coyote Valley, though, "the same places are supplied with fine homes, and large, commodious barns and sheds for the farmers' stock, and a mortgage is almost unheard of and a thing of the past." By placing "abundant" water at farmers' disposal, the Grand Ditch was making manifest the latent productivity and profitability of the lands it helped to irrigate. "It is a common occurrence," Anderson claimed, "for our farmers, especially those who cultivate potatoes and beets, to clean up, net, from a quarter section of land $4,000 to $6,000 in one year." Land prices had risen in consequence, from twenty to thirty dollars an acre in 1895, to sixty to one hundred dollars an acre in 1903.[11]

The Grand Ditch, Anderson reasoned, had amply repaid the optimism of Water Supply and its supporters. But beneath cold figures authenticating the Grand Ditch's economic benefits, Anderson also detected an unmistakable calculus of social progress: "Good schools," he declared, "are established at convenient distance for the education of

the children of the farmers living along" Water Supply's canals. "All
our people are prosperous and happy," Anderson concluded, "and the
future never appeared brighter than at present."[12]

Alas, the Water Supply president proved a poor prophet. In the early
years of the twentieth century, legal battles and financial difficulties
hampered work on the Grand Ditch. The company stayed afloat by
levying assessments on shareholders of $100 in 1903 and $150 in 1904.
Finally in 1905, the *Courier* reported that Water Supply was making
summer plans to "complete its stupendous Grand River ditch enterprise
by means of which a large volume of water will be added to the present
supply for irrigation purposes, making it possible to open up new farms
and adding to the population and wealth of the rural districts."[13]

And yet the ditch remained stuck in place. Further assessments in
1906 enabled contractors to extend the conduit to Tank Creek, but construction stalled there for more than two decades. Apart from a wood
covering built in the 1910s to keep rock slides and other debris from ob-
structing the channel, Water Supply performed "only maintenance and
repair work" on the Grand Ditch until the late 1920s.[14]

Behind the Ideal

Reclamation boosters imagined the Grand Ditch as an improvement that
would exemplify America's mastery over the Rocky Mountain landscape. The crews who built the conduit, though, experienced a different
reality. "Early ditch digging," historian James Hansen explains, "was a
grueling form of manual labor, particularly in the mountains. Lacking
modern machinery, and assisted only by teams of mules and horses,
work crews dug with picks and shovels, felled trees with axes," and yoked
teams of draft animals to an array of implements. No wonder longtime
Water Supply official Edward Baker called the ditch workers with whom
he labored in the early 1900s "strong, brutes of men—by God they had
to be." Workers struggled to overcome both the usual challenges of ditch
digging—recalcitrant draft animals, broken tools, autocratic foremen,
tension with fellow workers—and trials peculiar to laboring at elevations
exceeding 10,000 feet above sea level. Steep slopes, swollen streams,
scorching mountain sun, obstructions ranging from heavy timber to
rock outcrops, the famously harsh weather that led Arapaho Indians to
name the range across which the Grand Ditch meandered the Never

Summer Mountains, and "mosquitos big as hummingbirds" all awaited construction workers on the western slopes of the Coyote Valley. Despite these and other travails, workers fashioned a diversion canal that functioned well enough to keep Water Supply in business through several lean decades.[15]

The Grand Ditch materialized in stages. Engineers and survey crews finalized the canal's future course, planting flags, stakes, and signs that marked the waters of each stream the ditch intercepted as Water Supply's property. Gangs of transient, unskilled laborers followed, including Chinese and Japanese immigrants hired through labor contractors. Water Supply's Harvey Johnson remembered these manual workers as poorly paid but good workers: "You could hire those people for a dollar a day and board them," Johnson recalled, "and they'd work."[16]

Reclamation boosters were consummate Jeffersonians who believed that the project would put an end to water's wasteful ways. By making the Colorado River "do duty," the conduit would enable independent yeomen—the farmers who Jefferson famously celebrated as "the chosen people of God"—to turn Colorado's semiarid piedmont into a productive and orderly heartland. But water diversion also caused widespread ecological and hydrological change.[17]

Ditch workers began by clearing trees and other plants from the right-of-way, a hundred-foot-wide swath snaking along the Never Summers more than 1,000 feet above the North Fork of the Grand River. Lumber taken from the ditch route itself, though, hardly sufficed. Flumes, headgates, bridges, and other necessary structures all consumed timber cut from adjoining forests and then fed through portable sawmills. Logging and milling littered the landscape with slash and sawdust. Workers took food as well as building materials from the subalpine forests through which the canal twisted and turned. Though work on the ditch typically ended before Colorado's fall deer-hunting season opened, Edward Baker nonetheless quipped that the construction crews on which he labored as a young man "didn't object to killing a deer for a lot of food."[18]

The Grand Ditch's most significant ecological impacts, though, flowed directly from its raison d'être: improving on nature by channeling water across the Continental Divide. More water for piedmont farmers inevitably meant less for the Coyote Valley. Starting in the late nineteenth century, water tables on the valley floor began to fall gradually but inexorably. Peak flows on the Colorado River also started to dwindle—bad news, as later chapters show, for invertebrates, trout, and even willows. As far as anyone in Colorado during the early decades of the twentieth century was concerned, though, the biggest problem with the Grand Ditch was that it remained unfinished.[19]

Homesteading a Hard Land

Even as the doctrine of improvement was leading Water Supply and its workers to shove the hydrological hinterlands of the piedmont farming belt across the Continental Divide, much the same impulse was attracting homesteaders to the North Fork. Long after Frederick Jackson Turner's famous 1893 lament that the American frontier had closed, the Coyote Valley remained an open and untamed land.

About forty-two applicants filed homestead claims with the federal government to tracts within the Kawuneeche, and a few others purchased land from the government outright. John Hedrick, the first settler to claim a part of the North Fork as his own, initially settled on his land in July 1880; the last, Clarence Lee, entered his claim in June 1927. Seven other people joined Hedrick in filing claims during the 1880s, but all of them entered the North Fork after the mining rush crashed. Only six settlers filed entry papers in the 1890s, when Colorado suffered the worst economic depression in its history. Nine homesteaders entered valley lands in the 1900s, twelve in the 1910s, and seven in the 1920s.[20]

The agricultural settlement of the North Fork resembled a folk migration. Though boosters feverishly promoted homesteading elsewhere in the nation, neither railroads nor land companies played any significant role in advertising the Kawuneeche's charms. Instead, homesteaders chose to file claims to the valley's lands for reasons of their own—reasons that unfortunately went almost entirely unrecorded. The settlers' varied backgrounds shed little light on their motivations for coming to the valley. Six women filed homestead claims. Nova Scotia–born Mary Harbison numbered among the small contingent of immigrants to homestead in the North Fork, joined by a Dane and a trio of Germans. The American-born majority of homesteaders hailed mostly from older states such as Massachusetts, Virginia, and New York, as well as the Midwest (four came from Illinois and at least one each from Indiana, Ohio, Minnesota, Michigan, Kansas, Iowa, Missouri, and Nebraska).

Only one head of a homesteading household was born in Colorado. The settlers' ages also were mixed, ranging at the time of entry from twenty-four to seventy-one years old. Some homesteaders had been widowed; most were single or married. Several had children. In contrast to the sizable families characteristic of earlier American agricultural frontiers, though, the largest homesteading households in the Coyote Valley numbered just five members.[21]

Farmers and home seekers grappled with the same environmental conditions that had hampered the North Fork mining boom, as the documents they submitted to the General Land Office in the course of proving up their claims demonstrate. In contrast to mineral rush correspondents, who often portrayed the North Fork as a land of fertile pastures and prolific forests, would-be homesteaders depicted the valley as a place ill suited for agriculture. "Snow lies on [the] ground an average of 180 days of the year—often 200," Charles Seymour complained. Worse, he contended, the North Fork "never" experienced "more than 75 frostless nights" a year. Markus Christiansen lamented that "snow falls to a great depth making it impossible" to reach his tract "with a team . . . until late in the spring." And because "snow falls early," Christiansen continued, it was often "impossible to get a team out late in the fall." The "climatic conditions in the vicinity of this land," Christiansen concluded, "make it a hardship to reside on the land for a greater period of each year than five or six months." Even this hardy Scandinavian admitted that he "couldn't stand to stay there" during the winter because "it was snowy and the snow was deep." A former cook of Clinton DeWitt's painted an even grimmer picture; bad weather, Josephine Burton claimed, had made it impossible for her employer to venture "into the timber" to "get material and put up a house in which it would be safe to live without endangering his life."[22]

Homesteaders criticized the Coyote Valley's soils as well as its climate. Settler John Holzwarth Sr. disparaged the North Fork growing season as "short." Even in summer, Holzwarth griped, "nights . . . are very cool so that grains and other farm products will not mature and hay and pasture are the only crops that can be grown and the land is only fit for the growing of stock." For his part, Allen Hatter described his high-country tract as torture to cultivate. One portion contained "rough rocky hillside," with "absolutely no tillable land"; another stretch consisted "nearly all [of] hillside" and a "small strip [of] swamp." Hatter claimed that still other "flat, swampy" stretches of his claim suffered from a pair of serious liabilities: "natural sod too heavy and too deep to be cultivated" and "many beaver dams." Not surprisingly, Hatter proclaimed it "impossible to till the land and raise ordinary farm crops" in the Kawuneeche "owing to the high altitude, short seasons and the cold nights and the character and the surface of the soil."[23]

Settlers found that General Land Office bureaucrats often sympathized with their plight. Agency officials frequently allowed homesteaders extra time to prove up their claims. Even more important, they began in the 1910s to interpret the Homestead Act more loosely by accepting valid evidence of stock raising as sufficient proof that settlers had placed the land they claimed under "cultivation." Government latitude, however, failed to rescue many high-country settlers from failure.[24]

The Coyote Valley offered no refuge from hardship. Take Abram Macy, who filed on 160 acres of land in summer 1890. The following spring, Macy asked the land office if he could take a nine-month leave of absence from his tract because of "sickness and old age[. H]aving no person to live with me," the settler explained, "I have been obliged to move to the town of Grand Lake to get cared for and to have proper treatment." Though bureaucrats took pity on Macy, his illness showed no mercy. Less than a month after informing federal officials of his infirmity, Macy died.[25]

Abram Macy's fate was especially dire, but many other prospective homesteaders also struggled desperately to scratch out a living from the Colorado River headwaters. Robert Harbison, for instance, explained that he had "abandoned" his homestead because "the character of the land is such that it will not produce an agricultural crop in paying quantity and I am unable to make a living from said land, having no other means than my own labor, and the expense of putting said land into condition to produce paying crops would be such that I am unable to accomplish it." Some parcels proved so recalcitrant that it took a succession of settlers to tame them; one tract, for example, outlasted a total of five claimants between 1889 and 1920 before Andrew Christiansen finally succeeded at proving up his claim to it.[26]

No one ever attempted to homestead on the vast majority of the Coyote Valley's lands. Ultimately, just a small percentage of the North Fork ever passed from the public domain into private hands—perhaps 3,000 acres in a valley containing tens of thousand of acres in all. The

Kawuneeche's ferocious and recalcitrant environment necessitated a crucial change in federal policy: thwarted in its efforts to place all of the North Fork under settlers' control, the U.S. government would instead retain ownership over the vast majority of the valley's lands.

Improving the Valley

Public land laws required federal surveyors to impose a more or less rectilinear grid on the North Fork's intricate, highly irregular topography. The parcels on which settlers filed homestead claims invariably encompassed a range of geographic features, soils, and vegetation types. Most homesteads, however, shared a few essential features: frontage on the Colorado River or one of its tributaries; willow thickets on the lowest-lying ground; rich meadows where the vegetative communities settlers referred to as "native grass" or "native hay" flourished; and at least a dozen wooded acres on soils that were higher or dryer.

Most settlers claimed parcels along a contiguous strip of bottomlands near the North Fork that stretched from one to eight miles north of Grand Lake, a small resort town that offered opportunities to socialize as well as markets for the settlers' produce and labor. Only three homesteads occupied sites beyond the main cluster: the Holzwarth spread, a mile or so upriver; Sam Stone's place in the aptly named Big Meadows, several miles east of the river; and "Squeaky" Bob Wheeler's Hotel de Hardscrabble, at the foot of Milner Pass near the northern reaches of the Colorado River headwaters. Compared to their neighbors in the main strip of homesteads, Stone, Wheeler, and the Holzwarths faced greater isolation, higher transportation costs, and even harsher weather. Wheeler's land, after all, lay at an elevation of around 9,000 feet, and Stone's claim at Big Meadows towered a whopping 9,400 feet above sea level.

The few settlers who bought parcels from the government, like the somewhat larger group who purchased land from earlier homesteaders, could use the lands in their possession however they wanted. Those filing homestead papers, by contrast, could only receive a patent to their claim if they could convince federal officials that they had resided on their parcel and placed it under cultivation.

Homesteaders typically constructed homes from pines, either harvested from their own claims or taken from the adjoining public domain.

Settlers tended to start small, with rough-hewn log cabins of just a few hundred square feet. While homesteaders of the 1880s and 1890s often covered their cabins with simple dirt roofs, latter-day settlers usually opted for the added comfort and security of more expensive shingle roofs. As time passed, successful homesteaders added larger cabins to their lands, such as the four-room, twenty-by-forty-foot "Log House" the Holzwarth family built in the early 1920s.[27]

Unadorned simplicity typified the interior of every homestead cabin in the North Fork. The Hedricks, for instance, furnished theirs with "one cook stove, one heating stove, bedsteads, tables, chairs, and dishes and cooking utensils," all of which the family had possessed "since settlement." Another settler, Markus Christiansen, boasted to Land Office officials about his sixteen-by-twenty-four-foot cabin: "Why we have a good big table, 6 dining room chairs, 2 rocking chairs, 1 good bed, mattress, bedding and a range stove."[28]

Homesteads needed water as well as stoves and basic furnishings. Some settlers dug shallow wells to tap into the Kawuneeche's relatively shallow water table. Others, by contrast, dug ditches to carry water for domestic purposes from nearby streams; some of these canals also served to irrigate gardens and hay meadows.[29]

Federal regulations required homesteaders not just to make homes on their land but also to cultivate it. The Coyote Valley's settlers invariably practiced mixed husbandry, raising both plants and animals. Virtually every homesteader brought at least a few domesticated animals into the valley. Like mineral rush participants, homesteaders drew motive power and sustenance from the bodies of horses, cattle, chickens, and other creatures. Equally important, livestock and poultry could reproduce relatively rapidly; every time these creatures bore young, they effectively placed additional energy and wealth at their owners' disposal. The homesteaders' livestock presumably spent most of the warmer months grazing on the open ranges and fenced pastures of the North Fork meadowlands. Between mid-summer and late fall, settlers toiled to lay up sufficient hay from their own lands to keep their animals fed through the depths of winter. The Kawuneeche's haying operations, however, remained quite small; the wild grasslands on most homesteads spanned just a few dozen acres, and the largest encompassed only one hundred acres.[30]

Draft animals and farm implements helped homesteaders to turn willow thickets into hay meadows. "Harbison Ranch: Plowing in the Meadow," 1915, MSF Neg. 604, courtesy of the National Park Service.

The fortunes of homesteading households depended to no small degree on their ability to increase the size and productivity of their hay meadows. Settlers eked out more space for pasture and hay by clearing out the willow thickets that had covered much of the North Fork bottomlands for thousands of years. In some reaches of the valley, newcomers to the Kawuneeche also attempted to fell lodgepole pines and replace them with grass—an uncertain proposition since these conifers preferred dry sites and acidic, underdeveloped soils. Homesteaders quickly learned that clearing out shrubs and trees demanded backbreaking work. The deep, tightly entangled root systems that coursed beneath the North Fork's willow thickets proved especially stubborn; only with draft animals, heavy chains, and considerable patience could homesteaders break the hold of these hardy shrubs on their native soil.[31]

Clearing willow thickets and pine groves served larger ends. Settlers disparaged the Kawuneeche's "native hay" as unproductive, complaining that it lacked nutrition and was difficult to establish on freshly cleared ground. Homesteaders eschewed the North Fork's indigenous plants in favor of exotic grasses such as rye, timothy, and clover because these old-world cultigens (colloquially known as "tame hay" or "tame grass") generally delivered higher yields. Suspecting that plowing up the heavy, wet soils of the Colorado River bottomlands was a fool's errand, settlers generally chose instead to drag disks over "native hay" meadows and recently cleared lands alike before sowing "tame hay" species. A minority of settlers took their agricultural improvements a step further by digging ditches to irrigate their thirsty hay fields. Sam Stone, by contrast, sought to drain his boggy land by digging a ditch through Big Meadows. Clearing willow and pine enabled settlers to expand meadowlands. Planting tame hay and moderating moisture levels, meanwhile, helped settlers to increase their harvests. Native grasslands typically yielded just half a ton of hay per acre, while lands cultivated with exotic species typically produced at least a ton of hay per acre—and often more on irrigated or drained parcels.[32]

Many homesteaders sought to cultivate gardens, too. John Hedrick, the North Fork's pioneer gardener, raised turnips and "hardy vegetables" in the 1880s on "about an acre" of land he had "spaded" by hand. Henry Lehman, a longtime resident of Grand Lake, painted an almost cornucopian image of the valley's potential as a garden spot: "You can raise parsnips, turnips, carrots, you can raise lettuce of the finest, you can raise timothy, and oats, they have hay, you can raise cauliflower, and cabbage, raddishes [sic] and several other things." Though homesteaders rarely reaped as varied a bounty as Lehman described, even Robert Wheeler's high-elevation parcel could boast "a half acre of garden growing lettuce, radishes, onions, and rhubarb each year."[33]

Farming and gardening reconfigured intricate natural relationships that had evolved over many millennia. Clearing willows modified the hydrology of riparian areas. The shrubs' removal accelerated erosion, reduced habitat for a range of creatures, and forced beavers and elk to find alternative food supplies. The exotic species settlers introduced to the Coyote Valley, meanwhile, had a habit of venturing beyond homestead boundaries and onto public lands, where they often outcompeted and displaced native plants. Drainage ditches spurred other vegetational changes. When Sam Stone resolved to grow hay on a Big Meadows fen, he dug a channel roughly 500 meters long, half a meter wide, and a meter deep. Because boggy ecosystems need high water tables to maintain an-aerobic conditions, ecologist David Cooper and his colleagues explain, peat fens are "extremely sensitive" to "the hydrologic changes created by even small ditches or water diversions." By lowering water levels in the fen, Stone's ditch subjected the lands it drained to "a state of severe and prolonged drought for much of the twentieth century." These artificially arid conditions, in turn, altered the composition of the fen's soil and vegetation, with bluejoint and tufted hairgrass (both native to the North Fork) crowding out water-loving plants like Northwest Territory sedge and water sedge.[34]

At Big Meadows and other North Fork homesteads, an assortment of structures complemented ditches, gardens, meadows, and cabins. Many settlers built root cellars, chicken coops, and corrals; most also constructed wooden barns, sheds, and stables of varying designs and dimensions. Neighbors frequently helped each other to erect outbuildings as well as fences, just as they lent each other a hand to build houses and harvest hay. Homesteaders evidently obtained most of their building supplies from the local area. Lodgepole pine chopped down on the settlers' own claims usually sufficed for logs, poles, rails, and posts. But homesteaders sometimes purchased planks and boards from the Kawuneeche's small sawmill operations, as well as from Grand Lake lumberyards, which also sold fasteners and fittings freighted over the mountains.[35]

The Art of Shifting

Even in the context of the late 1800s and early 1900s, the North Fork's homesteads were small and primitive. Not a single settler raised more than one hundred acres of hay or one hundred head of cattle. Seven years after John Hedrick filed homestead papers he could count to his name just a dozen chickens, "one horse, one mule, one cow and two hei-ffers [*sic*]," while his year's harvest amounted to just twenty tons of hay, one ton of turnips, and "several bushels" of vegetables. After five years on the land, John Holzwarth Sr., who had extensive experience in ranching as well as the benefit of his full-grown son's labor, had planted just twelve acres of hay.[36]

Few settlers could have held on had they depended solely on the scanty produce of their own lands. To make do, settlers had to "shift"—to enlist family labor, leave the valley in search of seasonal work, and search out subsistence goods and marketable commodities beyond the boundaries of their homesteads. (In the early 1900s, some settlers also began to diversify in an even more consequential direction by marketing the wonders of Rocky Mountain nature to tourists—a story to which we return in Chapter 7.)

Resources drawn from the public domain helped to sustain most homesteaders in the Coyote Valley. Mrs. Rob Harbison described her family's travails as "a hard struggle on the ranch which they built from nothing." In truth, settlers drew heavily on energy and materials harvested from the surrounding government lands. "With 40 cows to feed," Rob Harbison admitted, "they cut hay wherever they could find it" and grazed their stock " 'any damn place they wanted to.' " After the creation of the Medicine Bow Forest Reserve in the early 1900s, though, settlers needed permits to graze stock or cut timber. In 1910, U.S. Forest Service officials allowed settlers to graze 500 cattle and 30 horses on lands under their control on the eastern slope of the Never Summers. Homesteaders also turned to public lands for game and fish, contributing to the decline of furbearers, large ungulates, native trout, and large predators throughout the Greater Rocky Mountain National Park Ecosystem.[37]

In the Coyote Valley, as on other homesteading frontiers, kinship ties and women's work figured centrally in household strategies. Newcomers who came to the Colorado River headwaters via chain migrations probably fared better than migrants who lacked kin or close associates in the Colorado high country. Andrew Christiansen and his father, Mark Christiansen, both proved up their claims, possibly with the help of Mark's brother Julius, who also lived in the area; Benjamin Mitchell received a favorable ruling from the General Land Office five months after his mother, Polly Ann Mitchell, successfully patented a claim initially filed by her husband; and Annie and Kate Harbison eventually received title to adjacent homesteads.[38]

Only scant traces document the travails of homesteading women in the North Fork. Evidence from other parts of the Colorado Rockies, though, shows how women's paid and unpaid labor could make the difference between success and failure. A northwestern Colorado ranch wife recalled days and nights of ceaseless toil: "You never run out of work on a farm—that's for sure." For North Fork women, cooking and

Members of the Harbison family, several of whom proved up homestead claims to the southern Kawuneeche Valley, served as the nucleus of this 1908 group photograph. MSF Neg. 704, courtesy of the National Park Service.

cleaning probably entailed many hours of labor each day. Baking in finicky woodstoves at high altitude required considerable skill; since most ovens of the era lacked temperature indicators, another Colorado ranch woman recalled that "you had to be a marvel at knowing your stove." During the annual roundup of late spring or summer and the fall haying season, homesteading women also had to feed hired hands and beneficent neighbors as well as their own families.[39]

The Coyote Valley, like other settlement frontiers, sometimes masqueraded as a gender-bending sort of place. The valley's women and girls often worked out-of-doors to raise chickens, care for dairy cattle, and plant gardens. They also sometimes undertook tasks that were traditionally gendered male such as grubbing out willows, hauling logs, and trapping beaver. Several of the valley's households were headed by women, and a few had no male members. On these homesteads, women presumably performed all or nearly all of the jobs that settlers in the Rocky Mountains typically considered "men's work."[40]

Chain migrations and Women's work notwithstanding, many North Fork settlers needed to supplement their household income by laboring for wages. An illustrative case involves "Squeaky Bob" Wheeler, who left his homestead during successive early twentieth-century winters to take a string of positions: cook in Estes Park, laborer in that same town, carpenter on the Grand Ditch, an unspecified job at a saw mill in the Kawuneeche, and an unknown posting on the Pacific Coast. Like Wheeler, Jacob Jones felt he had to hit the road to survive. Jones left his land in the valley in the 1880s "for the express purpose of earning money with which to live and to make improvements upon said land." John Hedrick, for his part, frequently left his family behind on the homestead; between 1880 and 1886, he often "worked for different parties, cut hay, cut wood, carried mail, and did odd jobs." In early winter 1886, Hedrick and his wife realized that "they could not stay" on their homestead, for they "had no provisions to last them through the winter and could get none there in the winter." The Hedricks, "obliged to seek employment as they could not make a living on the land," decided to move downriver to Kremmling. The family's star seemed to be rising when Hedrick found work with the Union Pacific Railroad, but tragedy struck when their young daughter took sick and died in spring 1887.[41]

A different kind of tragedy punctuated the ramblings of Benjamin Mitchell. Mitchell, who was apparently a single father, left his North Fork homestead in the early 1890s to set traps along St. Louis Creek on Middle Park's western edge; in subsequent years, he "worked on a ditch for five months," then went back to trap St. Louis Creek for five months more. But not long after he finally returned to his homestead, Mitchell killed a man in a fight and was sentenced to three years in prison for manslaughter. While Mitchell served time, his children were sent "here, there and everywhere and finally busted up and scattered." Once he was released, Mitchell gathered up his offspring. Though he succeeded at re-assembling his family, Mitchell nonetheless had to look for work beyond the North Fork. Leaving his children with his mother, who had homesteaded on an adjoining tract of the Kawuneeche, the ex-convict turned to punching cattle in Middle Park.[42]

Proving up a mountain homestead ultimately required a combination of backbreaking work, skill at turning the area's resources to maximum advantage, successful social networking, and no shortage of luck. By pursuing a wide range of subsistence and market activities—hunting, trapping, fishing, herding, lumbering, ditching, haying, gardening, labor migrations beyond the valley, and so forth—the men, women, and children who settled the North Fork resolved to turn the valley's unruly natural systems and Colorado's chaotic markets to their own advantage.

Those who succeeded in this intricate balancing act became the most permanent year-round inhabitants the valley has ever known.[43]

⊠ ⊠ ⊠

The building of the Grand Ditch and the extension of homesteading along the floor of the Coyote Valley together unfolded as part and parcel of a larger campaign by American settlers to tame and domesticate western lands. Water-hungry farmers on Colorado's northern piedmont and the significantly smaller group of settlers who pursued mixed husbandry on the valley floor brought fundamental changes to the North Fork's ecosystems and landscapes. In the final reckoning, though, we must be careful not to overestimate farming's impact on the valley environment. Most settlers and irrigation boosters knew only too well that their efforts at domestication and improvement remained precarious and incomplete. When it came to conquering and taming the West, nineteenth- and early twentieth-century Americans talked a big game. In the Coyote Valley, however, natural systems retained their age-old capacity to upset human designs, as conservationists were about to discover.

CONSERVATIONISTS

THE U.S. CONGRESS forever changed the course of the Coyote Valley's environmental history in January 1915 by establishing Rocky Mountain National Park on nearly 231,000 acres of land previously administered by the U.S. Forest Service. Most Colorado newspapers applauded the wisdom of federal lawmakers, with the *Rocky Mountain News* trumpeting the successful park bill as "the crowning result of one of the best organized and most efficiently managed campaigns ever conducted by Colorado people to obtain any benefit for the state." Piloting the campaign from start to finish was Enos Mills—a peculiar little tousle-haired gadfly who previously had labored as a cattle hand, mine worker, naturalist, lecturer, nature guide, and author.[1]

John Muir has always towered as an Olympian figure in national park mythology. The story of Enos Mills's painstaking efforts to build support for Rocky Mountain reminds us, however, that although Muir presided over the U.S. preservation movement like some latter-day Zeus, he remained just one spirit within a larger pantheon. National parks drew support, moreover, from a wide range of the American people, many of whom knew little about Muir and even less about his puritanical ways of thinking about nature and its preservation.[2]

Filmmaker Ken Burns is the latest in a long line of scholars and public intellectuals who have hailed the national parks as "America's best idea." The campaign Enos Mills led to create Rocky Mountain, though, demonstrates that early twentieth-century Americans held vague, flexible, and often contradictory ideas about national parks. Mills and the coalition of preservation advocates he began to assemble in fall 1909 built support for a federal park centered on Estes Park (directly across the Continental Divide from the Coyote Valley) by negotiating and compromising with their opponents. Park advocates recognized that only by making concessions could they generate the widespread support needed to secure Congressional action. Yet the resulting bargains reconfigured the borders of the preserve Mills proposed, reduced its size, and molded its regulations. When federal lawmakers placed most of the eastern half of the Coyote Valley within Rocky Mountain National Park in 1915, then, they invested these lands with an array of potentially conflicting ideas about the meanings and uses of nature in postfrontier America.[3]

Federal Forestry

The collapse of the North Fork mineral rush in the 1880s and the slow and uncertain progress of homesteading and water development in the succeeding decades together ensured that most of the Coyote Valley remained in the public domain as the twentieth century dawned. The persistence of federal ownership reflected, in turn, the emerging differences between the Mountain West and earlier U.S. frontiers. As a nation of farmers set its sights on the fertile lands of the Mississippi River valley in the late 1700s and early 1800s, no one could have predicted that a century later, the federal government would remain the largest landholder in the West. The all-important details of how the American nation should convert public domain lands seized from First Peoples and other imperial powers into private property spurred wrenching political and social conflicts. Americans from every class, party, and section did agree, however, that the ultimate goal of federal land policy should be to alienate federal lands, thus converting the public domain into private property.[4]

This presumption, however, began to clash with the new national geography ushered in by the Oregon Treaty (1846), the Treaty of Guadalupe Hidalgo (1848), the Gadsden Purchase (1854), the Alaska Purchase (1867), and the brutal wars of Indian dispossession that stretched from the 1830s into the 1880s. Land policies drafted to meet the needs of farmers in the eastern and central states fitted poorly with the environmental realities of the nation's newly acquired western realms, which were often too high, dry, cold, or rugged to support American-style agriculture. This was a lesson that the northeastern Nuche attempted to impress upon White River agent Nathan Meeker, but to no avail. And it was a lesson that the North Fork's homesteaders ignored at their peril. The Rocky Mountains comprised just one of the physiographical provinces that forced U.S. lawmakers and bureaucrats to rethink the wisdom of a national land system premised on privatizing the public domain.[5]

The advent of federal conservation in the Coyote Valley offers insights into the unintended consequences of an important shift in federal land policy in the 1890s and 1900s that consigned large swaths of the West to permanent government ownership and control. The Colorado River headwaters also offers a salutary case study in how federal foresters and national park advocates—overlapping constituencies that sometimes competed to impose differing visions of nature on the Kawuneeche— alternately cooperated and competed to carve out niches for their respective movements as part of a larger struggle to shape the destiny of the western landscape. Ultimately, the revolutionary reformulation of U.S. land policy and federal resource management turned the valley into a bizarre laboratory where a potent concatenation of ideas, institutions, practices, and anxieties vied for primacy.

The waters that first drew irrigation promoters to the Colorado River headwaters soon lured federal foresters and their supporters, too. These utilitarian conservationists shared with Water Supply and its farmer shareholders a driving desire to prevent the arid West from frittering away its lifeblood. Concern over the North Fork's snowbanks and streams, not its forests or scenery, motivated the federal government's 1902 move to temporarily withdraw from settlement more than 400,000 acres of public domain land in Wyoming and Colorado to create the Medicine Bow Forest Reserve. Three years later, President Theodore Roosevelt issued an executive order enlarging the reserve and making it permanent. Roosevelt's order closed most of the North Fork to homesteading, with the important exception of the Colorado River bottomlands. It also inaugurated direct federal management over the Coyote Valley.[6]

Hydrological arguments provided the main rationale for the Medicine Bow and other early federal forest reserves. Citizens of the piedmont farming region irrigated by Grand Ditch water began in 1892 to lobby for the creation of a federal forest reserve in the mountains to their west, petitioning the U.S. Department of the Interior to insure "the preservation of the timber from destruction by forest fires and from wanton depredations of mill men and speculators, to the end that protection be better afforded mountain snows, thereby providing for a more constant and regular supply of water for irrigation purposes." In an illuminating 1904 report, "The Proposed Medicine Bow Forest Reserve," federal foresters Smith Riley and J. H. Hatton made the same argument by likening the woodlands of the Rockies to "a great sponge, so perfectly is the office of absorption exemplified."[7]

Federal foresters and piedmont farmers agreed that only by defending standing forests could the government safeguard the water on which agriculture, industry, and urban growth all relied. The branches, leaves, and needles of standing trees provided shade to keep the sun from summarily melting winter's bounty, while subterranean root systems slowed runoff and prevented erosion. Trees felled by loggers or wildfires, by contrast, could no longer perform these vital functions. Many conservationists attributed woodland destruction to distribution-oriented land policies, aggravated by "timber thieves," firebugs, and other deviants. Keeping forested lands under government control, in short, struck conservationists as an essential maneuver in the crusade to defend the West's hydrological health.[8]

The future of irrigation in Colorado hinged on protecting the forest "sponge." "Rainfall on the adjacent eastward plains," Riley and Hatton explained in their 1904 study of the Medicine Bow, "is insufficient for agriculture, even for early-maturing crops." With ever more piedmont farmers choosing to plant potatoes, sugar beets, and vegetables instead of grains, settlers had begun to place "excessive demands . . . upon all water resources." Water Supply and other irrigation companies had built "extensive reservoir systems . . . to catch the surplus spring flow and hold it until needed in late July, August, and September." Riley and Hatton warned, however, that the specter of deforestation threatened these worthy efforts to reclaim Colorado's fertile soils from a barren fate. Without the forests' moderating influences, spring runoff seemed bound to accelerate. The resulting flooding and erosion would in turn jeopardize the irrigation systems constructed at such expense over the previous decades. Riley, Hatton, and other forest boosters cast federal conservation as the key to protecting the investments of Water Supply and other ditch companies. Watershed protection led the Forest Service to suppress wildfires, patrol boundaries, and enforce regulations on activities including logging, grazing, and hunting; as we learn in Chapter 9, the Forest Service also actively managed wildlife populations by eradicating predators and reintroducing elk to the Greater Rocky Mountain National Park Ecosystem.[9]

From the outset, some Coloradans fervently opposed federal forest conservation. "If you wonder why I oppose the Reserve," the owner of a sawmill within the Medicine Bow's proposed borders griped to Roosevelt, "it is because I love liberty, hate red tape, and believe in progress." A meeting of Larimer County citizens, meanwhile, responded to the reserve's creation with "an earnest, vigorous, and emphatic protest." An editorial in the *Fort Collins Courier* explained that Coloradans "are bitterly opposed to any change in present conditions relating to the forests." Reserving public lands "forever . . . from sale and settlement," the *Courier* contended, would permanently stunt population growth and deny local governments the future property-tax revenues that the ongoing conversion of the public domain into private property would have ensured. Because local settlers "fully appreciate the value and importance of the forest lands, from an economic standpoint," the editorial reasoned, "self-interest prompts them to take good care of them . . . without interference by the federal government."[10]

Though federal forestry continued to kindle misgivings in the years to come, a growing number of Coloradans warmed to the Medicine Bow reserve after Roosevelt made it permanent in 1905. The *Courier* attributed this change of heart to "new rules governing the regulation and protection of forest reserves," which it called "much more liberal than those at first promulgated." Forest Service liberality, though, soon generated a backlash of a different and ultimately more consequential character: a campaign led by Enos Mills to institute a new national park in the Colorado Rockies.[11]

The Campaign Begins

Mills self-consciously fashioned himself as John Muir's disciple. The man who has been praised as the "father of Rocky Mountain National Park" since the park's creation in 1915 frequently told audiences how a chance meeting with Muir changed his life. Mills moved to the Colorado mountains from a Kansas farm in 1884 as a self-described "sickly

The irascible Enos Mills spearheaded the campaign to create Rocky Mountain National Park. Denver Public Library, Western History Collection, Z-106.

boy of fourteen." The newcomer promptly regained his health by building himself "a little log cabin on the slope of Long's Peak." From this home base, Mills embarked on one adventure after another. By the early 1900s, he had traveled the Missouri and Mississippi Rivers "from source to sea"; he also had tramped through most of the American states and parts of Canada. Mills carried virtually nothing on these expeditions—sleeping under the open sky, "rarely following a schedule," and insistently observing the natural world in all its guises. Though Mills lived like a true ascetic, he recalled that he nonetheless had to "stop to earn my living" every "now and then." Ranch work did not agree with him, but mining did. Mills soon became a foreman and earned "big wages" before underground fires in the booming copper mines of Butte, Montana, caused Mills's employer to lay him off in fall 1889. Suddenly jobless, the young rambler lit off for the Pacific Coast.[12]

"I suppose fairies led me to California and John Muir," Mills would muse some years later. Finding Mills enraptured by a teeming tide pool south of San Francisco, Muir evidently recognized a kindred soul. After the older man introduced himself, Mills later claimed, the pair "walked back to San Francisco together, over the sand dunes." Muir, Mills recalled, "asked me questions about myself and my ambition and he advised me to study nature at every opportunity, everywhere, and to practice writing and speaking so I could tell what I saw." Muir also sought to recruit his new friend for the preservationist cause: " 'I want you to help me do something for parks, forests and wild life,' " Mills remembered Muir saying. From that point onward, Mills recounted that Muir "became *the* factor in my life."[13]

Mills had always cut a quirky figure with his "ruddy skin," weather-beaten face, and unruly shock "of brisk red hair which begins about half way back on his head and stands straight out." But after meeting the unconventional Muir, he gave his eccentricities full rein. Mills kept orphaned grizzly bears as pets, advocated unloosing the nation's schoolchildren to educate themselves amid the great outdoors, and lambasted porcupines for lacking "even rudiamentary [sic] ideas of conservation."[14]

Mills lionized Muir, calling him "the greatest genius that ever with words interpreted the outdoors." But Mills held himself in equally high esteem. Note how Mills conflated himself and his hero in these two passages, the first taken from an autobiographical sketch and the second from a paean Mills penned to Muir:

> Many a night, alone in the forest's depths, *I* have had wierd [sic] reveries by a campfire and felt like a wandering ancestor in the legend-making age.
> Many a night alone in the forest depths, *he* had weird reveries by a campfire and felt like a wondering [sic] ancestor in the legend-making age.

On occasion, Muir repaid Mills's adoration with avuncular encouragement: "I always feel good when I look your way: for you are making good on a noble career," Muir wrote Mills in 1913. "I glory in your success as a writer & lecturer & in saving God's park for the welfare of humanity."[15]

By the time Mills launched the campaign Muir praised so lavishly in this letter—the struggle to convince Congress to set aside Rocky Mountain National Park—the younger naturalist's celebrity almost rivaled Muir's. After further stints in the mines of Montana and Colorado, punctuated by journeys that took him to Alaska and Europe, Mills had purchased a ranch near Estes Park in 1902, renamed it the Long's Peak Inn, and "unconsciously evolved," as he later put it, "what is now known as Nature Guiding." But Mills, under constant strain to keep up with the inn's bills, soon sought other paying work. For several winters in the early 1900s, he held the title of Colorado State Snow Observer. As Mills trekked through the Rockies gathering snowpack data for state officials entrusted with forecasting irrigation conditions, he found a seemingly endless wellspring of material for his budding career as a lecturer and author. Mills progressed in the early 1900s from compiling summer resort news from Estes Park for Denver newspapers to placing feature articles in *Youth's Companion, Harper's, The Saturday Evening Post,* and other national magazines. Starting with *Wild Life on the Rockies* (1909), he also published a string of best-selling books. Mills was simultaneously earning a reputation as a spellbinding orator. After cutting his teeth at small Colorado venues, he became a fixture on the national lecture circuit after a widely lauded appearance at the 1906 annual convention of the General Federation of Women's Clubs. After Mills's "enthusiasm, eloquence and patent sincerity" had "captured his hearers" at that prominent affair, the *Chicago Inter-Ocean* reported that the wilderness wanderer was "besieged with invitations to address clubs all over the country."[16]

Lecturing paid well enough, and Mills needed the money. So each winter he hit the road, telling wild animal stories and singing the praises of forest conservation in front of packed houses across the United States. "Wherever and whatever he spoke of," one admirer declared, "he covered it with a mist and a glow of radiance which took the audience away from the commonplace of to-day and of the home place . . . into those immense spaces of mountain vistas and peaked horizons." Mills's oratorical talent attracted the notice of Gifford Pinchot, head of the U.S. Forest Service, who offered Mills a lucrative special position as lecturer in 1907. For the next two years, Mills "penetrated every nook and cranny of the country, addressing audiences on forest reserves, [and] forest preservation and reforestation, along the line of the government policies."[17]

But just two years after he started, Mills made an abrupt and angry break with Pinchot and utilitarian conservation. While Mills had previously lauded "a forest reserve" as "not only a thing of beauty and profit, but . . . strictly democratic," he now bemoaned that a national forest "is established chiefly for the purpose of using it to produce trees for the saw-mill and grass for the cattle." From the early 1910s until his death in 1922, Mills tirelessly bad-mouthed the Forest Service, condemning the agency as a "vicious," "devilish," "blackmailing organization" invested with "almost IRRESPONSIBLE power."[18]

Mills's antipathy toward the Forest Service led him to urge the Estes Park Improvement and Protective Association, a local civic group, to consider "how best to protect the wild birds, game and flowers" of the area. Ironically, it was Herbert Wheeler, chief of the Medicine Bow Forest Reserve, who took the floor at a fateful September 1909 gathering of the association to suggest the creation of a federal game preserve near Estes Park. Mills and other members of the improvement organization immediately took Wheeler's idea and ran with it. "This section," Mills lamented in a press release for the group, "is losing its wild charms. Extensive areas of primeval forests have been misused and ruined; the once numerous big game has been hunted almost out of existence, the birds are falling, the wild flowers vanishing, and the picturesque beaver, except where protected, are almost gone." Beautiful stretches of public land—Mills tellingly called them "scenes"—were "already extensively used as places of recreation. If they are to be permanently and more extensively used and preserved," he argued, "it will be necessary to hold them as public property and protect them." To prevent these "scenes" from being privatized, monopolized, and destroyed, the association proposed "convert[ing]" roughly 600,000 acres of Forest Service land into "a national park game preserve. Protected and used as a national park," the release explained, the area's "flowers, birds and especially its big game would increase and its resources thus used [would] serve more people and serve them better than any other use of them could give." Here Mills and his colleagues adapted Pinchot's utilitarian premise while redirecting it toward aesthetic ends. The improvement association recommended that permissive rules loosely based on Yellowstone's should govern the new "national park game preserve." Logging "under forest service regulations may be allowed for local use only," the group advised, "grazing should be restricted to local stock," and "the shooting of any bird or animal within the park should be prohibited." With these notable exceptions, "the use and ownership of private propearty [sic] would remain unchanged." From the outset, Mills and his Estes Park allies sought to neutralize opposition by emphasizing that their proposed preserve posed no fundamental threat to the status quo.[19]

Though the desire to protect flagging wildlife populations and preserve Estes Park's natural beauty clearly spurred the preserve idea, Mills and his allies also emphasized the economic benefits of preservation. A 1910 headline in the *Fort Collins Courier*—"How Estes Park Can Be Converted into a Gold Mine"—succinctly communicated this argument. In the article that followed, Mills pointed out that "aside from the ethical standpoint" for establishing a national park, "there is the commercial consideration." Federal wildlife protection would enhance the area's attractiveness; Yellowstone's game, Mills noted, "draws almost as many people as the geysers." Under proper protection, "wild animals" would soon "become so fearless" that the creatures would approach "within sight of the tourists." Mills quipped that while it took at least twenty acres of land to pasture a single cow in Estes Park, "2,000 tourists will do well on the same area." Turn Estes into "a National Park," Mills declared, "and it will sustain more homes than if used in any other way." Mills predicted that his park scheme could "run up" the estimated $150,000 of annual revenue tourism brought into the Estes Park economy "to anywhere from $10,000,000 to $20,000,000." The proposed national park, Mills concluded, represented "a big move to save some of our vanishing scenic wealth and also to make it productive."[20]

Federal funds for road construction figured centrally in Mills's calculus of improvement through preservation. By "promptly" building an "excellent system of roads and trails," a federal preserve would "increase [the area's] productivity many fold." Since local governments lacked the funds "to build roads, trails or bridle paths to the various attractive places," Mills worried that "another generation may come before some of these improvements" could be completed around Estes Park "unless Uncle Sam will take it and make a play ground of it." Mills and his allies always emphasized that the proposed national park would benefit the entire nation instead of an elect few. In another of the many articles and lectures he gave in 1910 to drum up support for the national park, Mills argued that the "wonderful scenic realm of Estes Park belongs to all people. The people of the whole United States as well as those of Colorado should feel righteously bound to keep this blessed place for the common good for all time."[21]

Mills's campaign emanated from Estes Park and always remained focused there, but it would have monumental—and almost entirely unintended—consequences across the Continental Divide in the Coyote Valley.

Coalitions and Compromises

Mills's efforts to portray Estes National Park as a "gold mine" and "play ground" soon attracted wider backing. Automobile tycoon Freelan Stanley and other influential Estes Park residents had touted the preserve from the outset. The "play ground" idea, though, also convinced many hoteliers, restaurateurs, automobile livery owners, realtors, and newspaper editors up and down the Front Range to lend their support to Mills's campaign. By 1910, a small but dedicated cadre of civic-minded activists had begun to champion the plan. In addition to John Muir, who praised Mills for his "good work in the cause of saving samples of God's best mountain handiwork for the benefit of humanity," the two most important of these were James Grafton Rogers, a Yale-educated Denver lawyer who drafted the many bills that park advocates placed before Congress, and J. Horace McFarland, head of the American Civic Association and the conservation movement's most effective lobbyist. The coalition spearheaded by Mills, Rogers, and McFarland would ultimately emerge triumphant, but it owed its success to repeated compromises on park boundaries and policies. What the coalition's triumph would portend for the newly renamed Kawuneeche Valley, however, remained anyone's guess.[22]

Mills and his allies differed most strenuously on the subjects of automobile tourism and the Forest Service. While Mills and Rogers saw no inherent conflict between scenic preservation, road building, and cars, McFarland expressed skepticism. "I am not so sure that I am in love with the automobile in the national parks," McFarland would later confide to Mills. The car, McFarland griped, behaved like "a rampacious [sic] grizzly bear on the average highway, snorting and stinking its way along, without regard to the highway which it destroys, the people whom it discomforts, or the decencies which it disregards. It does not need to be all these things, but at present it is." As for the Forest Service, Mills loathed the agency with all his being; Rogers and McFarland, by contrast, actively courted its support. Mills's two main allies repeatedly urged him to temper his shrill, even delusional attacks against federal foresters. "No good cause," McFarland advised, "ever got on well on a diet of hatred. It is poor food for a good man, and you are a good man." But Mills interpreted his friends' well-meaning counsel as apostasy. He broke off his previously cordial relationship with Rogers just weeks before Congress set aside Rocky Mountain National Park; by 1920, Mills also had destroyed his once close friendship with McFarland.[23]

Despite their differences, the leading lights of the park campaign heartily agreed on the need to thwart opposition from local landowners and the politicians who represented them. An early petition broaching the park idea to Colorado's congressional delegation, for instance, bent over backward to anticipate and neutralize local criticism: "No property is to be bought or sold; mining and prospecting are to continue as at present; fishing is to be allowed; timber cutting is to continue under forest service regulations; and grazing is to be restricted to local stock." The crux of the park-making process, however, hinged less on regulations than territory. What the national park would mean depended on where the government decided to place its borders.[24]

The peculiar origins of the proposed park led its advocates to play fast and loose with its boundaries. As we have seen, Mills's campaign had originated with local efforts to preserve the Estes Park area. Most of the land near that village, though, was already privately owned. This made it impractical and undesirable for Estes Park to be included within the park itself. Paradoxically, the main focal point of the preserve—supporters revealingly referred to it as Estes National Park until 1913—would remain forever outside the proposed park's borders. A second and even more momentous oddity of the Colorado park scheme was its guiding purpose. While previous national parks had typically centered on rare, even unique natural features such as Yellowstone's geysers, General Grant's immense sequoia trees, or Mount Rainier's lofty volcanic heights, Mills and his colleagues envisioned a park designed to protect and render accessible the scenery and wildlife that was characteristic of a vast region rather than concentrated in specific locale. This novelty would have immense consequences for the Coyote Valley. Because the natural features that Mills and his allies intended the park to preserve and highlight were distributed across a large stretch of the Colorado Rockies, park campaigners reckoned that instead of squandering their scarce political capital by squabbling over boundaries, it was more important to convince Congress to establish a national park somewhere in the northern Colorado Front Range—*anywhere*, really, as long as it adjoined Estes Park.[25]

Debates over the preserve's size and location showed that many Coloradans held fast to the old association of economic development with extractive industry instead of embracing Mills's claims about the potential benefits of preservation-oriented tourism. Mills's initial scheme involved around 1,000 square miles of lands stretching north from Mount Evans (immediately west of Denver) nearly to the Wyoming boundary. The open hostility of mining interests and local officials in Boulder and Grand Counties, though, impelled advocates to shrink the proposed preserve to 768 square miles by early 1910. The proposal for this reduced park died, however, when the chair of the Public Lands Committee in the U.S. House of Representatives quashed all national park bills on his committee's docket.[26]

With congressional approval of Estes National Park stalled for the foreseeable future, the executive branch took up the torch. Virtually every acre of the proposed park lay on national forestland, so the Forest Service launched an investigation of the plan's merits. In a 1910 report, forester Smith Riley expressed support in principle for Mills's proposal. But he also advised the Forest Service to secure three major concessions before signing on to the park scheme. First, Riley wanted to protect existing uses of any national forestlands included within the preserve. "The objects of those desiring the creation of the proposed National Park," Riley advised, could best "be secured without injury to present industries, by creating the Park more along the lines of a Game Preserve." Riley argued that sheep should be banned from the preserve; "cattle and horse grazing," by contrast, could be "allowed on the present scale to nearby owners of stock." He also recommended the continuation of mining and even limited logging under special use permits, unless these activities posed a nuisance to wildlife populations. Second, Riley advocated continuing Forest Service control over the preserve, assisted by state game wardens who would eradicate large predators (bear excepted) and otherwise "devot[e] their entire time and energy to the protection and propagation of game." Finally, Riley suggested scaling down the preserve to just 370 square miles.[27]

While Mills's initial boundaries stopped at the North Fork, Riley's extended several miles farther west to the crest of the Never Summers. This mountaintop border, he explained, would better match "natural topographical compartments," making the preserve's limits "more widely known, more easily established, and the likelihood of trespass greatly lessened." The forester dismissed the homesteads of the Colorado River headwaters as of "minor importance." Because "only the poorer classes of land remain," Riley claimed that the boundary he proposed "would not greatly affect agriculture." The forester underestimated the enduring allure of high-altitude homesteading—nearly half of the claims in the Kawuneeche were filed after 1910—yet he presciently realized that a national park would "greatly" enhance the revenues the North Fork's settlers could earn by catering to tourists. No less important, Riley's plan to reorient the proposed preserve on an Estes Park–Grand Lake axis impressed upon park supporters the advantages of avoiding "interfer[ence] with existing industries."[28]

Riley's revised national park plan drew acclaim from Grand County citizens. At a public meeting in Grand Lake in February 1910, "representative property owners of the community" expressed "unanimous" support for "the establishment of such a Park, provided it would not exclude miners and agricultural settlers, grazing and the conservative use of timber." The only feature of Riley's proposal that irked the crowd was its name: the forester embraced an audience member's suggestion that the preserve should be rechristened Colorado National Park, but Mills and his allies never embraced that moniker.[29]

Despite the promising reception Riley enjoyed at Grand Lake, enthusiasm for the preserve soon wavered. The Fort Collins Chamber of Commerce suspended its endorsement for the preserve after learning that Riley wanted "to extend the park into Grand county, taking in the headwaters of the Grand river and . . . much valuable farming land." Even in Estes Park, support appeared to be crumbling. When a petition "directed principally toward Enos Mills" circulated through town, the *Courier* reported that Mills "had trouble with one of the men who signed it" and lost his cool, leading to his arrest for assault and battery (charges were later dropped).[30]

Soon thereafter, Mills's campaign slumped toward its nadir. The equivocal support that Riley had received at Grand Lake had evaporated. A citizens' meeting called by the Grand County Board of Commissioners "protest[ed] against any portion whatever of Grand County Territory being taken over by the United States National Government to be named or known as Estes National Park or any other National Park." The petitioners detailed their economic and fiscal concerns about the proposed park. "It is well known to all informed persons," they huffed, "that Grand County is probably as undeveloped as any County in the state of Colorado." Only "by the development of its resources" could the county "pay off its now outstanding debt," which exceeded $100,000. As it stood, federal ownership of "practically eighty per cent of the entire area of Grand County" was making it very difficult for the county "to maintain the Government of this territory." Locals worried that park designation would derail the progress of a region "as yet in its infancy." The preserve, they claimed, would end homesteading on lands still "capable of great agricultural development" while stymieing the development of several mines "known" to contain "large bodies of low grade ore which only need transportation facilities to become paying properties." Perennially optimistic that their underdeveloped stretch of the Colorado Rockies was "liable at any time to become one of the greatest Mining Districts yet known," the people and public officials of Grand County declared that they "seriously object[ed]" to the North Fork "being taken into a National Park."[31]

Congressional committees, swayed by local concerns about preservation's impact on irrigation, lumber, grazing, and mining—concerns that were allegedly "strongest" in Grand County—killed another park bill in late 1911. But the dauntless Enos Mills continued to trumpet the proposal before anyone who would listen. He even made an appearance at "the White house[,] telling bear stories to President Taft" and "ask[ing] the president to join in the movement." With help from McFarland and Rogers, Mills's campaigning finally bore fruit in September 1912, when the U.S. Geological Survey decided to dispatch Chief Geographer Robert B. Marshall to investigate the Colorado park scheme.[32]

The enthusiastic, widely touted report Marshall submitted to the secretary of the interior in January 1913 inspired park supporters to redouble their efforts. Rogers, for instance, could hardly contain his delight that Marshall had "framed [the report] in such a way that we can

almost make it a campaign document in our work here." Astutely cal-
culating that expansive boundaries would spark greater local resistance,
the campaigners decided to shrink the preserve. By February 1913, they
had redrawn the park's boundaries so that they encompassed just 358.5
square miles, a far cry from the more expansive tract of roughly 700
square miles that Marshall had recommended. The resulting boundaries ignored forester Riley's recommendation that the preserve's western
border follow the ridgeline of the Never Summers. Instead, the preserve's
western border would reach to the cluster of homesteads along the
Colorado River headwaters. Marshall, like Riley before him, concluded
that the North Fork was too high, chilly, and snowy for farming or even
year-round ranching—though he did praise the valley as "an ideal
camping ground," predicting that if Congress agreed to establish the
park, settlers would soon "derive far greater revenue" from summer
tourism than they "could ever receive otherwise." From the Coyote Valley
to the eastern slope of the Front Range, the much-reduced park—now
renamed Rocky Mountain National Park on the recommendation of the
Department of the Interior and McFarland's American Civic Association—
consisted almost entirely of national forestland. By astutely reducing the
park's size and relocating its borders, Mills and his compatriots adeptly
quelled fears of federal overreach in the Colorado high country.[33]

The park coalition proved ready to deal on regulations as well as
boundaries. "After three years of fighting," the *Courier* hopefully noted
in February 1913, "the various factions have agreed upon the territory
to be made into a national park, as well as upon the terms which should
be embodied in the new law." Rogers could hardly contain his enthusiasm; "the Estes Park fight is won," he boasted to Mills. "In order to
unite all these various interests," Rogers admitted, "we had to make a
number of concessions in the way of mining rights, water rights, and so
on, but I think that these are all details which can be overlooked in the
general success of the project." The *Courier* summed up the most important of these "concessions": "There is to be no interference with those
who now have valid claims on homestead, mineral rights, rights of way
for any purpose whatever, waters arising in or flowing through the park
either for power or irrigation purposes, or any other rights which are
protected by laws of the United States at the present time." By negotiating with a range of stakeholders, Rogers, Mills, and their fellow park
advocates had generated widespread support. This, in turn, convinced

the Colorado legislature to send a memorial urging Congress to enact a bill to establish Rocky Mountain National Park.[34]

The exclusion of Grand Lake, the Colorado River bottomlands, and the Never Summer Range from the plan blunted discontent in Grand County. As the *Middle Park Times* emphasized in 1914, "all opposition to the establishment of the park has vanished. . . . In fact there is now a very strong sentiment in its favor." A desire to safeguard the beauties of the high country underpinned this about-face. If the "incomparable scenery" of the Rockies "is not preserved for future generations," the *Times* editor warned, "it will in course of time be destroyed." Such an outcome was regrettable in its own right, but it also would jeopardize Grand County's economic future by undermining its nascent tourist industry. A national park on the borders of Grand Lake, the *Times* prophesied, "will make that popular resort even more attractive than Estes park or even the National park itself." Of course, neither the *Times* editor nor the many other Coloradans who joined Enos Mills in equating preservation with development imagined that tourism itself might one day threaten the Coyote Valley's natural beauty.[35]

By early 1915, gerrymandered park borders and permissive regulations had neutralized virtually all opposition. "The proposed national park," Colorado senator Charles Thomas told reporters, "harmonizes with every practical interest and conflicts with none." Enos Mills hardly exaggerated when he crowed: "The people of Colorado want this park; thousands of visitors want it."[36]

Congress was finally ready to believe that it wanted the park, too. Senator Thomas and Representative Edward Taylor lined up a who's who of Colorado politicians to testify on the bill's behalf. Outgoing governor Elias Ammons promised that the state was already planning to build a road across the Continental Divide from Estes Park to Grand Lake. By passing the park bill, Senator John Shafroth remarked, Congress would make it easier for domestic tourists to "see America first," instead of spending their dollars abroad. Park boosters, however, were not content to let words do all their talking. Following a "stirring plea" from Enos Mills, they showed a series of "colored stereopticon pictures" that enabled congressmen to envision the high-mountain landscapes that Mills and his allies were striving to protect and publicize.[37]

In December 1914, bipartisan support from Colorado politicians buoyed the bill to establish Rocky Mountain National Park through the

A crowd of several hundred gathered in September 1915 to celebrate the park's establishment. Harry M. Rhoads, "Dedication of Rocky Mountain National Park," Denver Public Library, Western History Collection, Rh-259.

Senate. The House assented to the measure in January 1915 and passed it along to Woodrow Wilson. With a stroke of the president's pen, 230,907 acres previously managed by the Colorado and Arapaho National Forests were "forever withdrawn" from settlement or extractive uses, the *Fort Collins Courier* exalted, and "reserved exclusively for the playground of the American people." Only the eastern parts of the Coyote Valley were included within the borders of this new national "playground," but park supporters had always viewed the borders Congress established as subject to future expansion. Federal administrators at the newly created preserve, meanwhile, soon found reasons of their own for seeking to incorporate more of the Kawuneeche into Rocky Mountain.[38]

This was hardly the outcome that American settlers had envisioned when they clamored for Nuche dispossession in the 1860s and 1870s. The failure of both mining and agricultural settlement to thrive, however, opened the way for an alternative future for the Coyote Valley—one inspired less by the examples of Leadville or the Great Plains, and more by the preservationist principles first made manifest at Yellowstone and Yosemite. Over the long run, though, the most important legacies of the park campaign stemmed from the compromises Mills and his allies had made during six years of protracted negotiations over Rocky Mountain's boundaries and regulations.

Mixed Mandates

For more than a century, critics have disparaged the U.S. preservation movement as an elitist cabal that has enlisted state power to exclude local people and lock away productive natural resources, all so a privileged minority could revel in nature's glories. The story of Rocky Mountain National Park should compel us to rethink this caricature.

Enos Mills was no blueblood. Instead, he was a self-educated farm boy driven west by tuberculosis—an autodidact who mixed tramping adventures with work as a ranch hand, prospector, and mine foreman. The coalition Mills cultivated drew much of its heft from powerful, well-heeled urbanites like James Grafton Rogers. But it also encompassed progressive reformers like J. Horace McFarland, small-town editors, federal foresters, and common citizens. The willingness of Mills and his allies to alter Rocky Mountain's borders and rules played a critical role in assuaging antagonism toward the park from entrenched economic interests and local people alike.

From Herbert Wheeler's offhand suggestion to the Estes Park Improvement and Protective Association in 1909 onward, Mills and his allies cast their pet project in terms that dovetailed seamlessly with key words expressing the underlying ideals of settler colonialism and utilitarian conservation: Rights, Use, Development, Profit, and Accessibility.

To be sure, park campaigners sometimes waxed eloquent about beauty and sublimity, protection and permanence. From time to time, they even referred to Rocky Mountain National Park as a "wilderness." Yet the arsenal of other terms they deployed to draw support for their winning campaign—"game preserve," "wild gardens," "connecting link," "wonder-spot," "wonderland"—demonstrated that no single way of thinking about nature, and no unitary "national park ideal," propelled the park into existence. The *Denver Post* probably came closest to capturing how most Americans thought of the new reserve in a report that extolled Rocky Mountain as the "nation's newest playground," a term Mills and his allies had been trumpeting since 1910. This playground ideal was laudably inclusive, casting the park as a public space that belonged to and ostensibly welcomed anyone in search of escape and pleasure.[39]

The 1915 act setting aside Rocky Mountain National Park attempted to strike an elusive balance between protecting the natural world and encouraging visitation. It charged the reserve's administrators with providing for "the freest use of the said park for recreation purposes by the public and for the preservation of the natural conditions and scenic beauties thereof." This expansive mandate cast tourism, aesthetic enjoyment, and the perpetuation of undefined "natural conditions" as compatible goals of equal significance. This panoply of guiding objectives reflected, in turn, an astute move by preservationists to portray Rocky Mountain as both national and democratic—a site for the use, enjoyment, and edification of the American people. After Wilson signed the park into law, J. Horace McFarland and Enos Mills joined forces to lobby Congress to create an agency to administer the national parks. Their efforts bore fruit with the Organic Act of 1916, which invested the newly established National Park Service with the same paradoxical mission contained in the legislation authorizing Rocky Mountain: "to conserve the scenery, the natural and historic objects and the wildlife therein and to provide for the enjoyment of the same in such manner and by such means as will leave them unimpaired for the enjoyment of future generations."[40]

In the final reckoning, Colorado's new national park and the new federal agency charged with administering it together embodied a necessary but potentially problematic set of political compromises. Foremost among these was the potentially contradictory directive to provide for public "enjoyment" of Rocky Mountain National Park while keeping its "scenery," "natural and historic objects and . . . wildlife . . . unimpaired" for perpetuity. In the decades to follow, this dual mandate would garner broad popular affection and considerable political support for the Park Service and Rocky Mountain National Park alike. And yet it would also prompt seemingly endless challenges for the agency, its employees, and park visitors, as well as for other constituents of the Greater Rocky Mountain National Park Ecosystem.

The real trouble with the democratic vision that led Mills, McFarland, Rogers, and their allies to embrace compromise, then, was not that it cast the park as a sacred wilderness where human beings had no rightful place. Instead, the source of future trouble at Rocky Mountain emanated from the strategic decision made by the park's early advocates to place the desires of people and the demands of politics above the needs of the natural world. The model of tourist-oriented preservation on a relatively small tract of federal land under national park administration represented a triumph of preservationist realpolitik. But managers at Rocky Mountain would soon discover that for all its success, the park campaign nonetheless endowed them with only feeble, imperfect mechanisms for insulating the ecosystems and landscapes under their ostensible control from the incessant gales of historical change. Park officials would do their best to give the people what they wanted. But could the natural world abide the playground ideal?

III

FEDS

⫷ 7 ⫸

COMMON GROUND

AMERICANS tend to associate homesteading with the nineteenth-century expansion of farming onto the prairies and plains of Middle America. But the story of the Holzwarth family—probably the longest-lasting and certainly the best-documented clan to settle the Coyote Valley—reminds us that homesteading persisted well into the twentieth century, reached high into the Rocky Mountains, and entailed hosting tourists as well as raising crops. When the Holzwarths set out from their Denver home in 1916 to claim a piece of the Kawuneeche, they piled into a car, not a covered wagon. And though the Holzwarths initially came to the valley to raise livestock, they discovered during the 1920s that catering to national park visitors paid better than agriculture and offered greater security. The Holzwarths' story shows how the establishment of Rocky Mountain National Park proved a boon to many local settlers. It also illustrates the cordiality, cooperation, and interdependence that generally prevailed between the Park Service and homesteaders during the 1910s and 1920s.[1]

The Holzwarths' journey to the Coyote Valley began on Election Day in 1914, when a majority of Colorado voters passed a measure that would prohibit the sale of alcohol starting in 1916. The enterprising German-born saloon keeper John Holzwarth Sr. (known to his family simply as "Papa") had little choice but to shutter his tavern just south of downtown Denver. With the business Holzwarth had built up through a decade of hard work suddenly ruined, he decided to return to a calling that always had fascinated him: ranching. Holzwarth emigrated to the United States in 1879; just fourteen years old, he was apprenticed to a

St. Louis baker but soon ran away to Texas, where he worked as a sheep camp cook and ranch hand. Though he quickly distinguished himself as "an accomplished all-around horseman," Holzwarth grew tired of doing other men's bidding. He filed homestead papers on a tract of ranch land in Middle Park and spent several years struggling to establish a cattle operation while working stints as a cowhand and barkeep. In the early 1890s, though, "illness and financial embarrassment" forced Holzwarth to abandon his claim. Retreating to Denver, he found work at the Tivoli Brewery, where he met and eventually married Sophie Lebfromm, a fellow German emigrant. Sophie gave birth to five children, but only three of them survived into adulthood. By 1904, Holzwarth had saved enough from his brewery earnings to open his own saloon on Santa Fe Boulevard.[2]

Prohibition brought Holzwarth back to the Grand County range in 1917, when he purchased 160 acres of Kawuneeche Valley land just outside the boundary of Rocky Mountain National Park for $2,000; a year later, he filed a homestead claim to an adjacent 160 acres. The German's earlier failure at raising stock might have given him pause. But the Holzwarths, as John Holzwarth Jr. (known throughout his life as Johnnie) later recalled, "were too dumb and too stubborn to give . . . up." Like most homesteaders, the family set about trying to satisfy the Homestead Act's residence requirement, using nearby stands of lodgepole pine to build a cabin (later called the "Mama Cabin" after matriarch Sophie Holzwarth). Papa and Johnnie next turned to the law's cultivation requirement by grubbing willows from seven or eight acres along the Colorado River, where they began to cultivate "tame hay" to keep their cattle alive during the Kawuneeche's long winters.[3]

Just as things were finally looking up for the Holzwarths after several lean years, misfortune forced the family to diversify their operations. After a wagon accident in 1919 or 1920 permanently injured Papa Holzwarth's legs and hips, his wife and children rose to the occasion. Seventeen-year-old Johnnie immediately began to perform most of the heavier work on the homestead. Before long, he assumed day-to-day management of the ranch. Johnnie also opened what he called a "little woodpecker sawmill" that produced enough lumber to meet most of the Holzwarths' own needs while providing a surplus the family could sell or barter. The irrepressible Johnnie even laid more than one hundred miles of trap lines along streams that stretched over the Never Summer

Mountains into North Park; the resulting harvest of beaver, marten, and other species earned him several hundred dollars a year. Mama Holzwarth, who continued to leave the Kawuneeche each winter to seek wage work in Denver with her two daughters, took charge of the family's dairy throughout the rest of the year, producing butter and cheese for the local market from a herd Johnnie later praised as "the best milk cows in the valley." As for Papa, he "still tried to help with the work of building cabins or cutting and gathering hay," but his most important contributions to the household economy probably came from taxidermy, which he picked up thanks to a correspondence course he took following the wagon accident.[4]

The Holzwarths' sawmill, trapping, dairy, and taxidermy operations enabled them to hold on even after disease decimated the family's beef cattle. But it was national park tourism more than anything else that enabled the Holzwarths to fashion a home from the Coyote Valley. The family had arrived in the Kawuneeche possessing little sense of just how large the recently created Rocky Mountain National Park would loom in their future. Once they settled into the Coyote Valley, though, the Holzwarths undoubtedly noticed that some of their fellow settlers were already beginning to profit from the growing crowds of visitors who flocked to Rocky Mountain.[5]

As the Holzwarth family's saga hints, many of the major forces contending to control the destiny of the U.S. West writ large—settlement, reclamation, conservation, preservation, automobile tourism, and even metropolitan growth—met in microcosm in the twentieth-century Coyote Valley. It is tempting to believe that when these lines of force came into contact, only collision and conflict could result. Yet in the Kawuneeche, at least, these disparate vectors of change could also glance off each other; on occasion, they could even coalesce. If we think about the Colorado River headwaters as a kind of laboratory in which a series of experiments in the larger dynamics of western history unfolded in miniature, then we can start to glimpse the mechanics of regional change during the early twentieth century in a clearer light.

History is no science, though, and it is dangerous to confuse metaphors with realities. The Coyote Valley was not sterile but alive, and the forces that met in its confines were not controlled but contingent and chaotic, as the impact of Prohibition amendments and spooked draft horses on the Holzwarths illustrates. Whenever different people, groups, and institutions attempted to enact and realize their very different visions for the Colorado River headwaters, more-than-human forces persistently intruded on the drama. A cacophony of entities—fish and elk, coyotes and blizzards, pine beetles and soils, droughts and beavers, regional climatic shifts and unexpected genetic exchanges—impinged on the course of so-called human events. The resulting actions and interactions altered the valley's environments in ways that scientists, land managers, and historians have only begun to grasp.

The Genius of Squeaky Bob

Robert "Squeaky Bob" Wheeler was almost certainly the first to realize the Coyote Valley's touristic potential. In mid-June 1903, Wheeler pitched a tent at the foot of Milner Pass, in the valley's northern reaches just outside the new Medicine Bow Forest Reserve. Homesteading at 9,000 feet, however, proved slow work. During his first decade on the tract, Wheeler typically spent the first half of the calendar year laboring for wages beyond the Colorado River headwaters, then resided on his claim from mid-summer to early winter. He also began to accommodate summer visitors on his property, which he wryly called the Hotel de Hardscrabble. No doubt fed up with wandering, Wheeler resolved in 1913 to stay on his homestead year-round. He laboriously cleared and turned over a half-acre garden while also grubbing out dense lodgepole stands to create a hay meadow. From the beginning, his tame hay did poorly; five years later, Wheeler confessed to federal officials that his "cultivated land" was "just reach[ing] the production stage."[6]

For reasons that remain unclear, the Forest Service tried to convince General Land Office officials that Wheeler was violating the Homestead Act. Forester A. F. Potter alleged that Wheeler was more interested in cultivating the tourist trade than in tending his garden or hay meadow. Exhibit A in Potter's unsuccessful case against Wheeler was an illustrated pamphlet the settler used to market his Hotel de Hardscrabble. Apparently authored by Wheeler himself in the early 1910s, the pamphlet extolled the Coyote Valley in language reminiscent of correspondence from the 1880s mineral rush. "The scenery is so wonderful," Wheeler began, "that Enos Mills, the well-known writer, is seeking to have it included in the New Rocky Mountain National Park." Wheeler highlighted his property's excellent location "on the trail into Estes park," which made it "the natural and *only* stopping place" for tourists traveling between there and Grand Lake. Wheeler portrayed the Hotel de Hardscrabble as easy to reach, but he also represented it as an ideal place for visitors to experience the scenic wonders and marvelous wildlife of the high Rockies. "At the back of the Camp," his pamphlet bragged, "is a wonderful waterfall. The beavers have two large dams in the stream near by," while the wildflowers "are here in wonderful and untrampled profusion."[7]

Wheeler's pamphlet sought to tantalize the palate and pique the interest of travelers seeking active outdoor pursuits. At the Hotel de Hardscrabble, Wheeler bragged, "one may actually eat wild strawberry shortcake, and trout just pulled from the stream." The fishing was "good," and the locale "far enough from civilization to insure good hunting." In case the pleasures of shooting, angling, and feasting struck his readers as too placid, Wheeler assured them that untamed dangers still lurked nearby. The hotel's proximity to "mountain lion and wolves" turned a stay at Wheeler's wilderness "Camp" into a rugged escape from the mundane domesticity of modern America.[8]

Visitors enjoy a stop at Lake Irene along Milner Pass in the 1890s. William Henry Jackson, "Head Waters of N. Fork of the Grand River," MSF a, B14, S 05 C, Box 2, courtesy of the National Park Service.

After Congress set aside Rocky Mountain, Wheeler, the Holzwarths, and their neighbors suddenly occupied prime real estate on the threshold of a park that enjoyed instant popularity because of its proximity to Denver and the prosperous towns of the northern piedmont. Before the early 1910s, only a small trickle of adventurous travelers had penetrated the Coyote Valley (as Wheeler intimated when he declared the Hotel de Hardscrabble "the natural and *only* stopping place" between Estes Park and Grand Lake). In 1915, though, some 31,000 visitors would pass through Rocky Mountain's turnstiles; in 1918, when Wheeler received title to his homestead and the Holzwarths filed papers to theirs, more than 101,000 people toured the national park; and in 1920, Rocky Mountain's 240,000 visitors made it the most popular unit in the entire national park system. While it is impossible to know how many of these tourists set foot in the Kawuneeche, the extension of the Fall River Road was already making it significantly easier for automobile travelers to reach the valley from the piedmont and plains. Just a decade after Wheeler launched his Hotel de Hardscrabble, mass tourism had arrived in the Coyote Valley, opening up new opportunities for local settlers like the Holzwarths, even as it confronted the National Park Service and the Kawuneeche's ecosystems with unanticipated challenges.[9]

National Park Nature

Bob Wheeler's poorly recorded conflict with the Forest Service was more exceptional than typical. The early years of tourist-oriented federal preservation in the Coyote Valley witnessed only a few documented conflicts between the Park Service, settlers, and the U.S. Forest Service, in large part because it took so long for Rocky Mountain's administrators and rangers to introduce new land management practices to the Kawuneeche.

From the start, chronic underfunding prevented the Park Service from patrolling even the most heavily visited stretches of the national park, let alone its isolated western periphery. Indeed, neglect and inertia characterized early Park Service management in the Coyote Valley. Rocky Mountain's western borders remained unmarked for many years, and it took until 1922 for the Park Service to erect a station near Grand Lake to count the number of visitors who passed through the park's western entrance and distribute copies of park rules and regulations.

Well into the 1920s, a single ranger patrolled dozens of square miles of rugged parkland between the crest of the Front Range and the Colorado River. Park administrators left Estes Park each fall for Denver, where they waited out winter from their temporary headquarters in a down-town federal building. Not a single employee manned the park's Grand Lake Ranger District during the long cold season; frequent turnover in the ranger corps also occasionally left the post vacant during the summer high season. One of the district's first rangers, Al House, discharged the duties of his office from the comfort of his Kawuneeche Valley home-stead. Prior to 1922, neither roads nor telephone lines connected Grand Lake to Estes Park, which was already the focus of administrative effort and tourist interest at the park. Even then, deep snows made it impos-sible for at least six months of every year to travel between Rocky Moun-tain's eastern and western sides. Roger Toll declared 1929 "the first year that regular patrol work has been done in this park during the winter months."[10]

Hindered by these and other challenges, the National Park Service lacked both the will and the capacity to undertake any sweeping new initiatives in the Kawuneeche. Park regulations did restrict local resi-dents from harvesting furbearers and game in the Colorado River head-waters; some settlers also found that park administrators would not permit them to graze cattle or cut firewood within Rocky Mountain. With these relatively minor exceptions, the advent of federal preserva-tion brought few dramatic shifts in land use—and little conflict with local peoples. Park officials continued to suppress wildfires using the same tactics the Forest Service had instituted on the Medicine Bow re-serve in the early 1900s. The Park Service also perpetuated and even stepped up the long-standing predator eradication campaigns waged by settlers, state officials, and federal authorities. In 1917, Rocky Moun-tain's superintendent launched an all-out to eliminate mountain lions, coyotes, bobcats, and smaller predators from the park. This effort, ini-tiative subsequently escalated under U.S. Biological Survey guidance in the 1920s, was in line with the Park Service's broader policy. Stephen Mather, the borax mogul who served as the agency's first director, ex-plained that the national parks "play a very important part in the conser-vation of wild life, for in them all animals, *with the exception of predatory ones,* find safe refuge and complete protection." Mather's disregard for predators had shifted somewhat by 1926, when he called it "contrary of the policy of the service . . . to exterminate any species native to a park area." But Mather also hastened to add that he considered it "necessary to keep several of the predatory animals, such as wolves, mountain lions, and coyotes, *under control,* so that the deer, antelope, and other weaker animals may not suffer unduly from their depredations." The Park Service did not call off its antipredator crusade until the 1930s, by which time the combined efforts of settlers and federal trappers and hunters had exterminated gray wolves and grizzly bears from the northern Colorado Rockies while greatly diminishing populations of most other big meat eaters.[11]

Continuity also characterized the Park Service's attitude toward game and fish species in the Kawuneeche. In Chapter 9, we examine the steps park officials and their allies took to reintroduce elk to the Greater Rocky Mountain National Park Ecosystem. But fisheries management offers an equally clear-cut case of continuity and collaboration between settlers, utilitarian conservationists, and scenic preservationists, all of whom viewed fish as a resource to be manufactured and manipulated to satisfy tourist desires.[12]

Park officials eagerly perpetuated and even intensified long-standing efforts to plant hatchery-raised fish in the Kawuneeche's lakes and streams. After homesteader Harry Harbison opened the valley's first hatchery in 1894, an assortment of private, state, and federal stocking programs came and went. The Leadville National Fish Hatchery launched a small outdoor operation on Grand Lake's North Inlet in 1904; four years later, the Grand Lake Improvement Association erected a hatchery building. Both operations initially focused on raising Colorado River cutthroat trout, the only variety of trout that was indigenous to the Coyote Valley. But anglers complained that these fish made for poor sport, while hatchery managers disliked them because they took longer to mature than exotic trout species. And so Grand Lake's hatcheries began to propagate rainbow trout (which originated in the Sierra Nevada and other parts of the Far West) and brook trout (indigenous to eastern North America), faster-growing fish that were popular with sport anglers. Because rainbows, brookies, and Colorado River cutthroats spawned at different times of year, the hatcheries at the foot of the Kawuneeche began to raise all three.[13]

Rocky Mountain's first superintendent personally released rainbow trout at several spots in the valley's bottomlands in September 1916. The

National Park Service stocking programs perpetuated the introduction of non-native trout species to the Colorado River and its tributaries. "Planting Fish in Glacier Creek," 1932, MSF Neg. 4918, courtesy of the National Park Service.

next year, his successor planted 185,000 rainbow fry in the Colorado River and a smaller number of "native trout" in the inlets of Grand Lake. Thereafter, Rocky Mountain's growing trail network enabled park employees to plant trout in bodies of water that historically had lacked endemic fish populations because they lay above waterfalls or other natural obstructions that barred fish from migrating upstream.[14]

The Park Service's efforts to propagate and stock trout intentionally placed more—and more varied—fish in the streams and lakes of the Colorado River headwaters. Voracious rainbow and brook trout subjected the invertebrates that sustained all of the valley's trout species to added pressure. Brook trout exposed Colorado River cutthroats to especially stout competition. "In 1916," as homesteader John Holzwarth Jr. later recalled, "the brooks got into the beaver ponds and established themselves, and the natives stayed in the ponds I would say off and on for about 8 or 9 years." By the 1930s, Holzwarth claimed, "the cutthroats were gone." Colorado River cutthroats also began to interbreed with rainbows, muddying piscine gene pools in ways that continue to complicate "native" fish restoration efforts in the Greater Rocky Mountain National Park Ecosystem.[15]

During Rocky Mountain's first decade and a half, fisheries management consistently prioritized one plank in the Park Service's mandate— "to provide for the enjoyment" of the park by visitors—to the detriment of the complementary congressional directive to keep the park's lands and waters "unimpaired." This was just one of the many ways in which tourist-oriented preservation accelerated the pace of environmental change throughout the Greater Rocky Mountain National Park Ecosystem.

Roads to Paradise

Efforts to draw tourists to Rocky Mountain also spurred energetic road building atop the Continental Divide—a development that greatly increased visitation to the park's western side, much to the advantage of the Holzwarths and other settlers who were beginning to accommodate tourists. As both Enos Mills and Horace McFarland had anticipated, the needs and desires of automobile tourists soon came to exert outsized influences on resource management, economic development, and land use at Rocky Mountain, with consequences that rippled onto adjoining National Forest and private lands. Two main developments—the deindustrialization of Colorado's economy and the determination by park administrators and their allies that mass visitation offered a winning justification for park expansion—together moved road construction to the top of the agency's agenda for Rocky Mountain.

Mining, railroad development, and ore refining had driven heady growth in Colorado from the 1870s through the early 1900s. By the 1910s, though, coal production had plateaued, silver mining had collapsed, many railroads had gone bankrupt, and smelting had entered free-fall. With Colorado's traditional industries teetering on the brink of ruin, civic leaders and business elites embarked on a long, uncertain quest to place the regional economy on a sounder foundation. Automobile tourism joined irrigated agriculture, government employment, and the first stirrings of lifestyle-oriented suburbanization as key ingredients in the formula for renewal that distinguished the slow but steady growth Colorado enjoyed between World War I and the 1930s from the relative stagnation of other western states like Nevada and Montana.

Though Colorado had attracted wealthy American and European travelers since the 1860s, the popularization of automobiles in the wake of Henry Ford's 1908 unveiling of the Model T turned the state into a marquee destination for travelers of humbler means, too. By 1923, the influential *Overland Monthly and Out West Magazine* noted that "a vacation outing to the Colorado Rockies is considered one of the most alluring of all annual recreation jaunts." The high country, "with its wild and natural beauty and its associations of thrilling stories, grows stronger year by year . . . in popular fancy." With tourists chomping at the bit to visit Colorado's famous mountains, boosters touted road construction in the recreational hinterlands west of Denver as a key component in steering the region toward a postindustrial path to growth.[16]

As local civic and business leaders were embracing the potential economic benefits of automobile tourism, many leading lights in the U.S. national parks movement wanted to increase visitation to Rocky Mountain for political reasons. In the Hetch Hetchy fracas and other controversies, opponents of preservation cast park advocates as a rich and snobbish elite intent on enclosing the common patrimony of the public lands and preventing all but the wealthiest Americans from feasting their eyes on the West's scenic wonders. A growing chorus of preservationists responded to these damaging attacks by upholding automobile tourism as the key to popularizing and democratizing the national parks. Allen Chamberlain of the Appalachian Mountain Club, for instance, counseled Horace McFarland: "If the public could be induced to visit these scenic treasurehouses [*sic*], . . . they [would] soon come to appreciate their value and stand firmly in their defense." To Chamberlain and a growing chorus of other national park supporters, encouraging automobile tourism to the national parks would help the American people to feel more invested in protecting and expanding Rocky Mountain and other "scenic treasurehouses [*sic*]."[17]

Colorado boosters, of course, saw dollar signs in Park Service efforts to cultivate a popular constituency. Building roads to draw automobile travelers to Rocky Mountain and other parks would fuel regional growth while advancing America's democratic and egalitarian creed. Stephen Mather brought formidable business acumen to the Park Service's tourism campaign. "Our national parks are practically lying fallow," the director declared in 1915, "and only await proper development to bring them into their own." Attendance increased in the mid-1910s, slowed during World War I, then "leaped," as Mather himself put it, "to unprecedented figures" thereafter. The growing affordability, reliability, and comfort of cars underpinned the explosive growth in visitation to Rocky Mountain and other national parks, as Mather acknowledged in 1922, when he declared "the enlarged use of the automobile" to comprise "the principal factor in the travel movement in this country to-day." After experiencing the salutary effects of the nation's "great open breathing spaces," tourists "returned refreshed, rejuvenated, better men and women." An automobile-powered "exodus to the parks from the workshops and farms, the cities and towns," Mather crowed, had earned the National Park System "obvious" recognition "at the head of those worthwhile things in our national life that make for better citizens." By casting mass tourism as an instrument of economic and moral betterment for the entire nation, the Park Service leader demonstrated the ongoing influence of the ideology of improvement at the agency. Just as the Grand River could best "do duty" by being diverted into irrigation canals and onto farmers' fields, Rocky Mountain's scenery could only realize its full potential through an active program of road construction.[18]

But the Greater Rocky Mountain National Park Ecosystem comprised neither a blank canvas nor an inert stage setting. The very ruggedness and isolation that had first inspired Enos Mills and his comrades to campaign for the area's preservation greatly increased the difficulty and expense of building roads there. The Fall River Road—the first direct auto route to cross the Continental Divide between Estes Park and Grand Lake—took nearly eight years to finish because of interruptions occasioned by World War I, shaky funding, labor shortages, the short high-country construction season, and other problems. Paeans to the completed route suggest that most observers felt that the time, money, and energy invested in the Fall River Road had been well spent. By lauding the national park as "at once the most beautiful, most rugged, and most easily accessible spot in the entire Rocky Mountain region," travel writer Allan Osborne hinted at the wonder many observers experienced as they traversed "the world's highest sky-line automobile stretch"—a road that bridged "the Atlantic and Pacific watersheds in a way that even the Utes and Arapahoes [sic] in their wildest flights of fancy could hardly have pictured." Motor Travel magazine gushed that the route was destined to "become the most wonderful motor road in the world." Tourists "attract[ed] from all parts of the nation and from many foreign countries" took up the challenges presented by its sharp curves, steep inclines, precipitous drop-offs, and jarring potholes. The thrill of driving through the high Rockies at altitudes approaching 11,800 feet above sea level struck many visitors as the perfect counterbalance to the more sedate pleasures of taking in Rocky Mountain's sublime scenery. As the drive up and over the Continental Divide became the centerpiece of summer tourism at the park, hordes of travelers began to roll through the Coyote Valley.[19]

Even before the Fall River Road opened, it became a site for contentious exchanges between people and the mountain environment. Constructing the road required laborers and draft animals to modify the land in significant, long-lasting ways. Crews cleared trees and other vegetation, excavated and graded a right-of-way, bridged streams, and altered drainage patterns. Not even the most sanguine booster, though, claimed that all of this human and animal labor had conquered nature—far from it. The same forces that had hampered travel across the Continental Divide since Clovis peoples first pushed into the Greater Rocky Mountain National Park Ecosystem many thousands of years earlier—heavy rains, thick ice, deep snows, fierce storms, the inexorable workings of erosion—continually lashed against "modern" automobile roads, too. Rocky Mountain's superintendent groused in 1918 that the as-yet-unfinished Fall River Road was in "very bad shape" even on those stretches visitors were already using, "due to no repair work having been done and improper or practically no drainage, causing washing away of surfacing material." On one segment north of Grand Lake, the road had deteriorated so swiftly that "it was almost impossible to drive a wagon over it," let alone an automobile. To blunt the perils motorists faced, the Park Service and Colorado's highway department worked together throughout the 1920s, widening the road, reducing its grades, and installing safety walls along especially dangerous stretches.[20]

Neither the state nor federal governments, though, could do anything to stop winter from closing down the Fall River Road for at least half the year. Each June, Colorado newspapers regaled readers with stories of the epic assaults work crews directed against the snow and ice that submerged long stretches of the route. Dynamite helped with the herculean

The beginning of summer witnessed heroic attempts to dig, blast, and plow the snow off of the Fall River Road so that carloads of tourists could ascend the Continental Divide. Fred Payne Clatworthy, "Fall River Road at Big Drift," MSF Neg. 2333, Alb. 4036, courtesy of the National Park Service.

task of exhuming the road from drifts topping twenty feet or more. Legions of laborers hefting hand shovels then advanced to carve a passage over the Divide. The Park Service pushed hard to open the road by June 15. But even though workers frequently toiled every day for a month or more to clear the Fall River Road, they fell short of the agency's goal as often as they met it.[21]

Given the road's many shortcomings, it should come as no surprise that the Park Service and state engineers began to project a new route through the heart of Rocky Mountain just weeks after completing the Fall River Road in 1921. From its inception, Trail Ridge Road (so named, as journalists loved to point out, because it followed a ridge that several old Indian trails had followed across the Continental Divide) was hailed as "one of the most scenic possible drives within the National Park" and "a marvel of engineering skill and a sensation to the traveling public." Despite generous federal funding and the introduction of powerful earth-moving technology in the form of steam shovels, the new road did not open to travelers until summer 1932, when Trail Ridge eclipsed Fall River as the highest continuous automobile road in the world, capped by a seven-mile segment perched more than 12,000 feet above sea level.[22]

When a journalist remarked that Trail Ridge Road crossed "primeval territory where man has never yet traversed," he was trafficking in a peculiarly revealing kind of nonsense. Trail Ridge, like all roads, represented an undeniable product of human artifice. The Park Service, though, went to great lengths to induce the tourists who traveled atop this man-made structure to pay attention not to the road itself, but instead to the views it opened up. Every foot of Trail Ridge Road was carefully designed to blend into its surroundings. "Roadsides," Stephen Mather exulted, "have been cleaned . . . , old roads wiped out, the sloping of shoulders unusually well done, and in many places planting to cover up scars has been started." Motoring on the Fall River Road had delivered troubles and thrills in nearly equal measure. Driving on Trail Ridge Road, by contrast, struck most travelers as eminently pleasurable. As the trip over the backbone of the continent became easier and faster, tourists increasingly forgot about steam shovels, construction crews, and even the cars in which they were riding. The skill of the Park Service's landscape architects, who were becoming the most powerful professional cadre within the agency, enabled tourists to devote more of their attention than ever before to the stunning scenery that loomed just beyond the pavement's edge.[23]

Journeying on Trial Ridge became a convenient means for many automobile travelers to commune with wild nature. "This is the top of the world," Virginia S. Eifert later declared in *Nature Magazine*, "a world reached by means of a smooth highway." From Trail Ridge's carefully located pullouts and overlooks, Eifert expounded, travelers could see "a huge world . . . spread below. Dozens of mountain peaks rise more than eleven thousand feet high. Clouds build up mightily against a deep sapphire sky. Everything," in short, struck Eifert—and presumably other tourists who ventured into the Coyote Valley in automobiles—as "big and awe-inspiring, and cars seem beetle-like as they creep along the high roads." By laying bare what Eifert memorably called "man's own dwarfing in the presence of so much majesty," this "Road to the Top of the World" introduced the highway sublime to Rocky Mountain.[24]

Before Trail Ridge Road could offer park visitors the illusion of communion with the Rocky Mountain National Park environment, steam shovels and construction workers would have to impose significant changes on park landscapes and ecosystems. John "Mack" McLaughlin, "Fall River Road: Clearing for New Road," November 20, 1933, MSF Neg. 2402, Alb. 4006, courtesy of the National Park Service.

Down on the banks of the Colorado River, meanwhile, road construction was opening up new opportunities for work-worn settlers. Since the Kawuneeche bottomlands were only a few miles wide, almost all the valley's homesteads lay within a mile of a route traversed first by the Fall River Road, then by Trail Ridge. Homesteaders who filed claims *after* Rocky Mountain National Park's 1915 founding were more likely to drive cars into the Coyote Valley than wagons (though, for decades to come, horses and sleds remained the best—and sometimes the only— means of winter travel). The valley's inhabitants found that the new roads built after the designation of Rocky Mountain made it easier and cheaper to market dairy products, hay, and other goods at Grand Lake, which was quietly maturing into a thriving summer resort. No less important, roads were literally bringing national park visitors to the doorsteps of the valley's homesteads. By 1930, the tourist trade was playing an essential role in the economic strategies and land-use practices of old settlers and latter-day homesteaders alike.

The Dudes Abide

Tourists motoring through the valley on the Fall River Road in the late 1910s and 1920s were increasingly joined by a new kind of homesteader: the second home owner. The Holzwarths notwithstanding, most of the "settlers" who filed claims to tracts of Kawuneeche Valley land after 1915 had no intention of attempting to harvest a living from the land. Instead, they came in search of a place where they could periodically find refuge from their workaday lives. Clarence Lee, for example, bound books four days a week in Denver, then drove up to the Colorado River headwaters during warm-season weekends. World War I veteran Henry Nicholls, meanwhile, held down a steady job at Denver's Western Auto Supply Company between trips to his Kawuneeche homestead, where he played pioneer by tending his one-acre truck garden and building a "Log house." The General Land Office cut homesteaders much more slack in the late 1910s and 1920s than ever before. Veterans enjoyed especially smooth sailing; Nicholls, for instance, proved up his claim without presenting any evidence to show that he had satisfied the law by cultivating his land and residing on it year-round.[25]

Only a handful of visitors to the Coyote Valley filed homestead papers or purchased land from earlier settlers. The rest of the madding crowd, though, soon offered Holzwarth, Wheeler, Lee, and other local residents a lucrative supplement to mixed husbandry, wage work, and market production. More than any other settlers, the Holzwarths led the way. Johnnie Holzwarth (never a wholly reliable source—"You're not a good dude rancher," he later explained, "unless you can tell a story, and keep your guests entertained") recalled that his family's transformation from homesteading to dude ranching had begun not long after Papa's accident. On a Sunday afternoon in the summer of 1920, several of Papa's buddies drove up from Denver to pay Holzwarth a visit as he convalesced. Papa Holzwarth, ever the saloon keeper, poured his pals round after round of whiskey from his backyard still. Soon, the Holzwarths' guests had grown drunk, disorderly, and hungry. Though the trout of the Colorado River beckoned, Papa's friends were too soused or lazy to answer the fishes' call themselves. Johnnie, hopeful that a good solid meal might convince the loutish crew to head home, marched to the river bank, cast his line, and pulled in huge numbers of trout— 150 in one telling of the story, fifty in others. Soon thereafter, Papa's guests ate their fill, said their good-byes, and swerved onto the Fall River Road. That night, Johnnie and Sophie Holzwarth made a pact: never again would they offer their hospitality for free.

The Holzwarth Trout Lodge opened later that same year, advertising "room, board, horses, and diversions" at the price of two dollars a day or eleven dollars a week—somewhere between chump change and a king's ransom. By 1922, brisk business compelled the Holzwarths to outfit a rustic homestead cabin for overflow visitors. The crowds kept coming, though, and in 1924, the family erected several new guest cabins between the east bank of the Colorado and the Fall River Road, in a location that was sure to attract the attention of tourists driving to and from Rocky Mountain by car. The Holzwarths embarked on their largest expansion to date in 1929, when they debuted their three-story Never Summer Ranch. Instead of freighting the vegetables, chickens, and dairy products they produced to Grand Lake, the Holzwarths could now feed their ranch-raised foodstuffs to their own summer guests. Johnnie's knack with rod, reel, and rifle, meanwhile, kept the Never Summer Ranch's dining room tables flush with trout, deer, elk, grouse, rabbit, and other vestigial tastes of the Old West. Even so, the Holzwarths still required occasional financial support from Johnnie's sister, Julia, who held well-paying positions as an executive assistant with a succession of Denver firms.[26]

The Holzwarths had come to the Kawuneeche to live out Papa's dream of homesteading and raising cattle. By the start of the Great Depression, though, the family had become full-fledged dude ranchers who specialized in satisfying the desire of middle-class Americans to experience the bygone frontier.[27] By the time the Holzwarths opened their Never Summer Ranch, some of their neighbors were also accommodating tourists. The desire to commune with scenery, wildlife, and other elements of nature continued to draw overnight visitors to the Kawuneeche, just as it had when Bob Wheeler launched his Hotel de Hardscrabble. But tourists were also drawn to the Never Summer Ranch and its competitors by the lure of the mythic West. Vacationers came to the Colorado River headwaters to slough off their city skins. Tourists wanted to wake up in an early settler's cabin, take a morning ride through steep woodlands to explore Lulu City's ghostly remains, spend the afternoon mastering calves with a lasso, and while away the evening listening to actual cowboys tell tall tales about the open range before a crackling fire. The Holzwarths and the other Kawuneeche residents who catered to tourists simultaneously responded to and reinforced their guests' desires to experience the noble ways of their fabled frontier progenitors. Settlers were ideally situated to satisfy this impulse, which was not so different from the inspiration that first drew Papa Holzwarth and others to venture into the Kawuneeche.[28]

Between 1915 and 1930, the homesteading frontier and the national park system butted up against each other in the Coyote Valley. Scholars have documented widespread conflict between government conservation officials and local people in many other parts of the United States during the late 1800s and 1900s. In the Kawuneeche, by contrast, concord prevailed between settlers and the Park Service. Land management practices changed little after Rocky Mountain's establishment, while a shared interest in attracting visitors forged common ground between settlers and Park Service administrators. The park's expansion to the summit of the Never Summer Range in 1930, however, and the subsequent completion of Trail Ridge Road together began to sow seeds of dissension. After World War II, a new vision of Rocky Mountain as a place unsullied by human inhabitation gained traction. The Park Service responded by buying out private landowners and seeking to restore so-called natural conditions on these properties—an effort that eventually eradicated dude ranches like the Holzwarths' Never Summer Ranch, as well as other remnants of the interwar decades when homesteading and preservation coexisted and even harmonized.[29]

The Never Summer Boundary Extension

Conservationists greeted the rise of tourism at Rocky Mountain during the 1920s with a mix of approval and anxiety. Park Service officials cited the swelling ranks of national park visitors as an index of success. Other preservationists, however, worried that the onslaught of cars, tourists, and crass commercialism would mar the scenery and spoil the experience of communing with wild nature. Defenders and critics of automobile tourism could both agree, however, that a bigger park would be a better park.

The Never Summer extension of 1930, an Act of Congress that pushed the national park's border westward to incorporate most of the Coyote Valley, reflected the Park Service's commitment to protecting the all-important vistas from the Fall River Road and its successor, the route over Trail Ridge. As with the campaign that culminated in the 1915 law that established Rocky Mountain, however, efforts to extend the park's boundaries to the Never Summer ridgeline led advocates to make calculated compromises. As they licked their wounds after a failed 1925 expansion bid, park officials realized that extending Rocky Mountain's western border would remain a political nonstarter unless they made significant concessions to local landowners. By 1930, this strategy succeeded at reversing the opposition of the Water Supply and Storage Company, owners of the Grand Ditch, to a second boundary extension proposal. Almost a century later, the aesthetic and ecological consequences of the resulting bargain continue to haunt the Kawuneeche Valley.

From the inception of Enos Mills's park crusade in 1909, supporters had treated the preserve's borders as expedient and subject to future modification. National Park Service administrators ranging from the top brass in Washington to the superintendents of other parks and monuments across the United States expressed similar optimism; to them, as to James Gamble Rogers, the original boundaries of these federal preserves represented but a starting point for future expansion. Because most Park Service units adjoined national forests, enlarging parks and monuments typically hinged on transferring the management of these public lands from the Forest Service to the Park Service—a dynamic that exacerbated the already heated rivalry between the two agencies. By the 1920s, border controversies had erupted from Yellowstone to Yosemite, and from Glacier to Grand Canyon. Park Service and Forest Service leaders responded by convening the Coordinating Commission on National Parks and Forests, a joint committee intended to negotiate mutually acceptable solutions to these interagency conflicts.[30]

In 1925, the Coordinating Commission proposed a set of exchanges that would have placed nearly the entire Coyote Valley within Rocky Mountain, excepting only the Grand Ditch right-of-way and lands already claimed by or patented to settlers. Federal foresters were outraged by the commission's expansion proposal. Forest Supervisor J. V. Leighou objected to "some agitation by outside parties . . . for the inclusion of additional areas on the west side of the Continental Divide," a move for which he could see "no justification." The forester recalled that Mills's founding dream of a "game sanctuary" had constituted the "main reason for including" the eastern Kawuneeche within Rocky Mountain's original boundaries. After poring over correspondence exchanged in the early 1910s by Forest Service officials and park campaigners, Leighou could find "no contention" that the Colorado River headwaters lay "within the bounds of an area which was of National importance from a scenic stand-point." Leighou urged Forest Service leaders to fight annexation. He even advised them to press the Coordinating Commission to return the Park Service portion of the Coyote Valley to national forest administration. "Insofar as outstanding scenic features are concerned," he groused, "there are none within the area." The trough between the Never Summers and the Front Range, Leighou declared, was "merely an area similar to other areas within the Rocky Mountain region"— an ordinary mountain landscape rather than a place of exceptional aesthetic value.[31]

The Coordinating Commission, however, rejected such arguments. When it eventually announced its proposal to incorporate "the area at the headwaters of the Colorado River [the new moniker borne by the stream formerly known as the Grand River as a result of Colorado representative Edward Taylor's 1921 renaming bill]" into Rocky Mountain National Park, it noted that the Coyote Valley's "scenic character" made it "more suitable for park purposes than for forest purposes." Rocky Mountain superintendent Roger Toll used both aesthetics and economics to justify expanding the park's boundaries to the Never Summers. "Only superlative examples of American scenery," he explained, "are eligible to become a part of the national park system." The eastern flanks of the Never Summers, Toll contended, met these high standards. In Toll's view, "the national parks should consist only of lands that are scenic in the highest degree, and whose values for recreational and educational purposes are so great that all other lesser values may readily be waived to attain the development for which the areas are best suited." The landscapes of the Kawuneeche, Toll contended, could achieve their highest possible use only if Congress incorporated them into Rocky Mountain.[32]

The Forest Service was just one of the many entities to rally against the 1925 park expansion plan. Business and civic leaders in Boulder objected to another piece of the Coordinating Committee's proposal, which would have moved Rocky Mountain's southern border to encompass most of the Indian Peaks, a stunning stretch of Front Range splendor. Boulderites fretted that Congress might place Arapaho Glacier, the widely advertised source of their city's municipal water supply, under Park Service jurisdiction. Last but not least, Water Supply mounted what another forester later recalled as "considerable opposition," lodging "a strong protest against the transfer."[33]

The water company's concerns about park expansion reflected its recent decision to complete the Grand Ditch, which had remained stuck in place since the early 1900s. Water Supply resumed work on the project in the mid-1920s in response to legal developments, economic uncertainties, and climatic variations. Extreme drought in 1919 combined with booming prices for wheat, sugar beets, and cattle to prompt Water Supply's shareholders to call for larger and more stable diversions of Colorado River water. After the U.S. Supreme Court's 1922 *Wyoming v. Colorado* decision scaled back the company's claims to the Laramie River, Water Supply officers resolved to complete the Grand Ditch. In 1923, laborers began to clear timber from sections of right-of-way that Water Supply's precursor companies had located in the 1880s. The company's managers soon halted construction, though, realizing that they needed to build a new storage reservoir before extending the Grand Ditch. The best site for such a reservoir lay at the Long Draw site, part of which lay within Rocky Mountain's borders. Though Congress transferred the required lands to Water Supply in 1924 without any objection from the Park Service, company officials nonetheless remained wary that park expansion would prevent them from finally completing the Grand Ditch.[34]

The collective antagonism of Water Supply, Boulder boosters, and the U.S. Forest Service doomed the 1925 expansion plan, but the Park Service's defeat laid the foundation for success five years later. The agency's leaders honed their political tactics in a series of successful campaigns in the late 1920s that convinced Congress to create several new national parks and monuments, including Shenandoah, Great Smoky Mountains, Mammoth Cave, Grand Teton, Badlands, and Arches. By the time the Park Service announced a fresh proposal to expand Rocky Mountain in 1930, agency administrators had gained important experience in conciliating concerns of the sort that had sunk the 1925 proposal. Most crucially, they neutralized hostility from Boulder County by excluding the Indian Peaks from the expansion plan; no less important, their proposed legislation included several clauses to ensure that Water Supply could finish the Grand Ditch. Having appeased two key players in the coalition that had defeated the 1925 extension measure, Park Service officials proceeded to make a positive case for incorporating the west side of the Coyote Valley into Rocky Mountain. Park superintendent Edmund Rogers declared it a realm "of great scenic grandeur and geological interest"—"a natural unit of the Park" that would also protect the "winter grazing grounds of the park wild life."[35]

Federal foresters remained skeptical. J. V. Leighou again denounced park expansion, scoffing that "the only possible use that the tourists would be likely to make of this country would be to look at it from the . . . road." Leighou was hitting closer to the mark than he realized. By 1930, the Park Service wanted desperately to preserve the all-important vistas that Trail Ridge Road was poised to reveal. If the Forest Service opened the slopes of the Never Summers to logging, mining, or grazing, then tourists driving downhill into the Kawuneeche from the Continental Divide would experience a descent that was anticlimactic in more ways than one.[36]

Congress, unmoved by Forest Service grumbling, voted in 1930 to transfer most of its remaining lands in the Coyote Valley to Rocky Mountain National Park. The Never Summer boundary expansion act safeguarded Water Supply's long-postponed Grand Ditch; it also promised to draw additional visitors across the Continental Divide to the Colorado River headwaters. Yet the measure also placed the Kawuneeche's homesteaders and other private landowners in a pickle. The dude ranches, cabin resorts, and homesteads built by the Holzwarths and other settlers now lay almost entirely surrounded by a world-famous national park.

The Never Summer annexation probably brought more tourists to the Coyote Valley, but it was hardly an unalloyed boon for local residents. The Never Summer extension made it more difficult for many of them to make a living, since the Park Service had begun to regulate logging, hunting, grazing, and trapping more stringently than the Forest Service ever had. Even more important, the 1930 expansion act set in motion a gradual federal takeover of the Kawuneeche Valley floor. The Never Summer addition transformed the cluster of homesteads along the Colorado River into an isolated promontory of fee simple lands surrounded on three sides by Rocky Mountain. It also turned more isolated homesteads into inholdings—enclaves of privately owned land lying within the exterior boundaries of the national park. Fearful that these private lands could provide a beachhead for tawdry commercial development, the Park Service endeavored to reabsorb and eliminate the Coyote Valley's old settlement landscapes.

It did not take long for local residents to realize the threat they were facing. In November 1931, a joint meeting of citizens and the Grand County Board of Commissioners resolved to fight further efforts to en- large Rocky Mountain. "The people of Grand County," their petition declared, "are bitterly opposed to further additions of this nature," claiming that further expansion "would seriously interfere with the development and utilization of the valuable natural resources in the regions adjacent to the present National Park boundaries, and would im- pose serious hardships on private enterprises already established within and adjacent to these areas." The next month, a self-proclaimed "Old- Timer" griped in the *Middle Park Times* that the Never Summer extension "eliminates nearly every form of business activity and creates a play- ground." Local people were especially afraid that Park Service officials might attempt to extend Rocky Mountain into the Baker Gulch-Bowen Gulch area—a mineral-rich stretch of the Never Summers located south of the 1930 addition. Shrewdly gauging the political winds, the agency dropped this scheme in early 1932.[37]

Ever since, the Forest Service and the Park Service have held fast to adjoining bailiwicks on the Coyote Valley's western slopes. From 1930 onward, the main thrust of park expansion coursed not along the Never Summers, but up the heart of the old homesteading frontier along the Colorado River. The piecemeal transfer of former homesteads to na- tional park management was about to begin, and nothing could stop it.

◁| 8 |▷

RESTORING THE VALLEY PRIMEVAL

IN 1927, a Fort Collins banker convinced an ambitious farmer named Harvey Johnson to assume the mortgage on a 640-acre parcel irrigated by Water Supply. Neither Johnson nor the banker could have guessed it at the time, but the deal the two men sealed that day on the Colorado piedmont would have monumental consequences for the hydrology and ecology of the Coyote Valley. For under Johnson's leadership, Water Supply finally completed the Grand Ditch, thus laying the foundation for decades of wrangling with Johnnie Holzwarth and the National Park Service over the ditch's aesthetic and environmental consequences.

Harvey Johnson moved to Colorado in 1902 with his parents, Swedish-born immigrants who had heeded a preacher's advice to abandon the high plains of Kansas for the fertile lands below the Rocky Mountains. The Johnsons raised alfalfa, sugar beets, beef cattle, and dairy cows on a succession of rented farms. Harvey dropped out of school in sixth grade to help his dad and sisters with fieldwork. Several years later, after a miserable spell working on a Detroit automobile assembly line, he returned to Colorado and started farming on his own account. By the 1920s, Johnson's willingness to experiment with new crops and farming methods earned him a reputation as one of Larimer County's most progressive farmers. None of the innovations Johnson embraced, however, could reduce his dependence on irrigation. By 1927, Johnson had spent the majority of his life cultivating lands irrigated at least in part by Grand Ditch water. When he assumed the mortgage on a square mile of prime piedmont farmland that year, however, Johnson began to take much greater interest in the diversion canal that snaked along the distant Never Summer Mountains.[1]

As long as Johnson gave his crops "plenty of water," they flourished, yielding as much as twenty tons of sugar beets per acre. Yet in dry years like 1928, when Water Supply's ditches distributed water on just twenty-eight days in all, the small and jerry-built Grand Ditch simply could not supply enough water to Johnson and his fellow farmers in Larimer and Weld Counties. It was "good water," Johnson recalled, "but it was awful short." The drought's end failed to quell Johnson's doubts about his water supply. "When you went in debt for a farm," he explained, "and you had to raise a crop to meet that obligation, [it] put a terrible weight on you to find out why you didn't have enough water." Johnson had invested "his life savings" and "promised over a period of time to pay a debt." His financial commitment led him to ponder a tough question: "How am I going to do it without proper water?"[2]

This dilemma still gnawed at Johnson several years later, as he arrived at his first-ever meeting of Water Supply shareholders. After a fellow Swede unexpectedly nominated Johnson to the board, he consented to stand for election because he had "studied the company pretty well." The water company's newest board member made his inaugural journey to the Coyote Valley just months after winning a landslide victory. His gut still tied in knots from a harrowing automobile journey into the high country, Johnson's heart sank the instant he set eyes on the Grand Ditch. The all-important diversion canal on which his farm and his financial future depended was but a "little handmade ditch," so narrow "you could pretty well step across it." Though Johnson and Water Supply's other shareholders had invested some $1.5 million and an immeasurable sum of hope in the canal, the conduit nonetheless extended along just four miles or so of the sixteen-mile route that surveyors had staked out in the 1880s.[3]

In the years that followed, Johnson and his fellow board members redoubled their efforts to realize the diversion's full potential to "do duty." Under Johnson's leadership, Water Supply finally extended the Grand Ditch the full distance from La Poudre Pass to Baker Gulch. The piddling hand-dug ditch Johnson had discovered on his first journey to the Kawuneeche became an efficient, orderly canal during the late 1930s. Under Johnson's direction, Water Supply modernized the ditch and solidified its hold on the right-of-way the company had safeguarded in the negotiations leading up to the Never Summer addition of 1930. The water company's achievement, though, would come at a heavy cost to Johnnie Holzwarth, Rocky Mountain National Park, and the Coyote Valley environment.

By the 1930s, the Park Service, Forest Service, Water Supply, and roughly two dozen other landowners were all staking legal, economic, political, and moral claims to different parts of Kawuneeche. Each contender for this small stretch of the Colorado high country held fast to its own vision of what the valley was and what it might become: a playground where urbanites disenchanted with industrialism could restore their sagging spirits; a "forest sponge" that had to be protected from ruination; a source of life-giving water for the dry lands splaying out onto the plains from the foot of the Rockies; and a home place for raising hay, gardens, and livestock. As homesteaders, irrigators, conservationists, and preservationists grappled to manifest their disparate visions for the valley, a messy landscape grew messier still.

The Park Service sought to impose order on this chaos by extending and intensifying its grip over the Coyote Valley. From the Never Summer addition of 1930 through the buyout of the Holzwarths in the early 1970s, the agency purchased nearly all of the valley's private lands. Each acquisition, though, confronted the agency with a conundrum: How could it incorporate lands bearing obvious traces of earlier human uses—Native American inhabitation, mining, homesteading, water diversion, and tourist development—into a preserve that national park officials and visitors alike desperately wanted to see as primeval and unpeopled?

Gaining title to the former homesteads of the Colorado River bottomlands and extending park boundaries proved just the first and simplest stage in integrating settlement landscapes into Rocky Mountain. The Park Service resolved during the 1960s and 1970s to return the Kawuneeche to an imagined "pristine" or "natural" state. Paying little heed to the valley's deep environmental history, park officials endeavored to create something that never had actually existed—a place alternately envisioned as a postglacial landscape devoid of human beings *and* a mythical frontier safely tucked between the violence of Nuche removal and the traumas of modernity. The contradictions that permeated both the pristine and pioneer ideals, however, combined with the social and ecological complexities of this trickster place to frustrate the government's efforts to realize what park superintendent Roger Contor optimistically termed a "return to the pristine" in the Kawuneeche.[4]

Scar to Wound, and Wound to Parasite

Even as Harvey Johnson was making his maiden voyage to the Grand Ditch, construction crews were gearing up to extend the canal. Labor disputes halted work on two occasions—the militancy of American workers under the New Deal reached deep into the Rocky Mountain West—but the introduction of a steam shovel helped contractors make headway during the 1934 construction season. More strikes and a time-consuming spat between Water Supply and its main construction contractor then slowed the project again. Finally, in September 1936, crews completed the final leg of the canal. The "little handmade ditch" that so alarmed Johnson was just four feet wide. The newer sections excavated by steam shovel in the 1930s, though, measured eight feet across. Water Supply went on to widen the older portions of the canal, too. At any given moment, the new and improved ditch could divert some 20,000 acre-feet of water from the forests, meadows, and willow thickets of the Colorado River headwaters to thirsty crops on Colorado's northern piedmont.[5]

Rocky Mountain National Park officials, intent on sparing automobile tourists on the new Trail Ridge Road the disappointment of beholding shacks, construction detritus, and other signs that the Coyote Valley was not what it seemed, wasted no time in protesting the aesthetic impacts of ditch expansion. Even before construction was finished, they begged Water Supply to clean up—or at least hide—its mess. In 1936, for instance, park ranger Sterling Vaughn implored the company to remove abandoned cabins at ditch camps, dispose of trees and brush felled along the right-of-way, relocate a work camp that was "very much in evidence from the valley and from Trail Ridge Road" to a more secluded site, and locate any new structures it built in the future on ground "satisfactorily hidden from the public's view." Vaughn admitted that "to a Park Service landscape architect," the Grand Ditch "would still present a very unsightly appearance, but to one who has been familiar with the scene for the past two or three years it presents a one hundred percent improvement." Three decades later, Rocky Mountain's staff continued to beseech the ditch company to tidy up the unsightly vestiges of construction and maintenance along its right-of-way.[6]

The biggest problems, though, involved the ditch itself. A massive, plainly visible, man-made structure coursing through the heart of Rocky Mountain's west side offended visitors and Park Service employees alike. Yet the concessions the government had made to Water Supply in 1930 would continue to handcuff Rocky Mountain's administrators. "The ditch scar is there from now on," park superintendent David Canfield conceded in 1949, and "it must be considered practically impossible ever to obliterate it."[7]

This did not mean, however, that the Park Service had to accept all of the Grand Ditch's impacts. By the 1960s, conflict between the government and Harvey Johnson's Water Supply intensified. A succession of breaches in the 1960s and 1970s allowed debris-strewn waters to tumble down the slopes of the Never Summers, scouring out gullies and prompting the ire of the Park Service and private landowners.[8]

Even when state water officials collaborated with Water Supply to prevent breaches, such preventive measures sometimes caused more problems than they resolved. For example, after heavy summer rains filled Water Supply's Long Draw Reservoir to capacity in 1965, state engineers ordered the company to release water from the Grand Ditch into the creeks of the Kawuneeche. These releases of large quantities of water "caused serious erosion, besides uprooting and killing many trees." Man-made floods inflicted "considerable damage" on the Lulu City area, and then washed out several beaver dams along the Upper Colorado, inflicting losses of some $15,000 on the Holzwarths' Never Summer Ranch. An outraged Johnnie Holzwarth took on the ditch company. "We had problems," as Harvey Johnson later recalled, "not so much with the government," but instead with "a resort just below our system there"—the Never Summer Ranch—"that drawed [sic] us into several court hearings and several government projects . . . to get us out of the park." Like the Park Service, Johnnie Holzwarth was fighting mad at the Grand Ditch.[9]

These events led Superintendent Fred Novak to warn Johnson in 1966 that the Park Service would no longer tolerate "many practices" previously "taken for granted." Novak asked Water Supply's president to clean up unsightly debris dumps and "old construction camps,"

build crossings on several trails that traversed the canal "to accommodate horses and foot travel," reexamine Water Supply's procedures "to
further better management of our natural resources," and pay to remediate the harm done when the ditch company released "an abnormal
volume of water in an unnatural drainage." Novak justified his laundry
list of requests with a veiled warning: "We are all conscious," the superintendent intoned, "of a growing awareness in land conservation and
beautification among the American public." Novak was referring, of
course, to the surging tide of public activism that observers were just
starting to refer to as the environmental movement. By invoking the
newfound enthusiasm of the nation's citizenry for ecological protection, the superintendent sought to convey a veiled threat to Johnson:
while the Park Service itself had little power over Water Supply, the ditch
company was playing with fire if it continued to ignore the emerging
will of the American people.[10]

The complaints of W. C. Worthington, a tourist who visited Rocky
Mountain from Ohio in 1970, epitomized the "growing awareness"
Novak invoked. During Worthington's fall tour of the Kawuneeche,
heavy rains sent the Grand Ditch spilling over its banks once again.
"When one uses the various trails established by the Park Service on the
west side of the park," the Ohioan grumbled about the resulting breach,
"one can see the terrific amount of damage that has been done over the
years and continues, as a result of poor maintenance and management
of this open ditch." Worthington objected to the clear signs of "severe
erosion and the silting of the many valley streams." The tourist concluded his letter with a parting shot: "How a private, commercial, and
profit-oriented company is allowed to continually . . . cause irreparable
damage within the Rocky Mountain National Park, is beyond my com-
prehension." Visitors like Worthington assailed the Grand Ditch for
violating hallowed national park ideals.[11]

Rocky Mountain's Theodore Thompson sought to placate Worthington
by praising Water Supply. The company, he claimed, had responded to
the breach by performing "considerable general cleanup work" and
remedying "some remaining difficiencies [*sic*] in operating practices
and maintenance standards." Thompson predicted that "in the near
future," the Grand Ditch would "be brought to a standard that is [as]
acceptable as possible with this type of intrusion in an otherwise wilderness area." Yet Thompson may not have expressed such optimism if

This aerial view of the Kawuneeche Valley in midsummer 1972 shows the Grand Ditch "scar," with rubble from breaching clearly evident. Dwight L. Harris photo, MSF Neg. 7186, courtesy of the National Park Service.

he had given more thought to the forceful unpredictability of the high Rockies. In 1978, the Grand Ditch was "blown out" for the third time in thirteen years; as in previous breaches, this one sent "a large stream of water, boulders, and mud cascad[ing] down the mountainside."[12]

During the 1970s, Park Service officials and environmentalists also began to accuse the Grand Ditch of fundamentally altering the Coyote Valley's hydrology and depriving its rich riparian ecosystems of the water they needed to thrive. In 1986, a Park Service attorney hit the ditch company with a veritable litany of grievances. "Scars have appeared on the mountainside," he alleged, "banks and meadows have deteriorated, peat beds have been undercut and fallen into the stream channel, and the area has been strewn with large amounts of structural timber, abandoned tools and equipment, remains of old construction camps and a telephone line." This systemic critique of the diversion project reflected the Park Service's growing emphasis on scientific research. Yet it also responded to the unintended consequences of improvements that Water Service had made to the ditch at Harvey Johnson's behest. Frustrated with large losses to seepage because of the ditch's porous bed, Johnson oversaw an effort to line the conduit. This improvement deprived the Kawuneeche of additional water; an estimated 60 percent of the valley's water was now carried off to the Poudre watershed. Water tables throughout the Colorado River bottomlands have dropped as a result. Since time immemorial, the river had frequently burst its banks during the spring and summer snow melt or episodes of unusually heavy summer rains. Because of the Grand Ditch, however, flooding became less frequent and less intense. This, in turn, sapped the stream's capacity to perform the vital ecological work on which willows, benthic invertebrates, trout, and many other organisms directly or indirectly rely.[13]

Some of the Coyote Valley's riparian habitats deteriorated as the Grand Ditch rerouted precipitation from the eastern slopes of the Never Summers to piedmont farms such as the one worked by Harvey Johnson near Fort Collins. Especially hard-hit were wetlands; peat began to break down in some of the valley's fens, with the rate of decay accelerating during drought phases. The "continued use" of the Grand Ditch, researchers Jordan Clayton and Cherie Westbrook warned in 2008, had proven "detrimental to the health of the stream ecosystem of the upper Colorado River." The diversion canal may even have provided greenback cutthroat trout—a subspecies that evolved on the eastern slopes of the Front Range—to migrate across the Front Range and into the Kawuneeche. If some greenbacks indeed swam across the Great Divide, their journeys would have mixed gene pools that had been isolated for many thousands of years, further complicating subsequent efforts to restore "native" trout to the Greater Rocky Mountain National Park Ecosystem.[14]

As Harvey Johnson discussed his life and accomplishments with historian James Hansen in 1985, he could still conjure up the worries that had kept him up at night during the Dust Bowl years of the 1930s. "We had to have water," Johnson recalled of the anxieties that pressed down on him and his fellow farmers on northern Colorado's piedmont. "There was water up there in the mountains, and we were destitute, and we got it." To Johnson, the Grand Ditch constituted nothing less than "a monument to a fine group of farmers with great foresight and stamina to build."[15]

And so it was. Viewed from another perspective, though, the same man-made structure that Johnson celebrated also stands as a memorial to conflict. If the Grand Ditch commemorates the pluck and resourceful-ness of Harvey Johnson and everyone else who turned Water Supply into a wellspring of agricultural productivity and prosperity, the canal should also remind us of the labor struggles that erupted there during the New Deal, the breaches that gouged debris-strewn gullies down the slopes of the Never Summers, and the artificially imposed water scarcity that threatens the Coyote Valley's riparian zones with unprecedented harm.

The Culture and Nature of Dude Ranching

More than a thousand vertical feet separated the cluster of settlement on the floor of the Coyote Valley from the Grand Ditch above. And yet Water Supply and the private landowners on the valley floor nonethe-less shared a thirst for the same finite water supplies and a wariness born of occupying lands abutting or even enveloped by Rocky Moun-tain National Park. From the moment Squeaky Bob Wheeler accommo-dated the Hotel de Hardscrabble's first paying guest in the early 1900s through the shuttering of the Holzwarths' Never Summer Ranch in the early 1970s, the valley's settlers and latter-day locals eagerly embraced tourism. Indeed, the influx of visitor dollars enabled more than a few of the valley's homesteaders to maintain a foothold on lands they might otherwise have lost. Fifteen years after Rocky Mountain's creation, the Never Summer addition gave a welcome boost to the Coyote Valley's dude ranches, guest ranches, and cottage resorts. At the same time, though, park expansion also initiated a protracted federal campaign to eliminate private landholdings from the Colorado River headwaters. Every time the Park Service—an agency entrusted by Congress with preserving the nation's most treasured places—resolved to absorb a former homestead back into the public domain, it confronted difficult choices. What vestiges of settlement, park making, and tourism should it preserve, and which should it repurpose, remove, or destroy?

For the Holzwarth family and their neighbors, the 1930s and 1940s brought considerable challenges. After the 1929 expansion of their Never Summer Ranch, the family hosted as many as a hundred guests to the property on summer holiday weekends. Though a few visitors rented campsites, most stayed on the American Plan, which included a cabin or lodge room, three square meals of Sophie Holzwarth's home cooking, and a smorgasbord of rustic activities including horseback riding, fishing, hiking, hunting, and ranch chores. By the time John Holz-warth Sr. died in December 1932, the Great Depression had forced a huge decline in tourism. The Kawuneeche's settlers had little choice but to fall back on old habits of wage labor and resource diversification to stay afloat. Johnnie Holzwarth sold hay, cut ice from Grand Lake, and tirelessly ranged through the mountains setting mile after mile of tra-plines, "always" taking care to reinvest the proceeds in "improve-ments to the ranch." The Holzwarths also did all they could to trim expenses; starting in the 1930s, cabin guests would do their own cooking, wood chopping, and housekeeping.[16]

As the economy recovered, Rocky Mountain set new attendance rec-ords; in 1941, visitation exceeded 685,000—a far cry from the 255,874 who had entered the park at the low point of the Depression. The U.S. entry into World War II, though, again pushed tourism to the margins of American life. What Park Service director Newton Drury called "the handicaps of traveling under wartime conditions" reduced attendance at Rocky Mountain to 392,565 in 1942, followed by a mere 130,188 the following year. Mass mobilization for war also brought acute labor short-ages to the Colorado high country. With wranglers in short supply, the work guests performed at the Never Summer Ranch and its competitors became more important than ever before.

A war-weary public had begun flocking back to the national parks even before a giddy cowboy galloped up to the Coyote Valley from Grand Lake to deliver news of Japan's surrender on August 14, 1945. Although Rocky Mountain and other national parks had been "reduced," as Di-rector Drury aptly phrased it, "to hardly more than a custodial basis during the war," visitation nonetheless bounced back after the war's end, increasing from 204,253 in 1944 to 339,928 in 1945 and 808,115 in 1946. Pent-up consumer demand for rest, relaxation, and rugged play combined with rapidly rising incomes, a sharp upswing in automobile ownership, the construction of improved highways through the Col-orado high country, and skyrocketing metropolitan growth in Denver, Boulder, and other piedmont cities to propel dude ranch vacations in the Kawuneeche to new heights of popularity.[17]

Post–World War II baby boomers and their parents arrived at the gates of the Never Summer and neighboring tourist operations bearing expectations about the mythic West drawn from popular culture. Throughout the mid-twentieth century, a stampede of books, magazines, radio shows, films, and television programs schooled young and old alike in frontier nostalgia. Johnnie Holzwarth later recalled having spent many a frosty winter night reading Zane Grey novels with his father "by kerosene lamp." Indeed, Johnnie well understood the allure of the West served up by the likes of *Sunset,* Gene Autry, *True West,* John Wayne, *Gunsmoke,* and Bob Wills and the Texas Playboys. To give his guests a fuller taste of what they came for, Johnnie augmented his dude ranch's recreational lineup with Sunday rodeos and "starlit cookouts around crackling fires." The ranch's 1949 circular—addressed to potential visitors and printed on letterhead illustrated by a cowboy clinging to a bucking bronco—promised to ferry guests back to America's hallowed frontier past, where they could encounter wild nature. "Our location in Rocky Mountain National Park, with its scenic grandeur, is ideal," Johnnie assured the traveling public, "and we are experienced in anticipating the wants of our guests and knowing how to satisfy them. Dude ranching is our business—not a sideline." And so "the West as you 'dream it' is a *reality* at Holzwarth's!" Holzwarth went on to praise the ranch's location as "accessible by good roads and convenient to town, yet . . . within a half-hour by trail of country where it is not unusual to ride for days without seeing anyone but your own party." Holzwarth's, in short, was an "ideal spot for your 1949 vacation" because it was "comfortable, modern, informal"—a place that comfortably straddled the borderlands between the mythic West and the wilderness, the nation's settler-colonial past and its consumer-oriented present.[18]

By the early 1960s, much had changed in America, yet the Holzwarths continued to market their dude ranch using the same tried-and-true themes. A typical ad touted the Never Summer's "Majestic Scenery at [the] Headwaters of Colorado River," then extolled the former homestead as "One of Colorado's Oldest Dude Ranches" yet "Modern in Every Detail," with "excellent food" served "family style" and featuring "dairy products from the ranch." Offering the "best in saddle horses for novice or experienced rider[s]" alike, Holzwarth promised that visitors would not soon forget a ride on Rocky Mountain National Park's "many excellent trails." The Never Summer, in short, was "an ideal family ranch with true Western Hospitality" set in a "quiet, secluded location."[19]

An undated brochure for Holzwarths' reassured the leisure-loving parents of the atomic age by extending a warm western welcome to the little buckaroos who were proliferating in the American suburbs like

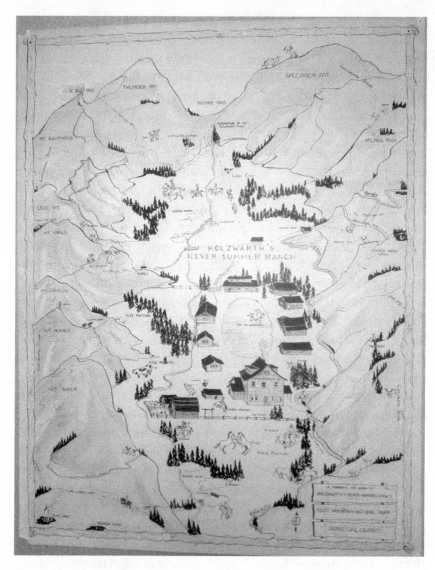

This undated hand-drawn poster of the Holzwarth's Never Summer Ranch depicts the entire Coyote Valley as a dude's paradise, replete with "Hoss Pasture," riding trails, and rodeo grounds. The only clear sign of the post–World War II boom in automobile tourism that sustained the Holzwarth family's guest operation is the winding course of Trail Ridge Road on the left side of the frame. MSF Neg. 10777, courtesy of the National Park Service.

summer wildflowers on the Rocky Mountain tundra. Young guests could have "lots of fun watching . . . the activities of regular ranch life." "Ranch pets from 'Trixie' the pony to 'Mamie' the calf" often performed "antics to the delight of youngsters," while the Never Summer's "equipped playground" tantalized even the fussiest junior cowpoke with "plenty of entertainment." With its "practical solid comfort in a romantic setting," Holzwarth's promised all the perks of "modern hotel service together with all the fun of a dude ranch!" A pair of photos captioned "Fun and Work for the Tenderfoot!" contrasted guests earnestly performing ranch chores with visitors clad in western wear enjoying a steak fry around the campfire. At the Never Summer Ranch, the brochure bragged, "Every One Is a Chef and a Star Performer."[20]

Promotional materials from the Coyote Valley's other dude ranches emphasized similar themes. The Phantom Valley Ranch, probably the Kawuneeche's second-largest dude ranch, cast the valley as an ideal place for visitors to encounter nature, experience the mythic West, revel in modern comfort, and enjoy family fun. As a "little boy," Irwin Beattie, the Phantom Valley's proprietor, had attended "the dedication of the park as a national playground" in 1915. Enraptured by Enos Mills's oratory, Beattie "dreamed the dream he one day would operate a lodge in the park." After turning his dream into a reality in 1941, Beattie distributed a classy eight-page color booklet to draw visitors. Beattie marketed Phantom Valley as a place where careworn Americans could "still find the friendly informality of the true West." Children, Beattie reassured anxious parents, would find the ranch a wonderland of wholesome, healthy diversion. "Even the tiniest tots" could ride on horseback under the expert supervision of a chief wrangler who had "been with us for years." The ranch boasted "lots of wildlife" for children "to enjoy," but Beattie also reassured potential guests that there was no danger of snakes or other "dangerous animals." And if parents wanted to enjoy a night out at Grand Lake, they could even hire one of the ranch's babysitters—"We only employ college girls," the booklet helpfully noted.[21]

Overshadowing babysitters, snakes, and wranglers in Phantom Valley's pitch, though, were the twin draws of national park nature and the mythic West of yesteryear. "Majestic snow-capped heights," Beattie's brochure exalted, "rise abruptly from this gentle valley where relaxing in the stimulating sunshine gives one a new lease on life." Whether on horseback or on foot, guests could ascend any of the "many fine trails"

of Rocky Mountain to reach a "beautifully timbered region of magnifi-
cent views." Interspersed between the booklet's text and photographs
were a hodgepodge of small, western-themed illustrations—cowboys,
spurs, Plains Indians, wagon wheels, fishing tackle, an old-fashioned
camping lantern, and so forth. The Kawuneeche, Beattie implied, offered a portal into the past. Thanks to federal "protection," he assured
potential visitors that "the wildlife and hundreds of varieties of wild
flowers are as plentiful as when the fur traders and the prospectors first
saw this mountain paradise." Guests at Phantom Valley could "enjoy an
unspoiled valley almost our own"—an unpeopled and pristine wilderness Eden that was nonetheless easy to reach via Colorado's "fine
highway system." As "one of the few remaining unspoiled beauty spots
in the country," the Kawuneeche loomed as a "pleasant, thrilling, [and]
almost perfect" destination.[22]

Beattie, the Holzwarths, and other dude ranchers marketed rustic vacations in the Colorado River headwaters by casting the ever-changing
Coyote Valley as three different places at once: a nostalgic frontier of
work and laborious play; a modern resort defined by convenience and
consumerism; and a prelapsarian wilderness. Though Phantom Valley,
the Never Summer, and their competitors sometimes fell short of the
nirvana their promotional materials depicted, many guests nonetheless
returned home with fond memories of their mountain vacations, as
shown by comments jotted down by twenty-first-century visitors on
their return to the Holzwarth historic site. For Diana Dufra Quantic, a
self-described "only child who loved the West," the weeks she spent at
the Never Summer in the summers of 1946 and 1947 were "like being
in heaven." Much as the booklet touting Phantom Valley's charms had
foretold, Linda Perry remembered Holzwarth's as "a wonderful place
for a child to dream dreams and enjoy nature." And Pamela Maughmer
still considered "staying at Never Summer Ranch" during her youth as
"the *best time of my life!*"[23]

Making a stay in the Kawuneeche's dude ranches live up to the
soaring expectations generated by materials promoting the valley required the brains and brawn of ranch proprietors, wranglers, babysitters,
cooks, and an array of other human workers. Fulfilling tourist longings
and sustaining tourist bodies also led dude ranch owners and employees
to build on and intensify the environmental changes of the settlement
era. Dude ranches drew lumber and firewood from local sources; for

"every building that is on this ranch," Johnnie Holzwarth bragged of the two dozen or so structures on his family's property, he had personally "cut the logs in the woods and saw-milled them." Supplying drinking water, disposing of waste and trash, and placing food on dining room tables imposed further impacts on the local environment. Some dude ranchers, for instance, supplied their dining room tables with local game; Holzwarth later swaggered that so many of his guests wanted venison for dinner that he had to hunt down as many as twenty-five deer each year.[24]

Perhaps the most intensive interactions between dude ranching and the Coyote Valley's ecosystems, however, stemmed from the tourist industry's dependence on horses and hay. Even as cattle became superfluous to the livelihoods of many of the valley's private landowners (Holzwarth sold off his herd in 1952), saddle and packhorses continued to play starring roles in the cowboy performances that ranch operators, wranglers, and dudes conspired to enact. Guests expected to pick from a wide selection of mounts; Holzwarth ordinarily had some seventy-five to one hundred horses on hand during the tourist season, but his herd occasionally swelled to 200 animals or more. Phantom Valley placed less emphasis on riding than the Never Summer, but Beattie nonetheless kept at least forty horses on his property each summer. With the rest of the Kawuneeche's private landowners presumably keeping several dozen additional steeds for themselves and their guests, the valley's horse population reached higher levels in the post–World War II era than at any point since Nuche removal.[25]

Feeding so many horses required dude ranchers to double down on their long-standing campaign to replace willow thickets and native grasslands with highly productive hay meadows. A 1950 real estate appraisal succinctly captured the connections linking tourism, horses, and hay at midcentury: "The principal land use in this area is for Dude Ranching, including grazing and the raising of hay for saddle and pack horses." Even though some ranch operators trucked or herded their horses to the lowlands of eastern Colorado or North Park to wait out the winter, the creatures nonetheless consumed large quantities of grass or hay throughout their warm-season stays in the Kawuneeche. Using new power machinery, private landowners altered the valley's riparian ecosystems in ways that would have made earlier homesteaders green with envy. In 1939, Johnnie Holzwarth started up a bulldozer and put it "to work clearing the Willows on the bottom land at his ranch intending to make a Hay Meadow." Aided by his dozer and a rented rotary plow, Holzwarth enlarged the Never Summer's cultivated meadows from just a few dozen acres to "200 acres of leveled, prime hayland." Landowners—guided by agricultural experts at the U.S. Soil Conservation Service and the Colorado Cooperative Extension—also deployed brawny gas-powered implements to fill in depressions, scrape off protuberances, and otherwise recontour their fields in order to maximize yields of exotic hay species. Conservation plans for the Pontiac Ranch, for instance, prescribed building "gradient ditches . . . to drain surface water," clearing out "invading willows," applying fertilizer, and "land smoothing." Such intensive cultivation methods seemed an unalloyed good to a horse lover like Johnnie Holzwarth: "When you've starved as many horses as I have in the early days," he explained, it came as a huge relief to "see this big hay growin'." Landowners like Holzwarth sensed that modern agriculture held the power to transform even this refractory landscape into a place of plenty.[26]

Catering to national park visitors, in short, led private landowners like Johnnie Holzwarth and Irwin Beattie to nip, tuck, and otherwise refashion the Kawuneeche environment to conform with the idylls they had promoted. At the same time, local people unwittingly played into the Park Service's hands even as they set the stage for the dilemmas Superintendent Contor and his colleagues confronted as they launched a campaign of their own to remake the settlement landscapes of the Coyote Valley floor.

Federalizing Settlement Landscapes

From the start, preservationists invariably saw private landholdings within or even adjacent to units of the national park system as so many Trojan horses lying in wait. Given the far-reaching legal privileges afforded to private property owners under American law, so-called inholdings stoked fears that commercial developers or even extractive industries might strike deep in the heart of the Coyote Valley and destroy Rocky Mountain's sacred wonderlands. "The development of private lands in any national park," Park Service director Arthur Demaray explained, "is contrary to the spirit and intent of the 1916 [National Park Service Organic] Act and to the extent that they exist the

National Park Service is unable to fulfill the obligation placed on it by Congress." It was thus "the policy of the Park Service," Demaray reminded his lieutenants at Estes Park in 1951, "to acquire the private lands as rapidly as funds are made available for that purpose."[27]

Demaray recognized that perhaps the most disruptive enclave of private land on Rocky Mountain's west side—the Grand Ditch—lay forever beyond the Park Service's reach. After decades of tight budgets, though, the director anticipated additional funding from Congress, some of which he intended to allocate for purchasing the cluster of old homesteads along the Colorado River headwaters. Alas, Demaray's prediction of congressional beneficence proved unduly optimistic. Several years passed before Congress finally appropriated the money the Park Service needed to strengthen its hold over the Kawuneeche. With the 1956 launch of Mission 66, an ambitious ten-year plan to rebuild and expand national park facilities worn thin by surging postwar tourism, though, the agency began to buy up all the land it could.[28]

The Park Service brought to the slow, halting process of land acquisition a long record of erasing the material vestiges of the Coyote Valley's human history. We have already seen how the agency's rangers, attorneys, and superintendents grappled with Harvey Johnson and Water Supply over the Grand Ditch "scar." During the Great Depression, Civilian Conservation Corps crews had pursued much the same ends at Lulu City, cleaning up the abandoned camp's "many old cabins, associated trash, [and] abandoned mining equipment." It should come as little surprise, then, that when the Park Service began to buy up the Kawuneeche's former homesteads in the late 1950s, the agency did all it could to eliminate signs of human lives and labors from these lands. Though the agency did convert some of the existing structures on certain tracts into employee housing, service buildings, and sites for historic interpretation, it razed the majority of dwellings, outbuildings, and fences that came into its possession.[29]

A combination of economic, legal, and administrative concerns led the Park Service to take aim at the physical remnants of American settlement. Preserving and maintaining jerry-rigged, weather-beaten structures took time and money, both of which were in short supply because of congressional parsimony. Park officials also feared that romantic relics of the Kawuneeche's frontier past would exert a magnetic pull on tourists—a worrisome proposition, since the defunct homesteads and

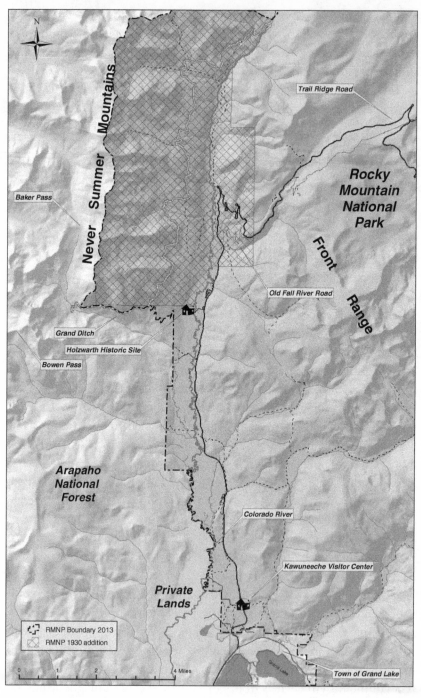

Park expansion, 1930–2013. Courtesy of the National Park Service.

guest operations dotting the valley bristled with dangers, including live electrical wires, faulty floors, unsound ceilings, and dangerous driveway intersections with Trail Ridge Road. By threatening tourists with harm, the historic buildings of the Colorado River headwaters also exposed the government to liability. Leveling these architectural artifacts seemed prudent in its own right, but it also eliminated the need to repair and keep up plumbing, electrical systems, roads, and all the other infrastructural elements that had enabled dude ranches to advertise (and recreational home owners to enjoy) cutting-edge comforts in the high country.[30]

But before managers at Rocky Mountain could demolish what remained of the Kawuneeche's settlement landscapes, they first had to secure title to these parcels. Two main problems slowed their progress. The first was the rapid postwar rise in land prices. A 1959 appraisal of Irwin Beattie's Phantom Valley Ranch attributed this "intrinsic and permanent trend toward increasing values" in the Kawuneeche to a veritable laundry list of factors: "the scenic attributes" of the Colorado River headwaters, rising "sales of fishing and hunting licenses in conjunction with shorter working hours," "the advent of new lakes" (a reference to Lake Granby and Shadow Mountain Reservoir, two U.S. Bureau of Reclamation water storage projects downstream from Grand Lake), "the ever-growing tendencies for mountain vacations," and the development of "faster modes of transportation" that rendered the valley "readily accessible to the fast growing metropolitan areas" of Colorado's Front Range. As the Colorado high country morphed into what historian William Philpott aptly calls "Vacationland," the Park Service struggled to convince Congress to foot the bill for buying out the Kawuneeche's private landowners.[31]

The reluctance of some residents to part with their property posed a second and even thornier problem. A case in point was Johnnie Holzwarth, who proposed to sell the government 614 acres of his 714 acres of land in 1963 in exchange for $810,000 and permission from the Park Service to continue living on the remaining one hundred acres of his family's land until his death. Regional Director George Baggley nixed this overture: "It seems obvious that we cannot give Mr. Holzwarth the assurance he desires," Baggley huffed, "nor can we agree to negotiate on his terms." Johnnie nonetheless remained "friendly" toward Rocky Mountain superintendent Allyn Hanks. The irascible dude rancher, however, also warned Hanks that he would seek "a public hearing on any proposal to enlarge the Park in that vicinity." In the ensuing standoff, Holzwarth emerged as the clear winner; safe in the knowledge that his land was becoming more valuable with every passing season, he continued to accommodate paying guests until the Park Service ponied up.[32]

Thereafter, Holzwarth and the Park Service eyed each other like a couple of wary poker players maneuvering for advantage. Testifying before Congress, an agency official complained that the Holzwarths recently had made "developments of a character not in keeping with the Mission 66 program of the National Park Service." Johnnie countered that he and his family had always strived "to be in keeping with the National Park building and operation policies," even though no law compelled them to do so. An "anonymous" memorandum to Rocky Mountain's staff that could only have come from Johnnie griped about "oppressive" park regulations that prevented local landowners from enjoying "freedom on our own private property." Any attempt by park officials to impose still more "control," Holzwarth warned, "would limit our way of profit and progress." Lurking in Holzwarth's antigovernment rhetoric lay an unmistakable threat: If the Park Service failed to up the ante, Johnnie would not hesitate to walk away from the table.[33]

The Park Service responded by trying to stay in the game even as the stakes rose. Developers subsequently offered Holzwarth more than $1 million for his property, but he turned them down flat. "Those realtors," Johnnie later recounted to the *Denver Post,* "tried to get me to consider the money-making aspects of the place, but I hadn't spent most of my life putting the place together just to see it pieced out again." Holzwarth now made a consequential change in tactics: instead of demonizing the Park Service as Big Brother, he began to curry favor from Colorado's burgeoning environmental movement. This emerging constituency, Johnny astutely calculated, now had the clout to pressure Congress into allotting additional funds to Rocky Mountain; they could also temporarily stake the federal government from their own coffers. "I was no conservationist when I first started," Johnnie confessed. "But as time went on," the one-time trapper, hunter, rancher, and sawmill operator claimed, "I realized what I had and how nature works things." As environmentalism reached its zenith in the early 1970s, Johnnie took pains to flatter the Park Service as the only rightful heir to the

legacy of private conservation he and his family had forged over the preceding half century.[34]

No one knows whether Holzwarth's sweet talk was just a bluff, but
his stratagem indeed paved the way for federal bureaucrats and lawmakers to double down. In 1972, the Park Service tendered the dude
rancher a deal he could not refuse: $750,000 for 135 acres of the Holz-
warth spread. Because this purchase still left Johnnie holding 639 acres
of prime bottomland, the Kawuneeche, as the *Post* explained, stood
poised "at a crossroads between development and a return to its natural
state. If the National Park Service can muster the funds, the valley at
the foot of the snowy, spectacular Never Summer Mountains will have
the curtain closed on its history as a resort area." If the agency fell
short, by contrast, the valley stood poised to go the way of so many
other old settlement landscapes in Colorado's burgeoning recreational
hinterlands, which developers were methodically carving up into so
many strip malls and subdivisions.[35]

Living History—and Erasing It

With the help of a timely loan from a national environmental group,
the Nature Conservancy, the Park Service purchased Holzwarth's remaining property for $1.625 million. As Johnnie Holzwarth "signed
away his Never Summer Ranch" in 1974, tears cascaded down the gruff
rancher's weather-beaten cheeks—an emotional response that out-
wardly echoed the sorrowful farewells that busted-out homesteaders,
failed miners, and northeastern Nuche had bade to the Coyote Valley
during the preceding century. In financial terms, though, Holzwarth
was walking away a big winner, having grossed $2.375 million for his
holdings. Nearly sixty years after Prohibition impelled Papa Holzwarth
to pursue his cowboy dreams in the Colorado River headwaters, the last
large tract of private land in the Kawuneeche returned to the public domain. At long last, the Park Service held property rights to the homestead
on which Johnnie and his family had struggled to get by and the dude
ranch that the Holzwarths had marketed as a modern gateway into unspoiled nature and the mythic West. Translating legal ownership into
practical control over the newest corner of Rocky Mountain, though,
would prove much trickier than federal officials had imagined.[36]

Even before the deal was complete, Superintendent Roger Contor was laying plans to incorporate the Holzwarth place into the national park. In a 1972 memo, Contor voiced a crucial distinction that would go on to shape most every element of Park Service efforts to transform landscapes thoroughly refashioned by settlement and tourism into places worthy of inclusion in one of the crown jewels of the nation's protected lands. "Care must be taken," Rocky Mountain's chief counseled, "to see that those structures with truly significant history be retained." What Contor dismissed as "marginal relics," by contrast, must "be disposed of to allow for the reclamation of the natural, prime resource scene." Contor never articulated what criteria distinguished "structures with truly significant history" from "marginal relics." Yet his bifurcated view of these material legacies of the Coyote Valley's past nonetheless led park staff to painstakingly preserve and restore some of the Holzwarths' improvements while casually obliterating others.[37]

Contor saw no reason why the Park Service should go to the trouble of saving structures associated with the Kawuneeche's long history as a tourist destination. And so within a year of closing on the second phase of the Holzwarth deal, crews leveled the dude ranch complex the Holzwarths had opened near the Fall River Road in 1929. An altogether different fate awaited the buildings clustering on the family's original homestead, which had been expanded during the 1920s into the Holzwarth Trout Lodge. Contor deemed it "perfectly acceptable" to accede to Johnnie's wishes by rehabilitating these structures to house a "Living History" site that would commemorate the travails endured by the Holzwarths and other early settlers. Neither Contor nor Holzwarth appeared to notice a key irony of destroying the Never Summer Ranch while preserving the Holzwarth homestead: Johnnie's old property was a lousy place to commemorate homesteading—the Holzwarths, after all, had come to the Kawuneeche *after* Rocky Mountain's establishment and they almost certainly would have gone bankrupt if not for the throngs of automobile visitors they began to accommodate in 1920—but an ideal site for interpreting the historical and ecological significance of dude ranching and national park tourism.[38]

The museum at the renovated homestead opened to visitors in June 1974. Two volunteers moved into the lodge's cabins and began to lead two-hour-long guided tours clad in what passed for period attire. Visitors could peruse Holzwarth family photo albums, enjoy tape record-

The interior of a cabin on the Holzwarth Living History Museum site contained rustic furniture, trophy heads prepared by John Holzwarth Sr., and portraits of Mama and Papa Holzwarth. August 1976, MSF Neg. 4716, courtesy of the National Park Service.

ings "of Johnnie's salty recollections," and snack on sourdough bread baked in an old oven. More than a thousand tourists visited the site that first summer—a mere trickle compared to the 10,849 who came in 1977. Not far away, the meadows grubbed out, cleared, planted, and mowed by the Holzwarths and their hired hands continued to produce hay. Determined to mow the meadows, costumed interpreters tried to hitch up a pair of Holzwarth's horses to old haying equipment bought from the rancher. The volunteers, though, lacked Johnnie's way with horses. Spooked, the creatures "ran away with the equipment and handler." Administrators, having elected to suspend the horsepowered haying "project . . . as hazardous to handler and stock," arranged for a Grand Lake rancher "to fertilize, irrigate, cut and bale the hay" on the Holzwarth place in exchange for 40 percent of the harvest. Until the Park Service severed this agreement in 1984, the Holzwarth homestead remained a "living history" site in two distinct senses: both a productive landscape, and a site where tourists were supposed to experience the past instead of just reading about it.[39]

Critics scolded the Park Service for inaccurately portraying homesteading as a distant and picturesque precursor to later twentieth-century developments rather than a contemporaneous complement to federal preservation and national park tourism. In the 1980s, Rocky Mountain officials responded by retooling interpretive programs at Holzwarth's to emphasize the family's long-running reign as the Kawuneeche's most successful dude ranchers. As the Park Service's discomfort with the historical significance of tourism wavered, administrators announced a new "objective" for the meadows Johnnie had done his darnedest to establish: instead of allowing hay production to continue on these lands, park staff signaled their goal of "returning much of the valley to more natural conditions." Larry Reed, Rocky Mountain's West Unit manager, predicted that the riparian lands of the old Holzwarth place would soon revert "to beaver ponds" once they were left alone Reed and other Park Service officials expected that beavers and other active forces would swiftly reclaim Holzwarth's hay fields and restore them—if not to a state of nature, then at least to what Reed frankly called "more natural conditions."[40]

In the 1980s, however, it already was becoming evident to informed observers that American settlement, federal preservation, and automobile-oriented tourism had fundamentally transformed the riparian ecology of the Coyote Valley. Reed expected busy rodents to turn back the clock to some unspecified historical baseline. Yet even as the Park Service was consolidating its control over the settlement landscapes of the Kawuneeche bottomlands, the valley's once-thriving beaver colonies were in dire straits.

Making Wilderness

Superintendent Contor's decision to clear most structures from freshly purchased tracts while turning one portion of the Holzwarth property into a dynamic monument to pioneer fortitude reflected the Park Service's ongoing struggle with a timeworn and nettlesome contradiction. Building support for park expansion and land acquisition required the agency to cast the Kawuneeche as simultaneously untouched and endangered—sufficiently intact and pleasing to the eye that it could merit inclusion within Rocky Mountain, yet also so threatened with ruination that it demanded immediate action. This way of thinking left little room for Park Service officials or park visitors to engage the Coyote Valley's rich and tumultuous human past in any meaningful way.

Park Service employees had repeatedly erased vestiges of the Kawuneeche's settlement history from the 1930s onward. The ascendance of wilderness ideals in the 1960s and 1970s made it even harder for Park Service managers to acknowledge that the Coyote Valley occupied a peculiar borderland where homesteading, tourism, and scenic preservation had overlapped and intermingled. Rocky Mountain's 1976 *Final Master Plan* epitomized a consequential shift in the metaphors guiding park policies. Whereas Enos Mills and his collaborators in the 1910s had hailed the national park as "America's playground," the rise of environmentalism inspired Park Service planners to reimagine the park as a place where, as the *Plan* put it, "man's impact must be minimized and controlled."[41]

Four years earlier, as Superintendent Roger Contor was mulling over how best to integrate Holzwarth's into Rocky Mountain, he noted in passing that the Coyote Valley was undergoing what he called a "return to the pristine." The "return" that Contor found so encouraging extended from trail system reforms to fisheries restoration and a proposal to include much of the Kawuneeche backcountry within a new federal wilderness area. Contor failed, however, to grasp the difficulties the Park Service would face when it attempted to re-create primeval conditions in landscapes and ecosystems transmuted by Nuche removal, agricultural settlement, federal preservation, mass tourism, and other historical processes. In the years to come, the "return to the pristine" that Contor had envisioned as the Kawuneeche's destiny would succumb to the combined forces of political resistance and ecological complexity.[42]

Already by the 1970s, an important distinction had emerged between Rocky Mountain's front country, which was oriented around the needs of automobile tourists, and its backcountry, where narrow, expertly designed footpaths traced faint contrails across a majestic and unpeopled wilderness. Rocky Mountain's Mission 66 plan had touted the need for "improved circulation of the visitors to points of outstanding scenic or scientific interest away from the roadways." Yet despite the construction of new trails and trailheads in the Kawuneeche, the Backpacking

Committee appointed in the early 1960s by Superintendent Novak blasted Rocky Mountain's trail network as "poorly located and . . . difficult to travel and maintain." More important, the committee signaled a newfound resolve to prevent the park's front country from encroaching on its backcountry. "New trail construction in an unmodified wilderness," it warned, "will not be considered a solution for relieving visitor congestion in already modified wilderness." To hold the line against "visitor congestion," the Backpacking Committee successfully argued that new trails in the backcountry should be narrower (eighteen inches across, as opposed to the thirty-six-inch standard the Park Service had used at Rocky Mountain since the 1920s). Slimmer trails were cheaper to build and had a smaller environmental impact. No less important, they effectively barred equestrian travel on new backcountry routes. Together with the decline of dude ranching, the removal of concessionaires' stables from inside park boundaries, and the growing popularity of hiking, this move privileged "foot trail use and back-country use" over horse travel. As the valley became a backpackers' paradise, the three-century reign of equestrianism in the Colorado River headwaters drew to an unceremonious close.[43]

An abortive attempt to designate much of Rocky Mountain a federally protected wilderness area, meanwhile, revealed that many Coloradans questioned Contor's vision of a "return to the pristine." In 1973, Contor (acting on instructions from his superiors) proposed that Congress include 238,000 acres of Rocky Mountain in the National Wilderness Preservation System—roughly 91 percent of the national park, including most of the Coyote Valley. But hearings in early 1974 exposed widespread public discontent. Citizens responded to the proposal by expressing fears that wilderness designation would limit access to the national park and hurt local residents whose livelihoods relied on tourism. Despite ardent support from environmentalists, backpackers, and some inhabitants of Grand and Larimer Counties, the Park Service decided not to pursue wilderness designation—a decision that reflected the agency's aversion to political controversy rather than any philosophical misgivings about "wilderness" as a guiding vision for management.[44]

Human beings, however, were hardly the only organisms who failed to comply with Contor's desire to turn back the clock to presettlement conditions. Heroic but only partially successful campaigns to restore native fish to the Colorado River watershed comprised a third and final

major plank in the agency's efforts to engineer a "return to a pristine."
During Rocky Mountain's early years, park rangers, local civic groups,
and state officials sought to conjure plentiful supplies of spirited trout
by planting the Kawuneeche's streams and lakes with hatchery-raised
rainbow trout, brook trout, and "native trout" (a term managers used
promiscuously in reference to several distinct subspecies of cutthroat
trout).[45]

The utilitarian assumptions underlying Rocky Mountain's stocking
program, however, came under fire starting in the late 1920s. A 1929
Park Service directive advised superintendents to leave at least some previously fish-free lakes and streams in their natural condition while re-
fraining from introducing new species to waters already possessing
breeding populations of fish. In 1936, Park Service director Arno Cammerer announced a new system-wide policy: "To bring all fish cultural
activities in the national parks and monuments within the general
policies applying to all other forms of animal life," Cammerer banned
further "introductions of exotic species of fish . . . in national park or
monument waters now containing only native species," and ordered
superintendents to encourage native species "in waters where native and
exotic species now exist."[46]

Sport angling, nonetheless remained the driving force in fisheries
management at Rocky Mountain in the ensuing decades. The 1962
Inter-Agency Lake Survey, for instance, championed "the objective of
providing for recreational angling while protecting basic Park fishery
resources," and Rocky Mountain's "Long Range Fishery Management
Plan" of 1965 celebrated the park's "fishery resources" as "significant for
the recreational opportunities they provide anglers to fish for wild trout
in the midst of the park's scenic surroundings."[47]

The 1965 plan's vague invocation of "wild trout"—as opposed to the
more precise nomenclature of "native" and "exotic" fish that Cammerer
had used in 1936—betrayed dawning confusion at Rocky Mountain
about which creatures counted as "native" and where. Decades of misguided and inconsistent ways of thinking about and manipulating
trout set the stage for environmental and genetic changes that researchers are just beginning to understand. Starting in 1938, the Park
Service insisted on stocking only "native trout" at Rocky Mountain.
Alas, the vast majority of the hatchery-raised fish planted in the park's
waters were Yellowstone cutthroats instead of greenback or Colorado

River cutthroats (subspecies indigenous to the eastern and western sides of the Continental Divide, respectively). Even in the 1940s, scientists and administrators expressed concern about this practice. Yet the closure of the Grand Lake hatchery in the early years of that decade had deprived the Park Service of its only source of Colorado River cutthroat hatchlings. Not until 1954 would the agency stop releasing Yellowstone-raised cutthroats in Rocky Mountain. No one knows, though, whether the Park Service's new Colorado supplier was raising Colorado River cutthroats, some other cutthroat subspecies, or hybrids thereof. Such confusion led the 1965 fisheries plan to confess that "modification of the aquatic environment and fish populations" at the park "has been so extensive that it is now difficult to determine the original composition and distribution of native fishes." Three decades after Cammerer's 1936 memo had expressed confidence in the power of research to guide efforts to "restor[e] . . . streams or lakes to their natural condition" and rehabilitate each "native species to its normal status," Rocky Mountain's fisheries managers were discovering that they lacked the means to reconstruct the genetic identities and ecological relationships that prevailed in the Colorado River headwaters prior to Nuche removal.[48]

The realization that there was no easy way to restore the park's aquatic ecosystems led Park Service officials to grope toward what expert Chris Kennedy of the U.S. Fish and Wildlife Service calls a "major shift in fisheries management" at Rocky Mountain: the 1969 declaration of a moratorium that effectively required that fish only be stocked into park waters where they were known to be indigenous. Where trout were concerned, though, fashioning a "return to the pristine" remained a daunting task even after the Park Service made the moratorium permanent in 1976. As Superintendent Contor himself would acknowledge that year in the park's aquatic resources management and action report, nonnative fish, "primarily brook trout," had "fill[ed] the normal biological carrying capacities of the waters" in virtually every stretch of Rocky Mountain.[49]

Taken together, the slow progress of fisheries restoration, the failure of wilderness designation, and the rise of the backpacker as Rocky Mountain's ideal backcountry visitor might have imparted an important lesson to Contor and his contemporaries: it was almost always easier to redraw the concepts and categories people carried around in their heads than it was to translate these shifting and sometimes contradictory ideas into material realities.

Troubled Waters

Two sets of Coyote Valley water stories—one pivoting on the challenges bedeviling the return of Colorado River cutthroat trout to their indigenous waters, the other involving the latest round of conflict between the Park Service and Water Supply—demonstrate how Rocky Mountain officials have grappled since the mid-1970s to address the irrepressible legacies of social and environmental change in the Coyote Valley. While many visitors, local residents, and Park Service officials continue to uphold Contor's "return to the pristine" at Rocky Mountain as a worthy objective or even a guiding vision, the recent histories of the Grand Ditch and native trout restoration lay bear the chimerical nature of Contor's quest.

The case of the Grand Ditch shows how the legacies of settler colonialism and conservation continue to act on the Kawuneeche environment. The 1930 Never Summer addition effectively gave Water Supply carte blanche over the diversion canal and its right-of-way. By the 1970s, though, the company Harvey Johnson had shepherded into the modern era seemed more responsive to pleas from dude ranchers, tourists, and the Park Service that it remediate the ecological and aesthetic damage the Grand Ditch inflicted on the ecosystems below. Since that time, however, the diversion canal has continued to sap water tables on the valley floor while periodically exposing the valley landscape to acute threats.

The largest of several major breaches to the canal opened above Lulu City in late May 2003 when ice dams forced water over the ditch's banks. Within minutes, raging torrents poured through the ditch's downhill bank and slashed a gully 167 feet across and 60 feet deep through a steep forest of "old growth lodgepole and spruce-fir." An estimated 48,000 to 60,000 cubic yards of rock and mud (enough to submerge an acre of land beneath ten yards of debris) reached the Colorado River. After the Park Service sued Water Supply, the two organizations reached an out-of-court settlement in 2008 by which the ditch company pledged $9 million in damages to Rocky Mountain. Park officials have used this money to fund a sweeping restoration program in the area affected by the breach, as well as a number of scientific studies to document the Grand Ditch's effects on the lands and waters below.[50]

Even as the Park Service was attempting to come to terms with the Grand Ditch's ongoing impact on the Coyote Valley, fisheries managers were continuing to butt up against the changes that decades of stocking had brought to the aquatic habitats of the Upper Colorado. In 1979, the Park Service initiated a plan to eliminate nonnative fish from the Kawuneeche and restock its waters with Colorado River cutthroats. Timber Lake and Timber Creek were the first sites targeted. After poisoning "non-native cutthroats and cutthroat x rainbow hybrids" there, the Park Service proceeded to introduce 1,080 "fry obtained from a pure strain of Colorado River cutthroat." Ironically, these genetically "pure" fish came from heavily polluted Clinton Gulch Reservoir at the Climax Mining Company's ore-processing operation near Leadville. Before long, though, Rocky Mountain officials and their collaborators had to turn to an even more unlikely source of Colorado River cutthroats: the Williamson Lakes in the High Sierra. Two helicopters and an airplane airlifted descendants of fish introduced to California from the Colorado River watershed decades earlier back to Bench and Ptarmigan Lakes in the Kawuneeche.[51]

Reagan-era budget cuts, though, hit the Park Service hard. During the lean years of the late 1980s and 1990s, fisheries scientists overcame tight federal budgets to make some notable gains. Most important, they discovered a breeding population of Colorado River cutthroats in Lake Nanita on the eastern slope of the Never Summers that seemed genetically pure. They also opened a hatchery to provide a more reliable and less expensive source of Colorado River cutthroats for restocking the Colorado River headwaters. New cooperative efforts launched in the late 1990s built on these earlier achievements, pooling funds from multiple state and federal agencies to wage a coordinated restoration campaign through much of the Colorado River cutthroat's original habitat in Colorado, Wyoming, and Utah.[52]

Though cooperative efforts have managed to eliminate brook trout and other exotic fish from parts of the Coyote Valley, it is still too early to know whether the Park Service and its partners will succeed at bringing Colorado River cutthroats back to their ancestral waters. As of 2005, the subspecies occupied just 10 percent of its historic habitat in the valley. Of the Kawuneeche's fourteen isolated populations of Colorado River cutthroats, ten had remained more or less intact since the nineteenth century, while four are believed to have been restored since the 1970s. Genetic studies on some of the latter populations, however, have recently cast a pall over the park's fisheries. Samples of DNA taken from trout in the Bench Lake and Ptarmigan Creek reintroduction sites high in the Kawuneeche strongly suggest that these fish are hybrids of Colorado River cutthroats airlifted to Colorado from the Sierra Nevadas, and Yellowstone cutthroats that survived the poisons used by fisheries experts to prepare these waters for the release of "native" fish. Some experts now doubt whether the indigenous trout of the Coyote Valley can elude extinction, since remaining populations of the subspecies are small and almost entirely confined to remote, disconnected habitats scattered throughout the high mountains.[53]

⊠ ⊠ ⊠

In retrospect, the National Park Service's efforts to achieve greater control over the Kawuneeche between the Never Summer addition and the early twenty-first century have yielded undeniable benefits. By buying up inholdings and expanding Rocky Mountain, the agency staved off both the second-home subdivisions and crass commercial developments that blanket many national park gateway regions. The Park Service also made the Colorado River headwaters accessible to more of the park-going public by extending trail networks and improving roads and other facilities. In the wake of Mission 66, the agency even began to address tourism's deleterious effects on the valley environment—designing trails for hikers instead of riders, razing old dude ranches, and reorienting the goal of fisheries management from entertaining sport anglers to reestablishing native trout. In short, no one can reasonably argue that the Kawuneeche's landscapes and ecosystems would have fared better if the Park Service had never determined to buy out private landholders after the Never Summer addition of 1930. Yet it is equally important to acknowledge that despite long-running, well-intentioned efforts to reestablish "natural conditions," and restore the Colorado River headwaters to their "pristine" state, the Coyote Valley's dynamism and complexity repeatedly thwarted the Park Service's best-laid plans.[54]

THE TRAGEDY OF THE WILLOWS

PRESENT-DAY VISITORS to the Coyote Valley might easily overlook an emergent crisis hidden in plain sight. Willows, which remain vigorous in most other stretches of the Mountain West, have declined within Rocky Mountain National Park since the 1980s. Thousands of the shrubs have died, and many of the rest are barely holding on. The deterioration of the park's willow thickets is depriving other organisms of energy, nutrients, and habitat. Beavers have been hit especially hard. At the dawn of World War II, when ranches and resorts still dominated the Kawuneeche Valley floor, a census by researcher Fred Packard estimated that more than 600 beavers inhabited Rocky Mountain's west side. In recent decades, beavers have vigorously reclaimed former habitats ranging from the slopes of Colorado's busiest ski areas to the old industrial corridor of Denver's Central Platte Valley. Today, though, not a single active colony remains in the protected lands of the Colorado River headwaters.[1]

The Coyote Valley's willows and beavers had together endured more than ten millennia of dramatic environmental and social change, outlasting the fur trade, the mineral rush, the homesteading boom, and the rise of automobile-oriented tourism. In the twenty-first century, however, the unprecedented collapse of willow and beaver populations is threatening to turn the valley into an altogether different place—one lacking any known precedent in the valley's deep history. Change, of course, is inherent to natural systems. But willow die-off and beaver abandonment jeopardize fundamental processes and relationships that have continuously made and remade the Colorado River headwaters since the end of the last Ice Age.

What is causing this crisis? The main culprits are elk and moose, rapidly growing populations of which began to overbrowse the valley's willow thickets in the 1970s, thus denying beavers the food and building material they need. The proliferation of large ungulates resulted, in turn, from the interplay of human actions and ecological dynamics during the twentieth century on scales ranging from the local to the national, and in venues that ranged from the Kawuneeche to the Greater Yellowstone Ecosystem to the halls of Congress. Predator eradication, elk reintroduction, moose introduction, the incorporation of settlement landscapes into Rocky Mountain, misguided wildlife management policies, water diversion, and global climate change have each played an essential role in willow die-off and beaver abandonment. Because the elk and vegetation management plan instituted by the Park Service in 2007 effectively addressed only some of these factors, the fate of the beavers, willows, and the riparian ecosystems that these organisms together support remains very much up for grabs at the dawn of Rocky Mountain National Park's second century.

Riparian Ecologies

Three ecological concepts—mutualism, ecosystem engineering, and trophic cascades—help us to understand the ecological causes and consequences of the beaver-willow crisis. Scientists consider two species to be mutualistic if interactions between them consistently benefit both. E. O. Wilson defines mutualism as a relationship of "intimate coexistence"—an elegant summary of the close interactions between beavers and willows that have undergirded the riparian ecology of the Kawuneeche since the end of the last Ice Age. The branches and leaves of willows have long nourished beavers and provided them with raw materials for construction. Beavers, in turn, have improved willow habitat through their work as ecosystem engineers in the riparian zone.[2]

A landmark 1994 study describes ecosystem engineers as "organisms that directly or indirectly modulate the availability of resources to other species." Natural scientists have long viewed beavers as archetypal ecosystem engineers because they "modify, maintain and create habitats."

Enos Mills's 1909 essay, "The Beaver and His Works," detailed the impact of these industrious rodents on the Coyote Valley. Having made "an extensive examination of some old beaver-works" in the Colorado River headwaters, Mills interpreted the Kawuneeche wetlands as material monuments to the beaver's skill and significance. Beaver dams, he explained, exerted a "decided influence on the flow of the water." These impoundments could "check and delay so much flood-water that floods are diminished in volume," resulting in "more even stream-flow at all times." Beaver ponds also increased sediment deposition. Because "the cream of the earth, that otherwise would be washed away and lost" instead accumulated behind beaver dams, willows found rich soil to colonize. Once "trash and mud" piled up, Mills observed, it was soon "covered with a mass of soil." On this rich foundation "shrubs of willow" would begin to grow, forming within just "a few years . . . a strong, earthy, willow-covered dam." Scientists have since confirmed and elaborated on Mills's core claim, showing how the ecological engineering of beavers has combined with beaver-willow mutualism to structure the hydrology, riparian ecology, and even the geomorphology of the Greater Rocky Mountain National Park Ecosystem.[3]

A third and final ecological concept, the trophic cascade, sheds further light on the mechanisms driving willow decline and beaver depopulation. Marine biologist Robert Paine first coined the term in 1980, but the roots of this way of thinking about relationships between predators, herbivores, and plants reach back to Aldo Leopold's famous—and largely apocryphal—epiphany about the tragic impact of wolf eradication on the deer herds of Arizona's Kaibab Plateau. A basic biological question shaped the emergence of the trophic cascade concept: Why is so much of the earth green? Why, in other words, do herbivores almost always stop short of completely denuding all available vegetation? Ecologists Nelson Hairston, Frederick Smith, and Lawrence Slobodkin offered a simple solution to this conundrum in an enormously influential 1960 article: herbivore populations, they hypothesized, were limited not by the amount of energy that vegetative communities could access, but instead by predation. Paine and other ecologists subsequently built on the so-called green-world hypothesis of Hairston, Smith, and Slobodkin by documenting how the growth and demise of predator populations affected herbivores and the plants they consumed.[4]

Beaver dams have shaped the hydrology and ecology of the Coyote Valley for many thousands of years. "Fishing in the Beaver Dams of the Colorado River," undated photograph, MSF Neg. 2816, Alb. 4014, courtesy of the National Park Service.

Three points about trophic cascades are especially important for understanding willow die-off and beaver depopulation in the Coyote Valley. First, trophic cascades link plants, herbivores, and predators, each of which occupies a distinct level within a food web. Paine's purposeful use of the term "cascade" highlights a second key attribute: The effects of shifting predator populations do not simply ramify through lower trophic levels. Instead, they flow with remarkable force to yield unpredictable, nonlinear effects. Last but hardly least, trophic cascades connect predators and prey not just through material exchanges of energy (as when a wolf eats an elk calf) but also through behavioral interactions that many ecologists and conservation biologists call "ecologies of fear." Prey species are afraid of getting eaten, and this fear changes how they behave. Since herbivores spend most of their waking hours grazing or browsing, the resulting behavioral shifts translate into altered herbivory (plant eating). When grizzly bears are present, for instance, moose in Wyoming seem to spend less time chomping on willow and other plants and more time watching for danger. Wolves in the Northern Rockies seem to exert similar influences on elk, especially where natural features block the ungulates' ability to flee to safer ground. Elk respond to wolves not only by staying on the move and devoting proportionally more time watching for danger but also by congregating in smaller groups and avoiding open terrain where wolves can most easily spot and stalk them.[5]

Armed with an understanding of willow-beaver mutualism, the crucial role beavers play as ecosystem engineers, and the trophic cascade concept, we can now consider the origins and evolution of the riparian ecosystems of the Colorado River headwaters.

From Indigenous Ecologies to American Conservation

Scientists sometimes take history for granted. In the case of trophic cascade research, though, this approach can dangerously oversimplify how we make sense of ecological dynamics in the past, present, and even the future. In the North American West, the tales scientists tell about trophic cascades typically hinge on just three species: a plant (either willow or aspen), an herbivore (with elk the prime antagonists), and a predator (usually the gray wolf, hero of many bold dreams about the "rewilding" of western places). For hundreds or even thousands of years, the story goes, a rough balance—what many ecologists would call a steady state— prevailed between wolves, elk, and the plants on which elk feed. The American conquest of native peoples, though, was soon followed by the rapid and remarkably thorough eradication of apex predators, which disrupted the relatively stable and harmonious set of interrelationships that had previously prevailed. Historically, wolves, bears, and mountain lions had kept populations of elk and other ungulates in check. But once settlers and their federal allies extirpated these and other meat eaters, large ungulates proliferated, with disastrous consequences for aspens and willows. The case of the Colorado River headwaters, though, demonstrates the pressing need for a more nuanced interpretation of trophic cascades and their history—one that does fuller justice to the complexities of ecological, political, and cultural change during the last century.

The ecological regimes that prevailed under the Nuche and their Mountain Tradition forebears offer a logical starting place. Upon inhabiting the Colorado River headwaters more than 13,000 years ago, native peoples effectively joined the Greater Rocky Mountain National Park Ecosystem's predator guild. Together with wolves, grizzlies, and mountain lions, First Peoples' hunters limited the growth of the area's ungulate herds while sustaining an ecology of fear. (As for the coyotes of the Coyote Valley, they presumably played the role of mesopredators— preyed upon by wolves, but prolific hunters of small mammals and occasional killers of larger ungulates including elk.) For millennia, thriving willow thickets supported healthy beaver colonies. The busy rodents returned the favor by engineering wetlands ideally suited for willows. Beaver-willow mutualism produced excellent habitat for an array of insects and birds; it also sustained aquatic ecosystems by preventing erosion, modulating stream flow, and providing shade for creatures ranging from tiny invertebrates to Colorado River cutthroat trout.[6]

The invasion of American fur trappers in the nineteenth century shook up the Coyote Valley's riparian ecosystems. Beaver populations along the Colorado River headwaters dropped precipitously by the 1830s, though little evidence documents the broader ecological impacts of their decline in the Kawuneeche. After U.S. troops forced the northeastern Nuche out of Colorado, American miners, hunters, ranchers, homesteaders, and tourists poured into the void that ethnic cleansing had opened. Like the Nuche, these newcomers kept dogs and horses; they also introduced other domesticated creatures to the Kawuneeche, including cattle, cats, and poultry. In the course of establishing novel agricultural ecosystems, homesteaders cut down lodgepoles and aspens, turned dozens of acres of willow thickets into meadows of tame hay, and otherwise changed the headwaters environment. Settlers also tried to eliminate competition from other members of the region's predator guild, most notably via wolf bounty programs supported by local governments, stockmen's associations, and the state of Colorado. Last but hardly least, the newcomers pushed elk to the brink of extinction, hunting the animals for food, sport, and sale, while building roads, ranches, towns, and other settlement features that fragmented many of Colorado's richest elk habitats.[7]

"Elk," the *Routt County Sentinel* lamented in 1907, "are practically exterminated as far as Colorado is concerned." Three years later, the state's once prodigious herds had diminished to just "10 small bands," numbering perhaps 500 to 1,000 animals in all, including a handful around Estes Park and roughly fifty head in and around Middle Park. If any elk remained in the Coyote Valley, which is far from certain, they would have faced stiff competition for browse from the settlers' cattle and horses. The ecology of fear would have persisted nonetheless, with elk moving frequently and exercising constant vigilance to avoid human hunters and their domesticated canines.[8]

Most informed observers reasoned that it was just a matter of time before Coloradans killed off the large ungulates. "The wild elk in the mountains," one journalist lamented, "have little chance for escape from extermination." In the nick of time, though, American conservationists rallied to save the elk. Colorado state game officials enacted a closed hunting season on the majestic creatures in 1913, a prohibition they would not lift until 1929. Enos Mills and other citizens concerned with the plight of Colorado's elk also lobbied the federal government to establish game reserves in the state, including Rocky Mountain National Park, which banned hunting from the get-go. Rescuing Colorado's dwindling elk herds from the threat of human predation, though, was just the first step in a larger suite of efforts that abruptly reversed the downward spiral of elk populations precipitated by the advent of American settler colonialism.[9]

Return of the Natives

Elk populations recovered swiftly—so swiftly, in fact, that some authorities began to express alarm by the 1920s about a different and altogether unanticipated kind of elk problem: though elk had teetered on the verge of extinction in the early 1910s, the creatures had bounced back so rapidly in the Greater Rocky National Park Ecosystem that they were starting to take a toll on the area's plant communities. Two key developments of the teens and twenties—elk reintroduction and predator eradication—explain this surprisingly rapid reversal. Alarm about the impact of resurgent elk on aspen, willows, and cultivated hay meadows eventually led the Park Service to enact an ungulate management policy known as lethal control, which empowered park rangers to restore predation to ecosystems where neither wolves, bears, nor human hunters had killed significant numbers of elk for several decades.[10]

The Coyote Valley's beaver populations continued to recover during these early twentieth-century decades despite ongoing efforts by settlers to establish and expand their hay meadows. The Holzwarths grubbed out seven or eight acres of willow thickets from the Colorado River bottomlands in the late 1910s, for instance, and other homesteaders tore up dozens of additional acres of the shrubs. Yet more than enough willow remained for beavers to reclaim much of their former territory.[11]

The animals' resumption of their ancient ecosystem engineering activities caused homesteaders and dude ranchers no end of headaches. Beaver dams often flooded roads, meadows, and other "improvements" that settlers had struggled to superimpose on the Colorado River bottomlands. A government inspector painted a grim view of the rodents' handiwork at Baker Creek, which "ha[d] been damed [*sic*] up by beavers in such a manner as to make this land a swamp" that was no longer "very suitable for stock"—and thus incapable of supporting the kind of mixed husbandry on which the agricultural settlement of the Coyote Valley depended. Such beaver-induced flooding jeopardized the efforts of many homesteaders to prove up their claims. In 1920–1921, Clinton DeWitt painstakingly "drained," "disced and drug" twenty-three acres of meadow. DeWitt was rewarded for his troubles the next year with a harvest of fifteen tons of hay. In 1923, though, beaver dams forced water onto DeWitt's meadows, reducing the settler's harvest to just ten tons. Like DeWitt, Harry Bruce Wiswall saw beavers as pests, complaining that they had "so infested the valley in which my homestead lies . . . that practically all of the hay land is continually flooded and cut up by beaver runs." Though the homesteader tried "repeatedly" to tear out the offending dams, this did "no good" because the beavers put the dams back "up over night." Wiswall and other desperate valley residents next turned to trapping. Indeed, between 1920 and 1941, the valley's settlers sold more than one hundred beaver pelts to the Colorado State Game Commission. Despite this onslaught, the rodents endured and even established new colonies.[12]

Elk, all but eliminated from the Kawuneeche by the early 1910s, experienced an even more dramatic boom. In what began as one of the great success stories in American wildlife conservation, cooperative efforts between federal agencies and local civic organizations transplanted dozens of elk from Greater Yellowstone to the Greater Rocky Mountain National Park Ecosystem. The creation of Yellowstone National

Park in 1872 and the establishment of the National Elk Refuge near
Jackson Hole in 1912 insured the survival of substantial elk herds in
northwestern Wyoming. By the 1910s, the protection afforded by federal reserves and the growth of cattle ranching combined to generate
an unexpected outcome. Elk, which had neared extinction just a few
years earlier, were fast overpopulating their range. Despite ongoing
poaching and a string of severe winters, 25,000 to 40,000 elk were
crowding into Jackson Hole by 1911; Yellowstone harbored many thousands more. Elk conservation advocates reasoned that they could solve
two problems at once by transplanting elk from Greater Yellowstone,
where the animals were now overcrowded, to other parts of the American West, where populations of elk and other large ungulates had
plummeted.[13]

Colorado proved the most enthusiastic beneficiary of federally spon-
sored elk reintroduction, with the Greater Rocky Mountain National
Park Ecosystem a major focus. Between 1912 and 1928, sportsmen,
the U.S. Forest Service, the Estes Park Improvement Association, and
other conservation advocates joined forces to bring in fourteen separate
shipments totaling about 350 elk from Greater Yellowstone to Colorado.
These included "20 cows and five bulls" released at Estes Park in
March 1913, as well twenty-four "two-year-old cows" let loose there the
following April. More than seventy additional elk were transplanted to
Nederland and Rollinsville, just across the Front Range from Grand Lake.
By 1927, National Park officials estimated Rocky Mountain National
Park's elk herd at 200 head. "Never before," crowed Superintendent
Roger Toll, "have such large numbers of deer and elk been seen at points
close to the public highways throughout the park." After possibly
breeding with remnant elk bands from Estes Park, Middle Park, and perhaps even Routt County, the descendants of elk brought in from Greater
Yellowstone almost certainly began to reclaim the Coyote Valley by the
late 1910s.[14]

Unprecedented shifts in predator-prey relationships propelled the
herds' expansion. Rocky Mountain's hunting ban and Colorado's closed
hunting season together brought human predation to a halt for the first
time in millennia. Federal conservation authorities, meanwhile, stepped
up their war against the West's large predators. Gray wolves and grizzly
bears had already been eliminated from the Kawuneeche years earlier.
But with the sanction of the National Park Service, the U.S. Biological

Survey effectively finished off the eradication campaign initiated by nineteenth-century American settlers. Populations of coyotes, mountain lions, bobcats, foxes, and smaller carnivores also dwindled. The Park Service finally disavowed predator eradication in the 1930s, but this change of heart came too late to save Colorado's wolves and grizzlies.[15]

By the time of the Never Summer addition, the Coyote Valley's elk, beaver, and willow were all flourishing. Yet the seeds of future trouble already were being sown. At Rocky Mountain, as at many other preserves, efforts to conserve wild game through predator eradication and game protection had alarming impacts on the plants large ungulates preferred, especially aspens and willows. As biologists and park managers grappled with the unintended consequences of elk conservation, they applied the insights of the emerging science of ecology to justify aggressive—and largely successful—human interventions.[16]

Lethal Control

Though the specter of elk extinction continued to haunt some conservationists into the 1920s, the nature of the nation's elk problem was already shifting decisively, from the fear of scarcity to the peril of overabundance. Efforts to remove elk from Jackson Hole and Yellowstone and reintroduce them elsewhere in the West undoubtedly saved the species from extermination. Yet elk conservation programs nonetheless flopped in two big ways. First, transplanting elk failed to prevent overpopulation in Greater Yellowstone. And, second, the troubling ecological dynamics first noted at Yellowstone in the 1920s began to spread to other reintroduction sites, including the Greater Rocky Mountain National Park Ecosystem.[17]

Rangers and scientists first expressed concern about the impact of elk on Rocky Mountain's plant communities in 1930—a year after the creatures' brisk recovery had begun to prompt alarm in Middle Park. In July 1929, Grand County commissioners complained to Colorado's game and fish commissioner that elk had grown "so numerous in Grand County as to . . . constitute a menace to the property of the ranchmen." The board unsuccessfully implored the commissioner to institute a "short open season" so that hunters could limit the herds' growth. Four months later, a prescient editorial in the *Middle Park Times* argued that despite the "commercial value," beauty, and "attractiveness" of elk to tourists, the

ungulates were acting like pests. "Protected as they are," elk were con-
suming "forage that would otherwise produce tame stock and they often
devour and destroy food raised on ranches." The creatures multiplied
so rapidly, moreover, that the editor claimed they were "becom[ing] a nuisance in some places. What," the editor wondered, "shall we do with
the surplus?"[18]

Transplanting "surplus" animals from Grand County to places where
elk remained scarce, the editor speculated, might temporarily slow the
herds' growth. State-licensed hunting offered an even surer way to check
elk populations, but this solution struck the editor as immoral and un-
remunerative. He assailed the state's first open elk season in sixteen
years as both "an orgy of killing," in which "many of the hunters . . .
mess[ed] the game," and "a poor business for state and county!" The editor proposed two alternative ways to control elk populations through
sport hunting. The state could either "send in each year expert huntsmen
who would quietly and skillfully shoot the surplus and in a business like
manner dispose of the animals," or it could allow local ranchers to kill
any elk who "stray[ed] to the ranches," provided that stockmen paid "a
certain amount for each one so killed. Thus the number would be kept
down, the ranchers would be protected and the state would receive some
value for its wards."[19]

Neither state nor federal officials seemed to pay any heed to the well-
meaning suggestions of the *Middle Park Times*. In 1932, Grand County's
commissioners begged the state game and fish commissioner to de-
clare another open season on deer and elk; any "further increase" in elk
populations, the board complained, "would work great damage to their
natural winter and summer range, as well as to the crops, range and hay
stacks of the ranchers." Four months later, still another petition from the
board fell on deaf ears.[20]

In the Coyote Valley, elk remained all but invisible to scientists and
land managers during the 1930s and 1940s. On the east side of Rocky
Mountain, by contrast, these decades witnessed an about-face in the
park's wildlife policies that did much to set the stage for the present-day
tragedy of the willows in the Colorado River headwaters. Despite the
Park Service's abandonment of predator eradication and the state's
declaration of open seasons on elk outside the national park's boundaries, resurgent ungulate populations nonetheless continued to devas-
tate aspen and willow around Estes Park. As ecological science gained

prominence within the Park Service, and as equally or even more troublesome irruptions (sudden population increases) raged elsewhere on the public lands, the Park Service turned from protecting Rocky Mountain's elk to shooting them. Aptly named lethal control, the agency's new strategy for managing elk entailed the animals' systematic slaughter within park boundaries through predawn hunts conducted by rangers or state game wardens deputized by the Park Service. In 1944, rangers began to gun down elk around Estes Park to reduce the size of the park's herd, a decisive break from Mills's founding vision of the park as a federally protected game refuge. Though the Park Service never deployed lethal control in the Coyote Valley, the program's suspension amid a political firestorm in the early 1960s nonetheless had immense implications for the beavers and willows in the riparian ecosystems of the Colorado River headwaters.[21]

This major shift in how the Park Service managed elk at Rocky Mountain originated not with Aldo Leopold, whose famous story about his Kaibab epiphany did not reach print until 1949, but instead with *Fauna of the National Parks of the United States*—more commonly referred to as *Fauna No. 1*. This blandly titled but pathbreaking report coauthored by George Wright, Joseph Dixon, and Ben Thompson transformed wildlife policy in the national parks by bringing new ecological understandings to bear. Wright and his associates articulated the rationale on which lethal control was premised. "In a National Park," they argued, the damage that overabundant ungulates inflicted on vegetative communities "cannot be undone by policing a boundary line." So-called "protection" work by park rangers, though "necessary," was powerless to "correct conditions already operative within the park," which had to "be sought out where they are doing damage and dealt with there. This is management, and the danger that it may be overdone is not sufficient reason for doing nothing. Recognition that there are wildlife problems," *Fauna No. 1* contended, "is admission that unnatural, man-made conditions exist."[22]

Wright and his colleagues considered it pointless under such circumstances for land managers to allow nature to take its course: "There can be no logical objection to further interference by man," the biologists reasoned, "to correct these conditions and restore the natural state." *Fauna No. 1* encouraged park managers to remedy "wildlife problems," including those involving overabundant herbivores, through vigorous

action. Ungulates "occupying a deteriorated range," an especially perti-
nent passage of *Fauna No. 1* pronounced, "shall not be permitted to ex-
ceed the reduced carrying capacity and, preferably, shall be kept below
the carrying capacity at every step until the range can be brought back
to original productiveness." Keeping elk populations "below the carrying
capacity" at Rocky Mountain—where large predators had been eradicated and where public sport hunting was banned by law—required the
Park Service to intervene directly and decisively. In lethal control's first
year at Rocky Mountain, rangers and deputized state game wardens
culled 301 elk and 113 mule deer from the park.[23]

Studies suggested that the policy worked. For instance, one official
at Rocky Mountain hailed the "heartening" findings of a 1955 report
that documented "the improvement in the vegetative cover that has resulted from control operations" on the park's east side. Decades before
trophic cascade researchers first wrote about the "ecology of fear," the
same study also noted that lethal control had broken up the large herds
that had previously congregated on the winter range around Estes Park.
By making browsers more fearful around humans, the policy "contributed much to range recovery. Perhaps," the author speculated, "this is
even more effective than killing the animals."[24]

Several factors kept the Park Service from extending lethal control
to the west side of the Coyote Valley, which remained cut off from the
Estes Park area for half the year and still lightly patrolled even during
the summer high season. Moreover, concern regarding the vegetative
impacts of skyrocketing elk populations initially centered on aspen,
which were mostly lacking in the Kawuneeche. Last and most important, the valley's elk populations had not yet caused any "noticeable
decrease in the beavers' food supply," as Fred Packard found when he
surveyed Rocky Mountain's beaver colonies on the eve of World War II.[25]

Though the Coyote Valley's elk herds almost certainly grew between
the 1930s and 1950s, the valley's willow and beaver continued to thrive
during these same decades. Anecdotal evidence from rangers' monthly
reports suggests that elk were coming to spend more of the year in the
Kawuneeche and in greater numbers. "There have been more elk seen
in this District," ranger Fred McLaren reported in summer 1938, "than
in years gone by. They have been reported in all valleys and along all
streams." The next month, another ranger described the Kawuneeche's
elk as "in fine condetion [*sic*] this year and are rangeing [*sic*] over a larger

area than I have ever seen before." Three years later, McLaren claimed: "Elk are increasing in this area very rapidly." Most documented elk sightings clustered near the homesteads on the valley floor, reflecting the creatures' strong preference for the grass, hay, and willows that dominated the Colorado River bottomlands. By the early 1940s, elk also were wintering in the Kawuneeche for the first time that long-serving park rangers like McLaren or old settlers like Johnnie Holzwarth could remember.[26]

The valley's growing elk herds increasingly competed for pasture and hay with the cattle and horses kept by private landowners. In 1938, for instance, McLaren reported that elk had torn into haystacks at the Fisher Ranch; he also fielded complaints from the Harbisons that elk were descending on their meadows before they could mow their hay. Even after the Park Service bought out local residents along the Colorado River and incorporated former homesteads into Rocky Mountain (as *Fauna No. 1* had recommended), rangers continued to irrigate hay meadows on these properties. "Several man days," McLaren noted in 1945, "were used in the irrigation of Elk pasture by both the Harbison and Selack [*sic*] ditches." Ironically, west-side rangers were irrigating "Elk pasture" just a year after their east-side counterparts had begun to shoot elk with high-powered rifles.[27]

Despite growing elk populations and escalating assaults from humans, the Kawuneeche's willow thickets and beaver colonies showed no signs of retreat during the mid-twentieth century. The mechanized farm equipment that supplanted horsepowered implements in the valley during the 1930s accelerated the transformation of native shrub lands into meadows of exotic timothy, rye, and alfalfa. Even second home owners saw willows as a nuisance; between 1941 and 1954, one family intent on obtaining an "unobstructed view toward Baker Mountain" grubbed out willows from their property on five separate occasions.[28]

Mechanized implements shifted the balance of power between private landowners and willow communities. Yet the persistence of thriving beaver populations indicates that the shrubs likely remained healthy. Beavers had recolonized the Coyote Valley's streams without direct human assistance; thereafter, their numbers grew with the help of protective legislation and predator eradication. By early 1939, when biologist Fred Packard launched his "investigations of wildlife problems in Rocky Mountain National Park," the beaver colonies of the Coyote

Valley had staged a dramatic comeback. Packard estimated that some 600 beavers inhabited the main branch of the Colorado, with additional colonies on the river's tributaries. "Almost every stream that can support beavers," Packard marveled, was either "stocked to capacity or . . . overpopulated." Packard attributed the beaver's recovery in the Kawuneeche to "an abundance of food and building material," especially willow. "Technicians who are familiar with conditions in other national parks," Packard reported, suspected "that Rocky Mountain National Park probably supports more beavers than any other."[29]

Settlers did not sit idly by as hundreds of busy rodents built dams, rerouted streams, and otherwise reengineered the riparian landscapes the Kawuneeche's human residents claimed as their own. "The Beaver are increasing so fast," ranger Fred McLaren asserted in 1940, "that they are giving the Ranchers on the North Fork of the Colorado River considerable trouble." Beaver dams, McLaren observed, were "flooding hay meadows and roads and daming [sic] irrigating ditches." Park rangers responded to local grievances by attempting to dislodge offending colonies. After several ranch owners "complained about Beaver Damage on their Property" in 1941, McLaren and an associate tore out several dams, then a trapper dispatched by the state game commission removed twenty-eight more of the animals from the Colorado watershed. But beavers quickly repossessed almost all of the sites from which rangers and trappers had attempted to eliminate them. Two years later, another ranger offered a breathless report of the widespread damage beavers were causing:

> At Phantom Valley they put a dam accross the river and threatened to flood their corral; at Holzwarth Ranch they put a dam accross the river and flooded their road; at Godchaux Ranch they damed an irrigation ditch; just below the bridge on the Bowen Gulch road they put a dam accross the river and floded the Saw Mill road; at the Harbison Ranch they continued to dam up their ditch causing it to overflow and flood timber land.

Beaver, in short, were doing well—too well, in the eyes of many of the valley's human inhabitants.[30]

As ranchers and park rangers continued to join in dubious battle against the beavers of the Colorado River headwaters, Park Service scientists were developing a new appreciation of the rodents' ecological significance. "A beaver is not just an animal which builds houses and dams," the authors of *Fauna No. 1* pointed out in 1933, but also a central player in many of the natural processes that the Park Service was charged with preserving and perpetuating. "Many different forms of wildlife," Wright and his colleagues noted, "follow in succession the changing habitats produced by the beaver cycle." No stage in "the beaver cycle," the biologists argued, should be considered "more destructive or more climax than the rest; it is a continuous chain of plant and animal succession, each phase of which leads naturally to the succeeding steps; any one moment in the cycle signified all the rest." For there "to be any permanent value in our parks," *Fauna No. 1* concluded, park ecosystems "must be allowed to run their orderly succession of change which produces the marvelous variety of life."[31]

Fauna No. 1 expressly decried aggressive control efforts like those conducted against the Coyote Valley's beaver colonies in the 1930s and 1940s. But rangers at Rocky Mountain continually flouted the report's nuanced, almost cosmic admiration for the beavers' ecosystem engineering. As late as 1958, ranger Wayne B. Cone would grouse that "beaver activities along Timber Creek and Onahu Creek continue to present a control problem." Though Cone accused beavers of damaging ranch lands and Park Service roads, he also made a more serious charge. Beaver, he claimed, were "threatening a fine group of aspen to extinction." Cone saw aspen trees felled by beavers not as a representative stage in an essential natural cycle, but instead as a threat to forest health and aesthetic values. Throughout the mid-twentieth century, beaver overpopulation struck park rangers and private landowners alike as the Kawuneeche's most pressing wildlife "problem." A sudden and deeply misguided shift in ungulate management in 1961, though, precipitated an outcome that decades of dynamiting and trapping had failed to produce: the eradication of beaver from the Colorado River headwaters.[32]

Toward Natural Regulation

Culling elk had always troubled officials at Rocky Mountain. Throughout the 1950s, superintendents feared that lethal control would prompt "public outrage" and "opposition." One superintendent explained that "considerable public relations work was necessary to acquaint the people at large, and especially the various sportsmen's organizations, with the need and purpose of the reduction." Park administrators sought political cover by collaborating with the U.S. Forest Service and Colorado's Game and Fish Department; keeping culling out of public view by conducting hunts before dawn and removing the carcasses of elk thus killed in tarpaulin-covered trucks; and enlisting "local sportsman associations" such as the Izaak Walton League to distribute meat butchered from these carcasses "to charitable groups," including schools, churches, and state institutions.[33]

Though these careful measures had sustained lethal control for nearly two decades, they failed to protect the policy from an unexpected reversal in the early 1960s. A veritable witch's brew of cultural, social, and political dynamics catalyzed a powerful public reaction that forced the sudden abandonment of culling at Rocky Mountain as well as other parks. The first public signs of trouble materialized at a pregnant moment for environmentalism, the National Park Service, and American political culture. The conservation movement had taken the offensive in 1961, after a successful fight against the Echo Park Dam in Colorado's Dinosaur National Monument. Citizen-activists spearheaded by the Wilderness Society pressured Congress to establish a new category of public land, so-called wilderness areas, which excluded both automobiles and mechanized development and recreation.[34]

The era's nascent environmentalists embraced wilderness as an antidote to the perceived failings of the national parks. Following World War II, tourism boomed at parks from coast to coast. Total visitation skyrocketed from 17 million in 1940 to 56 million in 1955. Congress, burdened by escalating defense spending and the strain of rebuilding Europe and Japan, refused to earmark additional funds for the Park Service. By the mid-1950s, a veritable chorus of critics was lamenting the overcrowded conditions and outdated facilities throughout the national park system. Bernard DeVoto, the conservation-minded editor of the influential *Harper's Magazine*, even argued that it would be better to shutter the system than to keep it open in its present disgraceful state. Park Service director Conrad Wirth successfully seized on these complaints, convincing Congress to fund a sweeping modernization program: the Mission 66 campaign, which touted an ambitious program of facilities construction as the best way to reconcile automobile tourism with the Park Service's obligation to preserve park landscapes in an "unimpaired" manner. By the early 1960s, though, more than a few conservationists had become disenchanted with Wirth's plan and the new visitor centers, comfort stations, campgrounds, and roads built under its auspices.[35]

The wilderness movement offered refuge for Mission 66's critics. But this was just one of the many signs that public faith in federal power and scientific authority were wavering as the 1960s dawned. After World War II and the Cold War had kindled fears that totalitarianism would infect the United States, growing (though still equivocal) federal support for the black freedom struggle and rankling controversies over New Deal liberalism combined to prompt renewed enthusiasm for states' rights. Meanwhile, a panoply of factors—including the 1959 discovery of radioactive strontium-90 in the milk Americans drank, the groundswell of work on the harms of organic pesticides and other environmental pollutants that Rachel Carson would draw upon in her epochal *Silent Spring* (1962), and the looming threat of nuclear annihilation—reinforced rising anxieties about what Dwight Eisenhower famously called "the military-industrial" complex in his January 1961 farewell speech. "In holding scientific research and discovery in respect," the outgoing president warned, "we must also be alert to the equal and opposite danger that public policy could itself become the captive of a scientific-technological elite."[36]

Distrust of federal science combined with the ascension of the wilderness idea and mounting disillusionment with the National Park Service to undermine lethal control's political efficacy. The elk management ruckus began quietly enough, when western state game commissioners urged the Park Service to allow recreational sport hunting within the lands under its control. As part of this larger effort, the Colorado Department of Fish and Game, long a crucial collaborator in lethal control at Rocky Mountain, announced that it would no longer lend its resources to the park's 1961 elk reduction campaign, nor would it help distribute the meat thus taken to needy citizens. That December, hunting columnist Jim Matlack of the Longmont *Times-Call* lambasted the Park Service's plan to kill some 200 elk from Rocky Mountain's eastern side. "Seems to me that the deer and elk belong to the public—not to the government," Matlack grumbled. "If a certain number must be killed each year," he concluded, then "the ordinary rank and file big game hunter should be allowed to put one into his own freezer." A few weeks later, Superintendent Allyn Hanks temporarily suspended lethal control at Rocky Mountain.[37]

What began as a relatively quiet local dispute became embroiled in a heated national controversy in January 1962. As Superintendent Lemuel "Lon" Garrison launched a massive campaign to kill roughly half of Yellowstone's northern herd—some 5,000 animals—"all hell broke loose," as Ted Trueblood of *Field and Stream* aptly recalled. The magnitude of the proposed slaughter at America's first national park prompted vitriolic complaints from conservationists, sportsmen, animal lovers, and politicians. By mid-January, newspapers throughout the West featured spirited debates on the Park Service's lethal control program. *Denver Post* hunting columnist Cal Queal declared: "Seldom has the National Park Service taken a worse public beating than it's now suffering. . . . Belted with charges of ineptness, stupidity, even of inhumanity, the NPS has been pictured as a ghoulish, kill-crazed monster with blood dripping from its bureaucratic jowls." Colorado senator Peter Dominick proclaimed it "the 'height of stupidity' to set aside public land for fishing and hunting and then to slaughter animals which could provide hunting." John A. Carver, Stewart Udall's assistant secretary of the interior, described the sudden backlash against lethal control as a "crisis in public relations," while the *Estes Park Trail* called the elk-reduction furor "one of the hottest controversies of the decade."[38]

The Park Service reacted to the clamor by digging in its heels. Acting regional director George F. Baggley, with "the strong support" of Secretary Udall and Director Wirth, ordered Rocky Mountain superintendent Hanks to pursue an "immediate resumption of the full-scale direct control program to assure reaching your planned reduction goal of 200 elk this winter." Baggley argued that only by culling could the Park Service "prevent another excessive buildup of an elk population which might result in a massive reduction program such as that presently being carried out at Yellowstone." Baggley assured Hanks that the Park Service "was 'over the hump' as regards public acceptance of these reduction programs." Citing "increasing support from many sources for our wildlife management policy," Baggley told Hanks there was no need to "relax our reduction goals."[39]

Despite Baggley's pleas, Hanks effectively mothballed lethal control. Implying that the park's reduction targets were based on shaky scientific foundations, he extended the moratorium on culling at Rocky Mountain, "pending the outcome" of two time-consuming bureaucratic maneuvers: first, the completion of a series of "cooperative elk studies" by park biologist Neal Guse and colleagues from the U.S. Forest Service and Colorado Fish and Game; and second, the development of "cooperative plans" with these same agencies "that included the possibilities of live trapping."[40]

Hanks's superiors redoubled their pleas for continued culling, but to no avail. "We plan to continue direct control on the strength of findings," Rocky Mountain's top official scolded, "rather than for the reasons of earlier predictions . . . or to satisfy deep seated convictions not to be swayed by political or public opinion developed without the benefit of facts." Lethal control would remain on hold, Hanks indicated, until a stronger body of scientific research had been assembled—and alternative strategies for removing the park's "surplus" elk exhausted.[41]

While Hanks temporized, Yellowstone's Garrison literally stuck to his guns. Despite mounting public outcry, Garrison's rangers continued to kill large numbers of elk. After Congress ordered a temporary halt to lethal control at Yellowstone, Secretary Udall appointed a blue ribbon advisory commission on wildlife management in the national parks chaired by Starker Leopold, Aldo Leopold's son and a noted biologist at the University of California at Berkeley. In March 1963, the commission released the influential Leopold Report. "Direct removal by killing," it declared in a ringing vindication of lethal control, "is the most economical and effective way of regulating ungulates within a park." Guided by the commission's findings, the Park Service entered into cooperative agreements with Montana and Wyoming that identified trapping and relocation as the preferred policies for limiting Yellowstone's herds. If these strategies failed to bring elk populations down to the park's estimated carrying capacity, though, the Park Service reserved the right to "dispose of the remaining surplus number of elk by direct reduction methods within Yellowstone National Park."[42]

Though the Leopold Report and the federal-state compacts subsequently negotiated with Montana and Wyoming offered a clear sanction for resuming lethal control, Hanks unflinchingly maintained his no-kill policy. An unexpected decision by Colorado wildlife officials to hold a special late elk season just outside Rocky Mountain's eastern boundaries in winter 1962–1963 brought an enthusiastic response from sportsmen. In the process, it bought Hanks the time and cover he needed. Roughly 220 of the 400 or so elk shot by hunters in the special season came from the so-called "Park herd"—more than the 200 head the Park

Service had initially set out to kill when the elk management brouhaha began. Hanks applauded the special hunt as "an effective management tool, both in the opinion of the Park and of the State," since it offered "a means of controlling surplus wildlife occupying critical winter range in the park, without actual subjection of public hunters to protected Park values." Yet Hanks also admitted that the special season was "only a temporary measure." Elk populations would inevitably bounce back, making it "necessary to lay plans for the undertaking of a similar project within the next three to five years."[43]

In the meantime, Park Service officials transplanted dozens of elk from Rocky Mountain to introduction sites in western Colorado. The agency and other entities participating in the cooperative elk studies launched in the early 1960s also tagged hundreds of other animals. The resulting research offered the best data yet assembled on the park's elk populations. Even so, park managers continued to overlook a key finding about elk migrations: the animals crossed the Continental Divide both more frequently and in larger numbers than anyone had previously realized. For more than three decades, the Park Service had assumed that Rocky Mountain's elk problem was restricted to the eastern slopes of the Front Range. New understandings about how elk actually moved across the high country should have forced managers to jettison this premise. Before that could happen, though, events at Yellowstone forced a paradigm shift in wildlife management throughout the national parks.[44]

The Park Service responded to the failure of trap-and-transplant schemes to control Yellowstone's elk by resuming culling there in 1966, as allowed by the cooperative agreements the federal government had signed with Montana and Wyoming. The political blowback to this move, however, soon led the agency to implement an untested and scientifically unsound policy. In the early 1960s, Park Service leaders had ardently defended the ecological principles undergirding lethal control. By spring 1967, though, agency officials caved in the face of high-level political pressure. After Senate hearings initiated by Wyoming's Gale McGee and backroom discussions between McGee, Stewart Udall, and Park Service director George P. Hartzog Jr., the agency abandoned lethal control—not just at Yellowstone, but system-wide.[45]

The Park Service subsequently strained to find scientific cover for its expedient capitulation to superior political force. In reports such as

"Natural Control of Elk," Park Service scientists argued that factors such as "winter food [scarcity], . . . periodic severe winter weather and native predators" would eventually restore a workable balance between ungulates and the plants they ate. In putting their own gloss on the Park Service's turn away from culling, officials at Rocky Mountain invoked both history and ecology. A typical defense began with an oblique gesture to the 1940s, when "it was decided that [anthropogenic] influences on the environment of the elk had so altered the ecosystem that natural regulations no longer limited the population." Up-to-date wildlife managers, this account contended, preferred the wisdom of nature's cycles to the arrogance and brutality of lethal control. "The elk herd," it explained, was now "being allowed to fluctuate naturally with an eventual equilibrium with the forage supply expected." In 1971, Yellowstone's head biologist, Glen Cole, termed the Park Service's let-live approach to ungulate management "natural regulation"—an oxymoronic but catchy moniker that quickly gained adherents.[46]

On the conceptual level, at least, the new policy possessed intrinsic appeal. Natural regulation reflected and reinforced Earth Day–era environmentalist thought in its implicit portrayal of "nature" as both a self-equilibrating entity gravely imperiled by heavy-handed human intervention and a hallowed escape from the social turmoil of the 1960s. The paradigm seemed to overturn musty truisms and eschew state-sponsored violence. At the same time, natural regulation forsook the liberal shibboleth that enlightened federal action could solve all America's ills. Advocates of natural regulation posited that ecosystems stripped of all predation could somehow regulate themselves in a "natural" manner.[47]

And yet the new policy rested on flawed understandings of ecology and history, as subsequent in the story of trophic cascades in the Coyote Valley would show. Until the early twentieth century, predation and hunting had limited ungulate populations in the Colorado River headwaters, enabling willows and beavers to flourish. Between the early 1910s and the early 1930s, though, game protection laws, elk reintroduction, and predator eradication campaigns led ungulate populations to soar. The advent of open hunting seasons outside the national park in 1929 and lethal control on Rocky Mountain's eastern slopes in 1944 had restored human predation to ecosystems stripped of wolves, grizzlies, and other meat eaters. But the ferocious backlash against government culling essentially replicated the disastrous conditions that

Populations of elk expanded rapidly because of changes in Park Service policies and the Kawuneeche Valley landscape. Russell Smith photograph, October 2010, courtesy of the National Park Service.

had driven rapid increases in large ungulate populations during the 1910s and 1920s.

For all their invocations of "nature," Park Service scientists and managers nonetheless understood that the control of Rocky Mountain's elk herds would continue to depend on human hunting—especially after the agency halted trap-and-transplant programs at Rocky Mountain in 1968. Culling, though, would now take place entirely outside of park borders, conducted by citizen-sportsmen instead of government employees. No one bothered to explain why private hunters hefting modern firearms into national forests on all-terrain vehicles qualified as agents of "nature," when park rangers and game wardens using rifles and helicopters did not.[48]

Further compromising natural regulation was the tendency of its supporters to deny the plasticity of elk behavior and the dynamism of national park landscapes. As the Park Service incorporated the erstwhile homesteads and dude ranches of the Kawuneeche into Rocky Mountain between the 1950s and early 1970s, the valley's elk no longer had to compete for browse with cattle and horses. Harassment by ranch dogs and opportunistic hunting by private landowners including Johnnie Holzwarth ceased, while the demolition of fences, outbuildings, houses, and cabins freed up additional riparian habitats for wildlife. As elk adjusted to shifting human land use in the Colorado River headwaters, they learned that they could find refuge from hunters within Rocky Mountain's borders. Land policies in the national park thus unwittingly enhanced the valley's attractiveness to elk. It was only a matter of time before Rocky Mountain's long-standing elk management problems crossed the Continental Divide and descended on the Coyote Valley.[49]

Because the Park Service had never actively managed elk within the Colorado River headwaters, natural regulation essentially carried forward the agency's existing policy of benign neglect. By the early 1990s, though, the Coyote Valley's willows and beavers showed clear signs of distress. Rapid increases in the valley's elk herds starting in the 1960s deserved most of the blame for this alarming development, but the introduction of a lumbering newcomer to the Kawuneeche in the late 1970s made a bad situation worse.

Making Moose

Even as the Coyote Valley's elk herds burgeoned, breeding populations of Shiras or Wyoming moose began to crowd into the Greater Rocky Mountain National Park Ecosystem for the first time in the region's deep history. The colonization of the Kawuneeche by moose exacerbated the ecological effects of resurgent elk herds, with devastating consequences for willows and beavers. Natural regulation was premised on the belief that ecosystems could heal themselves. The case of moose introduction, though, revealed the philosophical and practical shortcomings of the Park Service's new ungulate management paradigm.

Though state wildlife officials had first broached the idea of introducing moose to Colorado in the 1940s, sustained interest in the notion began with a 1967 article in *Colorado Outdoors* magazine. In "Moose for Colorado," Richard Denney, a former wildlife biologist for the department and participant in the cooperative elk studies of the 1960s, broached some tough questions: "How long has it been since moose have been in Colorado in any numbers, if ever? How much suitable moose habitat do we have in Colorado? How would moose fit in the general ecological scheme if they were released in Colorado? How much potential damage do they represent, and how can they be controlled?" Denney argued that these historical and ecological conundrums "would all have to be answered satisfactorily" before the state began to transplant moose into Colorado.[50]

Notwithstanding Denney's wariness, the idea of introducing moose to Colorado gained traction during the early 1970s. The Forest Service and ranchers worried "that there are already too many mouths eating the available forage," but staff at Rocky Mountain were eager to add the massive, oddly charismatic creatures to the park's bestiary. Under the dictates of natural regulation, though, the Park Service could participate in the state program only if it could show that moose had previously inhabited Rocky Mountain. After sifting through historical sources and consulting University of Colorado mammalogist David Armstrong, officials at Rocky Mountain were forced to concede that although bull moose had occasionally made solitary journeys from Wyoming and Utah, breeding populations of moose had never inhabited the Colorado high country. Natural regulation expressly barred Park Service managers from introducing new species to park ecosystems, so Superintendent Roger Contor had no choice but to "drop the moose reintroduction proposal."[51]

The Colorado Department of Wildlife forged ahead without the Park Service, but it had to make one important adjustment. Instead of releasing moose directly to the Coyote Valley, the state elected to transplant them to the western slopes of the Never Summers, an easy day's saunter from Rocky Mountain National Park's western border. Ironically, the Park Service's withdrawal from the introduction program actually eased the way for moose to colonize the Kawuneeche. Federal environmental laws passed in the early 1970s, after all, required the Park Service to draft environmental impact statements and hold public hearings regarding significant wildlife management actions inside park boundaries. Colorado's moose proposal probably would not have survived this strenuous review process. The Colorado Department of Wildlife, by contrast, had no legal obligation to weigh the ecological consequences of releasing the animals outside Rocky Mountain's borders.[52]

The state's transplantation program began in 1978, when wildlife officials trucked "three males, seven females, a yearling male, and a female calf" in wooden crates from Utah's Uinta Mountains to an intro-

To many national park visitors, moose seem like a natural part of the Kawuneeche Valley's ecology. In truth, they are recent arrivals that are subjecting willows such as those pictured in the foreground to unprecedented threats. Russell Smith photograph, June 2009, courtesy of the National Park Service.

duction site at "the willow-choked Illinois River drainage" across the Never Summers from the Coyote Valley. All that stood between Colorado's new moose herd and the Kawuneeche was a pair of gentle and relatively low divides covered with grass and browse, Bowen and Baker Passes. In early 1979, twelve more moose—"one male, six females, three yearling females, and two female calves"—were freighted from an inholding within Grand Teton National Park and released near the same transplantation site. By the next year, eighteen calves had been born in Colorado—a foretaste of the rapid population growth moose would enjoy in the absence of hunting and predation. By 1986–1987, Colorado boasted an estimated 100 to 130 moose.[53]

Proliferating moose swiftly expanded into new territories, starting with the Coyote Valley. The first recorded moose sighting in Rocky Mountain occurred in June 1980, near Onahu Creek. Seven more observations followed that same year, all in riparian areas flush with willow. Moose dispersal slowed in 1982 and 1983, but then accelerated in 1984. In 1985–1986, the "first documented over-wintering of moose in the park" occurred; the next year brought clear signs that moose were establishing breeding populations in the Colorado River headwaters.[54]

Park biologist David Stevens defended moose migration into Rocky Mountain as "simply . . . a form of natural pioneering by an animal very prone to expanding its range when favorable habitat is available." Trotting out the same tortured argument that state wildlife officials had devised to justify moose introduction, Stevens cast the species as a natural pioneer that "was expanding its range southward at the time of the arrival of European man." If "early settlers had not interfered with this movement," Stevens speculated, then "the moose would have become established on its own in the state." Importing moose from Utah and Wyoming, Stevens suggested, was simply a way of resetting the ecological clock back to the history that would have happened if white settlers had not upset nature's designs. This counterfactual fantasy attempted to spin moose introduction as the consummation of Rocky Mountain's presettlement environmental history. In truth, though, the story of how moose came to inhabit the park is more usefully understood as an object lesson in the contradictions of ungulate management after the demise of lethal control. Natural regulation was created by and suffused with human artifice (as any environmental policy inevitably must be). Worse, the policy hinged on the notion that Rocky Mountain and other national parks functioned like ecological islands—an untenable assumption that ignored the mobility of living things, the park's relatively small size, and the porousness of the its boundaries.[55]

The Plight of Beaver-Willow Mutualism

The Coyote Valley's teeming elk population and its new moose herds were overbrowsing willow thickets in the Colorado River headwaters by the early 1990s. Beavers declined alongside the shrubs that had long provided them with building material and nutriment. Though natural regulation had begun abruptly enough, the new paradigm showed surprising staying power. Despite clear evidence that natural regulation was failing to limit ungulate populations or prevent vegetative damage, the Park Service nonetheless held fast to the policy until the early 2000s.

Throughout natural regulation's heyday, the agency continued to pay little heed to elk in the Kawuneeche. But the valley's ungulate populations seem to have grown rapidly from the 1960s onward. As elk herds throughout the Greater Rocky Mountain National Park Ecosystem expanded, more of the animals presumably spent the winter in the Colorado River headwaters. A thorough 1980 census by park biologist Stevens estimated that "up to 10%" of Rocky Mountain's elk were spending the colder months in the Kawuneeche. Stevens's description of overwintering elk as "generally . . . distributed from Phantom Valley trailhead to Harbison Meadows" suggested that elk responded to the absence of hunters or predators by crowding into the willows along the Colorado River for a yearlong feast. Moose populations, meanwhile, burgeoned. The Department of Wildlife began to offer sport hunters the chance to bag a moose; it also transplanted some of the creatures from North Park to the San Juan Mountains. Yet more than sixty moose were nonetheless summering in Rocky Mountain by 2005, mostly on the west side. Each moose required tens of kilograms of vegetation a day to survive. A study of moose feeding habits in the Kawuneeche found that "six willow species comprised 91.3% of moose summer diets," a statistic with worrisome implications for the valley's riparian ecology.[56]

Few thoughtful advocates of natural regulation should have been surprised that proliferating elk and moose were beginning to harm the Coyote Valley's willows. Natural regulation was a policy, after all, premised on the belief that ungulates could be controlled from the bottom up through a four-stage scenario. As teeming herds of ungulates overexploited willows (stage 1), forage would decline (stage 2). Starvation, lower birth rates, higher juvenile mortality rates, and other mechanisms would then kick in (stage 3) and drive ungulate populations back down to more sustainable levels (stage 4). By the early 1990s, the first and second stages of this scheme were unfolding more or less as planned, with Park Service naturalists reporting from the Kawuneeche Valley "that elk have destroyed large willow stands in recent years." The combined effects of elk and moose even threatened some willow species with local extirpation. And yet there was no sign whatsoever that the all-important third stage—a reduction in ungulate numbers—was under way.[57]

As more elk and more moose inevitably consumed more willow, the Kawuneeche's beaver colonies struggled. The Park Service took little notice of this alarming development until the mid-1990s, when it became apparent that Rocky Mountain's beaver populations were declining drastically. A team of ecologists and hydrologists led by Bruce Baker set out to discover why. "Beaver-willow communities," they pronounced in a 2005 article, "have declined or failed to recover in riparian environments that have become heavily browsed by livestock or ungulates since European settlement." The biologists claimed that as domesticated livestock packed into the willow thickets of Rocky Mountain in the late 1800s and 1900s, these "additional herbivores" presented a "new level of competition" that was "unnatural to beaver-willow mutualisms, which likely evolved under relatively low herbivory in a more predator-rich environment."[58]

The timing of the beaver's decline in the Kawuneeche, though, shows that the beavers' plight was caused not by agricultural settlement, but instead by the unintended consequences of natural regulation. Growing herds of elk and moose subjected willow and beaver to far more pressure than cattle, horses, and homesteaders ever had. Fred Packard found some 600 beavers populating the Colorado River headwaters in 1939, and even in the 1950s, when the valley's domesticated herds likely neared an all-time high, the Kawuneeche's beaver colonies remained vigorous enough to provoke extensive and ongoing control efforts in the Colorado River headwaters. Beaver populations, then, only began to plummet *after* natural regulation and moose introduction brought hundreds of ostensibly wild ungulates to feed on the Kawuneeche's willow thickets, with especially severe consequences in winter, when snow buried most other plants.[59]

Baker and colleagues stood on firmer historical and ecological ground when they attributed the drastic recent drop in beaver populations at Rocky Mountain to trophic cascades. Beaver, they observed, were "largely absent from areas with heavy use by ungulates, especially elk," while most of the park's "most active beaver populations" inhabited sites "where ungulate use of riparian shrubs was least." Willows just outside the fence of an experimental research plot on Rocky Mountain's east side appeared "short and hedged due to 30 years of intense use by elk." Shrubs shielded from elk by the plot's high fence, by contrast, sustained "tall and vigorous" new growth, leading beavers to treat the fenced-off exclosure as a "food plot." The key conclusion of Baker's team was alarmingly simple: "In riparian systems where elk are overabundant they will outcompete and exclude beaver"—an insight that researchers could have extended to moose, too. The park's large ungulates and beaver all eat willow; yet elk and moose, unlike beaver, can meet their dietary needs by shifting to other kinds of vegetation when necessary.[60]

Baker and his fellow scientists painted a grim picture of the future that was bound to transpire if large ungulates continued to "outcompete and exclude beaver" in Rocky Mountain. "When beaver populations decline," they warned, "then . . . beaver-engineered wetlands will collapse." Beaver abandonment and willow decline resulted not from destiny, but instead from contingent historical interactions between people, institutions, animals, plants, and physical environments. The carefully orchestrated mutualism forged by beavers and willows endured American settlement and the rise of dude ranching in the Coyote Valley. By the 1990s, though, moose introduction and natural regulation were propelling the ecosystems of the Colorado River bottomlands toward a patently unnatural state.[61]

Culling Redux

The Park Service responded to the emerging crisis by launching a time-consuming collaborative planning process to develop a new elk management program. The first major benchmark in this still-unfolding process, the Elk and Vegetation Management Plan of 2007 (EVMP), represented a clear departure from natural regulation by resuming elk culling—rebranded as "lethal regulation"—within Rocky Mountain's boundaries. The EVMP revealed both the problems large ungulates were causing and the difficulties the Park Service faced in determining how best to keep their populations in check. The report contended that browsing by hungry elk "currently stunts the growth or kills all young aspen trees." This was true not just "on the core elk winter range" but also "in some parts of the Kawuneeche Valley." More ominous still, the report warned that elk "are severely inhibiting the ability of montane riparian willow to reproduce" and "suppressing" the growth of existing plants. By damaging Rocky Mountain's willow thickets, elk were making the park uninhabitable for beavers and damaging the "habitat for a large number of bird, butterfly, and plant species." The 2007 plan made clear that if the Park Service did not actively manage Rocky Mountain's elk, then the elk would continue to "manage" riparian ecosystems of their own accord.[62]

The environmental impact statement drawn up in the course of the planning process evaluated the advantages and demerits of three strategies for controlling elk populations: human hunting; limiting

John Marino's image captures the juxtaposition between two recent environmental-historical changes in the Coyote Valley: the mountain pine beetle infestation explained to park visitors by the sign in the foreground, and the threat to beaver-willow mutualism presented by the elk herd in the background. September 2009, courtesy of the National Park Service.

reproduction through contraception; and reintroducing wolves to restore the trophic cascades disrupted by predator eradication campaigns. By 2006, culling by rangers within park boundaries—essentially the same policy Superintendent Hanks had suspended in 1961—emerged as the Park Service's preferred option. A *New York Times* reporter described the drama at a "sometimes raucous public meeting" held at Estes Park, where the agency solicited comments on a proposed "20-year program of herd reduction and management that would involve shooting hundreds of elk, mostly at night in the park, using sharpshooters with silencers." Much of the ensuing discussion pivoted on different ways of thinking about the environment—how it worked, how people should value it, and what role, if any, people should play in it. "In Rocky Mountain," the *Times* reporter wryly noted, "natural is a tough thing to pin down."[63]

Many environmentalists decried the resumption of culling. Reintroducing wolves, some argued, offered an opportunity to "rewild" the Greater Rocky Mountain National Park Ecosystem, reinvigorating the relationships between large ungulates, predators, and plant species that prevailed prior to American settlement. The most ardent campaigners for reintroducing wolves to Rocky Mountain belonged to WildEarth Guardians, a Santa Fé–based group seeking "to foment the recovery of gray wolves." Restoring wild canids, WildEarth Guardians maintained, was "tremendously important to the living organisms they share the land with—so important, in fact, that without wolves many plants and animals risk local extinction." WildEarth Guardians clearly viewed Rocky Mountain as the beachhead for a larger campaign; the park "and surrounding federal lands," the group contended, "could provide a strong foothold for wolves in the Southern Rockies." "The time has come," the Guardians' *Vision for Wolves* (2009) declared, "to repatriate wolves to the hunting grounds of their ancestors in the Southern Rockies." WildEarth Guardians, like other wolf advocacy groups, celebrated the wolf's return to Yellowstone as both an unalloyed good and a talisman: "The time has come for managers at Rocky Mountain National Park to heed the examples from Yellowstone, to heed the need for wolves."[64]

After the Park Service decided in favor of using human hunters to cull elk from Rocky Mountain's herds, WildEarth Guardians filed suit to force the Park Service to reexamine its decision. The Tenth Circuit Court of Appeals in Denver dismissed this suit in January 2013, determining that the Park Service had acted properly in deciding not to reintroduce wolves to Rocky Mountain on the grounds that the park was too small, too close to large human populations, and too dominated by "steep, high-altitude terrain, which wolves dislike." Nor was the court persuaded by WildEarth Guardians' complaint that statutes banning hunting at Rocky Mountain made it illegal for the Park Service to use volunteers to kill elk. The Tenth Circuit Court's ruling meant that if wolves were to return to the Greater Rocky Mountain National Park Ecosystem, they would have to do so of their own volition.[65]

As this legal challenge was moving through the courts, Rocky Mountain's elk population began to contract. Rangers, volunteers, and Colorado Parks and Wildlife personnel began culling on the park's eastern side in 2008, killing thirty-three elk that year, followed by forty-eight in 2009–2010 and fifty in 2010–2011. Combined with a "high harvest of female elk during a 2006 elk hunting season" outside the park's boundaries and changing elk migration patterns driven by heavy winter snows, lethal regulation drove Rocky Mountain's elk population down to levels "consistent" with the EVMP's goal of a winter herd numbering 600 to 800 animals.[66]

And yet this downturn may not have come soon enough to help beavers or willows. Recent research strongly suggests that other ecological dynamics are aggravating the ongoing impacts of elk and moose in the Coyote Valley. More than a century of water diversion by the Grand Ditch has lowered the water table on the valley floor; a string of droughty years in the early 2010s linked to global climatic change then subjected willows to additional stress. Without sufficient water, the shrubs become vulnerable to a fungus spread by red-naped sapsuckers, a bird indigenous to the Greater Rocky Mountain National Park Ecosystem. Ecologist David Cooper and his colleagues "started noticing" that wherever sapsuckers had left "marks or wells . . . the stems above them were dead. . . . There's lots of sapsuckers," Cooper noted, which "feed on hundreds and hundreds of willows at a time." After sapsuckers "make these openings in the willow bark, . . . fungi get into those and the fungi are killing the stems."[67]

Hungry herbivores compound the effects of the *Cytospora* fungi spread by sapsuckers. After fungi kill virtually all of the young stems above the wells the birds drill, Cooper explained, "the willow will produce new shoots from below the point of death." These new shoots, though, "are very short." Once an elk or moose chomps them off, "there's no replenishment of tall stems." The troubles willows face in the Colorado River headwaters, then, are far from simple, resulting from intricate, weblike systems of dynamic interaction that encompass ungulates and rodents, hydrology and birds, climate and fungi, and, not least, human beings.[68]

CONCLUSION

SEEING THE FOREST *AND* THE TREES

THE DEEP HISTORY of the Coyote Valley reveals an unexpected and complex interplay between social and environmental change from the end of the Pleistocene through the dawn of the Anthropocene. Native Americans inhabited and interacted with the Kawuneeche's environments from the initial forays of Clovis peoples more than 13,000 years ago through the zenith of the northeastern Nuche bands in the second millennium CE. Yet none of these First Peoples wielded the power or the will to impose significant changes on the dynamic, forceful, and refractory landscapes and ecologies in which they lived and labored. After centuries of skillful Nuche adaptations to the challenges and opportunities presented by European and American colonialism, the Ute War and the subsequent dispossession of the People from their Colorado homelands enabled Americans to exploit and settle the Kawuneeche.

Miners and the homesteaders who followed in their wake, however, soon learned that the Coyote Valley remained a tricky place to eke out a livelihood. The vagaries of capitalism and the vicissitudes of the Rocky Mountain environment combined to constrain the efforts of American newcomers to domesticate and improve the Kawuneeche. The halting progress of settlement opened the way, in turn, for farmers from Colorado's northern piedmont, foresters intent on protecting the "sponge" provided by the valley's woodlands, and Enos Mills's coalition of tourist-oriented preservationists to harness the Kawuneeche and its natural systems to a trio of interrelated but distinct conservation projects: the

Grand Ditch, the Medicine Bow Forest Reserve, and Rocky Mountain National Park.

By the time Mills and his allies convinced Congress to set aside the park in 1915, the previous decades of conquest, settlement, and conservation had already fragmented the landscapes, ecosystems, and resources of the Coyote Valley in far-reaching ways. During the ensuing century, a range of stakeholders—including the Water Supply and Storage Company and its farmer-shareholders, the Forest Service, the National Park Service, tourists, scientists, and private landowners like the Holzwarths—grappled in a shifting array of conflicts and collaborations to remake the valley. Between 1930 and the 1970s, the Park Service attempted to fulfill its dual mandate of encouraging visitation and preservation by expanding Rocky Mountain's boundaries to encompass ever more of the Kawuneeche. The agency's officials eventually learned, however, that translating their newly acquired property rights into meaningful control over the valley environment was no simple task. Political contingencies such as the backlash against lethal control in the early 1960s, ecological complexities such as the poorly understood hybridization of cutthroat trout subspecies, and distorted views of the Coyote Valley's past together hampered even the most enlightened and well-intentioned Park Service initiatives.

How might understanding the deep environmental history of the Coyote Valley help us to grapple with the imminent prospects of massive environmental change that now confront it and every other part of the planet? "We may not experience ourselves as a geological agent," historian Dipesh Chakrabarty notes, "but we appear to have become one at the level of the species." The extraction and consumption of fossil fuels and the expansion and intensification of agriculture have pushed atmospheric concentrations of carbon dioxide, methane, and other greenhouse gases to their highest levels since the middle of the Pleistocene epoch. Global climate change is already exposing the ecosystems of the Coyote Valley to grave risks, as the case of willow die-off in the Colorado River headwaters has shown. Two final stories about past and future changes to the subalpine and alpine ecosystems of the Kawuneeche offer grounds for hope as well as despair.[1]

Tree Killers

Few visitors to Rocky Mountain National Park will discern the ecological shifts under way in the tundra ecosystems of the Never Summers and the Front Range. Most, though, will notice another consequence of the earth's changing climate: the mountain pine beetle epidemic that has killed limber pines in the Kawuneeche's subalpine zone and large swaths of lodgepole pine on the valley's floor and lower slopes.

At the start of the third millennium CE, populations of tiny, match head–sized beetles from the genus *Dendroctonus* (Latin for "tree killer") began to explode in the Coyote Valley. A decade and a half later, the epidemic is finally relenting. Though the outbreak of mountain pine beetle has killed thousands of acres of trees, it may also offer unexpected grounds for optimism. Many observers initially interpreted the bark beetle infestation as the start of a broader forest holocaust. But some researchers now predict that afflicted forests will become richer and more diverse because of the havoc beetles have wrought. Beetle-killed forests also promise to buffer the Kawuneeche's woodland ecosystems against wildfires and future insect outbreaks.

Dendroctonus has inhabited the coniferous forests of western North America for millions of years. The two most influential species in the Kawuneeche during the last several centuries have been the mountain pine beetle and its cousin, the spruce beetle. Both kinds of bark beetles share a similar life cycle. Beetle eggs hatch under the bark of infected trees. During the larval and pupal stages, bark beetles feed on the host tree's innermost bark layer (called phloem). Having reached adulthood, the beetles eat their way out of the tree, fly up to a mile away (even farther if winds are strong), alight on new hosts, and bore tunnels into their bark. The beetles next dig "galleries" or passageways through the tree's phloem, where they lay the eggs from which a new generation will emerge. Wherever pine beetles burrow, they introduce a blue stain fungus. In concert with the galleries beetles dig, this fungus kills trees by blocking the flow of water and sap through their tissues.[2]

Like other varieties of *Dendroctonus,* the species endemic to the Kawuneeche usually remain at endemic levels; periodically, though, their numbers explode. Mountain pine beetles greatly prefer older, more mature lodgepole pines. Because of the extensive stand-replacing fires the Coyote Valley experienced in the second half of the nineteenth century, the forests of the Colorado River headwaters probably made a poor habitat for the beetles well into the 1900s. Spruce beetle infestations, by contrast, apparently broke out in many subalpine forests in northern Colorado between 1882 and 1889 (though no documents from the Kawuneeche mention this epidemic). Park Service foresters reported both beetle species in Rocky Mountain during the late 1940s and early 1950s, but these epidemics were limited in extent. A more serious outbreak of mountain pine beetle began in the late 1960s and continued through 1986. Though Grand County was hit hard, most of the Coyote Valley remained unscathed.[3]

After a decade of diminution, bark beetle populations exploded again. "The dreaded mountain pine beetle," the *Denver Post* ominously intoned in 1996, "has returned." Like earlier epidemics, this one seemed to start in the ponderosa pine forests of the Front Range foothills. By 1997, though, state entomologist David Leatherman warned that mountain pine beetles were "already reaching epidemic status" in the lodgepole forests of the Vail Valley. A forest expert with the Rocky Mountain Forest and Range Experiment Station in Fort Collins acknowledged that the outbreak was rapidly carving a path from Colorado "to the West Coast" and called its scale "overwhelming."[4]

By the time the rate of destruction began to slow in the late 2000s and early 2010s, mountain pine beetles had indeed killed far more trees than even the gloomiest observers had prognosticated. "From New Mexico to British Columbia," the *New York Times* reported in 2008, "the region's signature pine forests are succumbing to a huge infestation of mountain pine beetles that are turning a blanket of green forest into a blanket of rust red." By 2010, more than 4 million acres of woodland in Colorado and southern Wyoming had been affected. Foresters have declared it "the largest known insect infestation in the history of North America"—a crisis of truly continental magnitude that has afflicted well over 60 million acres of woodland in the United States, Canada, and Mexico, with lodgepole pines especially hard-hit.[5]

Observers in the Coyote Valley first noted the mountain pine beetle epidemic around 2001. This "synchronous and widespread" outbreak moved quite gradually through the Colorado River headwaters until about 2005, then rapidly accelerated to its peak in 2007–2008. Having quite literally eaten their way out of house and home, pine beetles have subsequently declined.[6]

The mechanisms driving cyclical fluctuations in pine beetle populations remain poorly understood. Some observers initially blamed the outbreak on failed federal forest policy. In the first year of the outbreak, for example, Wayne Shepperd of the Rocky Mountain Forest and Range Experimental Station argued: "While beetle infestations are part of a natural cycle, they're probably more severe now because humans have circumvented nature by suppressing fires that historically thinned America's forests."[7]

By the 2000s, though, a string of studies on the fire history of subalpine forests collectively undermined what is known as the "fire exclusion/fuel buildup" model—the notion that present-day lodgepole forests in Colorado had become unnaturally dense and weak due to government-led fire suppression campaigns begun during the heyday of the conservation movement. In reality, climate, not fire suppression, accounted for two key ingredients in the epidemic: (1) vast swaths of even-aged lodgepole pines and (2) the recent infestation of these forests by pine beetles. Hot, dry weather fueled the massive, stand-replacing fires that struck many Colorado woodlands in the late 1870s and 1880s (the same fires that American settlers and White River agent Nathan Meeker blamed on the northeastern Nuche). A century later, greenhouse gas emissions almost certainly played a pivotal role in causing unusually warm and arid conditions once again. Drought weakened the defenses that pine trees have evolved to combat insect pests. Even more important, because winter and nighttime temperatures rose even more rapidly than summer and daytime temperatures, deep cold snaps—which historically had served to check the growth of bark beetles, especially in late fall and early spring—became less frequent.[8]

Research on the Greater Rocky Mountain National Park Ecosystem offers a case study in the entanglements that connect forests, climate change, and the mountain pine beetle outbreak of recent decades. The Nuche and other native peoples did not use fire to actively manage subalpine forests. Wildfires nonetheless erupted in the Kawuneeche, but they did so infrequently—at intervals of 145 to 273 years in lodgepole forests and even less frequently in subalpine fir-Englemann spruce woodlands—and almost always in immense conflagrations that consumed many thousands of acres of trees. During the past several centuries, severe fire seasons within the present-day boundaries of Rocky Mountain have correlated closely with prolonged droughts; these, in turn, seem to be driven by large-scale climatic patterns (especially the El Niño/Southern Oscillation, Atlantic Multidecadal Oscillation, and Pacific Decadal Oscillation). Throughout the twentieth century, fire dynamics in the Coyote Valley remained well within the long-term historic range of variability. Lodgepole forests characterized by "high stand densities"—the much maligned "doghair pines" that cover the ground with a coniferous fur of skinny, bristly trees—were probably as common in the 1600s and 1700s as they are today. The scientific consensus, then, holds that fire suppression did not contribute to the pine beetle epidemic of the early 2000s.[9]

Tourists and locals alike have tended to make another erroneous assumption about wildfire and mountain pine beetle in the Kawuneeche: that beetle-killed forests act as giant outdoor tinderboxes that might erupt any time into blazes of unprecedented scope and severity. The view that the bark beetle outbreak will inevitably lead to catastrophic fire seasons, though, is about as reliable as the old chestnut that fire suppression set the stage for the epidemic. Soon after bark beetles and blue stain fungus kill trees, they enter the so-called red phase in which their needles turn red and they become more flammable. One to three years later, though, the needles of beetle-killed trees turn gray; from that point on, these woodlands remain harder to ignite than living forests. As fire ecologist Jason Sibold, foremost expert on the fire history of the Greater Rocky Mountain National Park Ecosystem, noted, "You're probably less likely to have a fire following an outbreak."[10]

Doom, Resilience, and the Road Ahead

In the years since the height of the pine beetle epidemic, two main interpretations of the Coyote Valley's ecological future have begun to take shape. The first is regional in scope and forecasts doom ahead, as global climate change unleashes transformations more intense and dramatic than anything the Rocky Mountain high country has experienced in many thousands of years. The second, by contrast, adopts a local scale and paints a much more optimistic picture—one emphasizing the ecological resilience of subalpine forests affected by mountain pine beetles.

Nearly every reputable climate researcher concurs that anthropogenic climate change is already underway in the American West. What remains less clear, however, is the probable pace, severity, and consequences of the changes ahead. Several studies make especially alarming predictions about the future of the West's forest and tundra ecosystems. A study of the Greater Yellowstone Ecosystem (GYE), for instance, contends that revolutionary ecological transformations may be afoot. Models designed to forecast the impact of warmer, drier, and more erratic climatic conditions there strongly suggest that "continued warming could completely transform the GYE's fire regimes by the mid-21st century, with profound consequences for many species and for ecosystem services including aesthetics, hydrology, and carbon storage." Researchers even warn there is "a real likelihood" that Yellowstone's forests will be "converted to nonforest vegetation during the mid-21st century" because more-frequent wildfires "would likely preclude postfire tree generation."[11]

Broader-scale predictions about the ecological effects of climate change raise fears of a still bleaker future for the Greater Rocky Mountain National Park Ecosystem. The realization undergirding these dire forecasts, a recent review article notes, is that "long-lived tree species" like those that dominate the montane and subalpine forests of the Coyote Valley are characterized by "slow rates of migration," meaning that it takes them a very long time to colonize new soil. The far-reaching climatic changes already under way in the Mountain West will almost undoubtedly grow more severe in the decades ahead. As climatic change outpaces the ability of trees to colonize new ground, the region's forest ecosystems seem bound to experience "a mismatch between the climate to which trees are currently adapted and the climate the trees will experience in the future." Once standing trees are "exposed to climate conditions outside their climatic niches," they will suffer from "compromised productivity and increased vulnerability to disturbances, such as insects and pathogens." Over time, these factors will extirpate many vegetative communities in the cordilleras of the western United States. A 2012 study by the U.S. Forest Service's Rocky Mountain Research Station contends that even under relatively conservative projections—a mean temperature increase of 2.1 to 5.7 degrees Celsius and a −3 percent to +14 percent change in precipitation—an estimated "55% of future landscapes" across the region "likely will have climates that are incompatible with the vegetation types that now occur on those landscapes."

The subalpine forest and tundra biomes of the Rocky Mountains will either decline "substantially (>97%)" from their current ranges by 2090, or disappear altogether. Such profound and far-reaching transformations even have led some conservation biologists to propose that land managers begin to plan for "assisted migration," "facilitated migration," or "assisted colonization" to help species and communities move to more-suitable habitats in response to climatic change. Alas, those destinations where long-term conditions seem most likely to sustain the denizens of the tundra biome after their extirpation from the Coyote Valley lay hundreds of miles north of Rocky Mountain National Park.[12]

Considerable uncertainty permeates attempts to model future climate and vegetation; future precipitation trends are especially hard to predict. If the assumptions underlying today's models prove robust, though, lodgepole pine forests will either die off or push their range up the slopes of the Never Summers and Front Range. Vegetation communities resembling the present-day shrub-grasslands of the northern Great Basin in Nevada, Idaho, and Oregon, meanwhile, may well come to dominate the old hay meadows and willow thickets of the Kawuneeche bottomlands. Such transformations would dwarf any and all of the ecological changes the valley has experienced since the Colorado River Glacier retreated more than 12,000 years ago. In the face of this and the other heartrending ecological catastrophes that global climate models prophesy, it is tempting to take refuge—as so many Americans have—in denial or technological utopianism. Confronted with the prospects of extreme environmental change, some are even finding solace in sophistry. For if "nature" has always been a human construction—a mere figment of our collective imagination—then why should we lament its domestication and destruction when we might instead celebrate—or at least accept—the brave new world of the Anthropocene, with its radically altered landscapes, ecosystems, and processes?[13]

There still remains ample opportunity, however, to embrace less-cynical responses to the dilemmas now confronting humanity and the places we call home. The Coyote Valley, this trickster place, may just offer grounds for hope.

In the aftermath of the worst bark beetle outbreak in North America's known history, lodgepole pine forests have regenerated with surprising swiftness. Fir, spruce, and aspen are all faring well in the wake of the infestation. Forests in the Kawuneeche have become more het-

erogeneous, with more varied "age structures, tree densities, and species compositions at the landscape scale" than the uniform stands of
doghair pines they are supplanting. One study, for instance, forecasts
that while lodgepole pine will continue to dominate those parts of the
Colorado River headwaters "where it formed pure stands prior to the
epidemic," mixed forests containing spruce, fir, and aspen are emerging
in many beetle-killed areas. The aspens' renaissance is especially encouraging since these deciduous trees have been displaced by conifers
in much of the Southern Rockies in recent decades.[14]

Collectively, this research on the ecological consequences of
the mountain pine beetle infestation emphasizes the resilience of the
Kawuneeche's ecosystems in the face of intensive regional-scale events.
In contrast to the even-aged stands of lodgepole pines that took root after
the widespread and intense wildfires of the late 1800s, the postoutbreak
forests that are currently regenerating will likely prove much less vulnerable to future bark beetle infestations. This leads forest ecologists
to predict that the Coyote Valley "is likely to remain forested with a
modest change in species composition"—a sharp departure from the
much gloomier scenarios posited by regional-scale models warning
that climatic change is bound to force profound ecological transformations, ranging from the upward elevational shift of some biomes to the
complete eradication of others. "From a purely ecological standpoint,"
two leading authorities on Rocky Mountain forests explain, the "dead
and drying trees" that cover the slopes of the present-day Colorado
high country "do not necessarily represent poor 'forest health.' They
may instead reflect a natural process of forest renewal."[15]

Which future will actually materialize in the Kawuneeche: the ominous scenario predicted by models of climatic and vegetational change,
or the more sanguine view portrayed by field ecologists documenting
the recovering of the Coyote Valley's forest ecosystems following the
mountain pine beetle outbreak? Only time will tell. The precautionary
principle, however, wisely directs us to do all in our power to address
the underlying causes of anthropogenic climate change even as we yearn
with all our might that maybe—just maybe—Coyote still has a few tricks
in store for the valley that bears his name.

⊰ NOTES ⊱

ABBREVIATIONS

Works frequently cited in the notes have been identified by the following abbreviations:

ARCIA	Annual Reports of the Commissioner of Indian Affairs
ARDNPS	Annual Reports of the Director of the National Park Service
DPL	Denver Public Library
FCC	*Fort Collins Courier*
GLO Records	General Land Office Records, National Archives and Records Administration, Washington, D.C.
NARA	National Archives and Records Administration
RMN	*Rocky Mountain News* (Denver, Colorado)
RMNP	Rocky Mountain National Park
RMNP Archives	Rocky Mountain National Park Archives, Estes Park, Colorado
RMR	Ranger's Monthly Reports, RMNP Archives
SMR	Superintendent's Monthly Reports, RMNP Archives

INTRODUCTION

1. William Blake, "Auguries of Innocence," in *The Poems of William Blake, Comprising Songs of Innocence and Experience together with Poetical Sketches and Some Copyright Poems Not in Any Other Collection,* new ed. (London: Pickering and Chatto, 1887), 145; Henry D. Thoreau, *Walden; or, Life in the Woods* (Boston: Ticknor and Fields, 1854); Aldo Leopold, *A Sand County Almanac, and Sketches Here and There* (New York: Oxford University Press, 1949); William J. Cronon, "Kennecott Journey: The Paths Out of Town," in *Under an Open Sky: Rethinking*

America's Western Past, ed. William Cronon, George A. Miles, and Jay Gitlin (New York: Norton, 1992), 28–51; and Terry Tempest Williams, *Refuge: An Unnatural History of Family and Place* (New York: Pantheon, 1991).

2. For an extraordinarily helpful discussion of the larger scaling-up of which trends in environmental history comprise just one small vector, see Sebouh Aslanian et al., "AHR *Conversation:* How Size Matters: The Question of Scale in History," *American Historical Review* 118 (2013): 1431–1472.

3. On climate change, see Naomi Oreskes, "The Scientific Consensus on Climate Change: How Do We Know We're Not Wrong?" in *Climate Change: What It Means for Us, Our Children, and Our Grandchildren,* ed. Joseph F. C. Dimento and Pamela Doughman, 2nd ed. (Cambridge, MA: MIT Press, 2014), 105–148; Intergovernmental Panel on Climate Change, "Climate Change 2014 Synthesis Report: Summary for Policy Makers," ed. Core Writing Team, Rajendra K. Pachauri, and Leo Meyer, available at http://www.ipcc.ch/pdf/assessment-report/ar5/syr/AR5_SYR_FINAL_SPM.pdf The first articulation of the "Anthropocene" concept is Paul J. Crutzen and Eugene F. Stoermer, "The Anthropocene," *International Geosphere-Biosphere Programme Newsletter* 41 (2000): 17.

4. William Bright, *Colorado Place Names,* 3rd ed. (Boulder, CO: Johnson Books, 2004), 40.

5. The resolution was published as Committee on Interstate and Foreign Commerce, *Change Name of Grand River to Colorado River,* H.R. Rep. No. 67–97; *Renaming of the Grand River, Colo., Hearing before the Committee on Interstate and Foreign Commerce of the House of Representatives on H.J. Res. 460,* 66th Cong. (1921).

6. An especially salient example from this vast literature is Philip L. Fradkin, *A River No More: The Colorado River and the West* (New York: Knopf, 1981).

7. My critique here follows that laid out by William Cronon, "The Trouble with Wilderness; or, Getting Back to the Wrong Nature," in *Uncommon Ground: Rethinking the Human Place in Nature,* ed. William Cronon (New York: Norton, 1995), 69–90.

8. Rogers quoted in Andrew Cowell, "Arapaho Placenames in Colorado: Indigenous Mapping, White Remaking," *Names* 52 (2004): 27. On the Toll Expedition, see Oliver W. Toll, *Arapaho Names and Trails: Report of a 1914 Pack Trip* (n.p., 1962). The first codification of the Colorado Mountain Club's (CMC's) naming project is U.S. Geological Survey, *Topographical Map of Rocky Mountain National Park,* surveyed by R. B. Marshall (Washington, DC: Government Printing Office, 1919). Harriet W. Vaille, Toll's cousin, elaborated on the agenda that drove Colorado's Anglo-American population to color the state's emerging vacationlands with place names salvaged form aging Arapaho informants: "Before the last old Indian dies," she told anthropologist Alfred Kroeber, "we desire to preserve as many Indian traditions as possible." Harriet W. Vaille to Alfred Kroeber, January 7, 1915, Box 7, James Grafton Rogers Collection, MS 536, History Colorado, Denver.

For more on Sage, see Jeffrey D. Anderson, *One Hundred Years of Old Man Sage: An Arapaho Life* (Lincoln: University of Nebraska Press, 2003).

9. For this transliteration and the quote, see Andrew Cowell and Alonzo Moss Sr., "Arapaho Place Names in Colorado: Form and Function, Language and Culture," *Anthropological Linguistics* 45 (2003): 357. Other versions can be found at Cowell, "Arapaho Placenames in Colorado," 27; and the folder on Harriet Vaille in Box 7, Rogers Collection. Despite Coyote's central role in the oral and written literatures of many Native American peoples, there is no single synthesis of the large body of scholarship relating to this figure.

10. In using "Nuche," I follow the convention of several other historians, who prefer this straightforward Anglicized transcription of the Ute word in favor of *núuci,* Noochee, or alternate spellings; T. Givón, ed., *Ute Traditional Narratives* (Ignacio, CO: Ute Press, 1985), 1; Uintah-Ouray Ute Tribe, *Stories of Our Ancestors: A Collection of Northern-Ute Indian Tales* (Salt Lake City: University of Utah Printing Service, 1974), 24, 35. For the sake of convenience and clarity, I employ Nuche when referring to multiple individuals, instead of the linguistically correct *núuci-u.* Harriet Vaille may have hinted at why the Colorado Mountain Club paid little attention to the limits of the Arapaho traditional territories: "We Coloradans . . . feel that of all the Indian tribes, the Arapahoes [*sic*] belong peculiarly to us," Vaille to Kroeber. On "captivity economies" between the Nuche and Plains Indians, see Brandilyn Denison, "Remove, Return, Remember: Making Ute Land Religion in the American West" (PhD diss., University of North Carolina, 2011), 50. Alas, most Nuche toponyms for north-central Colorado have been lost. On Native American place names in the U.S. West more generally, see Keith H. Basso, *Wisdom Sits in Places: Landscape and Language among the Western Apache* (Albuquerque: University of New Mexico Press, 1996).

11. "The Indians of Long Ago," in Uintah-Ouray Ute Tribe, *Stories of Our Ancestors,* 22 (quoted); see also "Coyote Steals Fire," ibid., 13–18. Subsequent quotes from "Coyote *(Yur-g:er-vuech)* Lets the Animals *(Pee-see-yaff)* Out of the Cave," in Uintah and Ouray Ute Tribe, *The Way It Was Told* (Salt Lake City: University of Utah Printing Service, 1977), 27–29.

12. Uintah-Ouray Ute Tribe, *Stories of Our Ancestors,* 68.

13. Bertha Groves, "Sinawav Names the Trees and Bushes," recorded September 29, 1985, translated by Bertha Groves, transcribed by T. Givón, in Givón, *Ute Traditional Narratives,* 49. For more on Coyote's role in Nuche oral literature, see T. Givón, introduction to ibid., 6. My approach to Native American oral traditions and historical reconstruction is informed by Roger C. Echo-Hawk, "Ancient History in the New World: Integrating Oral Traditions and the Archaeological Record in Deep Time," *American Antiquity* 65 (2000): 267–290; and Marsha L. Weisiger, *Dreaming of Sheep in Navajo Country* (Seattle: University of Washington Press, 2011), ch. 3.

14. See Audrey DeLella Benedict, *The Sierra Naturalist's Guide: Southern Rockies* (San Francisco: Sierra Club Books, 1991); Cornelia Fleischer Mutel, *From*

Grassland to Glacier: The Natural History of Colorado and the Surrounding Region,
2nd ed. (Boulder, CO: Johnson Books, 1992); and Scott A. Elias, *Rocky
Mountains* (Washington, DC: Smithsonian, 2002).

15. Benedict, *Sierra Naturalist's Guide,* 378–381; Patrick C. Trotter, *Cutthroat: Native Trout of the West* (Boulder: Colorado Associated University Press, 1987),
151–162.

16. Benedict, *Sierra Naturalist's Guide,* 427, 435.

17. Ibid., ch. 22; figures from 462, 464.

18. For a thoughtful plea urging historians to rethink the limits of their disci-
pline because of the pressing demands of anthropogenic climate change,
see Dipesh Chakrabarty, "The Climate of History: Four Theses," *Critical
Inquiry* 35 (2009): 197–222.

19. The only synthesis yet published is Andrew Nikiforuk, *Empire of the Beetle:
How Human Folly and a Tiny Bug Are Killing North America's Great Forests* (Van-
couver: Greystone Books, 2011). On mountain pine beetle at Rocky Mountain, see the conclusion herein.

20. Fred M. Packard, "A Survey of the Beaver Population of Rocky Mountain
National Park, Colorado." *Journal of Mammalogy* 28 (1947): 219–227.

21. Jordan A. Clayton and Cherie J. Westbrook, "The Effect of the Grand
Ditch on the Abundance of Benthic Invertebrates in the Colorado River,
Rocky Mountain National Park," *River Research and Applications* 24 (2008):
975–987.

22. Key studies include Barbara J. Bentz et al., "Climate Change and Bark Bee-
tles of the Western United States and Canada: Direct and Indirect Effects,"
BioScience 60 (2010): 602–613; Isabel W. Ashton, *Observed and Projected
Ecological Response to Climate Change in the Rocky Mountains and Upper Columbia
Basin: A Synthesis of Current Scientific Literature* (Fort Collins, CO: U.S. Depart-
ment of the Interior, National Park Service, Natural Resource Program
Center, 2010), 21–25.

23. Works advocating the "national park idea" include Alfred Runte, *National
Parks: The American Experience,* 4th ed. (Lanham, MD: Taylor Trade, 2010);
Ken Burns, "America's Best Idea: The National Parks" (PBS Home Video,
2009); and Dayton Duncan, *The National Parks: America's Best Idea: An Illustrated History* (New York: Knopf, 2009). For a trenchant critique, see James
Morton Turner, "Rethinking American Exceptionalism: Toward a Transnational History of National Parks, Wilderness, and Protected Areas," in Andrew C. Isenberg, ed., *Oxford Handbook of Environmental History* (New York:
Oxford University Press, 2014), 282–309. More critical—and hence more
useful—environmental histories of national parks and the National Park
Service (NPS) are cited throughout the body of this book.

24. As the esteemed historian Ann McGrath has recently put it, "the micro
and macro are not only companions, but can also be one and the same
creature. . . . In specific locations," she goes on to argue, "stratigraphic lay-
erings of time can reveal both the everyday and the exceptional, poten-

tially linking the local and the global." In Aslanian et al., "AHR *Conversation*," 1436. On microhistory, see James F. Brooks, Christopher R. N. DeCorse, and John Walton, eds. *Small Worlds: Method, Meaning, and Narrative in Microhistory* (Santa Fe: School for Advanced Research Press, 2008). On deep history, see Daniel Lord Smail, *On Deep History and the Brain* (Berkeley: University of California Press, 2008); Daniel Lord Smail and Andrew Shryock, "History and the 'Pre,'" *American Historical Review* 118 (2013): 709–737. On the history of Rocky Mountain National Park more generally, see Lloyd K. Musselman, *Rocky Mountain National Park: Administrative History, 1915–1965* (Washington, DC: U.S. Office of History and Historic Architecture, Eastern Service Center, 1971); C. W. Buchholtz, *Rocky Mountain National Park: A History* (Boulder: Colorado Associated University Press, 1983); and Jerry J. Frank, *Making Rocky Mountain National Park: The Environmental History of an American Treasure* (Lawrence: University Press of Kansas, 2013).

1. EMERGENCE

1. I take my inspiration here from Brian M. Fagan, *Writing Archaeology: Telling Stories about the Past*, 2nd ed. (Walnut Creek, CA: Left Coast Press, 2005). Most studies cited here rely on radiocarbon dating, but researchers typically use calibration programs to translate radiocarbon dates into calendar years. This, together with shifting conventions regarding the appropriate benchmark—Before the Common Era or Before Present—usually accounts for disparities between the dates used here and those that readers may encounter elsewhere.

2. Scott A. Elias, *The Ice-Age History of National Parks in the Rocky Mountains* (Washington, DC: Smithsonian Institution Press, 1996); William A. Braddock and James C. Cole, *Geologic Map of Rocky Mountain National Park and Vicinity, Colorado* (Reston, VA: United States Geological Survey, 1990); A. R. Nelson et al., "Radio-Carbon Dated Upper Pleistocene Glacial Sequence, Fraser Valley, Colorado Front Range," *Geology* 7 (1979): 410–414.

3. Charles C. Mann, *1491: New Revelations of the Americas before Columbus* (New York: Alfred A. Knopf, 2005), 160.

4. John McPhee, *Annals of the Former World* (New York: Farrar, Straus and Giroux, 1998), 312–313. See also Keith Heyer Meldahl, *Rough-Hewn Land: A Geologic Journey from California to the Rocky Mountains* (Berkeley and Los Angeles: University of California Press, 2011), 181, 188; Braddock and Cole, *Geologic Map*; Omer B. Raup, *Geology along Trail Ridge Road: A Self-Guided Tour for Motorists* (Estes Park, CO: Rocky Mountain Nature Association, 2005), 18, 64.

5. Raup, *Geology along Trail Ridge Road*, 18; Halka Chronic, *Time, Rocks, and the Rockies: A Geologic Guide to Roads and Trails of Rocky Mountain National Park* (Missoula, MT: Mountain Press 1984).

6. Meldahl, *Rough-Hewn Land*, 188 (quoted). See also Chronic, *Time, Rocks, and the Rockies*, 67; and McPhee, *Annals of the Former World*, 313. Braddock and

Cole, *Geologic Map,* argue that "at least the southern part of the valley existed prior to deposition of the Troublesome Formation," which they date to 29–23 million years BP.

7. Katherine Lee Knox, "The Never Summer Igneous Complex: Evolution of a Shallow Magmatic System" (master's thesis, University of Colorado–Boulder, 2005); Raup, *Geology along Trail Ridge Road,* 18. Many authors argue that mid-Tertiary volcanism continued in the Never Summers until 24 or 25 million years ago, but Knox's dating seems definitive. See also Lon Abott and Terri Cook, *Geology Underfoot along Colorado's Front Range* (Missoula, MT: Mountain Press, 2012).

8. Meldahl, *Rough-Hewn Land,* 170, 196–199.

9. Quotes from ibid., 204–207. See also McPhee, *Annals of the Former World,* 313–315. The most thorough synthetic approach to the exhumation is Robert S. Anderson et al., "Facing Reality: Late Cenozoic Evolution of Smooth Peaks, Glacially Ornamented Valleys, and Deep River Gorges of Colorado's Front Range," in *Tectonics, Climate, and Landscape Evolution,* ed. S. D. Willett, N. Novius, M. T. Brandon, and D. M. Fisher, Special Paper 398, Penrose Conference Series (Boulder, CO: Geological Society of America, 2006), 397–418. Here, I subsume more-complicated factors into a simpler driving force, but Meldahl persuasively attributes the Exhumation to "(1) passive uplift caused by erosion, (2) active uplift caused by a hot, buoyant mantle beneath the Rockies, and (3) climate change that delivered bigger floods to the Rocky Mountain rivers"; Meldahl, *Rough-Hewn Land,* 207. By 11 million years ago, "evidence of a paleo-Colorado River" appears; scientists generally agree that the Colorado River had become an integrated system by 5 or 6 million years ago. See Karl E. Karlstrom et al., "Introduction: CRevolution 2: Origin and Evolution of the Colorado River System II," *Geosphere* 8, no. 6 (2012).

10. Abott and Cook, *Geology Underfoot,* 51; Anderson et al., "Facing Reality," 406–409. Mountain glaciation may have begun as long as 3 million years ago; see Meldahl, *Rough-Hewn Land,* 210. The most authoritative recent study argues that the most recent glacial phase in the Central Rockies lasted from 23,000 BP to 16,000 BP. Oliver A. Chadwick, Robert D. Hall, and Fred M. Phillips, "Chronology of Pleistocene Glacial Advances in the Central Rocky Mountains," *Geological Society of America Bulletin* 109 (1997): 1443.

11. On dates for the end of the last Ice Age, see Elias, *Ice-Age History,* 143; Byron M. Straw, "Glacial and Periglacial Deposits of the Lake of the Clouds Cirque, Never Summer Mountains, Colorado" (master's thesis, University of Northern Colorado, 2010), iii, 80–81; Jared M. Beeton, "Post-Pinedale Glacial and Periglacial Deposits of the Snow Lake and Nokhu Cirques, Never Summer Mountains, Colorado" (master's thesis, University of Northern Colorado, 2003), 15, 17. On the global timing of the Younger Dryas, see R. B.

Alley, "The Younger Dryas Cold Interval as Viewed from Central Green-land," *Quaternary Science Reviews* 19 (2000): 213–226.

My use of the Greater Rocky Mountain National Park Ecosystem merits explanation, since the term previously has appeared in print just once; see Dave Hallock, "Wildlife Trends on the Urban-Rural Fringe," in *Issues and Technology in the Management of Wildlife: Proceedings of a National Symposium,* Thorne Ecological Institute Conference in Glenwood Springs, Colorado, February 6–8, 1989, 17, 18, 21. The "greater ecosystem" concept, like so much else relating to the national parks, originated at Yellowstone. Its underlying premise is simple but profound: national park boundaries are political and historical, not ecological; effective management in these environments thus requires that we constantly remember that national parks are inextricably connected to the lands beyond their borders. Despite the many important differences between Rocky Mountain and Yellowstone, there is nonetheless good reason to think about the Coyote Valley as an integral part of a larger mosaic. Imagine the Greater Rocky Mountain National Park Ecosystem not as a singular, self-contained ecological entity, but instead as a shifting set of entangled relationships that, Coyote-like, has assumed different configurations depending on historical circumstances and the questions we ask about them. Three adjoining areas loom especially large in my analysis: Estes Park and the eastern side of Rocky Mountain National Park; Middle Park, a large, irregular expanse of relatively flat land down-river from Grand Lake; and the Cache La Poudre watershed, which begins just north of the Kawuneeche.

12. Elias, *Ice-Age History,* 143–151; and E. C. Pielou, *After the Ice Age: The Return of Life to Glaciated North America* (Chicago: University of Chicago Press, 1991), pt. 4.

13. On timing, see J. Tyler Faith and Todd A. Surovell, "Synchronous Extinction of North America's Pleistocene Mammals," *Proceedings of the National Academy of Sciences* 106 (2009): 20641–20645. On causes, see Anthony D. Barnosky et al., "Assessing the Causes of Late Pleistocene Extinctions across the Continents," *Science* 306 (2004): 71.

14. On beavers and willows, see H. Raul Peinetti, Bruce W. Baker, and Michael B. Coughenour, "Simulation Modeling to Understand How Selective Foraging by Beaver Can Drive the Structure and Function of a Willow Community," *Ecological Modeling* 220 (2009): 998–1012. For a critical take on the ability of beavers to engineer landscapes, see L. Persico and G. Meyer, "Holocene Beaver Damming, Fluvial Geomorphology, and Climate in Yellowstone National Park, Wyoming," *Quaternary Research* 71 (2009): 340–353. For a persuasive rebuttal focused on RMNP, see Lina E. Polvi and Ellen Wohl, "The Beaver-Meadow Complex Revisited—The Role of Beavers in Post-Glacial Floodplain Development," *Earth Surface Processes and Landforms* 37 (2012): 332–346. For studies that largely confirm the significance

of beavers as geomorphological agents, see Lina Eleonor Polvi Pilgrim, "Biotic Controls on Post-Glacial Floodplain Dynamics in the Colorado Front Range" (PhD diss., Colorado State University, 2011); and Natalie Kramer, "An Investigation into Beaver-Induced Holocene Sedimentation Using Ground Penetrating Radar and Seismic Refraction: Beaver Meadows, Rocky Mountain National Park, Colorado" (master's thesis, Colorado State University, 2011).

15. Wilderness Act of 1964, 16 U.S.C. § 1131–1136 (1964). The best brief for the intensive humanization of American environments is Mann, *1491*. For an important study of "wilderness" in post–World War II culture and politics, see James Morton Turner, *The Promise of Wilderness: American Environmental Politics since 1964* (Seattle: University of Washington Press, 2012).

16. Mann, *1491*, 160 (quoted), 169; Alan D. Reed and Michael D. Metcalf, *Colorado Prehistory: A Context for the Northern Colorado River Basin* (Denver: Colorado Council of Professional Archaeologists, 1999), 61–62; Robert H. Brunswig, *Prehistoric, Protohistoric, and Early Historic Native American Archaeology of Rocky Mountain National Park*, vol. 1, *Final Report of Systemwide Archaeological Inventory Program Investigations by the University of Northern Colorado (1998–2002)*, National Park Service Project ROMO-R98-0804 (Greeley: University of Northern Colorado, 2005), 70, 106–107.

17. Brunswig, *Prehistoric, Protohistoric, and Early Historic Native American Archaeology of Rocky Mountain National Park*, 71–73, 108. For support on glacial advances, see Straw, "Glacial and Periglacial Deposits," iii, 80; Beeton, "Post-Pinedale Glacial and Periglacial Deposits," 15, 17. In Middle Park, Folsom sites are as dense as anywhere in North America—probably because the area provided year-round forage for *Bison antiquus* pushed out of the high country by neoglaciation; Robert H. Brunswig, "Paleoindian Cultural Landscapes and Archaeology," in *Frontiers in Colorado Paleoindian Archaeology: From the Dent Site to the Rocky Mountains*, ed. Robert H. Brunswig and Bonnie L. Pitblado (Boulder: University Press of Colorado, 2007), 274–275.

18. Brunswig, "Paleoindian Cultural Landscapes and Archaeology," 278. Revealingly, "Nearly half (47.1 percent) of RMNP's thirty-four late Paleoindian components are situated above tree line on sites associated with what are inferred as warm-season tundra hunting territories"; ibid., 290. On the Holocene altithermal, see Kramer, "Investigation into Beaver-Induced Holocene Sedimentation," 14.

19. Quotes from Bonnie L. Pitblado and Robert H. Brunswig, "That Was Then, This Was Now: Seventy-Five Years of Paleoindian Research in Colorado," in *Frontiers in Colorado Paleoindian Archaeology*, ed. Brunswig and Pitblado, 50; Brunswig, *Prehistoric, Protohistoric, and Early Historic Native American Archaeology of Rocky Mountain National Park*, 76–77, 232–233. On Big Horn Flats, see ibid., 111. Mark Stiger interprets a classic archaeological essay as defining "tradition" based on "temporal continuity in technologies or other systems of related forms." Mark Stiger, *Hunter-Gatherer Archaeology of the Colorado*

High Country (Boulder: University Press of Colorado, 2001), 18. Kevin D. Black defines the Mountain Tradition as an "adaptation to upland terrain, over an extended length of time and covering a broad geographical area"; "Archaic Continuity in the Colorado Rockies: The Mountain Tradition," *Plains Anthropologist* 36 (1991): 4. Though Brunswig, *Prehistoric, Protohistoric, and Early Historic Native American Archaeology of Rocky Mountain National Park*, refers to "foothill-mountain traditions" to recognize the likelihood that these were complex and multifarious groups, I prefer Black's "Mountain Tradition" because it is simpler and better encompasses transhumance rounds that linked the Kawuneeche to areas to the valley's north and west, as well as the Rockies' eastern foothills. See also Bonnie L. Pitblado, "Angostura, Jimmy Allen, Foothills-Mountain: Clarifying Terminology for Late Paleoindian Southern Rocky Mountain Spear Points," in *Frontiers in Colorado Paleoindian Archaeology*, ed. Brunswig and Pitblado, 328; Brunswig, "Paleoindian Cultural Landscapes and Archaeology," 294; Reed and Metcalf, *Colorado Prehistory*, 57, 68–69. On game drive sites, see E. Steve Cassells, "Hunting the Open High Country" (PhD diss., University of Wisconsin–Madison, 1995), as well as the voluminous work of archaeologist James B. Benedict, for example, *The Game Drives of Rocky Mountain National Park* (Ward, CO: Center for Mountain Archeology, 1966); "Getting Away from It All: A Study of Man, Mountains, and the Two-Drought Altithermal," *Southwestern Lore* 45 (1979): 1–12; "Footprints in the Snow: High-Altitude Cultural Ecology of the Colorado Front Range, U.S.A.," *Arctic and Alpine Research* 24 (1992): 1–16; and "Effects of Changing Climate on Game-Animal and Human Use of the Colorado High Country (U.S.A.) since 1000 BC," *Arctic, Antarctic, and Alpine Research* 31 (1999): 1–15.

20. Brunswig, *Prehistoric, Protohistoric, and Early Historic Native American Archaeology of Rocky Mountain National Park*, 80, 114–115 (quoted); Reed and Metcalf, *Colorado Prehistory*, 32, 71, 88, 97.

21. Brunswig, *Prehistoric, Protohistoric, and Early Historic Native American Archaeology of Rocky Mountain National Park*, 82, 115–119. This correlates with Beeton's "Triple Lakes Advance" of 5,200–3,000 radiocarbon years BP; "Post-Pinedale Glacial and Periglacial Deposits," 19.

22. Brunswig, *Prehistoric, Protohistoric, and Early Historic Native American Archaeology of Rocky Mountain National Park*, 89, 96; James P. Doerner, "Late Quaternary Prehistoric Environments of the Colorado Front Range," in *Frontiers in Colorado Paleoindian Archaeology*, ed. Brunswig and Pitblado, 11–38; Reed and Metcalf, *Colorado Prehistory*, 22, 32, 89, 96.

23. Benedict, "Footprints in the Snow." On the likelihood that Mountain Tradition practitioners who inhabited the Kawuneeche spent winters to the West, see Reed and Metcalf, *Colorado Prehistory*, 89; Brunswig, *Prehistoric, Protohistoric, and Early Historic Native American Archaeology of Rocky Mountain National Park*, ch. 7. On the lack of seasonal campsites used repeatedly over long stretches of time, see ibid., 230. On astronomy at RMNP sacred sites, see

Robert Brunswig, Sally McBeth, and Louise Elinoff, "Re-enfranchising Native Peoples in the Southern Rocky Mountains: Integrated Contributions of Archaeological and Ethnographic Studies on Federal Lands," in *Post-Colonial Perspectives on Archaeology,* ed. Peter Bikoulis, D. Lacroix, and M. Pueramaki-Brown (Calgary, AB: Chacmool Archaeological Association, 2009), 55–69.

24. Mountain Tradition foragers probably also sought out bulbs of Geyer's onion, seeds from alpine sunflower, and the bulbs, roots, and seeds of the mariposa lily. John A. Brett, *Ethnographic Assessment and Documentation of Rocky Mountain National Park* (Denver: University of Colorado, Denver Department of Anthropology, 2002), 67–73; Brunswig, *Prehistoric, Protohistoric, and Early Historic Native American Archaeology of Rocky Mountain National Park,* 236–242.

25. The assumptions underlying this paragraph's argument are discussed and cited in Chapter 9; they also figure centrally in recent management decisions, see, United States Department of the Interior, National Park Service, *Elk and Vegetation Management Plan—Rocky Mountain National Park, Colorado* (Washington, DC: Government Printing Office, 2007), 7–8. Considerable controversy attends the unexpectedly low frequency of elk in faunal remains from prehistoric archaeological sites in the Rocky Mountain West, with Charles Kay claiming that the near-total absence of elk means "'the elk weren't there'"; quoted in Mann, *1491,* 321. See also Charles E. Kay, "Are Ecosystems Structured from the Top-Down or Bottom-Up: A New Look at an Old Debate," *Wildlife Society Bulletin* 26 (1998): 484–498; and Charles E. Kay, Brian Patton, and Cliff A. White, "Historical Wildlife Observations in the Canadian Rockies: Implications for Ecological Integrity," *Canadian Field-Naturalist* 114 (2000): 561–583. For two critiques of this work, see Michael J. Yochim, "Aboriginal Overkill Overstated," *Human Nature* 12 (2001): 141–167; and R. Lee Lyman, "Aboriginal Overkill in the Intermountain West of North America," *Human Nature* 15 (2004): 169–208. On the potential for overexploitation of ungulates at game-drive sites, see Stiger, *Hunter-Gatherer Archaeology,* 164–167.

26. Brunswig, McBeth, and Elinoff, "Re-enfranchising Native Peoples."

27. On fire, see William L. Baker, "Indians and Fire in the Rocky Mountain Landscape: The Wilderness Hypothesis Renewed," in *Fire, Native Peoples, and the Natural Landscape,* ed. Thomas R. Vale, (Washington, DC: Island Press, 2002), 41–76; William L. Baker, *Fire Ecology in Rocky Mountain Landscapes* (Washington, DC: Island Press, 2009); and more detailed evidence presented in Chapters 2 and 3 herein.

2. ENDURANCE

1. Thomas James, *Three Years among the Indians and Mexicans,* 1846 ed. unabridged, with an introduction by A. P. Nasatir (1846; Philadelphia: Lippincott, 1962), 90–92.

2. Ibid. Lechat may have owed his name to his possible role as a so-called Cat Man—a headman who policed the Bear Dance, the most important ceremony in the Nuche calendar. See Ralph Cloud, "The Way the Bear-Dance Used to Be Done," May 7–8, 1981, translated by Sunshine Smith, transcribed by T. Givón, in *Ute Traditional Narratives*, ed. T. Givón (Ignacio, CO: Ute Press, 1985), 228.

3. James, *Three Years*, 90–92.

4. Ibid.

5. Ibid.

6. Ibid.

7. Daniel Lord Smail and Andrew Shryock, "History and the 'Pre,'" *American Historical Review* 118 (2013): 709–737. On Comanche success at reshaping the Interior West during this era, see Pekka Hämäläinen, *The Comanche Empire* (New Haven, CT: Yale University Press, 2008).

8. Useful overviews include Robert L. Bettinger, "Cultural, Human, and Historical Ecology in the Great Basin: Fifty Years of Ideas about Ten Thousand Years of Prehistory," in *Advances in Historical Ecology*, ed. William Balee (New York: Columbia University Press, 1998), 179–181; and David Rhode and David B. Madsen, "Where Are We?" in *Across the West: Human Population Movement and the Expansion of the Numa*, ed. David B. Madsen and David Rhode (Salt Lake City: University of Utah Press, 1994), 213–222. On continuity and in situ development, see Alan D. Reed, "Ute Cultural Chronology," in *Archaeology of the Eastern Ute: A Symposium*, ed. Paul R. Nickens, Occasional Paper No. 1 (Denver: Colorado Council of Professional Archaeologists, 1988), 80.

9. Virginia McConnell Simmons, *The Ute Indians of Utah, Colorado, and New Mexico* (Niwot: University Press of Colorado, 2000); Ned Blackhawk, *Violence over the Land: Indians and Empires in the Early American West* (Cambridge, MA: Harvard University Press, 2006); and Hämäläinen, *Comanche Empire*.

10. The 1400 CE date comes from Uncompahgre Brown Ware at RMNP sites; Robert H. Brunswig, *Prehistoric, Protohistoric, and Early Historic Native American Archaeology of Rocky Mountain National Park*, vol. 1, *Final Report of Systemwide Archaeological Inventory Program Investigations by the University of Northern Colorado (1998–2002)*, National Park Service Project ROMO-R98–0804 (Greeley: University of Northern Colorado, 2005), 88.

11. On family groups, see Julian H. Steward, *Ute Indians I: Aboriginal and Historical Groups of the Ute Indians of Utah: An Analysis with Supplement* (New York: Garland, 1974), 7. On the presence of Yampa or Yamparika Utes in the Kawuneeche, see Sally McBeth, *Native American Oral History and Cultural Interpretation in Rocky Mountain National Park* (Greeley: University of Northern Colorado, 2007), 25; on Uncompahgre, Yampa, and Grand River Nuche there, see John A. Brett, *Ethnographic Assessment and Documentation of Rocky Mountain National Park* (Denver: University of Colorado–Denver, Department of Anthropology, 2002), 11, 40. For more on precontact Nuche

social organization, Ute bands, and their locations, see Simmons, *Ute Indians*, 15–23; and Donald Callaway, Joel Janetski, and Omer C. Stewart, "Ute," in *Handbook of North American Indians*, vol. 11, *Great Basin*, ed. Warren L. D'Azevedo (Washington, DC: Smithsonian Institution, 1986), 336–340, 353. On American confusion about Nuche bands, see Hubert Howe Bancroft, *Native Races*, vol. 1, *Wild Tribes* (San Francisco: A. L. Bancroft, 1883), 463–465.

12. On mythology as cultural unifier, see Anne M. Smith, *Ethnography of the Northern Ute* (Santa Fe: Museum of New Mexico, 1974), 19. On land use and band identity, see John Wesley Powell, "Report on the Indians of Numic Stock," in *Anthropology of the Numa: John Wesley Powell's Manuscripts on the Numic Peoples of Western North America 1868–1880*, ed. Don D. Fowler and Catherine S. Fowler (Washington, DC: Smithsonian Institution Press, 1971), 38. After the late 1600s, a shared pursuit of equestrian lifeways distinguished the Nuche from Southern Paiutes. Steward, *Ute Indians I*, 10.

13. Callaway, Janetski, and Stewart, "Ute," 336–367; Steward, *Ute Indians I*, 29; Thomas G. Andrews, "Tata Atanasio Trujillo's Unlikely Tale of Utes, Nuevomexicanos, and the Settling of Colorado's San Luis Valley," *New Mexico Historical Review* 75 (2000): 21–23; Marvin K. Opler, "The Southern Utes of Colorado," in *Acculturation in Seven American Indian Tribes*, ed. Ralph Linton (New York: Appleton Century, 1940), 119–207.

14. Alan D. Reed and Michael D. Metcalf, *Colorado Prehistory: A Context for the Northern Colorado River Basin* (Denver: Colorado Council of Professional Archaeologists, 1999), 153–154; James B. Benedict, *The Game Drives of Rocky Mountain National Park* (Ward, CO: Center for Mountain Archeology, 1966); and James B. Benedict, "Effects of Changing Climate on Game-Animal and Human Use of the Colorado High Country (U.S.A.) since 1000 BC," *Arctic, Antarctic, and Alpine Research* 31 (1999): 1–15.

15. It is very difficult to determine unequivocally, of course, whether ceramics manufactured outside the Rockies were used by Nuche peoples or traders and travelers from other groups. Brunswig, *Prehistoric*, 124–128, 208, 224–227.

16. On corn in the Southwest, see William L. Merrill et al., The Diffusion of Maize to the Southwestern United States and Its Impact," *Proceedings of the National Academy of Sciences* 106 (2009): 21019–21026. On the introduction of maize to present-day Colorado, see Reed and Metcalf, *Colorado Prehistory*, 142; and E. Steve Cassells, *Archaeology of Colorado*, rev. ed. (Boulder, CO: Johnson Books, 1997), 145, 192, 195, 212–213. On maize and violence, see Christy G. Turner II and Jacqueline A. Turner, *Man Corn: Symbolism and Violence in the Ancient Southwest* (Salt Lake City: University of Utah Press, 1999). On drought, see David M. Meko et al., "Medieval Drought in the Upper Colorado River Basin," *Geophysical Research Letters* 34 (2007), available at http://onlinelibrary.wiley.com/doi/10.1029/2007GL029988/full. On Ancestral Puebloan tumults, see Craig Childs, *House of Rain: Tracking a Vanished Civilization across the American Southwest* (New York: Little, Brown,

2007); Stephen H. Lekson, *A History of the Ancient Southwest* (Santa Fé, NM: School of American Research Press, 2009); and James F. Brooks, "Women, Men, and Cycles of Evangelism in the Southwest Borderlands, AD 750 to 1750," *American Historical Review* 118 (2013): 738–764. On Fremont people and maize, see David B. Madsen, *The Fremont* (Salt Lake City: Utah Museum of Natural History, 1989). On Grand County's short growing season, see Reed and Metcalf, *Colorado Prehistory,* 17, figs. 2–4.

17. Paul W. Mapp, *The Elusive West and the Contest for Empire, 1713–1763* (Chapel Hill: University of North Carolina Press, 2011), ch. 2; John Tutino, *Making a New World: Founding Capitalism in the Bajío and Spanish North America* (Durham, NC: Duke University Press, 2011), 126–140, 213–222. Callaway, Janetski, and Stewart, "Ute," 354, lumps all "eastern Utes" together as having been "in contact with Spaniards at least by the early 1600s," but the northeastern Nuche appear only very rarely in Spanish records.

18. David J. Weber, *The Spanish Frontier in North America* (New Haven, CT: Yale University Press), 28–29 (quoted); Alfred Barnaby Thomas, "Spanish Expeditions into Colorado," *Colorado Magazine,* November 1, 1924, 290. Some scholars assume that the Ute experienced severe epidemics during the early colonial period without providing firm evidence to back this claim, for example, Charles Wilkinson, *Fire on the Plateau: Conflict and Endurance in the American Southwest* (Washington, DC: Island Press, 1999), 128. Reed and Metcalf, *Colorado Prehistory,* 162–163, postulate that a reduction in the frequency of Ute archaeological sites dating from 1650 through 1750 may reflect disease effects, but this hypothesis is conjectural. Later epidemic outbreaks are amply recorded; David Rich Lewis, *Neither Wolf nor Dog: American Indians, Environment, and Agrarian Change* (Lincoln: University of Nebraska Press, 1994), 36; Russell Thornton, *American Indian Holocaust and Survival: A Population History since 1492* (Norman: University of Oklahoma Press, 1987), 100.

19. The northeastern bands almost certainly acquired horses before their Comanche neighbors began to obtain the animals around 1700. Simmons, *Ute Indians,* 29–31; Blackhawk, *Violence over the Land,* 30; Reed and Metcalf, *Colorado Prehistory,* 149; Demitri B. Shemkin, "The Introduction of the Horse," in *Handbook of North American Indians,* 517–23.

20. Elliott West, *The Contested Plains: Indians, Goldseekers, and the Rush to Colorado* (Lawrence: University of Kansas Press, 1998), 50–55; N. Scott Momaday, *The Names: A Memoir* (Tucson: University of Arizona Press, 1976), 28.

21. Sally J. Cole, *Legacy on Stone: Rock Art of the Colorado Plateau and Four Corners Region* (Boulder: Johnson Books, 1990), 223–252; Virginia DeJohn Anderson, *Creatures of Empire: How Domestic Animals Transformed Early America* (New York: Oxford University Press, 2004).

22. Lewis, *Neither Wolf nor Dog,* 30. Major interpretations of the slave trade in the Southwest make virtually no mention of northeastern Nuche; James F. Brooks, *Captives and Cousins: Slavery, Kinship, and Community in the Southwest*

Borderlands (Chapel Hill: University of North Carolina Press, 2002); and Blackhawk, *Violence over the Land.*

23. Smith, *Ethnography of the Northern Ute,* 54, 238, 252; Lewis, *Neither Wolf nor Dog,* 30; S. Lyman Tyler, "The Yuta Indians before 1680," *Western Humanities Review* 5 (Spring 1951): 153–163. On the quality of Nuche-prepared hides, see Rufus B. Sage, *Rocky Mountain Life; or, Startling Scenes and Perilous Adventures in the Far West, during an Expedition of Three Years* (Boston: Wentworth, 1857), 232.

24. West, *Contested Plains;* Blackhawk, *Violence over the Land;* Andrews, "Tata Atanasio Trujillo's Unlikely Tale"; Hämäläinen, *Comanche Empire;* and Pekka Hämäläinen, "The Rise and Fall of Plains Indian Horse Cultures," *Journal of American History* 90 (2003): 833–862.

25. Pekka Hämäläinen, "The Politics of Grass: European Expansion, Ecological Change, and Indigenous Power in the Southwest Borderlands," *William and Mary Quarterly* 67 (2010): 173–208; Dan Flores, "Bison Ecology and Bison Diplomacy: The Southern Plains from 1800 to 1850," *Journal of American History* 78 (1991): 465–485; West, *Contested Plains,* 51–53; and Elliott West, *The Way to the West: Essays on the Central Plains* (Albuquerque: University of New Mexico Press, 1995), 21–36. Increased bison hunting on the Plains may have propelled another, more speculative shift: smaller harvests of elk and other quarry from the Colorado high country. The Nuche, unlike the Comanche, Cheyenne, and other peoples, are not known to have lost any of their plant lore during the shift to equestrianism.

26. Elizabeth John, *Storms Brewed in Other Men's Worlds: The Confrontations of Indians, Spanish, and French in the Southwest, 1540–1795* (College Station: Texas A&M, 1975). For contrasting examples, see Hämäläinen, "Rise and Fall"; West, *Contested Plains;* Richard White, *The Roots of Dependency: Subsistence, Environment, and Social Change among the Choctaws, Pawnees, and Navajos* (Lincoln: University of Nebraska Press, 1983); and Steven Michael Fountain, "Big Dogs and Scorched Streams: Horses and Ethnocultural Change in the North American West, 1700–1850" (PhD diss., University of California–Davis, 2007).

27. Quoted in David J. Weber, *The Taos Trappers: The Fur Trade in the Southwest, 1540–1846* (Norman: University of Oklahoma Press, 1971), 23.

28. Quoted in Brooks, *Captives and Cousins,* 154–155. See also Andrews, "Tata Atanasio Trujillo's Unlikely Tale." Fray Escalante wrote that his party's interpreter and guide, Andrés de Muñiz, was afraid of offending the Nuche "lest he 'lose the ancient friendship which they maintain with them through the vile commerce in skins.'" Weber, *Taos Trappers,* 23–24.

29. James, *Three Years,* 90–92. Contrast this case with the classic interpretation in William J. Cronon, *Changes in the Land: Indians, Colonists, and the Ecology of New England* (New York: Hill & Wang, 1983), ch. 5.

30. Hiram Martin Chittenden, *The American Fur Trade of the Far West* (New York: Francis P. Harper, 1902), 1:11; Richard White, *The Middle Ground: Indians,*

Empires, and Republics in the Great Lakes Region, 1650–1815 (New York: Cambridge University Press, 1991); David J. Wishart, *The Fur Trade of the American West: A Geographic Synthesis 1807–1840* (Lincoln: University of Nebraska Press, 1979), 122.

31. Steven G. Baker, "Historic Ute Culture Change in West-Central Colorado," in *Archaeology of the Eastern Ute*, 166. Though Baker posits a "middle contact" phase characterized by increased trade and more plentiful trade goods, he offers no archaeological evidence to support its existence.

32. Quotes from Wishart, *Fur Trade of the American West*, 145; Sage, *Rocky Mountain Life*, 232. On fur deserts, see Eric Jay Dolin, *Fur, Fortune, and Empire: The Epic Story of the Fur Trade in America* (New York: W. W. Norton, 2010), ch. 14.

33. Chittenden, *American Fur Trade of the Far West*, 2:730, 772. The Nuche, for instance, burned Fort Robidoux; they also killed U.S. Army explorer John Gunnison.

34. James A. Hanson, "The Myth of the Silk Hat and the End of the Rendezvous," in *Rethinking the Fur Trade: Cultures of Exchange in an Atlantic World*, ed. Susan Sleeper-Smith (Lincoln: University of Nebraska Press, 2009), 420–438; Dolin, *Fur, Fortune, and Empire*, ch. 14; Wishart, *Fur Trade of the American West*, 166; Fred M. Packard, "A Survey of the Beaver Population of Rocky Mountain National Park, Colorado," *Journal of Mammalogy* 28 (1947): 219–227.

35. White, *Roots of Dependency*; Andrew C. Isenberg, *The Destruction of the Bison: An Environmental History, 1750–1920* (New York: Cambridge University Press, 2000); West, *Contested Plains*.

36. The starkest contrast here is with the Cheyenne case; see West, *Contested Plains*.

37. Richard Irving Dodge, *Thirty-Three Years' Personal Experience among the Red Men of the Great West: A Popular Account of Their Religion, Habits, Traits, Exploits, etc., with Thrilling Adventures and Experiences on the Great Plains and in the Mountains of Our Wide Frontier* (Hartford, CT: A. D. Worthington, 1882), 442; Blackhawk, *Violence over the Land*, 181–182; Simmons, *Ute Indians*, 29–46.

38. Andrews, "Tata Atanasio Trujillo's Unlikely Tale"; Blackhawk, *Violence over the Land*, chs. 6–7; Simmons, *Ute Indians*.

39. Charles S. Marsh, *People of the Shining Mountains: The Utes of Colorado* (Boulder, CO: Pruett, 1982).

40. Powell reported hearing this story both on the Kaibab Plateau and among the White Rivers in Colorado in 1868–1869. In Powell's version, both brothers were referred to as Shin-au-av. Though Powell repeatedly called Shin-au-av the "Progenitor of the Wolf nation," other texts clarify that the younger of these two brothers is known as Coyote (Yurg:ervuech). See Powell, "Report on the Indians of Numic Stock," 80. See also Powell's *Sketch of the Mythology of the North American Indians*, in Smithsonian Institution Bureau of Ethnology, *First Annual Report* (Washington, DC: Government

Printing Office, 1881), 44; Simmons, *Ute Indians*, 1; and the modernized adaptation of the story Powell recorded published in "Coyote (Yurg:ervuech) and Senawahv Discuss Matters of Importance to the People," in Uintah-Ouray Ute Tribe, *Stories of Our Ancestors: A Collection of Northern-Ute Indian Tales* (Salt Lake City: University of Utah Printing Service, 1974), 7–8.

41. On First Peoples and labor history, see Thomas G. Andrews, "Work, Nature, and History: A Single Question That Once Moved like Light," in *The Oxford Handbook of Environmental History*, ed. Andrew Isenberg (New York: Oxford University Press, 2014), 429–431.

42. Classic studies on the Ute bear dance include Verner Z. Reed, "The Ute Bear Dance," *American Anthropologist* 9 (1896): 237–244; and Julian H. Steward, "A Uintah Ute Bear Dance, March, 1931," *American Anthropologist*, 34 (1932): 263–273. On Nuche migrations, see William N. Brown to General John Pope, August 30, 1877, in *Letter from the Secretary of the Interior, Transmitting in Compliance with a Resolution of the Senate: Correspondence concerning the Ute Indians in Colorado*, Ex. Doc. 31, 46th Cong., 2d Sess. (Washington, DC: Government Printing Office, 1880), 117. On the Ute fondness for Middle Park, see Frank Hall, *History of the State of Colorado* (Chicago, IL: Blakely, 1895), 4:136.

43. William B. Butler, *The Historic Archaeology of Rocky Mountain National Park* (Estes Park, CO: U.S. National Park Service, 2005), 50–54; Oliver W. Toll, *Arapaho Names and Trails: Report of a 1914 Pack Trip* (n.p., 1962).

44. Smith, *Ethnography of the Northern Ute*, 40; Reed and Metcalf, *Colorado Prehistory*, 161.

45. Smith, *Ethnography of the Northern Ute*, 34–38, 42, 123; Reed and Metcalf, *Colorado Prehistory*, 160; Douglas D. Scott, "Conical Timbered Lodges in Colorado or Wickiups in the Woods," in *Archaeology of the Eastern Ute*, 45–53.

46. Smith, *Ethnography of the Northern Ute*, 97 (quote). On basketry, see ibid., 91. On pottery, see Reed, "Ute Cultural Chronology," 81; and Reed and Metcalf, *Colorado Prehistory*, 155. On pitch, see Wilson Rockwell, *The Utes: A Forgotten People* (Lake City, CO: Western Reflections, 1998), 43.

47. Smith, *Ethnography of the Northern Ute*, 15, 64, 107, 109, 112–113, 115.

48. Brett, *Ethnographic Assessment*, 68–71; Smith, *Ethnography of the Northern Ute*, 64–66.

49. Smith, *Ethnography of the Northern Ute*, 64–66; Brett, *Ethnographic Assessment*, 68–71; Reed and Metcalf, *Colorado Prehistory*, 154.

50. On deer and bear, see Smith, *Ethnography of the Northern Ute*, 52; and Powell, "Report on the Indians of Numic Stock," 47.

51. Powell, "Report on the Indians of Numic Stock," 47–48.

52. Brett, *Ethnographic Assessment*, 72; Smith, *Ethnography of the Northern Ute*, 57, 61, 252.

53. Powell, "Report on Indians of Numic Stock," 48; Smith, *Ethnography of the Northern Ute*, 49, 78; Charlie Wash, "Council on the Seasons, 1936–1937,"

trans. Anne M. Smith, in *Ute Tales*, collected by Anne M. Smith, assisted by Alden Hayes (Salt Lake City: University of Utah Press, 1992), 36.

54. Smith, *Ethnography of the Northern Ute*, 48–49, 80–81 (quoted); Janet Lecompte, *Pueblo, Hardscrabble, Greenhorn: Society on the High Plains, 1832–1856* (Norman: University of Oklahoma Press, 1978), 160.

55. Quotes from Jared Farmer, *On Zion's Mount: Mormons, Indians, and the American Landscape* (Cambridge, MA: Harvard University Press, 2008), 52; T. Givón, *Ute Reference Grammar* (Amsterdam: John Benjamins, 2011), 409; Jay Miller, "Numic Religion: An Overview of Power in the Great Basin of Native North America," *Anthropos* 78 (1983): 339, 341; and Alex K. Carroll, M. Nieves Zedeño, and Richard W. Stoffle, "The Ghost Dance: A Cartography of Numic Ritual," *Archaeological Method and Theory* 11 (2004): 129, 142. Edward Sapir translated *puwa* as "supernatural power"; "Texts of the Kaibab Pauites and Uintah Utes," *Proceedings of the American Academy of Arts and Sciences* 65 (1930): 317.

56. Smith, *Ethnography of the Northern Ute*, 155 ("various animals"); Powell, "Report on Indians of Numic Stock," 69 ("progenitors"); Clifford Duncan, "Rabbit's Fireball and the Creation of the Rocky Mountains and the Colorado [Grand] River," in McBeth, *Native American Oral History*, 40 ("When we say"). See also James A. Goss, "Ute Language, Kin, Myth, and Nature: A Demonstration of a Multi-Dimensional Folk Taxonomy," *Anthropological Linguistics* 9 (1967): 9; Smith, *Ethnography of the Northern Ute*, 47.

57. Nuche relationships with other beings, things, and forces mesh well with Eduardo Viveiros de Castro's notion of "perspectival multi-naturalism," which is most fully explicated in *Cosmological Perpectivism in Amazonia and Elsewhere: Four Lectures Given in the Department of Social Anthropology, University of Cambridge, February–March 1998* (Chicago, IL: HAU Books, 2015).

58. Powell, "Report on Indians of Numic Stock, 75. Powell's description sounds remarkably like the accounts of Eastern Algonquins in Calvin Martin, *Keepers of the Game: Indian-Animal Relationships and the Fur Trade* (Berkeley: University of California Press, 1978).

59. Contrast this interpretation of the northeastern Nuche with Blackhawk, *Violence over the Land*, which is at its most persuasive when addressing the southeastern Nuche and their Great Basin kin.

60. Richard White, in William Cronon and Richard White, "Indians in the Land," *American Heritage* 37 (1986): 18–25.

61. Charles C. Mann, *1491: New Revelations of the Americas before Columbus* (New York: Alfred A. Knopf, 2005), 3–4.

62. Mann, *1491*, 249. Mann appears to premise his conclusions largely on Cronon, *Changes in the Land;* and Stephen J. Pyne, *Fire in America: A Cultural History of Wildland and Rural Fire* (Seattle: University of Washington Press, 1997). Ironically, Omer Stewart, perhaps the first anthropologist to draw attention to the importance of native burning, spent his career studying the Nuche. See Omer C. Stewart, *Forgotten Fires: Native Americans and the*

Transient Wilderness, ed. Henry T. Lewis and M. Kat Anderson (Norman: University of Oklahoma Press, 2004).

63. William L. Baker, "Indians and Fire in the Rocky Mountains: The Wilderness Hypothesis Renewed," in *Fire, Native Peoples, and the Natural Landscape,* ed. Thomas R. Vale (Washington, DC: Island Press, 2002), 70. See also Chapter 3 and conclusion, herein.

3. DISPOSSESSION

1. Robert C. Black III, *Island in the Rockies: The History of Grand County, Colorado, to 1930,* Grand County Historical Society (Boulder, CO: Pruett, 1969), 181–182; Kathy Naples, "Tabernash," Grand County History, available at http://www.grandcountyhistory.com/article/tabernash-0.

2. Naples, "Tabernash"; *Letter from the Secretary of the Interior Transmitting Copy of Evidence Taken before White River Ute Commission,* H. Exec. Doc. 83, 46th Cong., 2nd Sess. (1880), 47. The last source gives the rancher's name as Elliott and claims that he was killed by Piah.

3. Naples, "Tabernash"; Black, *Island in the Rockies,* 181–182. See also *RMN,* September 1, 1878, 4. On the Ute War, see Marshall Sprague, *Massacre: The Tragedy at White River* (Boston: Little, Brown, 1957); and Peter Decker, *"The Utes Must Go!": American Expansion and the Removal of a People* (Golden, CO: Fulcrum, 2004).

4. Elliott West, *The Contested Plains: Indians, Goldseekers, and the Rush to Colorado* (Lawrence: University of Kansas Press, 1998), esp. 115–201; Hubert Howe Bancroft, *History of Nevada, Colorado, and Wyoming, 1540–1888,* vol. 25, in *The Works of Hubert Howe Bancroft* (San Francisco: History, 1890), chs. 3–5; Rodman Paul, *Mining Frontiers of the Far West, 1848–1880,* rev., expanded edition by Elliott West (1963; Albuquerque: University of New Mexico Press, 2001), ch. 6; Kathleen A. Brosnan, *Uniting Mountain and Plain: Cities, Law, and Environmental Change along the Front Range* (Albuquerque: University of New Mexico Press, 2002), 10–63. Figures on migration and "go backs" from West, *Contested Plains,* 145, 175; and Carl Abbott, Stephen J. Leonard, and Thomas J. Noel, *Colorado: A History of the Centennial State,* 4th ed. (Boulder: University Press of Colorado, 2005), 52.

5. Carl Abbott, Stephen J. Leonard, and David McComb, *Colorado: A History of the Centennial State,* rev. ed. (Boulder: Colorado Associated University Press, 1982), 54–57; West, *Contested Plains,* 108–113, 225; Brosnan, *Uniting Mountain and Plain,* 10–13; Stephen J. Leonard and Thomas J. Noel, *Denver: From Mining Camp to Metropolis* (Niwot: University Press of Colorado, 1990), 8–12; Duane A. Smith, "Mother Lode for the West: California Mining Men and Methods," in *A Golden State: Mining and Economic Development in Gold Rush California,* ed. James J. Rawls and Richard Orsi (Berkeley and Los Angeles: University of California Press, 1999), 149–173.

6. Bancroft, *History of Nevada, Colorado, and Wyoming*, 376–384; Black, *Island in the Rockies*, 33–35; Frank Hall, *History of the State of Colorado* (Chicago: Blakely, 1895), 4:138.

7. Frederick Merk, *Manifest Destiny and Mission in American History: A Reinterpretation* (New York: Knopf, 1963); Conrad Cherry, ed., *God's New Israel: Religious Interpretations of American Destiny* (1971; repr. Chapel Hill: University of North Carolina Press, 1998), pt. 3; Thomas Hietala, *Manifest Design: Anxious Aggrandizement in Late Jacksonian America* (Ithaca, NY: Cornell University Press, 1985); Anders Stephanson, *Manifest Destiny: American Expansionism and the Empire of Right* (New York: Hill and Wang, 1995).

8. Quote from Bancroft, *History of Nevada, Colorado, and Wyoming*, 332. On ores and smelting, see James E. Fell, *Ores to Metals: The Rocky Mountain Smelting Industry* (Lincoln: University of Nebraska Press, 1979); and Rodman Wilson Paul, "Colorado as a Pioneer of Science in the Mining West," *Mississippi Valley Historical Review* 47 (1960): 34–50.

9. ARCIA 1865, 147 (quoted); Richard Slotkin, *Regeneration through Violence: The Mythology of the American Frontier* (Middletown, CT: Wesleyan University Press, 1973); Robert F. Berkhofer Jr., *The White Man's Indian: Images of the American Indian from Columbus to the Present* (New York: Knopf, 1978); Richard Drinnon, *Facing West: The Metaphysics of Indian-Hating and Empire-Building* (Minneapolis: University of Minnesota Press, 1980); Reginald Horsman, *Race and Manifest Destiny: The Origins of American Racial Anglo-Saxonism* (Cambridge, MA: Harvard University Press, 1981); Brian W. Dippie, *The Vanishing American: White Attitudes and U.S. Indian Policy* (Middletown, CT: Wesleyan University Press, 1982).

10. ARCIA 1870, 163.

11. Ibid.

12. Ibid., 163–164.

13. Thomas G. Andrews, *Killing for Coal: America's Deadliest Labor War* (Cambridge, MA: Harvard University Press), ch. 1.

14. ARCIA 1866, 156. On the "persistence of natives," see Patricia Nelson Limerick, *The Legacy of Conquest: The Unbroken Past of the American West* (New York: Norton, 1987), ch. 6.

15. On southeastern Nuche, see ARCIA 1864, 182; Thomas G. Andrews, "Settling the San Luis Valley: Ecology, Society, and 'Beautiful Roads' in the Hispanic Colonization of Conejos and Costilla Counties, Colorado" (master's thesis, University of Wisconsin–Madison, 1997).

16. West, *Contested Plains*, ch. 9; Brosnan, *Uniting Mountain and Plain*, chs. 2–3; Alvin T. Steinel, *History of Agriculture in Colorado: A Chronological Record of Progress in the Development of General Farming, Livestock Production and Agricultural Education and Investigation, on the Western Border of the Great Plains and in the Mountains of Colorado, 1858 to 1926* (Fort Collins, CO: State Agricultural College for the State Board of Agriculture, 1926), 31–45, 53–58, 63–67.

17. Stan Hoig, *The Sand Creek Massacre* (Norman: University of Oklahoma Press, 1961); Jerome A. Greene and Douglas D. Scott, *Finding Sand Creek: History, Archaeology, and the 1864 Massacre Site* (Norman: University of Oklahoma Press, 2004); Ari Kelman, *A Misplaced Massacre: Struggling over the Memory of Sand Creek* (Cambridge, MA: Harvard University Press, 2013).

18. Quotes from ARCIA 1864, 223–224; 1865, 181 and 178. See also *RMN*, October 26, 1865, 3.

19. For reports of Nuche hunting bison on the Plains, see ARCIA 1869, 264; 1871, 556; 1873, 258; 1874, 272 and 274; and 1875, 230. The People also hunted antelope near Denver. See ARCIA 1867, 223; and *RMN*, August 10, 1867, 4.

20. ARCIA 1861, 135. See also ARCIA 1861, 102.

21. ARCIA 1862, 236; 1866, 155; 1868, 181–182; and 1869, 262. The Nuche's buffalo hunt actually had met with success that year. See *RMN*, October 26, 1869, 4.

22. ARCIA 1862, 236. Contrast this with the Cheyenne case in West, *Contested Plains*.

23. ARCIA 1865, 178 ("ten sacks"); ARCIA 1874, 271 ("best market"); ARCIA 1874, 230 ("the attention" and "the glorious annual"). On intertribal "buffer zones" and game proliferation, see Harold Hickerson, "The Virginia Deer and Intertribal Buffer Zones in the Upper Mississippi Valley," in *Man, Culture, and Animals: The Role of Animals in Human Ecological Adjustments*, ed. Anthony Leeds and Andrew P. Vayda (Washington, DC: American Association for the Advancement of Science, Pub. No. 78, 1965), 43–66; Elliott West, *The Way to the West: Essays on the Central Plains* (Albuquerque: University of New Mexico Press, 1995), 61. On trading posts, see ARCIA 1873, 256; 1876, 21; 1877, 46; 1878, 19; and 1879, 18–19. News accounts of Nuche trading visits to Denver include *RMN*, March 15, 1865, 4; July 23, 1869, 4; and April 30, 1870, 4. On Nuche trading in Canon City, see *RMN*, March 29, 1865, 2. Denver's role as territorial capital also made it an important site for negotiations with state and federal officials. See *RMN*, February 12, 1866, 4; April 12, 1866, 4; May 20, 1867, 4; January 15, 1868, 4; January 21, 1875, 4; and January 28, 1879, 4. On Nuche sipping sodas, see *RMN*, May 11, 1874, 4; and May 20, 1874, 4. For descriptions of Nuche camps in Denver, see *RMN*, June 6, 1868, 4; and July 20, 1872, 4. On Nuche trading horses in Denver, see *RMN*, August 20, 1878, 4.

24. ARCIA 1871, 556–557; 1873, 262.

25. ARCIA 1866, 161.

26. ARCIA 1863, 123–124.

27. Ibid., 124–125.

28. Ibid.; ARCIA 1866, 158; 1877, 45. Colorado editors repeated this doctrine; see, *RMN*, September 12, 1868, 4.

29. Treaty with the Utah-Tabeguache, October 7, 1863, 13 Stat. 67, in *Indian Affairs: Laws and Treaties*, compiled and edited by Charles J. Kappler, 57th

Cong., 1st sess., Sen. Doc. 452, vol. 2:856–859; Nicolay in ARCIA 1863, 149–150.

30. ARCIA 1866, 155 (quote); Black, *Island in the Rockies,* 46, 57; Virginia Mc-Connell Simmons, *The Ute Indians of Utah, Colorado, and New Mexico* (Niwot: University Press of Colorado, 2000), 117–126.

31. Treaty with the Ute, 1868, 15 Stat. 619, in *Indian Affairs,* 2:990–996. Eugene H. Berwanger ludicrously calls this "the most generous treaty ever made between the U.S. government and any Native American group"; Berwanger, *The Rise of the Centennial State: Colorado Territory, 1861–76* (Urbana: University of Illinois Press, 2007), 39. On continuing Nuche use of Middle Park, see Black, *Island in the Rockies,* 116. For helpful context, see C. Joseph Genetin-Pilawa, *Crooked Paths to Allotment: The Fight over Federal Indian Policy after the Civil War* (Chapel Hill: University of North Carolina Press, 2012), ch. 3.

32. ARCIA 1869, 259; 1873, 259; Helen Hunt Jackson, *A Century of Dishonor: A Sketch of the United States Government's Dealings with Some of the Indian Tribes* (New York: Harper and Brothers, 1881), 343–356. On agency cattle and northeastern Nuche reluctance to embrace husbandry, see ARCIA 1872, 551; 1875, 232–234; 1876, 20; 1877, 47; 1879, 177; and 1880, 15.

33. ARCIA 1863, 123; Black, *Island in the Rockies,* 77; *RMN,* August 9, 1870, 4; *RMN,* August 15, 1870, 4; Simmons, *Ute Indians,* 126, 141.

34. *Daily Central City Register,* July 6, 1873; *Georgetown Weekly Miner,* July 14, 1874; ibid., October 10, 1874; ibid., November 21, 1874; ibid., July 31, 1875; Black, *Island in the Rockies,* 79, 85–89; Louise C. Harrison, *Empire and the Berthoud Pass* (Denver, CO: Big Mountain Press, 1964); William Wyckoff, *Creating Colorado: The Making of a Western American Landscape, 1860–1940* (New Haven, CT: Yale University Press, 1999), ch. 2; Mary Lyons Cairns, *Grand Lake: The Pioneers* (Denver, CO: World Press, 1946) and *Grand Lake in the Olden Days* (Denver, CO: World Press, 1971); Michael M. Geary, *A Quick History of Grand Lake: Including Rocky Mountain National Park and the Grand Lake Lodge* (Ouray, CO: Western Reflections, 1999). The Grand County Board of Commissioners' first substantive act set tolls on the Rollinsville and Middle Park Wagon Road. Entry for November 9, 1874, *Proceedings of the Grand County Board of Commissioners,* Grand County Record Office Hot Sulphur Springs, CO, 1:1–2.

35. Black, *Island in the Rockies,* 131, 171.

36. U.S. Census statistics, 1870 and 1880; Andrews, *Killing for Coal,* chs. 1–2.

37. ARCIA 1879, 170.

38. Nathan Meeker to Henry Moore Teller, Folder 207, Box 1, Henry Moore Teller Papers, Denver Public Library; ARCIA 1879, 176. Meeker took this case to the people of Colorado; see *RMN,* May 24, 1878, 1, and May 25, 1878, 2. "Citizens of Grand and Routt counties," reported that Colorado governor John Routt agreed "the Indians have been badly treated." Routt to Teller, December 17, 1877, Folder 72, Box 1, Teller Papers. See also Frank A. Hinman to Teller, February 24, 1878, Folder 199, Box 1, Teller Papers.

39. Meeker to Teller, April 17, 1878, Folder 207, Box 1, Teller Papers; Brandilyn Denison, "Remove, Return, Remember: Making Ute Land Religion in the American West" (PhD diss., University of North Carolina, 2011), 67–76.

40. ARCIA 1878, 19; 1879, 19.

41. ARCIA 1879, 19, 176.

42. Ibid., 19; ARCIA 1878, 18 (Southern Ute); ARCIA 1881, 328 (Tabeguache); Meeker to Commissioner of Indian Affairs, March 3, 1879, in *Letter from the Secretary of the Interior*, 137. On horses and status at Uintah, see ARCIA 1883, 140 (Uintah).

43. ARCIA 1879, 17–18 (first and third quotes); Nathan Meeker to Henry Teller, December 28, 1878, *Letters Received by the Office of Indian Affairs 1824– 81, Colorado Superintendency, 1861–1880*, National Archives Microfilm M-234, Roll 212 (second and fourth quotes). Ironically, the Nuche themselves had initially objected to the old agency site, claiming that "it would frighten all their game away, the White River region being the best portion of all their hunting-grounds." See ARCIA 1870, 170.

44. Accusations of Native American wastefulness would later reappear in conservationist discourse. Louis S. Warren, *The Hunter's Game: Poachers and Conservationists in Twentieth-Century America* (New Haven, CT: Yale University Press, 1997); Mark David Spence, *Dispossessing the Wilderness: Indian Removal and the Making of the National Parks* (New York: Oxford University Press, 1997); Karl Jacoby, *Crimes against Nature: Squatters, Poachers, Thieves, and the Hidden History of American Conservation* (Berkeley: University of California Press, 2001).

45. Petition from Grand County citizens, August 30, 1877, in *Letter from the Secretary of the Interior*, 118.

46. ARCIA 1876, 20; 1862, 236; Wilson Waldren paraphrased in *Colorado Miner*, July 17, 1880, 3.

47. ARCIA 1877, 46; 1880, 18; William L. Baker, "Indians and Fire in the Rocky Mountains: The Wilderness Hypothesis Renewed," in *Fire, Native Peoples, and the Natural Landscape*, ed. Thomas R. Vale (Washington, DC: Island Press, 2002), 53–57. Arid conditions also likely increased the frequency and danger of dry lighting strikes. Accusations tendered by a Hayden settler against the White Rivers in July 1879 suggest that the People did set fires to cabins and other structures built by settlers; James B. Thompson to CIA, July 21 and August 13, 1879, *Letters Received, Colorado Superintendency*, Roll 212. For an earlier accusation of Nuche fire setting, see George K. Otis to CIA, August 31, 1864, in ARCIA 1865, 255.

48. Frederick Pitkin to CIA, July 5, 1879; Nathan Meeker to CIA, July 7, 1879 (two letters), in *Letter from the Secretary of the Interior*, 143–145. See also Meeker to CIA, July 15, 1879, in ibid., 148–149. The same document contains a variety of statements both in support of and opposing the portrait of Nuche game wasting and fire setting; see 59–61, 66–67.

49. Arvila Meeker testimony in *White River Ute Commission*, 22; Meeker to Hayt, August 31, 1879, in ibid., 52. On Meeker's refusal to allow off-reservation hunting expeditions, see ibid. and Meeker to CIA, September 6, 1879, in *Letter to the Secretary of the Interior*, 234.

50. *White River Ute Commission*, 12–13. An exasperated secretary of the interior, Carl Schurtz, later griped: "They can clear themselves . . . only by pointing out and surrendering the guilty parties. They must all be made to understand that unless this is done the whole tribe must be held responsible and be dealt with accordingly." Ibid., 51.

51. Quotes from *White River Ute Commission*, 41; Meeker to Commissioner of Indian Affairs, February 3, 1879, ibid., 135; and ibid., March 3, 1879, 136.

52. Denison, "Remove, Return, Remember," 81–82. Johnson denied that he struck Meeker: "I was not mad at him," he told federal investigators; *White River Ute Commission*, 8.

53. *White River Ute Commission*, 8 and Wilson M. Stanley to Commissioner of Indian Affairs, telegram of October 5, 1879 and letter of October 15, 1879, *Letters Received, Colorado Superintendency*, Roll 212.

54. George Sherman to CIA, August 16, 1880, *Letters Received, Colorado Superintendency*, Roll 214. On removal, see Simmons, *Ute Indians*, 189–197; Decker, *"The Utes Must Go!"* chs. 6–7.

55. Quotes from ARCIA 1875, 359; and Francis McKinley interview by Leslie Kelen, August 11, 1988, Folder 6, Box 2, Ute Indian Interviews, Marriott Library, University of Utah, Salt Lake City, 11, 6, 20. For earlier, mostly positive assessments of Uintah, see ARCIA 1862, 199 and 202; 1865, 147. For a concurring opinion on the Utah reservations' unsuitability for grazing, see ARCIA 1881, 328. On tensions, see ARCIA 1881, 157 and 332; 1882, 150; 1883, 20 and 140. More generally, see David Rich Lewis, *Neither Wolf nor Dog: American Indians, Environment, and Agrarian Change* (Lincoln: University of Nebraska Press, 1994), chs. 2–3.

56. McKinley interview, 6; ARCIA 1881, 332; Tommy Appah interview with Sandra Fuller, November 14, 1983, transcript, Folder 1, Box 1, Ute Indian Interviews, 24 (both quotes); Clifford Duncan, interview with Leslie G. Kelen, August 30, 1982, Folder 7, Box 1, Ute Indian Interviews, 9; Ruby (Antwine) Black interview with Leslie G. Kelen, November 13, 1983, Folder 2, Ute Indian Interviews, 37. On the immense horse wealth of the Colorado Nuche on the eve of removal, see Christopher Gilson to Ranald S. Mackenzie, April 13, 1880, *Letters Received, Colorado Superintendency*, Roll 214. On the skill of one Nuche horsewoman, see Carleen Kurip interview, Folder 4, Box 2, Ute Indian Interviews, 2, 4. On conflicts between Northern Ute hunters and Colorado game authorities, see *Denver Times*, October 19, 1898, 2; October 22, 1898, 1; October 24, 1898, 2; October 25, 1900, 2; October 28, 1900, 16–17; October 30, 1900, 5; November 18, 1900, 17; November 29, 1900, 2; December 2, 1900, 1; December 5, 1900, 7; and December 9, 1900, 1.

4. MINERS

1. Susan Baldwin, *Historic Resource Study: Dutchtown and Lulu City, Rocky Mountain National Park, Colorado* (Boulder, CO: Creative Land Use, 1980), 14.

2. On estimated town populations, see Robert C. Black, *Island in the Rockies: The History of Grand County, Colorado, to 1930* (Boulder, CO: Pruett, 1969), 278. Buchholtz claims that Gaskill never housed more than fifty. See C. W. Buchholtz, *Rocky Mountain National Park: A History* (Niwot: University Press of Colorado, 1983), 98. The 1880 census recorded 417 residents in Grand County; by 1884, Grand County listed 416 voters; *Proceedings of Grand County Board of Commissioners*, January 8, 1885, 1:152–153.

3. For a now classic articulation of this argument, see Patricia Nelson Limerick, *The Legacy of Conquest: The Unbroken Past of the American West*, 1st ed. (New York: Norton, 1987), ch. 4. Also useful are Duane A. Smith, *Mining America: The Industry and the Environment, 1800–1980* (Lawrence: University Press of Kansas, 1987); Andrew Isenberg, *Mining California: An Ecological History* (New York: Hill and Wang, 2005); Timothy J. LeCain, *Mass Destruction: The Men and Giant Mines Who Wired America and Scarred the Planet* (New Brunswick, NJ: Rutgers University Press, 2009); and Kent A. Curtis, *Gambling on Ore: The Nature of Metal Mining in the United States, 1860–1910* (Boulder: University Press of Colorado, 2013).

4. Frank Jones Burnett, *Golden Memories of Colorado* (New York: Vantage, 1965), 155 (quoted); Baldwin, *Historic Resource Study*, 28; "Alfred A. Edwards Tells of the Valley as It Was When He Came in 1869," *Fort Collins Express*, September 29, 1935.

5. Burnett, *Golden Memories of Colorado*, 155; Buchholtz, *Rocky Mountain National Park*, 93. Burnett later claimed that Baker had "located a 160 acre ranch at the head of the Grand River," but GLO records contain no account of this filing.

6. Burnett, *Golden Memories of Colorado*, 155; Buchholtz, *Rocky Mountain National Park*, 93.

7. Frank Fossett, *Colorado: A Historical, Descriptive and Statistical Work on the Rocky Mountain Gold and Silver Mining Region* (Denver: Daily Tribune Steam Printing House, 1876), 420; Rossiter W. Raymond, *Statistics of Mines and Mining in the States and Territories West of the Rocky Mountains Being the 8th Annual Report* (Washington, DC: Government Printing Office, 1877), 319.

8. Elliott West and Rodman Paul note that "mining camps were the most sexually imbalanced, diverse, and transient gatherings recorded in American history." See Rodman Wilson Paul and Elliott West, *Mining Frontiers of the Far West, 1848–1880* (Albuquerque: University of New Mexico Press, 2001), 209.

9. Ibid.; Rodman Wilson Paul, "Colorado as a Pioneer of Science in the Mining West," *Mississippi Valley Historical Review* 47 (1960): 34–50; Otis E. Young Jr., *Black Powder and Hand Steel: Miners and Machines on the Old Western Frontier*

(Norman: University of Oklahoma Press, 1976); and James E. Fell, *Ores to Metals: The Rocky Mountain Smelting Industry* (Lincoln: University of Nebraska Press, 1979).

10. *Colorado Miner,* July 24, 1880; and August 14, 1880, 3.

11. Leo Marx, *The Machine in the Garden: Technology and the Pastoral Ideal in America* (New York: Oxford University Press, 1964); Richard White, *The Organic Machine* (New York: Hill and Wang, 1995); Benjamin R. Cohen, *Notes from the Ground: Science, Soil, and Society in the American Countryside* (New Haven, CT: Yale University Press, 2009); Mark Fiege, *The Republic of Nature: An Environmental History of the United States* (Seattle: University of Washington Press, 2012). ch. 4.

12. *Colorado Miner,* November 8, 1879, 3; and September 18, 1880, 1; *FCC,* November 18, 1880, 2; and September 4, 1884, 1; Sarah Keyes, "'Like a Roaring Lion': The Overland Trail as a Sonic Conquest," *Journal of American History* 96 (2009): 19–43.

13. "Letter from Lulu," *FCC,* February 10, 1881, 2; "Middle Park," *Colorado Miner,* November 8, 1879, 3.

14. *Colorado Miner,* March 19, 1881, 8.

15. Richard White, "Animals and Enterprise," in *The Oxford History of the American West,* ed. Clyde A. Milner, Carol A. O'Connor, and Martha A. Sandweiss (New York: Oxford University Press, 1994), 237–273; Ann Norton Greene, *Horses at Work: Harnessing Power in Industrial America* (Cambridge, MA: Harvard University Press, 2008). A huge literature underpins my metabolic approach; a recent synthesis is Vaclav Smil, *Harvesting the Biosphere: What We Have Taken from Nature* (Cambridge, MA: MIT Press, 2013).

16. Few sources detail livestock practices in detail; this paragraph interpolates from John M. Crowley, "Ranches in the Sky: A Geography of Livestock Ranching in the Mountain Parks of Colorado" (PhD diss., University of Minnesota, 1964); John M. Crowley, "Ranching in the Mountain Parks of Colorado," *Geographical Review* 65 (1975): 445–460; Warren P. Clary and John W. Kinney, "Streambank and Vegetation Response to Simulated Cattle Grazing," *Wetlands* 22 (2002): 139–148; J. W. Bartolome, "Impacts of Grazing Intensity and Grazing Systems on Vegetation Composition and Production," in *Developing Strategies for Rangeland Management* (Boulder, CO: Westview, 1984), 917–925; Andrea C. Mayer and Veronika Stöckli, "Long-Term Impact of Cattle Grazing on Subalpine Forest Development and Efficiency of Snow Avalanche Production," *Arctic, Antarctic, and Alpine Research* 37 (2005): 521–522.

17. "Middle Park," *Colorado Miner,* November 8, 1879, 3; "Letter from Lulu," *FCC,* February 10, 1881, 2. In very rough figures, 5,000 tons of hay should have been enough to feed 275–700 cows through the winter, or a larger number of horses and smaller stock. See Andrea Zippay, "Feeding Beef Cows during Winter Months Can Tear Up Farm Budget Book," *Farm and Dairy,* August 8, 2002, available at: http://www.farmanddairy.com/news

/feeding-beef-cows-hay-during-winter-months-can-tear-up-farm-budget
-book/748.html.

18. Kathryn Morse, *The Nature of Gold: An Environmental History of the Klondike Gold Rush* (Seattle: University of Washington Press, 2003), 182.

19. *Grand Lake Prospector,* July 31, 1886, 3; Mrs. Macfarland-Hightower to Mr. Tom Thomas, February 1968, Ferrell Atkins Files, RMNP Archives.

20. George Crofutt, *Grip-Sack Guide of Colorado* (Omaha, NE: Overland, 1881), 116; *Colorado Miner,* August 23, 1879, 2.

21. J. S. Perky, *Larimer County Homes and Mines—Where to Outfit for North Park and Middle Park Mining Districts* (Fort Collins, CO: Courier, 1880), 17; Burnett, *Golden Memories of Colorado,* 158; "Lulu's Progress," *FCC,* July 29, 1880, 1.

22. McFarland-Hightower to Thomas; "Lulu City," *FCC,* July 15, 1880, 2; Wilson Waldren, paraphrased in *Colorado Miner,* July 17, 1880, 3. See also Alan Taylor, "'Wasty Ways': Stories of American Settlement," *Environmental History* 3 (1998): 291–310.

23. On fuel, see Thomas G. Andrews, *Killing for Coal: America's Deadliest Labor War* (Cambridge, MA: Harvard University Press), ch. 2.

24. *Colorado Miner,* June 11, 1881, 3; *RMN,* June 26, 1882, 3; *Colorado Miner,* March 31, 1883, 3. See also William Butler, *Historic Archeology of Rocky Mountain National Park* (Estes Park, CO: National Park Service, Rocky Mountain National Park, 2005), 216; *FCC,* February 19, 1880, 2; *FCC,* July 8, 1880, 2; *RMN,* July 15, 1880; *Colorado Miner,* September 18, 1880, 1; *FCC,* November 18, 1880, 2; *Denver Republican,* January 1, 1881, 2; and January 22, 1881, 2; *Colorado Miner,* June 11, 1881, 3; *Ft. Collins Express,* July 21, 1881, 2; *Colorado Miner,* April 15, 1882, 3; *RMN,* June 26, 1882, 3; *Colorado Miner,* March 31, 1883, 3; *Grand Lake Prospector,* July 18, 1885; *Colorado Miner,* March 19, 1881, 3. These accounts provide little information on the species cut, the locations logged, or the overall quantity of wood consumed.

25. On mining and forest fire, see William L. Baker, *Fire Ecology in Rocky Mountain Landscapes* (Washington, DC: Island Press, 2009), 357. Relevant fire histories of the Colorado Front Range include ibid., 367–370; Thomas T. Veblen and Diane C. Lorenz, "Anthropogenic Disturbance and Recovery Patterns in Montane Forests," *Physical Geography* 7 (1986): 1–24; and Thomas T. Veblen and Diane C. Lorenz, *The Colorado Front Range: A Century of Ecological Change* (Salt Lake City: University of Utah Press, 1991). On fire history in the Kawuneeche, see Jason S. Sibold, "Multi-Scale Subalpine Forest Dynamics, Rocky Mountain National Park, Colorado" (PhD diss., University of Colorado at Boulder, 2005), 28, 41–42.

26. I draw most of this from studies of other regions; see especially William Cronon, *Changes in the Land: Indians, Colonists, and the Ecology of New England* (New York: Hill and Wang, 1983), ch. 6.

27. Andrews, *Killing for Coal*, 41, 77; Katherine A Brosnan, *Uniting Mountain and Plain: Cities, Law, and Environmental Change along the Front Range* (Albuquerque: University of New Mexico Press, 2002), 146–148. The dead trees also may have been killed by mountain pine beetle.

28. Contrast this approach with Kent A. Curtis, "Producing a Gold Rush: National Ambitions and the Northern Rocky Mountains, 1853–1863," *Western Historical Quarterly* 40 (Autumn 2009): 275–297.

29. On freight costs, see Andrews, *Killing for Coal*, 56–57.

30. Black, *Island in the Rockies*, 167; Petition, July 2, 1877, in *Proceedings of Grand County Board of County Commissioners*, 1:37; "Road to the Park," *FCC*, July 10, 1879, 2.

31. Butler, *Historic Archaeology of Rocky Mountain National Park*, 59–112.

32. Ibid. On the use of draft animals for road construction, see *Proceedings of Grand County Board of County Commissioners*, January 16, 1882, 1:131.

33. Nell Donathan Pauly, *Ghosts of the Shootin'* (Grand Lake, CO: privately published, 1961), 181.

34. Black, *Island in the Rockies*, 170–171. The closest railroad tracks ever reached was Granby, some twenty miles down valley from Grand Lake.

35. Andrews, *Killing for Coal*, ch. 2.

36. Probably the best example of this is presented by the Denver and Rio Grande. See Robert Athearn, *Rebel of the Rockies: A History of the Denver and Rio Grand Western Railroad* (New Haven, CT: Yale University Press, 1962). More generally, see Richard White, *Railroaded: The Transcontinentals and the Making of Modern America* (New York: W. W. Norton, 2011). On smelting consolidation, see Fell, *Ores to Metals*.

37. MacFarland-Hightower to Thomas.

38. Butler, *Historic Archaeology of Rocky Mountain National Park*, 120–121, 143.

39. *Colorado Miner*, August 30, 1879, 3. Bernd Brunner, *Bears: A Brief History*, trans. Lori Lantz (New Haven, CT: Yale University Press, 2007), 153–154; and Peter S. Alagona, *After the Grizzly: Endangered Species and the Politics of Place in California* (Berkeley: University of California Press, 2013), ch. 1.

40. Charles Hedrick, "Memoirs of Charles Hedrick, 1874–1950," unpublished, RMNP Archives, 2–3. I gesture here toward a landmark essay in cultural history and animal history; see Robert Darnton "Workers Revolt: The Great Cat Massacre of the Rue Saint-Séverin," in *The Great Cat Massacre and Other Episodes in French Cultural History* (New York: Basic Books, 1984), 75–106. For more on marten, see Steven W. Buskirk and Leonard F. Ruggiero, "American Marten," in *American Marten, Fisher, Lynx, and Wolverine in the Western United States: The Scientific Basis for Conserving Forest Carnivores*, ed. Leonard F. Ruggiero et al., USDA Forest Service General Technical Report RM-254 (Fort Collins, CO: Rocky Mountain Forest and Range Experiment Station, 1994), 7, 22; Ian D. Thompson, John Fryxell, and Daniel J. Harrison,

"Improved Insights into Use of Habitat by American Martens," in *Biology and Conservation of Martens, Sables, and Fishers: A New Synthesis*, ed. Keith B. Aubry et al. (Ithaca, NY: Cornell University Press, 2012), 228. For more on predator control, see Chapters 7 and 9 herein.

41. For quotes and figures on population density, see Buskirk and Ruggiero, "American Marten," 15. Buskirk, a leading authority on American marten, told me that Hedrick's story has "the tinny clank of apocrypha," since "nothing in the scientific literature would speak to this" scenario. Steven W. Buskirk, personal communication with author, August 13, 2013.

42. *Fort Collins Express*, July 21, 1881, 2; *Colorado Miner*, January 5, 1884, 3. All of these observers tended to see sinister designs in bears' evident tendency to lurk at the fringes of human settlement—a behavior driven by the creatures' fondness for trash.

43. *RMN*, August 12, 1880, 2; "Lulu City," *FCC*, July 15, 1880, 2.

5. FARMERS

1. Diversified crops required about twice the average annual precipitation that fell on Colorado's northern piedmont; Oliver Knight, "Correcting Nature's Error: The Colorado-Big Thompson Project," *Agricultural History* 30 (1956): 158.

2. The surveyors also had been instructed "to determine as to the feasibility of turning the waters of Grand Lake eastward into the St. Vrain and Boulder Creeks," but this ambitious pumping scheme proved impractical. See "Storage of Water," *FCC*, January 22, 1885, 4.

3. James E. Hansen, *The Water Supply and Storage Company: A Century of Colorado Reclamation, 1891–1991* (Fort Collins, CO: Water Supply and Storage Company, 1991), 9–12; C. E. Tait, "Storage of Water on Cache La Poudre and Big Thompson Rivers," U.S. Department of Agriculture, Office of Experiment Stations, Bulletin No. 134 (Washington, DC: Government Printing Office, 1903), 33; *FCC*, July 25, 1885, 1; and "More Water," *FCC*, July 25, 1889, 1. Water Supply envisioned the Grand Ditch as one component within a larger system, including a short canal on Specimen Mountain and a stillborn canal on the western slopes of the Never Summers.

4. *FCC*, August 23, 1894, 1 (quoted); Russell N. Bradt, "Foreign Water in the Cache La Poudre Valley" (master's thesis, Colorado State College of Education, 1948), 3. The Water Supply and Storage Company refused to grant me permission to consult the company's archives. Apparently, though, their first record book commenced on July 23, 1891; Betty Jane Kissler, "A History of the Water Supply and Storage Company" (master's thesis, Colorado State College of Education, 1952), 40.

5. *FCC*, October 1, 1902, 5 (quoted); Bradt, "Foreign Water," 5–6; and Hansen, *Water Supply and Storage Company*, 15.

6. Tait, "Storage of Water," 36, reported that the company had issued 600 shares. By 1965, the Water Supply and Storage Company still had "600 shares of stock outstanding" held by "approximately 230 individual share holders who own varying numbers of shares dependent upon their irrigated acreage." J. R. Barkley to John Holzwarth, December 1, 1965, copy, doc. W-24, in National Park Service Water Resources Division, "Documents Relating to the Grand River Ditch in Rocky Mountain National Park," vol. 1, RMNP Archives.

7. *FCC,* August 29, 1901, 7. See also *FCC,* July 25, 1901, 6.

8. *FCC,* August 10, 1893, 1 (first quote); September 24, 1896, 5 (second quote). Also invoking the same phrase is *FCC,* September 23, 1903, 11.

9. William Cronon, "Landscapes of Abundance and Scarcity," in *Oxford History of the American West,* ed. Clyde A. Milner II, Carol A. O'Conor, and Martha A. Sandweiss (New York: Oxford University Press, 1994), 613.

10. *FCC,* December 30, 1903, 7. See also *FCC,* September 23, 1903, 11. For more on the union of nature and artifice in western irrigation projects, see Mark Fiege, *Irrigated Eden: The Making of an Agricultural Landscape in the American West* (Seattle: University of Washington Press, 1993).

11. A. A. Anderson, "Does Irrigation Pay?" *FCC,* January 14, 1903, 3. On the value irrigation added, see E. S. Nettleton, "The Reservoir System of the Cache La Poudre Valley," U.S. Department of Agricultural Experiment Stations, Bulletin No. 92 (Washington, DC: Government Printing Office, 1901), 107. On improvement, see Chapter 4, as well as David E. Nye, *American Technological Sublime* (Cambridge, MA: MIT Press, 1994). For an acknowledgment of natural limits on irrigation in northern Colorado, see *FCC,* October 22, 1902, 2.

12. Anderson, "Does Irrigation Pay?"

13. *FCC,* January 4, 1905, 2 (quoted). Rising share values may have eased the burden of such assessments; *FCC,* August 26, 1903, 2.

14. Bradt, "Foreign Water," 9; Edward Baker interview by Ferril Atkins, June, 1966, transcript, Tape No. 1 of 2, Ferril Atkins Papers, RMNP Archives.

15. Hansen, *Water Supply and Storage Company,* 14, quoting *FCC,* July 25, 1901, 3 (first quote); Baker interview with Atkins (second quote). On the challenges snow posed, for instance, see *FCC,* September 3, 1902, 8; June 7, 1905, 7; and May 2, 1906, 15. On ditch and canal diggers, see Peter Way, *Common Labour: Workers and the Digging of North American Canals, 1780–1860* (New York: Cambridge University Press, 1993); and Ryan L. Dearinger, "Frontiers of Progress and Paradox: Building Canals, Railroads, and Manhood in the American West (PhD diss., University of Utah, 2009).

16. Harvey Johnson interview with James Hansen, August 27, 1985, transcript, Folder 8, Box 1, Harvey Johnson Papers, Colorado Agricultural Archives, Morgan Library, Colorado State University, Fort Collins, 107 (quoted); significantly, Johnson was referring to the 1930s. On Asian workers, see ibid.,

105; Baker interview; John Wiley, "Five Days on Horseback in Rocky Mountain National Park," *Hotel Monthly* 24 (October, 1916), 45; "Grand River Ditch–July 1955," n.d., Doc. W-43 in NPS Water Resources Division, "Documents Relating to the Grand River Ditch in Rocky Mountain National Park," vol. 1, 105. Virtually all of the workforce of ten to twelve men responsible for maintaining the canal during the 1910 irrigation season were native-born Americans. U. S. Census, 1910, manuscript rolls for Grand County.

17. Thomas Jefferson, *Notes on the State of Virginia* (London: John Stockdale, 1787), 274; Henry Nash Smith, *Virgin Land: The American West as Symbol and Myth* (Cambridge, MA: Harvard University Press, 1950).

18. Baker interview (quoted). In 1907 alone, workers milled 197,000 board feet of lumber from the ditch line. J. V. Leighou to District Forester, Denver, April 29, 1930, Folder 427—"Rocky Mountain National Park," Box 91, "Historical Files, 1900," Arapaho-Roosevelt National Forest Papers, Record Group 95, Records of the U.S. Forest Service, NARA–Denver. On refuse, see Chapter 8.

19. Chris Kennedy interview with author, November 24, 2010, in author's possession; Sandra Ryan and Nel Caine, *Effects of Flow Diversion on Downstream Channel Form in Mountain Streams*, Completion Report No. 176 (Fort Collins: Colorado Water Resources Research Institute, 1993); Jordan Clayton and Cherie Westbrook, "The Effect of the Grand Ditch on the Abundance of Benthic Invertebrates in the Colorado River, RMNP," *River Research and Applications* 24 (2008): 975–987.

20. The information in this and the following paragraph comes from data assembled by researcher Brandon Luedtke from the GLO Records. Twenty-two applicants succeeded in proving up their claims under the Homestead Act; eighteen failed. In a handful of other cases, the final result is unclear from extant documents. Five other households purchased land from the government outright. These success rates were roughly comparable to national success rates. This suggests that the story of homesteading in Coyote Valley was more typical than aberrant. Hedrick did not file his claim until 1884, but he claimed to have entered in 1880.

21. Mary E. Harbison case, ibid. Leon Giggey's family had five members in total; there were also five Holzwarths, but one daughter spent most of her time in Denver.

22. Charles Seymour, Mark Christiansen, and Clinton DeWitt cases, ibid.

23. John G. Holzwarth Sr. and Allen Hatter cases, ibid.

24. In the North Fork, at least, the GLO also proved much more accommodating to World War I veterans than to men who had fought in previous American wars.

25. Abram Macy case, GLO Records.

26. Robert A. Harbison case, ibid. (quoted); Andrew Christiansen case, ibid.

27. Holzwarth case, ibid. In at least one instance, a settler household actually downsized with the passage of time—from a twenty-four-by-twenty-eight-foot structure "of hewed logs" to a "dwelling house" of twelve by fourteen feet. Hedrick case, ibid.

28. Hedrick case; Mark Christiansen case, ibid.

29. Benjamin J. Mitchell case, ibid.

30. The largest documented holding of meadowland was Charles Hertel's of "about 100 acres of hay." Charles Hertel case, ibid.

31. GLO Records for most parcels document the grubbing out of willows; on pines, see Wheeler case.

32. On "tame grass," see Holzwarth case, GLO Records; on "tame hay," see Jacob Jones case, ibid. On hay, livestock, and history, see William P. Headden, "Colorado Hays and Fodders," *Colorado Agricultural Experiment Station General Bulletin* 93 (1904); and S. C. Dinsmore and P. B. Kennedy, "Digestion Experiments with the Native Hay of the Truckee Meadows," *University of Nevada Agricultural Experiment Station Bulletin* 64 (1907): 23. On Stone's ditching, see David J. Cooper et al., "Hydrologic Restoration of a Fen in Rocky Mountain National Park, Colorado, USA," *Wetlands* 18 (1998): 335–345. Many cases in the GLO Records mention irrigation ditches; none mention drainage canals, suggesting that settlers waited to prove up their claims before draining their fields. Comparative hay yields are estimated from various figures in GLO Records. These figures comport with hay yield data published in the 1970s, though by that time, sedges and rushes (most of them native to the Rockies) had recolonized many high-country meadows in Colorado's Middle Park. See John M. Crowley, "Ranching in the Mountain Parks of Colorado," *Geographical Review* 65 (1975): 452.

33. Hedrick case, GLO Records; Mitchell case, ibid.; Wheeler case, ibid.

34. Cooper et al., "Hydrologic Restoration," 335, 343. For a comparative case, see Mark Fiege, "The Weedy West: Mobile Nature, Boundaries, and Common Space in the Montana Landscape," *Western Historical Quarterly* 36 (2005): 22–47.

35. On help with house building, see Henry Nicholls case, GLO Records. Other claims in this paragraph are documented extensively in GLO Records.

36. Hedrick case, ibid. (quoted); Holzwarth case, ibid.; SMR, June 1916.

37. Mrs. Rob Harbison quote from Ferrel Atkins, summary of interview with Robert Harbison and Mrs. Robert Harbison, July 17, 1962, Folder 20: "History, West Side," Box 1, Atkins Papers, RMNP Archives. Rob Harbison quotes from ibid., 2, 4. For corroboration on the wandering ways of Harbison's cattle, see John G. Holzwarth II interview by Roger and Susan Contor, January 20, 1974, "Holzwarth Ranch: Homestead Historical Notes, Compiled 1974–1978," RMNP Archives. On grazing in the valley under U.S. Forest Service management, see Grazing Card, Henry Schnoor, April 15 to October 15, 1906, Box 75: "Special Use Permits and Directories, Maps, and

Land Status 1906–1969"; Arapaho-Roosevelt National Forest Papers and H. N. Wheeler, "Supplemental Report on That Portion of Proposed Estes National Park Lying West of the Continental Divide, within the Arapahoe National Forest," May 1910, Folder 402: "Roosevelt—General," Box 587: "Historical Files, 1900," ibid. On fur trapping, see Chapter 9, as well as the Hedrick journal referenced in Chapter 4.

38. See the relevant cases in GLO Records.

39. Mary Birovchak Levkulich interview in Julie Jones-Eddy, *Homesteading Women: An Oral History of Colorado, 1890–1950* (New York: Twayne, 1992), 66 (first quote); Janet Mortimer Eberle interview in ibid., 52 (second quote). See also Stella La Force Rector and CeCilia Sullivan Knott interviews in ibid., 38, 60. Helpful context appears in Katherine Harris, "Homesteading in Northeastern Colorado, 1873–1920: Sex Roles and Women's Experience," in *The Women's West,* ed. Susan Armitage and Elizabeth Jameson (Norman: University of Oklahoma Press, 1987), 165–178; Julie Jones-Eddy, *Homesteading Women: An Oral History of Colorado, 1890–1950* (New York: Twayne, 1992); Chad Montrie, "'Men Alone Cannot Settle a Country': Domesticating Nature in the Kansas-Nebraska Grasslands," *Great Plains Quarterly* 25 (Fall, 2005): 245–258; and Katherine Benton-Cohen, *Borderline Americans: Racial Division and Labor War in the Arizona Borderlands* (Cambridge, MA: Harvard University Press, 2009).

40. See especially Susan Lee Johnson, *Roaring Camp: The Social World of the California Gold Rush* (New York: Norton, 2000); and Matthew Basso, Laura McCall, and Dee Garceau, eds., *Across the Great Divide: Cultures of Manhood in the American West* (New York: Routledge, 2001).

41. Wheeler case, GLO Records (first quote); Hedrick case, ibid. See also Jones and Wiswall cases, ibid.

42. Mitchell case, ibid.

43. While native peoples always left the Kawuneeche when winter descended, some American homesteaders resided in the Colorado River headwaters year-round.

6. CONSERVATIONISTS

1. Quoted in Lloyd K. Musselman, *Rocky Mountain National Park: Administrative History, 1915–1965* (Washington, DC: U.S. Office of History and Historic Architecture, Eastern Service Center, 1971), ch. 2. On Mills, see Alexander Drummond, *Enos Mills: Citizen of Nature* (Niwot: University Press of Colorado, 1995).

2. The best biography of Muir is Donald Worster, *A Passion for Nature: The Life of John Muir* (New York: Oxford University Press, 2008).

3. For a recent and influential pair of examples, see Ken Burns, "America's Best Idea: The National Parks" (PBS Home Video, 2009); Dayton Duncan with Ken Burns, *The National Parks: America's Best Idea: An Illustrated History,*

1st ed. (New York: Alfred A. Knopf, 2009). Of the many scholarly critiques of the "best idea" school of national parks historiography and hagiography, the most trenchant is James Morton Turner, "Rethinking American Exceptionalism: Toward a Transnational History of National Parks, Wilderness, and Protected Areas," in *The Oxford Handbook of Environmental History*, ed. Andrew C. Isenberg (New York: Oxford University Press, 2014), 282–308.

4. Paul Wallace Gates, *History of the Public Land Law Development* (Washington: Government Printing Office, 1968); Malcolm J. Rohrbough, *Trans-Appalachian Frontier: People, Societies, and Institutions, 1775–1850*, 3rd ed. (Bloomington: Indiana University Press, 2008).

5. E. Louise Peffer, *The Closing of the Public Domain: Disposal and Reservation Policies, 1900–50* (Stanford, CA: Stanford University Press, 1951). To be sure, violent territorial conquest marked the history of U.S. relations with indigenous nations from the 1770s through the end of the reservation period, but Jacksonian removal policies brought about a decisive intensification of this dynamic.

6. J. W. Morrill, "Birth of the Roosevelt National Forest," March 1, 1943, Folder 72A, Box 13, "Historical Files, 1900," Arapaho-Roosevelt National Forest Papers, RG 95, NARA–Denver.

7. Paraphrase of 1892 petition, in "Unanimous for the Reserve," *FCC*, December 29, 1898, 4; Smith Riley, and J. H. Hatton, "The Proposed Medicine Bow Forest Reserve, Colorado," 1904, Folder 327: "Boundaries—Roosevelt," Box 75: "Historical Files, 1900 Arapaho-Roosevelt National Forest Papers. On early proposals, see also *Colorado Transcript* (Golden, CO), January 23, 1895, 8; and "Unanimous for the Reserve," *FCC*, December 29, 1898, 4.

8. L. G. Carpenter, "Forests and Snow," *Agricultural Experiment Station of the Agricultural College of Colorado Bulletin 55* (Fort Collins, CO: Experiment Station, 1901); and Enos A. Mills and W. G. M. Stone, *Forests and Trees (Illustrated)* (Denver: Denver Chamber of Commerce, 1905).

9. Riley and Hatton, "Proposed Medicine Bow Forest Reserve"; C. M. Granger, "Report on Proposed Boundary Changes on the Arapaho National Forest, Colorado," June 25, 1909, Folder: "L-Boundaries 1908–09," Box 1: "Arapaho-Roosevelt National Forest, Alpha Files 1907–1973," Arapaho-Roosevelt National Forest Papers. The Medicine Bow Reserve became the Medicine Bow National Forest in 1907; in 1910, the North Fork area was placed into the Colorado National Forest; and in 1932, the remaining Forest Service lands in the Kawuneeche became part of Roosevelt National Forest. C. W. Buchholtz, *Rocky Mountain National Park: A History* (Boulder: Colorado Associated University Press, 1983), 28–29; Scott Thybony, Robert G. Rosenberg, and Elizabeth Mullett Rosenberg, *The Medicine Bows: Wyoming's Mountain Country* (Caldwell, ID: Caxton, 1985). 49.

10. Letter quoted in Buchholtz, *Rocky Mountain National Park*, 127; *FCC*, June 13, 1901, 2; and September 3, 1902, 2. On antireserve sentiments, see H. J. M. Mattis, "The Everlasting Timber Racket," *FCC*, June 20, 1901, 1; June 27,

1901, 2; August 15, 1901, 2; October 29, 1902, 2; and Michael McCarthy, *Hour of Trial: The Conservation Conflict in Colorado and the West, 1891–1907* (Norman: University of Oklahoma Press, 1977).

11. *FCC,* May 24, 1905, 2.

12. Typescript autobiographies in Folder 37, Box 1, Enos A. Mills Papers, CONS 250, Conservation Collection, Western History and Genealogy Department, DPL.

13. Quotes from ibid.; and Fred L. Holmes, "Enos A. Mills—Nature Guide and Author," *Independent* (Dearborn, MI), n.d. clipping, Folder 97, ibid.

14. Quotes from "Interest Children in Nature, Says Mills," *Omaha World Herald,* January 4, 1914; "The Tree Killer," typescript, Folder 65, Box 1, Mills Papers. On pet grizzlies, see "Lectures on Life in the Open," *Omaha Bee,* January 4, 1914, in Folder 75; on childhood education, see "Interest Children in Nature."

15. Emphasis added; quotes from Mills, "John Muir," undated typescript in Folder 42, Box 1, Mills Papers; undated notes in Folders 37 and 42, ibid.; and John Muir to Enos Mills, February 16, 1913, Muir Family Papers, HM 57349–57497, Huntington Library, San Marino, CA, available at http://digitalcollections.pacific.edu/cdm/ref/collection/muirletters/id/17867.

16. Typescript autobiography, Folder 37, Mills Papers; "Books and Men Who Make Them," *Chicago Inter-Ocean,* April 10, 1909, clipping in Folder 84, Box 1, Mills Papers.

17. H. Clark Brown, "When the Spirit of the Rockies Came to the Prairies," Folder 87, Box 1, Mills Papers. See also the press excerpts in *Enos A. Mills: Author, Speaker, Nature Guide* (Longs Peak, CO: Trail Book Store, 1921), 22.

18. Mills and Stone, *Forests and Trees* ("forest reserve"), 13; Enos Mills, "National Forests vs. National Parks," typescript in Mills Papers; Mills to J. Horace McFarland, August 19, 1911, Series: American Civic Association, 1901–1950, Box 18, J. Horace McFarland Papers, MG-85, Pennsylvania State Archives, Harrisburg ("vicious" and "devilish"); Mills to McFarland, May 7, 1913, ibid. ("blackmailing organization"); and Mills to McFarland, March 17, 1914, ibid. ("IRRESPONSIBLE power").

19. "Estes Park Should Be a National Park," *FCC,* September 22, 1909, 13. On Wheeler's suggestion and subsequent support, see Buchholtz, *Rocky Mountain National Park,* ch. 5; Jerry J. Frank, *Making Rocky Mountain National Park: The Environmental History of an American Treasure* (Lawrence: University Press of Kansas, 2013), 11; "How Estes Park Can Be Converted into a Gold Mine," *FCC,* February 10, 1910, 11. Mills later claimed that he originated the idea around 1906, on a visit to J. Horace McFarland's Mount Pleasant Press print shop—an epiphany McFarland did not recall. Mills to McFarland, February 12, 1915, Box 18, McFarland Papers; McFarland to Mills, February 17, 1915, ibid.

20. "How Estes Park Can Be Converted into a Gold Mine."

21. "Colorado's Climate and Scenic Resources," reprinted from *Denver Republican, Telluride Journal,* March 24, 1910, 1; Enos Mills, "From Enos A. Mills," letter dated January 26, 1910, published in *Longmont Ledger,* February 4, 1910, 4; "Discussions of Estes National Park," ibid., January 14, 1910, 1. For a debate on national parks and economic development, see Alfred Runte, *National Parks: The American Experience* (Lincoln: University of Nebraska Press, 1979), and Richard W. Sellars et al., "The National Parks: A Forum on the 'Worthless Lands' Thesis,'" *Journal of Forest History* 27 (July 1983): 130–145. On national parks and roads, see Paul Sutter, *Driven Wild: How the Fight against Automobiles Launched the Modern Wilderness Movement* (Seattle: University of Washington Press, 2002); David Louter, *Windshield Wilderness: Cars, Roads, and Nature in Washington's National Parks* (Seattle: University of Washington Press, 2006).

22. Muir to Mills, August 14, 1912, Muir Family Papers, available at http://digitalcollections.pacific.edu/cdm/ref/collection/muirletters/id/8620; Enos Mills, *Story of Estes Park* (Longs Peak and Estes Park, CO: Author, 1911), 102; Buchholtz, *Rocky Mountain National Park,* 120–137; Frank, *Making Rocky Mountain National Park,* 7–20.

23. Quotes from McFarland to Mills, October 29, 1917, Box 18, McFarland Papers; McFarland to Mills, April 20, 1912, ibid. On severed ties, see McFarland to Mills, December 28, 1914, ibid.; McFarland to Mills, September 25 and October 11, 1920, and Mills to McFarland, October 6, 1920, ibid.; and Mills to Rogers, May 3, 1914, Box 7, James Gamble Rogers Papers, History Colorado, Denver.

24. Quoted in "Let Every Man Sign Petition for Estes National Park," *FCC,* March 31, 1910, 1.

25. On Estes Park's strategic exclusion, see McFarland to R. B. Marshall, January 31, 1913, Box 18, McFarland Papers.

26. "Estes Park Should Be a National Park"; "The National Park," article reprinted from *Boulder Herald* in *FCC,* February 10, 1910, 13; "Estes National Park Discussed: County Commissioners Do Not Want Boulder County Land Included," *Range Leader* (Hugo, CO), February 12, 1910, 1; "Favors Estes Park Preserve: Denver Chamber of Commerce Anxious to Have It Established," *Oak Creek Times,* March 3, 1910, 4. On new park size, see "Discussions of Estes National Park"; "No Show for Estes National Park: Congressman Taylor Says State Must First Cede Territory to Government," *FCC,* February 10, 1910, 13. The park bill was further slowed by the conviction shared by McFarland and other preservationists that establishing new parks was a task that should await the establishment of a Bureau of National Parks. McFarland to Thorndike Deland, December 19, 1910, Box 18, McFarland Papers.

27. Smith Riley, "Report on Area Included within the Proposed Estes National Park," March 1910, Folder 424: "RMNP, 1910–1917," Box 90, "Historical Files, 1900," Records of Arapaho-Roosevelt National Forest.

28. Ibid.

29. Ibid.

30. "Commercial Body Reconsiders Plan for National Park," *FCC,* January 5, 1911, 1; "National Park Has Not Been Forgotten," *FCC,* May 12, 1911, 6. Mills saw the Forest Service lurking behind every discouraging word uttered about the national park. See, for example, Mills to McFarland, February 19–20, 1911, Box 18, McFarland Papers.

31. Minutes, January 3, 1911, *Proceedings of the Grand County Board of County Commissioners,* 2:n.p.

32. "To Make Estes Park a National Park," *Summit County Journal and Breckenridge Bulletin,* December 9, 1911, 8 ("strongest"); "Plan a National Park for Northern Colorado," *Aspen Democrat-Times,* December 21, 1911, 1 ("sitting . . ."); "The President and Estes Park," *FCC,* January 5, 1912, 6 ("asking . . ."); and Mills to McFarland, April 24, 1912, Box 18, McFarland Papers ("This campaigning").

33. R. B. Marshall, "Report on an Examination of the Area of the Proposed Rocky Mountain (Estes) National Park, Colorado," January 9, 1913, "Local History" folder, Box 13, "RMNP Correspondence, 1927–1953," Records of Rocky Mountain National Park, RG 79, Records of the National Park Service, NARA–Denver. On press coverage, see "U.S. Geographer Favors 'Rocky Mountain National Park' in Big Estes Region," *Denver Republican,* September 24, 1912, clipping in *Scrapbook, 1899–1906;* R. B. Marshall to McFarland, January 27, 1913, Box 18, McFarland Papers; "Bill Framed for Mountain National Park," *FCC,* February 7, 1913.

34. James Gamble Rogers to R. B. Marshall, January 29, 1913, Box 7, James Gamble Rogers Papers, History Colorado, Denver; Rogers to Mills, February 6, 1913, Box 7, Rogers Papers; "Bill Framed for Rocky Mountain National Park." On the size of different proposals, see Buchholtz, *Rocky Mountain National Park,* 135–136. On the name "Rocky Mountain," see McFarland to Mills, November 10, 1911, Box 18, McFarland Papers; and Mills to McFarland, September 16, 1912, ibid. On federal ownership of reduced park, see "National Park Bill to Be Introduced at Once," *Fort Collins Review,* repr. Estes Park *Trail,* July 4, 1914, 29.

35. "Another National Park," repr. from *Middle Park Times,* in *Steamboat Pilot,* January 14, 1914, 2.

36. Thomas quoted in "The National Park," *Steamboat Pilot,* January 27, 1915, 4; Enos A. Mills, "The Rocky Mountain National Park," *Estes Park Trail,* August 15, 1914, 32.

37. Buchholtz, *Rocky Mountain National Park,* 136; Musselman, *Rocky Mountain National Park,* ch. 2; "Boundaries of the New Nat'l Park," *FCC,* January 22, 1915, 2.

38. "Boundaries of the New Nat'l Park."

39. On "wilderness," see Mills in "Discussions of Estes National Park"; "Natural History: Notebook," typescript autobiographical essay, Folder 37, Box 1, Mills

Papers. For other terms, see "Colorado's Climate and Scenic Resources" (wild gardens); "Boundaries of the New Nat'l Park" ("connecting link"); "Estes Park a National Playground," *Denver Republican,* January 7, 1910, n.p., clipping in *Scrapbook, 1899–1906,* Box 2, Mills Papers ("wonder-spot" and "wonderland"); Denver *Post* quoted in Buchholtz, *Rocky Mountain National Park,* 136. On playground, see also "Estes Park a National Playground"; "Would Make Estes Park a National Playground," *Steamboat Pilot,* November 23, 1910, 6; "Parks and Playgrounds," *Steamboat Pilot,* February 24, 1915, 5. In a stock speech, Mills drew from a range of metaphors: "Nature is the kind, just mother of all. I imagine if she were to speak to us today she would say: 'Make Parks of my best wild gardens and I will help you. These playgrounds, real wonderlands, will be matchless schools for your children.'" See "Natural History: Notebook," Folder 89, Box 1, Mills Papers. In a later piece, Mills declared a "National Park . . . a university, a library, a museum, a zoo, and an art gallery in one." Enos A. Mills, "National Parks and National Life," undated typescript, in *Scrapbook, 1899–1906,* ibid. Contrast my emphasis here on the "playground" metaphor with the sharp critique of wilderness and its shortcomings as the basis for American environmental politics offered by William Cronon, "The Trouble with Wilderness; or, Getting Back to the Wrong Nature," in *Uncommon Ground: Rethinking the Human Place in Nature,* ed. William Cronon (New York: W. W. Norton, 1995).

40. U.S. Congress, Act of Jan. 26, 1915, 38 Stat. 798; U.S. Congress, Act of Aug. 25, 1916, 39 Stat. 535. Mills figured more centrally in the 1916 legislation than scholars have previously acknowledged; Mills to McFarland, November 19 and 28, and December 20, 1915, Box 18, McFarland Papers; McFarland to Mills, November 20, 1915, ibid. On the act and its legacies, see Donald C. Swain, "The Passage of the National Park Service Act of 1916," *Wisconsin Magazine of History* 50 (Fall 1966): 4–17; Robin W. Winks, "The National Park Service Act of 1916: 'A Contradictory Mandate'?" *Denver University Law Review* 74 (1997): 575–623; Richard West Sellars, *Preserving Nature in the National Parks: A History* (New Haven, CT: Yale University Press, 1997), 7–46; John C. Miles, *Wilderness in National Parks: Playground or Preserve* (Seattle: University of Washington Press, 2009), 3–41.

7. COMMON GROUND

1. Brian Q. Cannon, "Homesteading Remembered: A Sesquicentennial Perspective," *Agricultural History* 87 (2013): 1–29.

2. James D. Mote, *Holzwarth Homestead: Historic Structure Report and Historic Furnishing Study, Rocky Mountain National Park, Colorado* (Denver: Department of the Interior, National Park Service, 1982), 3, 5; Holzwarth case, GLO Records; quotes from oral interviews with John Holzwarth Jr., in Grand

Lake Area Historical Society, "Meet Papa Holzwarth," available at http://grandlakehistory.org/wp-content/uploads/2012/12/Holzwarth-Meet-Papa-Holzwarth.pdf.

3. "Conservationist Can 'Take It with Him,'" *Denver Post,* March 17, 1974 (quoted); Mote, *Holzwarth Homestead,* 14; and Holzwarth case, GLO Records.

4. Quotes from "Living the Life of a Dude," *Denver Post,* December 1, 1974; Kathleen Means, comp., "The Holzwarth Family: Holzwarth Trout Lodge, Holzwarth Ranch, Never Summer Ranch, 1917–1974, RMNP," May 2001, typescript report from Fleshuts Cabin, Kawuneeche Valley, RMNP, 7. See also ibid., 20–21; and Lynn Mohn, "Raising Pansies, Radishes, and Hell," *National Parks and Conservation Magazine* 49 (1975): 11; Grand Lake Area Historical Society, "Meet Papa Holzwarth."

5. On the demise of the family's cattle, see "John Holzwarth: Mr. Dude Rancher," *Denver Post,* December 1, 1974.

6. Wheeler case, GLO Records.

7. "Camp Wheeler: The Different Resort on the Grand River, Colorado," n.d., brochure enclosed in A. F. Potter to Commissioner, GLO, May 15, 1918, in Wheeler case, GLO Records.

8. Ibid.

9. Rocky Mountain National Park, "Park Statistics," available at http://www.nps.gov/romo/parkmgmt/statistics.htm. Park attendance figures from these early years are quite unreliable.

10. Quote from ARDNPS 1929, 119. On the stringing of telephone line, see SMR, July 1922; "Fall River Road Improvements Are Being Pushed Rapidly," *Estes Park Trail,* August 25, 1922. On winter headquarters, see SMR, October 1921, November 1922; and ARDNPS 1929, 116. On boundary marking, see SMR, July 1917; on the checking station, see SMR, July 1922; on rangers, see SMR, November and December 1918; December 1921; and January and December 1922.

11. ARDNPS 1922, 22 (emphasis added); and 1926, 14 (emphasis added). See also ARDNPS 1924, 10. On debates within the American Society of Mammalogists regarding whether federal campaigns against predators were going too far, see Thomas R. Dunlap, *Saving America's Wildlife: Ecology and the American Mind, 1850–1980* (Princeton, NJ: Princeton University Press, 1988), 50–52; and Peter S. Alagona, *After the Grizzly: Endangered Species and the Politics of Place in California* (Berkeley: University of California Press, 2013), 76–81.

12. My interpretation in this regard is inspired by Joseph E. Taylor III, *Making Salmon: An Environmental History of the Northwest Fisheries Crisis* (Seattle: University of Washington Press, 1999).

13. Christopher M. Kennedy, "An Outline of the History of Fisheries Management on the West Side of Rocky Mountain National Park" (unpublished typescript in author's possession, 2011), 1–3. This document references a

wide range of primary and secondary sources, and I rely heavily on the research and interpretations it presents. Grand Mesa Lakes and Trappers Lake were likely the major sites for the collection of Colorado River cutthroat trout eggs, with streams above Grand Lake playing a more minor role. Chris Kennedy interview with author, November 24, 2010, in author's possession and in RMNP Archives.

14. SMR, October 1916; October 1917; and September 1918; *Estes Park Trail,* September 3, 1926, quoted in Kennedy, "Outline of the History of Fisheries Management," 3.

15. Quote from Means, "Holzwarth Family," 19. See also Jerrett James Frank, "Marketing the Mountains: An Environmental History of Tourism in Rocky Mountain National Park" (PhD diss., University of Kansas, 2008), 205–207; Kennedy, "Outline of the History of Fisheries Management," 1–2. Kennedy attributes this competitive advantage to brook trout's larger size during the summer feeding season than cutthroats, which spawn in the spring. Ibid., 3. Fishery-reared rainbows were more likely to interbreed with Colorado River cutthroats than rainbows spawned in situ; Jessica L. Metcalf, Matthew R. Siegle, and Andrew P. Martin, "Hybridization Dynamics between Colorado's Native Cutthroat Trout and Introduced Rainbow Trout," *Journal of Heredity* 99 (2008): 149.

16. "Rocky Mountain National–Estes Park," *Overland Monthly and Out West Magazine,* July 1923, 18. William Philpott locates the rise of Colorado's modern tourist industry in the post–World War II era, but I emphasize earlier roots. See William Philpott, *Vacationland: Tourism and Environment in the Colorado High Country* (Seattle: University of Washington Press, 2013), 11–19.

17. Quoted in Alfred Runte, *National Parks: The American Experience* (Lincoln: University of Nebraska Press, 1979), 90.

18. Stephen T. Mather, "The National Parks on a Business Basis," *American Review of Reviews* 51 (April 1915): 429–430; ARDNPS 1922, 14; and 1921, 12; David Louter, *Windshield Wilderness: Cars, Roads, and Nature in Washington's National Parks* (Seattle: University of Washington Press, 2006), chs. 1–2.

19. Quotes from Allan B. Osborne, "Where the Rockies Reign Supreme," *Illustrated World* 37 (August 1, 1922): 876, 878; Florence M. Pettee, "The Motorist's Colorado," *Motor Travel* 11 (1919): 12. Sources documenting the road's construction include "Convicts Working on the Fall River Road," *FCC,* December 19, 1913; "Fall River Road Work Going at Slow Rate," *FCC,* September 22, 1916; "The Fall River Road," *Middle Park Times,* July 6, 1917; "Fall River Road Work Resumed," *FCC,* August 3, 1917; SMR, October 1919; "Fall River Road to Be Opened Today," *Summit Daily News* (Breckenridge, CO), September 25, 1920; "Fall River Road to Be Completed During Summer," *Steamboat Pilot,* April 13, 1921.

20. SMR, June 1918; August 1920; and October 1918. For a pathbreaking environmental history of automobiles, see Christopher W. Wells, *Car*

Country: An Environmental History (Seattle: University of Washington Press, 2012).

21. "Fall River Road Is Expected to Open on About Schedule Time," *FCC,* June 10, 1921; SMR, June 1921; and June 1922; "Snow Removed in Fall River Road," *FCC,* June 20, 1923; ARDNPS 1925, 120; and 1926, 131.

22. "Secretary Fall Greatly Pleased with Fall River Road," *Estes Park Trail,* September 30, 1921; "Trail Ridge Road to Cost Million," ibid., December 6 1929. On funding and techniques, see ARDNPS 1930, 141. On Indian trails and Trail Ridge, see, for example, "New Fall River Road Is Scenic," *Steamboat Pilot,* April 19, 1929; and "Trail Ridge Road Complete This Year," ibid., June 12, 1931.

23. "Trail Ridge Road Complete This Year"; ARDNPS 1930, 3.

24. Virginia S. Eifert, "Road to the Top of the World," *Nature Magazine* 46 (1953): 321.

25. Clarence Lee and Henry Nicolls cases, GLO Records. See also Charles Clark case, ibid.

26. Mote, *Holzwarth Homestead,* 19–21. In 1928, daughter Julia Holzwarth supplied a $13,500 loan for construction of the Never Summer Ranch; Mohn, "Raising Pansies, Radishes, and Hell," 17.

27. Means, "Holzwarth Family," 27 (quoted); Mohn, "Raising Pansies, Radishes, and Hell," 11; Thomas B. Muths, "Holzwarth Ranch, Rocky Mountain National Park: Historic Structures Report, Architectural Section" (Jackson, WY: AIA and Associates, Restoration Architects and Planners, 1979), 4–5; Earl Pomeroy, *In Search of the Golden West: The Tourist in Western America* (Lincoln: University of Nebraska Press, 1957), 168.

28. Lawrence Borne, *Dude Ranching: A Complete History* (Albuquerque: University of New Mexico Press, 1983).

29. For examples of antagonism between rural land users and state conservation authorities, see Karl Jacoby, *Crimes against Nature: Squatters, Poachers, Thieves, and the Hidden History of American Conservation* (Berkeley: University of California Press, 2001).

30. On the commission, see Hal K. Rothman, *On Rims and Ridges: The Los Alamos Area since 1880* (1992; Lincoln: University of Nebraska Press, 1997), 158; and Stephen R. Mark, *Domain of the Cavemen: A Historic Resource Study of Oregon Caves National Monument* (Oakland, CA: National Park Service, Pacific West Region, 2006), 72.

31. J. V. Leighou to District Forester, Denver, April 11, 1925, Folder 422: "RMNP, 1925–26," Box 90: "Historical Files, 1900," Arapaho-Roosevelt National Forest Papers, Record Group 95, Records of the U.S. Forest Service, NARA–Denver. See also C. W. Buchholtz, *Rocky Mountain National Park: A History* (Niwot: University Press of Colorado, 1983), 165.

32. Roger Toll, "Proposed Park and Forest Boundary Changes," December 8, 1925, Folder 40: "Chronological Survey of the Boundary Revision Proposals, 1925," Box 5, Series 2: L1417, RMNP Archives.

33. Quote from Allen Peck to Chief of the U.S. Forest Service (USFS), April 23, 1930, Folder 427, Box 91, Arapaho-National Forest Papers. On Boulder opposition, see Buchholtz, *Rocky Mountain National Park*, 165.
34. Russell N. Bradt, "Foreign Water in the Cache La Poudre Valley" (master's thesis, Colorado State College of Education, 1948), 10–12; *Wyoming v. Colorado*, 259 U.S. 419 (1922); James E. Hansen, *The Water Supply and Storage Company: A Century of Colorado Reclamation, 1891–1991* (Fort Collins, CO: Water Supply and Storage Company, 1991), 17–18.
35. Edmund B. Rogers to National Park Service (NPS) Director, January 17, 1930, Folder 37: "Chronological Survey of the Boundary Revision Proposals, 1930," Box 5, Series 2: L1417, RMNP Archives. On ongoing mistrust of RMNP by water interests, see "Colorado News of Interest," *Aspen Daily Times*, October 12, 1928.
36. J. V. Leighou to District Forester, Denver, April 29, 1930, Folder 427: "Rocky Mountain National Park," Box 91: "Historical Files, 1900," Arapaho-Roosevelt National Forest Papers; Richard Sellars, *Preserving Nature in the National Parks: A History* (New Haven, CT: Yale University Press, 1997), 52–53; Lloyd K. Musselman, *Rocky Mountain National Park: Administrative History, 1915–1965* (Washington, DC: U.S. Office of History and Historic Architecture, Eastern Service Center, 1971); Ethan Carr, *Wilderness by Design: Landscape Architecture and the National Park Service* (Lincoln: University of Nebraska Press, 1999).
37. R. O. Throckmorton, Clerk of the Board of County Commissioners, Grand County, to the Director, National Park Service, November 17, 1931, Folder 36, Box 5, "Chronological Survey of the Boundary Revision Proposals, 1931," Series 2: L1417, Boundary Adjustments, Rocky Mountain National Park: Land Records, 1915–1990, RMNP Archives; "Old-Timer," "Objects to Giving More Land to Park," reprinted in *Steamboat Pilot*, December 4, 1931. See also File 602, "Resume of Proposals to Change the Authorized Boundaries of Existing Areas," and "Report on Boundary Revision Proposals 1915–1947," RMNP. For a response, see Ray Lyman Wilbur to R. O. Throckmorton, Clerk of the Board of County Commissioners, Grand County, November 25, 1931, Series 2: L1417, Boundary Adjustments, Rocky Mountain National Park: Land Records, 1915–1990, RMNP Archives. For public expressions of NPS respect for private property rights in the area, see Edmund Rogers letter, quoted in "Grand Lake and National Park," *Steamboat Pilot*, January 23, 1931.

8. RESTORING THE VALLEY PRIMEVAL

1. Transcript, Harvey Johnson Interview with James Hansen, August 27, 1985, Folder 8, Box 1, Harvey Johnson Papers, Colorado Agricultural Archives, Morgan Library, Colorado State University, 6–9.
2. Ibid., 36, 73.

3. Ibid., 39–40, 79–80, 103. Johnson gave conflicting information on chronology, alternately stating that he was elected in 1934 and 1937.

4. Roger Contor, Memorandum to Director Midwest Region, May 14–15, 1972, Folder 56, Box 5, ROMO Land Records, RMNP Archives.

5. Russell N. Bradt, "Foreign Water in the Cache La Poudre Valley" (master's thesis, Colorado State College of Education, 1948), 14–16; Patrick McKnight, "The Water Rights of Rocky Mountain National Park: A History," typescript (n.p., 1983), 39; Johnson interview, 79–80; on volume, see "Grand River Ditch—July 1955," W-43, National Park Service (NPS) Water Resources Division, "Documents Relating to the Grand River Ditch in Rocky Mountain National Park," vol. 1, RMNP Archives.

6. Quotes from Vaughn, "Operations of the Water Supply and Storage Co., on the Grand Ditch," July 31, 1936, Report 2, "Water Supply and Storage Company" folder, Box 18: "General Correspondence Files, 1927–1953," Records of Rocky Mountain National Park, NARA–Denver. See also Reports 1 and 3, ibid.; Richard T. Hauff to WSSC c/o Ward Fischer, August 10, 1966, W-135, NPS Water Resources Division, "Documents Relating to the Grand River Ditch in Rocky Mountain National Park," vol. 2.

7. Canfield to Regional Director, Region 2, August 23, 1949. On persistent NPS complaints of the ditch as a "scar," see Jeffrey S. Hickey, "An Uneasy Coexistence: Rocky Mountain National Park and the Grand Ditch" (master's thesis, University of Colorado at Boulder, 1988), 178–181.

8. Robert W. Woods to Phillip R. Iversen, June 29, 1966, W-138, NPS Water Resources Division, "Documents Relating to the Grand River Ditch in Rocky Mountain National Park," vol. 2.

9. Granville B. Liles to Harvey Johnson, October 18, 1965, W-163, ibid; John Holzwarth to Wayne Aspinall, August 10, 1965, W-32, in ibid., vol. 1; Johnson interview, 136. See also Don H. Sherwood, petition, *In the matter of John G. Holzwarth vs. the Water Supply and Storage Company*, n.d., enclosure in Johnnie Holzwarth to George Hartzog, January 11, 1967, W-4, ibid. The Holzwarth family sometimes spelled the ranch Neversummer.

10. Fred J. Novak to Harvey Johnson, September 23, 1966, W-15, NPS Water Resources Division, "Documents Relating to the Grand River Ditch in Rocky Mountain National Park," vol. 1. A Google N-gram of "environmental movement" demonstrates that the word entered widespread English usage around 1968.

11. W. C. Worthington to Walter J. Hickel, Secretary of the Interior, October 12, 1970, W-91, ibid.

12. Theodore R. Thompson to William E. Hinshall, n.d. [1970], W-93, ibid.; Telephone message record, June 16, 1978, W-81, ibid.

13. Memorandum concerning Trip Report—Chambers Lake, Long Draw Reservoir, and Grand Ditch from Chief, Water Rights Branch, Water Resources Division to Thomas Lucke, August 8, 1986, Box 11, Folder 52: "L34-

General," Series 4: L24 Encroachment Files to L3417 Hiking and Riding, Rocky Mountain National Park: Land Records, 1915–1990, RMNP Archives; Jordan A. Clayton and Cherie J. Westbrook, "The Effect of the Grand Ditch on the Abundance of Benthic Invertebrates in the Colorado River, Rocky Mountain National Park," *River Research and Applications* 24 (September 2008): 975–987, esp. fig. 5.

14. Woods estimates the maximum drop in water table at 20 cm; his research shows that the water table was most affected near the Colorado, and less affected near toe-slope areas, where other sources recharged groundwater; Scott W. Woods, "Ecohydrology of Subalpine Wetlands in the Kawuneeche Valley, Rocky Mountain National Park, Colorado" (PhD diss., Colorado State University, 2001), 20–30. On peat bogs, see Rodney Chimner and David Cooper, "Carbon Dynamics of Pristine and Hydrologically Modified Fens in the Southern Rocky Mountains," *Canadian Journal of Botany* 81 (2003): 488. On greenback migration, see Christopher M. Kennedy, "An Outline of the History of Fisheries Management on the West Side of Rocky Mountain National Park," March 2011, unpublished typescript in author's possession, 2. More generally, see Sandra Ryan, "Effects of Transbasin Diversion on Flow Regime, Bedload Transport, and Channel Morphology in Colorado Mountain Streams" (PhD diss., University of Colorado at Boulder, 1994).

15. Johnson interview, 113–114, 177.

16. Lynn Mohn, "Raising Pansies, Radishes, and Hell," *National Parks and Conservation Magazine* 49 (1975): 12–17 (quote on 12); Lawrence Borne, *Dude Ranching: A Complete History* (Albuquerque: University of New Mexico Press, 1983), 4; Lawrence Borne, "Dude Ranching in the Rockies," *Montana: The Magazine of Western History* 38 (Summer 1988): 14–27; Jim Weir, "Dude and Guest Ranches in Grand County: Who, What, When, and Where," *Grand County Historical Association Journal* 6 (1986): 3–31; Kathleen Means, comp., "The Holzwarth Family: Holzwarth Trout Lodge, Holzwarth Ranch, Neversummer Ranch, 1917–1974, RMNP," May 2001, typescript report from Fleshuts Cabin, Kawuneeche Valley, RMNP, 7. On later hay sales, see "Ranch Owner Challenges Testimony," *Denver Post,* March 28, 1965; Dick Prouty, "Conservationist Can 'Take It with Him'", *Denver Post,* March 17, 1974.

17. Drury quoted in ARDNPS 1943, 207; and 1946, 307. For visitation numbers, see ARDNPS for the relevant years. On post–World War II tourism, see Borne, "Dude Ranching," 176; William Philpott, *Vacationland: Tourism and Environment in the Colorado High Country* (Seattle: University of Washington Press, 2013).

18. Mohn, "Raising Pansies, Radishes, and Hell," 12 ("starlit"); other quotes from John G. Holzwarth to Daniel C. Varty, n.d. [1949], copy in "Neversummer Ranch" binder at Fleshuts Cabin, Kawuneeche Valley, RMNP

(emphasis in original). On the Holzwarths' literary tastes, see Means, "Holzwarth Family," 8. More generally, see Robert G. Athearn, *The Mythic West in Twentieth-Century America* (Lawrence: University Press of Kansas, 1986).

19. Undated advertisement in "Neversummer Ranch" binder.

20. "Out among the Peaks and Pines of the Glorious Rockies," n.d., in "Guest Ranches" binder.

21. "R. L. Wheeler of Dude Ranch Fame Is Dead," undated clipping from unidentified newspaper, in ibid. ("little boy"); Pasquale Marranzino, "Gates Swing Shut," typescript copy of article from *RMN,* September 7, 1960, in ibid. ("dreamed the dream"); "Phantom Valley Ranch 1926–1960," n.d., copy in ibid. (brochure quotes). For more on Beattie and his background, see Pasquale Marranzino, "All from Hotel de Hardscrabble," typescript copy of article from *RMN,* 1958, in ibid.

22. "Colorado's Phantom Valley Guest Ranch," n.d., copy in ibid. Advertising brochures from other guest operations in the valley hit on similar themes as those emphasized by the Never Summer and Phantom Valley ranches. See untitled brochure for Kawuneeche Ranch, n.d.; Onahu Ranch, "Onahu Ranch: The Way to a Wonderful Vacation," n.d.; "Supplementary Information and Rate Schedule of Onahu Ranch," n.d.; and Green Mountain Ranch," n.d., all in ibid.

23. Diane Dufra Quantic, Linda Perry, and Pamela Maughmer, n.d., in "Memories: I Remember When . . ." binder, in ibid. Stephanie Fox Wetherill concurred, proclaiming her annual summer stays at "this place and the pack trips we took . . . by far the best times of my childhood." See Stephanie Fox Wetherill, n.d., in ibid.

24. Quoted in Means, "Holzwarth Family," 22. On deer, see ibid., 26. On the Holzwarth water system, see "Historic Chronology, Holzwarths," typescript in "Neversummer Ranch" binder.

25. On Holzwarth's sale of his beef cattle, see "John Holzwarth: Mr. Dude Rancher," *Denver Post,* December 1, 1974. The Never Summer appears to have continued to keep dairy cattle thereafter. On the size of Holzwarth's horse herd, see "A Dude Ranch Is . . . 1874–1986," *Grand County Historical Association Journal* 6 (1986): 13; Means, "Holzwarth Family," 21. On Phantom Valley, see Marranzino, "Gates Swing Shut."

26. Memorandum to Superintendent, Rocky Mountain National Park, Appraisal Report on Tract No. 314," January 25, 1950, Folder 5, Box 46, Records of Rocky Mountain National Park, RG 79, Records of the U.S. National Park Service, NARA–Denver ("principal use"); RMR, November 1939 ("to work"); Roger Contor, Memorandum to Allyn Hanks, September 6, 1963, Folder 006: "L1417 Boundary Adjustments—Boundaries 06/01/1963–03/27/1968," Box 4, Series 2: ROMO land records, RMNP Archives ("200 acres . . ."); Middle Park Soil Conservation District, Soil and Water Conservation Plan, Pontiac Ranch, May 29, 1963, Folder 41: "Housman," Box 8,

ibid.; Joseph T. Shubert, Appraisal of Housman Property, June 25, 1974 (quotes on Pontiac Ranch); interview, 1965, quoted in Prouty, "Conservationist Can 'Take It with Him'" ("When you've . . ."). On wintering horses, see Dan Abernathy, "Souvenirs of a Cowboy," *American Cowboy* (August 1996): 54; excerpt of Nick Brown to [NPS], n.d., in "Memories: I Remember When . . ." See also Jane Stotts, *Footprints on a Mountain Landscape: Tracking the History of 160 acres in the Kawuneeche Valley of Rocky Mountain National Park* (Estes Park, CO: Rocky Mountain Nature Association, 2005), 55–56.

27. A. E. Demaray, memorandum "Private Land Policy: Rocky Mountain National Park," October 1, 1951, copy in Folder 54: "Neversummer Ranch Appraisal," Box 7, ROMO Land Records.

28. Ibid. On the Park Service's travails during this period, see Ethan Carr, *Mission 66: Modernism and the National Park Dilemma* (Amherst: University of Massachusetts Press, 2007), ch. 1, 228.

29. On the Civilian Conservation Corps (CCC), see William Butler, "The Civilian Conservation Corps in Rocky Mountain National Park," 2005, typescript report on file at RMNP Archives, 2.

30. See, for example, Richard Ward, Memorandum to RMNP Superintendent, August 31, 1972, Folder 82, Box 9, RMNP Archives.

31. Victor C. Huffaker, "Appraisal: Phantom Valley Ranch (Tract 309) Grand County, Colorado," December 1, 1959, Folder 2, Box 7, ROMO Land Records; Philpott, *Vacationland*. For another accounting, see George McCaslin, "Green Mountain Ranch Appraisal," February 1, 1963, Folder 36, Box 8, RMNP Papers, NARA–Denver.

32. George Baggley, Memorandum to Allyn Hanks, August 2, 1963, Folder 006, Box 4, ROMO Land Records; Allyn Hanks, Memorandum to George Baggley, September 26, 1963, ibid. See also Allyn Hanks, Memorandum to George Baggley, July 26, 1963, ibid.

33. "Ranch Owner Challenges Testimony," *RMN,* March 28, 1965; Memorandum to park officials, n.d., Folder 56, Box 5, ROMO Land Records. The author's family was "going into the forty-sixth year of operation"—a statement that probably applied only to the Holzwarths.

34. Prouty, "Conservationist Can 'Take It with Him.'"

35. Steve Wynkoop, "Kawuneeche Valley Fate in the Air: Development vs. Return to Nature," *Denver Post,* February 3, 1974; "Rancher Sold Land to Save It," ibid., March 14, 1974. See also Lincoln Bramwell, *Wilderburbs: Communities on Nature's Edge* (Seattle: University of Washington Press, 2014).

36. "Holzwarth Ranch Bought for Parkland," *RMN,* March 14, 1974.

37. Roger Contor, Memorandum to Director Midwest Region, May 14–15, 1972.

38. Ibid.

39. For visitation numbers, see "Holzwarth Homestead Final Report for 1977," Folder 2, temp. Box 130, RMNP Archives. On haying, horses, and the Bruton

arrangement, see Larry D. Reed to Assistant Superintendent, May 18, 1984, Folder 6, Box 16, Ser. 5, RMNP Land Records, RMNP Archives.

40. Ibid.; James. B. Thompson to Kenneth L. Bruton, June 12, 1984, ibid.; James D. Mote, *Holzwarth Homestead: Historic Structure Report and Historic Furnishing Study, Rocky Mountain National Park, Colorado* (Denver: Department of the Interior, National Park Service, 1982), 27; Borne, "Dude Ranching."

41. National Park Service, *Rocky Mountain National Park: Final Master Plan* (Washington, DC: National Park Service 1976), 1.

42. Contor, Memorandum to Director Midwest Region, May 14–15, 1972.

43. National Park Service, *Mission 66 Prospectus, Rocky Mountain National Park and Shadow Mountain Recreation Area, 1957,* RMNP Archives, 5–6; U.S. Department of Interior, "A Report to the Superintendent for a Back Country Management Plan in Rocky Mountain National Park," May 1965, on file at RMNP Library, 48; National Park Service, *Rocky Mountain National Park: Final Master Plan,* 24 ("foot trail and backcountry use"). On older trail standards, see William Ramaley, "Trails and Trailbuilders of Rocky Mountain National Park," undated manuscript on file, RMNP Library, 39.

44. Jerritt James Frank, "Marketing the Mountains: An Environmental History of Tourism in Rocky Mountain National Park" (PhD diss., University of Kansas, 2008), 154–157.

45. Frank, "Marketing the Mountains," 216–217; Kennedy, "Outline of the History of Fisheries Management," 1–2; Richard Sellars, *Preserving Nature in the National Parks: A History* (New Haven, CT: Yale University Press, 1997).

46. Arno B. Cammerer, Office Order No. 323 ("The Fish Policy"), April 13, 1936, quoted in Kennedy, "Outline of the History of Fisheries Management," 4; Horace M. Albright, Memorandum to All Park Superintendents, August 6, 1929, paraphrased in ibid., 3.

47. R. A. Azevedo and O. L. Wallis, *Inter-Agency Lake Surveys and Trout Investigations, Rocky Mountain National Park, 1961, Including Ten Year Stocking Schedule* (Washington, DC: U.S. Department of the Interior, National Park Service, 1961); N. Guse and O. L. Wallis, *Long Range Fishery Management Plan, Rocky Mountain National Park, 1965–1974* (Estes Park, CO: U.S. Department of the Interior, National Park Service, 1965).

48. Frank, "Marketing the Mountains," 226–228; Kennedy, "Outline of the History of Fisheries Management," 4–6; Guse and Wallis, *Long Range Fishery Management Plan,* 1.

49. Kennedy, "Outline of the History of Fisheries Management," 6. Frank, "Marketing the Mountains," 230, 248; Roger J. Contor, "Aquatic Resources Management: Management Action Description" (Estes Park, CO: U.S. Department of the Interior, National Park Service, Rocky Mountain National Park, 1976), 1–2; United States Fish and Wildlife Service, "Rocky Mountain National Park Fisheries Management Report, 1979" (Lakewood, CO: Colorado Fisheries Assistance Office, 1979).

50. See http://www.nps.gov/romo/parkmgmt/grand_ditch_breach_rest_eis
.htm; http://www.nps.gov/romo/parknews/grand_river_ditch.htm; and
http://www.nps.gov/romo/parknews/pr_wssc_justice.htm.

51. United States Fish and Wildlife Service, "Rocky Mountain National Park
Fisheries Management Report, 1979," 9, 11; Bruce D. Rosenlund, Chris Kennedy and K. Czarnowski, *Fisheries and Aquatic Management: Rocky Mountain
National Park* (Lakewood and Estes Park, CO: U.S. Department of the Interior, Fish and Wildlife Service, Colorado Fish and Wildlife Assistant Office,
and National Park Service, Rocky Mountain National Park, 2001), 153; Kennedy, "Outline of the History of Fisheries Management," 6–7.

52. Kennedy, "Outline of the History of Fisheries Management," 7; Colorado
River Cutthroat Trout Task Force, *Conservation Agreement and Strategy for
Colorado River Cutthroat Trout* (Oncorhynchus clarkii pleuriticus) *in the States
of Colorado, Utah, and Wyoming* (Fort Collins: Colorado Division of Wildlife,
2001); *Conservation Strategy for Colorado River Cutthroat Trout* (Oncorhynchus
clarkii pleuriticus) *in the States of Colorado, Utah, and Wyoming* (Fort Collins:
Colorado Division of Wildlife, 2006).

53. Michael K. Young, *Colorado River Cutthroat Trout* (Oncorhynchus clarkii
pleuriticus): *A Technical Assessment* (Fort Collins, CO: USDA Rocky Mountain Research Station, 2008), 2, 4–6; Daniel C. Dauwalter et al., "Identifi-
cation and Implementation of Native Fish Conservation Areas in the Upper
Colorado River Basin," *Fisheries* 36 (2011): 278–279; Christine L. Hirsch,
Shannon E. Albeke, and Thomas P. Nesler, "Range-Wide Status of Colorado
River Cutthroat Trout *(Oncorhynchus clarkii pleuriticus)*" (Fort Collins: Colo-
rado Division of Wildlife, 2005), 14; Jessica L. Metcalf et al., "Across the
Great Divide: Genetic Forensics Reveals Misidentification of Endangered
Cutthroat Trout Populations," *Molecular Ecology* 16 (2007): 4445–4454; "Our
View," editorial, *Colorado Springs Gazette,* September 13, 2007; Chris Kennedy
interview with author, November 24, 2010, in author's possession and in
RMNP Archives; Jack E. Williams et al., "Potential Consequences of Climate
Change to Persistence of Cutthroat Trout Populations," *North American Journal
of Fisheries Management* 29 (2009): 533–548; Z. E. Underwood, C. A. Myrick,
and K. B. Rogers, "Effect of Acclimation Temperature on the Upper Thermal
Tolerance of Colorado River Cutthroat Trout *Oncorhynchus clarkii pleuriticus:*
Thermal Limits of a North American Salmonid," *Journal of Fish Biology* 80
(2012): 2431; Matt Hildner, "A Warning for Fish and Game," *Pueblo Chieftain,*
November 18, 2012.

54. A 1993 study of sedimentation in the valley could have applied to most any
other dimension of the Kawuneeche environment: "The valley," researchers
concluded, "should not be regarded as a pristine, undisturbed, watershed."
Terrence Toy, Donna Ryder, and David Longbrake, "Identification of Potential
Sediment Sources in Kawuneeche Valley Using a Geographic Information
System," *Proceedings of the Symposium on Geographic Information Systems and Water
Resources* (Mobile, AL: American Water Resources Association, 1993), 145.

9. THE TRAGEDY OF THE WILLOWS

1. Fred M. Packard, "A Survey of the Beaver Population of Rocky Mountain National Park, Colorado," *Journal of Mammalogy* 28 (1947): 225–226. A 2007 report, for instance, declared beaver populations to be "stable or increasing" throughout the Rocky Mountain region. Steve Boyle and Stephanie Owens, *North American Beaver* (Castor Canadensis): *A Technical Conservation Assessment*, USDA Forest Service, Rocky Mountain Region (2007), available at http://www.fs.fed.us/r2/projects/scp/assessments/northamericanbeaver .pdf, 3, 13.

2. Edward O. Wilson, *The Diversity of Life* (Cambridge, MA: Belknap Press of Harvard University Press, 1992), 178; J. L. Bronstein, "Our Current Understanding of Mutualism," *Quarterly Review of Biology* 69 (1994): 31–51; N. Thompson Hobbs and David J. Cooper, "Have Wolves Restored Riparian Willows in Northern Yellowstone?" in *Yellowstone's Wildlife in Transition*, ed. P. J. White, Robert A. Garrott, and Glenn E. Plumb (Cambridge, MA: Harvard University Press), 180–181.

3. Enos Mills, "The Beaver and His Works," in *Wild Life on the Rockies* (Boston and New York: Houghton Mifflin, 1909), hypertext at: http://abob.libs.uga .edu/bobk/beavwork.html. On the concept, see Clive G. Jones, John H. Lawton, and Moshe Shachak, "Organisms as Ecosystem Engineers," *Oikos* 69 (1994): 373–386; Clive G. Jones, "Positive and Negative Effects of Organisms as Physical Ecosystem Engineers," *Ecology* 78 (1997): 1946–1957; Justin P. Wright and Clive G. Jones, "The Concept of Organisms as Ecosystem Engineers Ten Years On: Progress, Limitations, and Challenge," *BioScience* 56 (2006): 203–209; Clive G. Jones et al., "A Framework for Understanding Physical Ecosystem Engineering by Organisms," *Oikos* 119 (2010): 1862–1869; Kim Cuddington et al., eds., *Ecosystem Engineers: Plants to Protists* (Amsterdam and Boston: Academic Press, 2011); Clive G. Jones, "Ecosystem Engineers and Geomorphological Signatures in Landscapes," *Geomorphology* 157 (2012): 75–87. See also A. M. Gurnell, "The Hydrogeomorphological Effects of Beaver Dam-Building Activity," *Progress in Physical Geography* 22 (1998): 167–189.

4. Robert T. Paine, "Food Webs: Linkage, Interaction Strength, and Community Infrastructure." *Journal of Animal Ecology* 49 (1980): 666–685. The best popular account is Cristina Eisenberg, *The Wolf's Tooth: Keystone Predators, Trophic Cascades, and Biodiversity* (Washington, DC: Island Press, 2010). For an anthology of scientific syntheses, see John Terborgh and James. A. Estes, eds., *Trophic Cascades: Predators, Prey, and the Changing Dynamics of Nature* (Washington, DC: Island Press, 2010). On Leopold, see Susan L. Flader, *Thinking like a Mountain: Aldo Leopold and the Evolution of an Ecological Attitude toward Deer, Wolves, and Forests* (Lincoln: University of Nebraska Press, 1974); Thomas R. Dunlap, "That Kaibab Myth," *Journal of Forest History* 32 (1988):

60–68; Christian C. Young, *In the Absence of Predators: Conservation and Controversy on the Kaibab Plateau* (Lincoln: University of Nebraska Press, 2002); Neil Prendergast, "Tracking the Kaibab Deer into Western History," *Western Historical Quarterly* 39 (2008): 413–438; and especially Susan Flader, "Searching for Aldo Leopold's Fierce Green Fire," *Forest History Today* (Fall 2012): 26–35.

5. Nelson G. Hairston, Frederick E. Smith, and Lawrence B. Slobodkin, "Community Structure, Population Control, and Competition," *American Naturalist* 94 (1960): 421–425; John Terborgh, "The Green World Hypothesis Revisited," in *Large Carnivores and the Conservation of Biodiversity*, ed. Justina Ray et al. (Washington, DC: Island Press, 2005), 82. On the ecology of fear, see Eisenberg, *Wolf's Tooth*, 39–42; Joel S. Brown, William Laundré, and Mahesh Gurung, "The Ecology of Fear: Optimal Foraging, Game Theory, and Trophic Interactions," *Journal of Mammalogy* 80 (1999): 385–399; W. J. Ripple and R. L. Beschta, "Wolves and the Ecology of Fear: Can Predation Risk Structure Ecosystems?" *BioScience* 54 (2004): 755–766; Joel Berger, *The Better to Eat You With: Fear in the Animal World* (Chicago: University of Chicago Press, 2008); Joel Berger, "Fear-Mediated Food Webs," in *Trophic Cascades*, ed. Terborgh and Estes, 241–254. Research on trophic cascades has stimulated roiling debates and controversies, particularly in the Greater Yellowstone Ecosystem. There, the resurgence of apex predators in recent decades has coincided with apparent improvements in the vitality of aspen and willow communities and rising beaver populations. Some scientists, however, hesitate to credit the return of wolves for these shifts. On these debates, see Matthew J. Kauffman, Jedediah F. Brodie, and Erik S. Jules, "Are Wolves Saving Yellowstone's Aspen? A Landscape-Level Test of a Behaviorally Mediated Trophic Cascade," *Ecology* 91 (2010): 2742–2755; Robert L. Beschta and William J. Ripple, "Are Wolves Saving Yellowstone's Aspen? A Landscape-Level Test of a Behaviorally Mediated Trophic Cascade: Comment," *Ecology* 94 (2013): 1420–1425; Matthew J. Kauffman, Jedediah F. Brodie, and Erik S. Jules, "Are Wolves Saving Yellowstone's Aspen? A Landscape-Level Test of a Behaviorally Mediated Trophic Cascade: Reply," *Ecology* 94 (2013): 1425; Robert A. Garrott, Daniel R. Stahler, and P. J. White, "Competition and Symbiosis: The Indirect Effects of Predation," in *Yellowstone's Widlife in Transition*, ed. White, Garrott, and Plumb, 104–105; Hobbs and Cooper, "Have Wolves Restored Riparian Willows?" 179. On recent impacts of predation by wolves outside of Yellowstone National Park, see Arthur D. Middleton et al., "Animal Migration and Shifting Patterns of Phenology and Predations: Lessons from a Yellowstone Elk Herd," *Ecology* 94 (2013): 1245–1256. On willow, aspen, and beaver, see Hobbs and Cooper, "Have Wolves Restored Riparian Willows?" 187–193; D. B. Tyers, "The Beavers of Yellowstone," *Yellowstone Science* 16 (2008): 4–14; and M. T. Tercek, R. Stottlemyer, and R. Renkin, "Bottom-Up Factors Influencing Riparian

Willow Recovery in Yellowstone National Park," *Western North American Naturalist* 70 (2010): 387–399.

6. Eisenberg, *Wolf's Tooth,* 42–45. I consider *all* humans to be animals; contrast this perspective with settler-colonial conflations of wolves and Indian peoples. Karl Jacoby, "'The Broad Platform of Extermination': Nature and Violence in the Nineteenth Century North American Borderlands," *Journal of Genocide Research* 10 (2008): 249–267.

7. On predator eradication, see Jon T. Coleman, *Vicious: Wolves and Men in America* (New Haven, CT: Yale University Press, 2004), 210–211; Thomas R. Dunlap, *Saving America's Wildlife: Ecology and the American Mind, 1850–1990* (Princeton, NJ: Princeton University Press, 1988), 5–61; Donald Worster, *Nature's Economy: A History of Ecological Ideas,* 2nd ed. (New York: Oxford University Press), ch. 12.

8. Quote from "A Routt County Elk Preserve," item from *Denver Republican,* reprinted in *Routt County Sentinel* (Steamboat Springs, CO), August 2, 1907. See also Lloyd W. Swift, "A Partial History of the Elk Herds of Colorado," *Journal of Mammalogy* 26 (1945): 114, 118; "Elk in Routt County," *Yampa Leader* (Steamboat Springs, CO), August 3, 1907; *Routt County Republican* (Steamboat Springs, CO), January 17, 1913.

9. Quote from "A Routt County Elk Preserve."

10. State game officials did allow limited elk hunts because "they are so numerous in some parts of the state that winter forage for them is hard to find." *Leadville Herald Democrat* quoted in "Steamboat Elk Meat," *Steamboat Pilot,* January 2, 1918.

11. Holzwarth case, GLO Records.

12. Charles Clark case, GLO Records; Clinton DeWitt case, ibid.; Harry B. Wiswall case, ibid.; Colorado State Game and Fish Commission, *Record of Beaver Hides,* 19237A, Colorado State Archives, Denver. On beaver abundance, see RMR, October 1939; Packard, "Survey of the Beaver Population," 225–226.

13. These population figures refer only to elk wintering in Jackson Hole; "A Plea for the Elk," *Telluride Journal,* November 2, 1905; *Aspen Democrat-Times,* February 24, 1911; *Durango Wage Earner,* October 5, 1911.

14. First quotes from Neal R. Guse et al., "Rocky Mountain Cooperative Elk Studies: Preliminary Report, 1962–1963," April 1, 1964, typescript in Folder N1427: "Wildlife 1963–1964," Box 14, Numerical Subject Files, Records of Rocky Mountain National Park, RG 79, Records of the National Park Service, NARA–Denver, 12. Population estimate and Toll quote from Jerry J. Frank, *Making Rocky Mountain National Park: The Environmental History of an American Treasure* (Lawrence: University Press of Kansas, 2013), 124. On transplantation, see also *FCC,* April 11, 1913; and March 20, 1914; Pete Barrows and Judith Holmes, *Colorado's Wildlife Story* (Denver: Colorado Division of Wildlife, 1980), 257; Russell L. Robbins, Don E. Redfearn, and

Charles P. Stone, "Refuges and Elk Management," in *Elk in North America: Ecology and Management,* comp. and ed. Jack Ward Thomas and Dale To-weill (Harrisburg, PA: Stackpole Books, 1982), 491; Swift, "Partial History of the Elk Herds of Colorado," 115. Small remnant populations of elk may have remained in the Kawuneeche as of 1913, but we have little clear evidence of their presence. George M. Wright, Joseph S. Dixon, and Ben H. Thompson, *Fauna of the National Parks of the United States: A Preliminary Survey of Faunal Relations in National Parks,* Contribution of Wild Life Series Fauna No. 1 (Washington, DC: Government Printing Office, 1933), 48.

15. The state's last recorded grizzly kill occurred in 1952. David Petersen, *Ghost Grizzlies: Does the Great Bear Still Haunt Colorado,* rev. and updated ed. (Boulder, CO: Johnson Books, 1998); Coleman, *Vicious,* 211–216; Michael J. Robinson, *Predatory Bureaucracy: The Extermination of Wolves and the Transformation of the West* (Boulder: University Press of Colorado, 2005); Peter S. Alagona, *After the Grizzly: Endangered Species and the Politics of Place in California* (Berkeley: University of California Press, 2013), chs. 1–3.

16. Horace M. Albright, "The National Park Service's Policy on Predatory Mammals, 1931," *Journal of Mammalogy* 12 (1931): 185–186, reprinted in Lary M. Dilsaver, *America's National Park System: The Critical Documents* (London: Rowman and Littlefield, 1994), 87–88; Wright, Dixon, and Thompson, *Fauna of the National Parks,* 110.

17. William Cronon, "Landscapes of Abundance and Scarcity," in *The Oxford History of the American West,* ed. Clyde A. Milner, Carol A. O'Connor, and Martha A. Sandweiss (New York: Oxford University Press, 1994), 603–637; M. P. Skinner, "The Elk Situation," *Journal of Mammalogy* 9 (1928): 309–317; P. J. White and Kerry A. Gunther, "Population Dynamics: Influence of Resources and Other Factors on Animal Density," in *Yellowstone's Wildlife in Transition,* ed. White, Garrott, and Plumb, 49; and James A. Pritchard, *Preserving Yellowstone's Natural Conditions: Science and the Perception of Nature* (Lincoln: University of Nebraska Press, 1999), 26–34.

18. Petition to the State Game and Fish Commissioner, July 1, 1929, *Proceedings of the Grand County Board of County Commissioners,* 4:214; *Middle Park Times,* November 21, 1929. On early problems around Estes Park, see Jerritt James Frank, "Marketing the Mountains: An Environmental History of Tourism in Rocky Mountain National Park" (PhD diss., University of Kansas, 2008), 281; and Guse et al., "Rocky Mountain Cooperative Elk Studies," 14.

19. *Middle Park Times,* November 21, 1929.

20. Resolutions, May 2 and September 6, 1932, *Proceedings of the Grand County Board of County Commissioners,* 4:342.

21. Through the 1990s, Park Service studies and reports on elk at Rocky Mountain focused exclusively on the park's east side. Stanley E. Broman, Memorandum to RMNP Superintendent, "Report on the 1953–54 Elk-Deer

Reduction Program in Rocky Mountain National Park," December 14, 1954, Folder N 1427: "Wildlife, Elk," Box 14, Rocky Mountain National Park Papers, NARA–Denver; "Elk Management Plan: Rocky Mountain National Park," January 1, 1961, ibid.; "Long Range Management Plan for the Eastern Rocky Mountain Elk and Deer," October 2, 1961, ibid.; Neal R. Guse, "Effective Management Program Requirements for Eastern Rocky Mountain Deer and Elk Herds," ibid.

22. Wright, Dixon, and Thompson, *Fauna of the National Parks*, 19–21.
23. Ibid. Figures quoted are for 1944–1945. The policy actually began in winter, 1943–1944, but "lacked general public support and was abandoned without much success." In 1949–1950, another 340 elk were killed; thereafter, "an average of 50 animals" were culled in each year of the 1950s. Guse et al., "Rocky Mountain Cooperative Elk Studies," 15–16. See also Frank, *Making Rocky Mountain National Park*, 128. The best recent interpretation of *Fauna No. 1* and its role in national park wildlife management is Alagona, *After the Grizzly*, 81–87.
24. John S. McLaughlin to RMNP Superintendent, January 4, 1955, Folder N 1427: "Wildlife, Elk," Box 14, Numerical Subject Files, 1953–1965, RMNP Papers, NARA–Denver.
25. Packard, "Survey of the Beaver Population," 227.
26. Quotes from RMR, June 1938, July 1938, and November 1941. See also RMR, December 1938, February 1943, and January 1949. *Fauna No. 1* had recommended in the 1930s that the park's western boundary be extended southward to encompass the winter ranges used by west-side elk, suggesting that McLaren and Holzwarth may have exaggerated the novelty of elk wintering along the Colorado; Wright, Dixon, and Thompson, *Fauna of the National Parks*, 107–108.
27. RMR, October and December 1938; quote from RMR, July 1945.
28. Jane Stotts, *Footprints on a Mountain Landscape: Tracking the History of 160 Acres in the Kawuneeche Valley of Rocky Mountain National Park* (Estes Park, CO: Rocky Mountain Nature Association, 2005), 45.
29. Packard, "Survey of the Beaver Population," 225–226. See also RMR, October 1939; and Barrows and Holmes, *Colorado's Wildlife Story*, 291.
30. RMR, September 1940 and September 1941 (McLaren quotes), November 1943 ("At Phantom Valley," all misspellings in original). See also RMR, October 1940. For more on the State Trappers Service, see Barrows and Holmes, *Colorado's Wildlife Story*, 297. Since landowners typically received 50 percent of the furs taken by lethal trapping, they had some incentive to lean on the National Park Service (NPS) to bring in state trappers.
31. Wright, Dixon, and Thompson, *Fauna of the National Parks*, 112–113. This section of the report would be quoted at length in correspondence regarding beaver management at RMNP; NPS Regional Director, Memorandum for RMNP Superintendent, November 9, 1942, copy in "Beaver

Studies" folder, Wildlife Management Monitoring Research, Natural Resource Archives, RMNP Archives.

32. RMR, October 1958. See also RMR, September 1956. The emphasis on beaver control remains widespread; see, for example, Dietland Müller-Schwartze, *The Beaver: Its Life and Impact,* 2nd ed. (Ithaca, NY: Comstock of Cornell University Press, 2011), ix, 181.

33. Quoted in Frank, *Making Rocky Mountain National Park,* 129–130.

34. Mark W. T. Harvey, *A Symbol of Wilderness: Echo Park and the American Conservation Movement* (Albuquerque: University of New Mexico Press, 1994); Paul Sutter, *Driven Wild: How the Fight against Automobiles Launched the Modern Wilderness Movement* (Seattle: University of Washington Press, 2002); James Morton Turner, *The Promise of Wilderness: American Environmental Politics since 1964* (Seattle: University of Washington Press, 2012), ch. 1.

35. Bernard DeVoto, "Let's Close the National Parks," *Harper's* 207 (October 1953): 49–52; John C. Miles, *Guardians of the Parks: A History of the National Parks and Conservation Association* (Washington DC: Taylor and Francis, in cooperation with the National Parks and Conservation Association, 1995), 185–219; Ethan Carr, *Mission 66: Modernism and the National Park Dilemma* (Amherst: University of Massachusetts Press, 2007). Figure quoted from ibid., 4.

36. *Public Papers of the Presidents of the United States, Dwight D. Eisenhower: Containing the Public Messages, Speeches, and Statements of the President, January 20, 1953 to January 20, 1961* (Washington, DC: Government Printing Office, 1958–1961), 1039; Rachel Carson, "A Reporter at Large: Silent Spring I," *New Yorker,* June 16, 1962, 35–99; Kim Phillips-Fein, *Invisible Hands: The Businessmen's Crusade against the New Deal* (New York: Norton, 2009), chs. 3–5; Paul S. Boyer, *By the Bomb's Early Light: American Thought and Culture at the Dawn of the Atomic Age* (Chapel Hill: University of North Carolina Press, 1994), 352–355.

37. Jim Matlack, "Were Those Shots Really Necessary?" *Longmont Times Call,* December 1, 1961; Allyn F. Hanks to Regional Director, January 15, 1962, Folder N 1427: "Wildlife, Elk," Box 14, NARA–Denver; "State Game Dept. Assails Shooting of RM Park Elk," *Ft. Collins Coloradoan,* January 12, 1962; and Folder N 1427, Box 14, NARA–Denver. For more on the larger conflict between the National Parks Conservation Association, NPS, state game officials, and sport hunters, see Miles, *Guardians of the Parks,* 219–222; Richard Sellars, *Preserving Nature in the National Parks: A History* (New Haven, CT: Yale University Press, 1997), 195–199.

38. Ted Trueblood, "Too Many Elk," *Field and Stream* (July 1963), 36; Cal Queal, "Limited Park Hunt Needed," *Denver Post,* January 21, 1962; Dominick quote from ibid.; Carver quoted in Sellars, *Preserving Nature in the National Parks,* 200; "How Many to an Acre?" *Estes Park Trail,* January 12, 1962.

39. George F. Baggley to Superintendent, January 1, 1962, Folder N 1427: "Wildlife, Elk," Box 14, NARA–Denver.

40. Allyn F. Hanks to Regional Director, January 15, 1962, ibid.

41. Allyn F. Hanks to Regional Director, February 7, 1962, ibid.

42. A. Starker Leopold et al., *Wildlife Management in the National Parks: The Leopold Report,* March 4, 1963, available at: http://www.nps.gov/history/history/online_books/leopold/leopold7.htm; last phrase quoted in Senate Committee on Appropriations, *Department of the Interior, National Park Service: Hearings before a Subcommittee of the Committee on Appropriations, . . . First Session on Control of Elk Population, Yellowstone National Park* (Washington, DC: Government Printing Office, 1967), George Hartzog testimony, 15, and full agreement at 102–106. For incisive analyses of the Leopold Report, see Sellars, *Preserving Nature in the National Parks,* 214–217, 243–246; Alagona, *After the Grizzly,* 92–95. Though in "keeping with 'scientific' management," continued culling at Yellowstone "was, to say the least biopolitically insensitive." James R. Peek, Richard J. Pedersen, and Jack Ward Thomas, "The Future of Elk and Elk Hunting," in *Elk of North America,* comp. and ed. Thomas and Toweill, 611.

43. Hanks to Regional Director, February 25, 1963, Folder, N1427: "Wildlife Jan. 1963–Dec. 1964 Elk," Box 14, NARA–Denver.

44. SMR, February 1964; R. Bruce Gill, "Elk Seasonal Movements," in R. N. Denney et al., *Job Completion Report* (n.p.: Colorado Department of Game and Fish, 1967), 192–200.

45. Sellars, *Preserving Nature in the National Parks,* 246–247.

46. Quotes from ibid., 247; and Karl Hess, *Rocky Times in Rocky Mountain National Park: An Unnatural History* (Niwot: University Press of Colorado, 1993), 22. See also Glen F. Cole, "An Ecological Rationale for the Natural or Artificial Regulation of Native Ungulates in Parks," draft paper prepared for the Thirty-Sixth North American Wildlife and Natural Resources Conference, Portland, Oregon, March 7–10, 1971. Cole was a leading researcher on the ecological roles predators played in the Greater Yellowstone Ecosystem. Peter Steinhart, *The Company of Wolves* (New York: Vintage, 1995), 243; Etienne Benson, *Wired Wilderness: Technologies of Tracking and the Making of Modern Wildlife* (Baltimore, MD: Johns Hopkins University Press, 2010), 73–80.

47. Adam Rome, *The Genius of Earth Day: How a 1970 Teach-In Unexpectedly Made the First Green Generation* (New York: Hill and Wang, 2013).

48. On transplanting, see *Control of Elk Population,* 15, 102.

49. East-side elk populations increased from around 1,000 head in the 1960s to perhaps 3,000 head in 1982. Hess, *Rocky Times in Rocky Mountain,* 26. Unfortunately, elk researchers continued to pay little attention to the Kawuneeche. For a suggestive anecdotal mention, though, see SMR, January 1964.

50. Richard N. Denney, "Moose for Colorado?" *Colorado Outdoors,* March–April 1967, 16. A 1949 study mentioned "the proposed stocking of moose." Gil-

bert N. Hunter and Lee E. Yeager, "Big Game Management in Colorado," *Journal of Wildlife Management* 13 (October 1949), 409. Underlying Denney's concern was a dynamic first noted by the pioneering ecologist Adolph Murie at Michigan's Isle Royale National Park in 1930: Americans had eradicated predators from the island, so when moose colonized it in the early 1900s, their numbers soon exploded, with disastrous consequences for the island's plant communities. Adolph Murie, *The Moose of Isle Royale,* University of Michigan Museum of Anthropology (Ann Arbor: University of Michigan Press, 1934), 39–44.

51. Denney, "Moose for Colorado?" 19; David M. Armstrong, *Rocky Mountain Mammals: A Handbook of Mammals of Rocky Mountain National Park and Vicinity,* 3rd ed. (Boulder: University Press of Colorado, 2008), 217–218; Fred Brown, "Opposition to Moose Diminishes," *Denver Post,* January 21, 1978, 2; David R. Stevens, "Moose in Rocky Mountain National Park," 1988, typescript in file: "Shiras Moose-Reintroduction," Natural Resources Box LL, Wildlife Management/Monitoring Research Records, RMNP Archives, 1–3. Ironically, state wildlife officials almost lost faith in the scheme; Hoover to Joe Van Wormer, March 18, 1970, copy appended to Denney, "Moose for Colorado?" in ibid.

52. On protected lands and endangered species protection, see the excellent Alagona, *After the Grizzly.*

53. Stevens, "Moose in Rocky Mountain National Park," 3 (quoted) and 9. Moose usually give birth to a single calf. Yet, in an indication of what one reporter termed their "penchant for Colorado," seven sets of twins were born in just the first five years after introduction. Karen Hinton, "Moose Herd in Colorado Grows to 85," *Rocky Mountain News,* September 6, 1983, 16; "North Park Moose Herd Booming," *Wildlife News* 12 (May–June, 1987), 4.

54. Stevens, "Moose in Rocky Mountain National Park," 6–15.

55. Ibid. 1–2. According to a recent in-house history of the Department of Wildlife, moose "appeared to be moving slowly southward; in 1978 the Division speeded up the process." See Barrows and Holmes, *Colorado's Wildlife Story.*

56. David R. Stevens, *The Deer and Elk of Rocky Mountain National Park: A Ten-Year Study,* NPS Service Report ROMO-N-13, 50–51, 62; Barrows and Holmes, *Colorado's Wildlife Story,* 265–266; Gary Gerhardt, "State Wildlife Division Aims to Cull Moose in North Park," *Rocky Mountain News,* April 16, 1992, 10; J. D. Dungan and R. G. Wright, "Summer Diet Composition of Moose in Rocky Mountain National Park, Colorado," *Alces* 41 (2005): 139. Stevens claimed that up to 30 percent of the elk herd actually wintered on "alpine tundra," including the Specimen Mountain area. Several factors probably contributed to growing elk populations in the Kawuneeche under the "natural regulation" mandate. First, some elk migrated across the divide because of a combination of "push" (overpopulation and range

deterioration on the east side) and "pull" (the elimination of the settlement landscape in the Kawuneeche, which eliminated competition with domesticated livestock and rendered private and national forestlands stressful, even dangerous places for elk) factors. Second, some elk from Middle Park probably sought refuge in the Kawuneeche as recreational development, housing, and water storage projects covered other stretches of Grand County.

57. Hess, *Rocky Times in Rocky Mountain,* 36.
58. Bruce W. Baker et al., "Interaction of Beaver and Elk Herbivory Reduces Standing Crop of Willow," *Ecological Applications* 15 (2005): 110–118.
59. Elk and cattle are "socially compatible"; and while the former focus on browse, the latter specialize in grass. Jack R. Nelson, "Relationships of Elk and Other Large Herbivores," in *Elk of North America,* 415–423.
60. Bruce W. Baker et al., "Why Aren't There More Beaver in Rocky Mountain National Park?," in *Wildlife and Riparian Areas: Colorado Riparian Association Seventeenth Annual Conference* (Estes Park, CO: Colorado Riparian Association, 2004), 85–90.
61. Ibid.
62. U.S. Department of the Interior, National Park Service, *Elk and Vegetation Management Plan—Rocky Mountain National Park, CO* (Washington, DC: Government Printing Office, 2007), vi–vii.
63. Kirk Johnson, "Plan for Sharpshooters to Thin Colorado Elk Herd Draws Critics," *New York Times,* May 28, 2006, available at http://www.nytimes .com/2006/05/28/us/28elk.html?_r=1&.
64. WildEarth Guardians, "Wolves in the American West," available at http:// www.wildearthguardians.org ("strong foothold"); and Rob Edwards, *A Vision for Wolves: A Report from WildEarth Guardians* (n.p.: WildEarth Guardians, 2009), i ("The time has come").
65. *WildEarth Guardians v. National Park Service,* 703 F.3d 1178 (10th Cir. Colo. 2013).
66. National Park Service, "Elk and Vegetation Management Plan Fact Sheet," last updated August 2012, available at http://www.nps.gov/romo/park mgmt/elkveg_fact_sheet.htm. The carcasses were distributed to the needy through a lottery system; thanks to the Great Recession, more than 5,200 people applied in spring 2009 to receive one of the thirty-three elk culled that winter. "National Park Sees a Stampede for Free Elk Meat," *National Public Radio All Things Considered* (March 14, 2009), transcript available at www.npr.org.
67. Woods estimates the drop in the valley's water table at 20–30 cm. Scott W. Woods, "Ecohydrology of Subalpine Wetlands in the Kawuneeche Valley, Rocky Mountain National Park, Colorado" (PhD diss., Colorado State University, 2001), 20–30; David Cooper interview with author, October 1, 2010, transcript in author's possession and in RMNP Archives; Kristen M. Kaczynski, David J. Cooper, and William R. Jacobi, "Interactions of Sap-

suckers and *Cytospora* Canker Can Facilitate Decline of Riparian Willows," *Botany* 92 (2014): 485–493.

68. Kaczynski, Cooper, and Jacobi, "Interactions of Sapsuckers and *Cytospora* Canker Can Facilitate Decline of Riparian Willows"; Cooper interview with author. My conclusions here align closely with Arthur Middleton, "Is the Wolf a Real American Hero?" *New York Times,* March 10, 2014, A21, New York edition.

CONCLUSION

1. Dipesh Chakrabarty, "The Climate of History: Four Theses," *Critical Inquiry* 35 (2009): 221. Observed levels of carbon dioxide at Hawaii's Mauna Loa in 2008 far exceeded those derived from air bubbles trapped in Antarctic ice cores that record more than 800,000 years of atmospheric change. National Oceanic and Atmospheric Administration, "Global Climate Change Indicators," available at http://www.ncdc.noaa.gov/bams-state-of-the-climate /2009.php.

2. Bark beetles and the fungi with which they associate date back at least to the Triassic. K. B. Sturgeon and J. B. Mitton, "Evolution of Bark Beetle Communities," in *Bark Beetles in North American Conifers,* ed. J. B. Mitton and K. B. Sturgeon (Austin: University of Texas Press, 1982), 350–384; Scott DiGuistini et al., "Genome and Transcriptome Analyses of the Mountain Pine Beetle-Fungal Symbiont *Grosmannia clavigera,* a Lodgepole Pine Pathogen," *Proceedings of the National Academy of Sciences of the United States of America* 108 (2011): 2504. The primary fungus is *Grosmannia clavigera,* but *Ophiostoma* is also present. Ibid., 2505.

3. Sarah J. Hart et al., "Drought Induces Spruce Beetle Outbreaks across Northwestern Colorado," *Ecology* 95 (2014): 936; "Annual Forestry Report, 1948," January 3, 1949 and "Rocky Mountain National Park 1951 Annual Forestry Report," January 21, 1952," in Folder 207–13, Box 18, Rocky Mountain National Park General Correspondence Files, Record Group 79, National Archives and Records Administration, Denver, CO; "Man and Nature Team Up to Defeat Mountain Pine Beetle in 1986," *RMN,* November 4, 1986, 14. On the mountain pine beetles' preference for trees above six inches in diameter at breast height (DBH), see J. A. Beal, "The Black Hills Beetle, a Serious Enemy of Rocky Mountain Pines," U.S. Department of Agriculture, Farmers' Bulletin No. 1824 (Washington, DC: Government Printing Office, 1939), 2; and Kellen N. Nelson, "The Effect of Mountain Pine Beetle Caused Mortality on Subalpine Forest Stand and Landscape Structure in Rocky Mountain National Park, CO" (master's thesis, Colorado State University, 2009), 11. Nelson goes on to point out that over the course of the current mountain pine beetle (MPB) outbreak in the Kawuneeche Valley, the beetles have grown less selective, now opting for smaller-diameter trees between 15 and 25 cm DBH (14–15, 19). *Dendroctonus*

ponderosae will even infect and kill trees as narrow as 10 cm DBH. See Niklas Björklund and B. Staffan Lindgren, "Diameter of Lodgepole Pine and Mortality Caused by the Mountain Pine Beetle: Factors That Influence Their Relationship and Applicability for Susceptibility Rating," *Canadian Journal of Forest Research* 39 (2009): 913.

4. Guy Kelly, "Return of the Pine Beetle: Epidemic Starting, Say Officials, with Trees from Vail Valley to South Park Infested," *RMN,* October 26, 1997, 20a (quoted). See also Gary Gerhardt, "Beetles Make a Comeback: Mountain Pine Beetle Infesting State's Trees," ibid., September 5, 1996, 24a; Gary Gerhardt, "Time Is Critical to Stem Epidemic of Pine Beetle," ibid., June 27, 1999, 32a. For authoritative accounts on broader and narrower scales, see, respectively, *Bark Beetle Outbreaks in Western North America: Causes and Consequences,* ed. Barbara J. Bentz (Salt Lake City: University of Utah Press, 2009); and Teresa B. Chapman, Thomas T. Veblen, and Tania Schoennagel, "Spatiotemporal Patterns of Mountain Pine Beetle Activity in the Southern Rocky Mountains," *Ecology* 93 (2012): 2175–2185. On the larger pattern of worldwide insect outbreaks, see Hugh Raffles, *Insectopedia* (New York: Vintage, 2010), 325.

5. Quotes from Jim Robbins, "Bark Beetles Kill Millions of Acres of Trees in West," *New York Times,* November 18, 2008. See also W. H. Romme et al., *Recent Forest Insect Outbreaks and Fire Risk in Colorado Forests: A Brief Synthesis of Relevant Research* (Fort Collins, CO: Colorado Forest Restoration Institute, 2006); Robbins, "Bark Beetles Kill Millions of Acres"; Nathan Rice, "Western Pine Beetles Munch Eastward," *High Country News,* April 22, 2011, available at http://www.hcn.org/blogs/goat/western-pine-beetle -munches-eastward; Catherine I. Cullingham et al., "Mountain Pine Beetle Host-Range Expansion Threatens the Boreal Forest," *Molecular Ecology* 20 (2011): 2157–2171; Christopher J. Fettig et al., "Changing Climates, Changing Forests: A Western North American Perspective," *Journal of Forestry* 111 (2013): 222. A slightly more measured assessment comes from a team of scientists assembled by the Nature Conservancy in 2008: "Many believe the mountain pine beetle epidemic, now nearly a decade in duration, might be unprecedented at least in recent centuries." Merrill R. Kaufmann et al., *The Status of Our Scientific Understanding of Lodgepole Pine and Mountain Pine Beetles: A Focus on Forest Ecology and Fire Behavior,* GFI Technical Report 2008–2 (Arlington, VA: Nature Conservancy, 2008), unillustrated version, 2. Byron J. Collins et al., "Post-Harvest Seedling Recruitment Following Mountain Pine Beetle Infestation of Colorado Lodgepole Pine Stands: A Comparison Using Historic Survey Records," *Canadian Journal of Forest Research* 40 (2010): 2452. One group of scientists claims that mountain pine beetle was "subsiding in 2008" in the Kawuneeche; see Matthew Diskin et al., "Forest Developmental Trajectories in Mountain Pine Beetle Disturbed Forests of Rocky Mountain National Park, Colorado,"

Canadian Journal of Forest Research 41 (2011): 788. The most recent study estimates that pine beetles have damaged roughly 3.4 million acres of forest in Colorado; Colorado State Forest Service, "Aerial Survey Shows Spruce Beetle Activity Escalating, Mountain Pine Beetle Declining," February 6, 2015, available at http://csfs.colostate.edu/2015/02/06/aerial -survey-shows-spruce-beetle-activity-escalating-mountain-pine-beetle -declining/.

6. Diskin claimed that the epidemic was "most severe" on the west side of Rocky Mountain as of 2008. Matthew Diskin, "Forest Regeneration Trajectories in Mountain Pine Beetle-Disturbed Forests of Rocky Mountain National Park" (master's thesis, Colorado State University, 2010), 6. Jeff Connor, personal communication with author via e-mail, September 21, 2011, in author's possession.

7. Kelly, "Return of the Pine Beetle."

8. Gerhardt, "Time Is Critical"; Romme et al., *Recent Forest Insect Outbreaks;* T. R. Karl et al., eds., *Global Climate Change Impacts in the United States* (Cambridge: Cambridge University Press, 2009). Nelson has since found that even after "broad-scale forcing [that is, drought] subsided in the middle stage of the eruption . . . this did not suppress populations [of beetles] because a positive feedback cycle had begun and beetles were able to overcome the defenses of healthy trees." See Nelson, "Effect of Mountain Pine Beetle," 18.

9. Jason S. Sibold, "Multi-Scale Subalpine Forest Dynamics, Rocky Mountain National Park, Colorado" (PhD diss., University of Colorado at Boulder, 2005), 28, 34–40, 48, 258–260. See also Rosemary L. Sherriff, Thomas T. Veblen, and Jason S. Sibold, "Fire History in High Elevation Subalpine Forests in the Colorado Front Range," *Écoscience* 8 (2001): 369–380; Thomas T. Veblen, William H. Romme, and Claudia Regan, "Regional Application of Historical Ecology at Ecologically Defined Scales: Forest Ecosystems in the Colorado Front Range," in *Historical Environmental Variation in Conservation and Natural Resource Management* (Chichester, UK: Wiley, 2012), 149–165; Dennis C. Odion et al., "Examining Historical and Current Mixed-Severity Fire Regimes in Ponderosa Pine and Mixed-Conifer Forests of Western North America," *PLOS ONE* 9 (2014): e87852.

10. Jason Sibold interview with author, November 22, 2010, copy in author's possession. "The limited available evidence," William L. Baker concludes, "suggests that fires will not be substantially changed in intensity or extent" because of bark beetle infestations." See Baker, *Fire Ecology in Rocky Mountain Landscapes* (Washington, DC: Island Press, 2009), 114. See also Wesley G. Page, Michael J. Jenkins, and Justin B. Runyon, "Mountain Pine Beetle Attack Alters the Chemistry and Flammability of Lodgepole Pine Foliage," *Canadian Journal of Forest Research* 42 (2012): 1643–1645.

11. Anthony L. Westerling et al., "Continued Warming Could Transform Greater Yellowstone Fire Regimes by Mid-21st Century," *Proceedings of the National Academy of Sciences* 108 (2011): 13169.

12. Fettig et al., "Changing Climates, Changing Forests," 219–220 ("mismatch" to "pathogens"); Megan M. Friggens et al., "Modeling and Predicting Vegetation Response of Western USA Grasslands, Shrublands, and Deserts to Climate Change," in *Climate Change in Grasslands, Shrublands, and Deserts of the American West: A Review and Needs Assessment*, ed. Deborah M. Finch (Fort Collins, CO: U.S. Department of Agriculture, U.S. Forest Service, Rocky Mountain Research Station, 2012), 1; Mountain Research Initiative EDW Working Group, "Elevation-Dependent Warming in Mountain Regions of the World," *Nature Climate Change* 5 (2015): 424–430. On modeling and assumptions, see Friggens et al., "Modeling and Predicting Vegetation Response of Western USA Grasslands, Shrublands, and Deserts to Climate Change," 3–4. The predicted years of disappearance are 2060 for alpine tundra in the Rockies, and 2090 for current subalpine cover. Fettig et al. estimate the future ecosystem "mismatch" only slightly more conservatively than Friggens et al., at 48 percent instead of 55 percent (219).

13. For a helpful discussion of this term and a defense of its application to the period since 1800, see Will Steffen et al., "The Anthropocene: Conceptual and Historical Perspectives," *Philosophical Transactions of the Royal Society A* 369 (2011): 842–867. Some largely celebratory accounts include Paul Kevin Wapner, *Living through the End of Nature: The Future of American Environmentalism* (Cambridge, MA: MIT Press, 2010); Michael Shellenberger and Ted Nordhaus, eds., *Love Your Monsters: Postenvironmentalism and the Anthropocene* (n.p.: Breakthrough Institute, 2011); and Emma Marris, *Rambunctious Garden: Saving Nature in a Post-Wild World* (New York: Bloomsbury, 2011). The best study of climate change deniers remains Naomi Oreskes and Erik M. Conway, *Merchants of Doubt: How a Handful of Scientists Obscured the Truth on Everything from Tobacco Smoke to Global Warming* (New York: Bloomsbury, 2010).

14. Sibold, "Multi-Scale Subalpine Forest Dynamics," 100–103, 106; Diskin, "Forest Regeneration Trajectories," iv, 13–14, 17, 39, 44–47; Diskin et al., "Forest Developmental Trajectories," 782, 788; Collins et al., "Post-Harvest Seedling Recruitment," 2455; Nelson, "Effect of Mountain Pine Beetle," 16; Dan Binkley, "Age Distribution of Aspen in Rocky Mountain National Park, USA," *Forest Ecology and Management* 255 (2008): 797–802; D. M. Kashian, W. H. Romme, and C. M. Regan, "Reconciling Divergent Interpretations of Quaking Aspen Decline on the Northern Colorado Front Range," *Ecological Applications* 17 (2007): 1296–1311; J. J. Worrall et al., "Rapid Mortality of *Populus Tremuloides* in Southwestern Colorado, USA," *Forest Ecology and Management* 255 (2008): 686–696; Dominic Kulakowski et al., "Compounded Disturbances in Sub-Alpine Forests in Western Colorado Favour Future Dominance by Quaking Aspen *(Populus tremuloides),*" *Journal of Vegetation Science* 24 (2013): 168–169.

15. Diskin et al., "Forest Developmental Trajectories," 791 (first quote); Veblen and Romme quoted in Allen Best, "A Sucker Punch to the Stomach: When Trees Turn Red," *High Country News*, August 17, 2009, available at http://www.hcn.org/wotr/a-sucker-punch-to-the-stomach-when-trees -turn-red. See also Nelson, "Effect of Mountain Pine Beetle," 1–2, 20.

◁ ACKNOWLEDGMENTS ▷

Many people and institutions have helped me bring this book to fruition. Mark Fiege, a wonderful friend and all-around force for good, first planted the seeds for *Coyote Valley* many years ago, when he called to ask me whether I had any interest in writing a contract report for the National Park Service (NPS) on the environmental history of the Kawuneeche Valley. Mark has proven an endless fount of energy and enthusiasm ever since. I hope very much that he, Maren Bzdek, and their colleagues will do me the kindness of claiming this book as a publication of the Public Lands History Center at Colorado State University.

The report on which much of this book is based was funded by Rocky Mountains Cooperative Ecosystem Studies Unit, Cooperative Agreement H12000040001. An enormous thank-you to Daniel Knowles and Brandon Luedtke, my indefatigable research assistants in the early stages of this project. Without their resourcefulness, skill, and hard work, I would have been up Coyote Creek with nary a paddle in sight. At the National Park Service, Cheri Yost got me started and never failed to respond to my requests for help. Paul McLaughlin provided a wealth of valuable feedback during the NPS review of my work. Ben Bobowski and Judy Visty advocated for the project from its inception, and I am very grateful for all of the help they have provided. Tim Burchett, former Rocky Mountain National Park (RMNP) archivist, helped me and my assistants delve into the park's wonderful cache of documents, photographs, and other sources. I also want to thank park staff for graciously hosting me on a number of visits, ranging from day trips in the Kawuneeche Valley to a couple of extremely productive writing retreats at McGraw Ranch. Though I sometimes take a critical stance toward the National Park Service in the pages that follow, I want to express my respect and gratitude for the difficult, essential, and often thankless work that NPS employees do.

The staffs of the Denver Public Library, the National Archives and Records Administration branch in Denver, the Grand County Clerk and Recorder's Office, the Grand County Judicial Center, and a number of other libraries and archives played critical roles in helping me and my researchers find the various historical sources that serve as the basis for this book. David Cooper, Chris Kennedy, and Jason Sibold shared their immense knowledge of riparian ecology, fisheries, and fire history, respectively. The University of Colorado Denver's History Department and College of Liberal Arts and Sciences also offered financial and logistical support during the report stage. JoAnn Porter helped navigate contractual challenges, while Dean Dan Howard and Marjorie Levine-Clark provided funding. I especially appreciate all of the many ways in which Myra Rich championed this project. I can never repay her for helping to bring me back to Colorado, but I hope this book can stand as a small token of my gratitude.

In the three and a half years that it has taken to transform the contract report I completed for the NPS into *Coyote Valley,* I have accrued many additional debts. Kathy Cahill and Rich Fedorchak of RMNP provided crucial assistance. My wonderful colleagues at the University of Colorado's Denver and Boulder campuses were always willing to lend an ear. Fellowships from the John Simon Guggenheim Memorial Foundation and the University of Colorado Boulder's Center for Humanities and the Arts, and a sabbatical from the College of Arts and Sciences, afforded me the time I needed to complete additional research, reorganize the manuscript, and thoroughly redraft every portion of it. Emily Seitz kindly gleaned documents on the campaign to create RMNP from the Pennsylvania State Archives. Coi Gehrig helped with photographs and engravings from Denver Public Library's collections. Ron Thomas and Isabelle Lewis devoted their cartographic talents to making the maps contained herein. Thanks also to Sherri Sheu for indexing the book.

I presented portions of the manuscript to historians at Syracuse University, Montana State University, Harvard's Charles Warren Center, and the Clements Center for Southwest Studies at Southern Methodist University; special thanks to Joyce Chaplin, Andrew W. Cohen, Edward Countryman, Andrew Graybill, Chris Kyle, Tim LeCain, Michael Reidy, Brett Walker, and their students and colleagues for making these visits so productive. I also profited from less formal discussions of this project at the Huntington Library's Institute for California and the West, as well as the West Network's 2013 gathering at Pingree Park. Andrew Cowell shared his illuminating work on Arapaho linguistics, thus laying the foundation for much of my introduction. Peter Alagona, Katherine Benton-Cohen, Kevin Black, Flannery Burke, Pekka Hämäläinen, David Rich Lewis, Pamela Riney-Kehrberg, Ian Tyrrell, Tom Veblen, George Vrtis, and Phoebe Young offered sharp and constructive criticism on individual chapters. Paul Sutter upped the ante by helping me rethink much of Part III; he also listened patiently as I tried to talk my way through many of the book's arguments. John T. Andrews—my father and a quaternary geologist extraordinaire—steered me through the unfamiliar terrain of the Kawuneeche's deep past. Martha Andrews discussed this project with me on several occasions; like my father, she generously shared her knowledge of various fields related to past human-environment interactions in the Colorado high country. I hope that all of these experts will recognize the fruits of their counsel in the preceding pages; surely, each will also wince more than once at advice I failed to heed. I am especially grateful for Ari Kelman. Ari was kind enough to read through a long, rough, and rambling report. Better still, he convinced me that there just might be a book hidden within. Ari also read several portions of *Coyote Valley,* always helping me to hone my thinking and my prose.

Holly and Rich Spurlin kindly shared their Grand Lake cabin, offering me the peace and quiet I needed to meet an important deadline. The McMasters and the DeLisis lent my family and me plenty of support along the way. Kathleen McDermott was gracious enough to take a chance on this book, and I am thankful for her faith in it and me, as well as for her keen editorial eye. Two anonymous reviewers from Harvard University Press did an admirable job of letting me know where my manuscript went astray—and where it was right on track.

I still get goose bumps whenever I contemplate the good fortune I have enjoyed ever since my family and I landed in Denver's Whittier neighborhood nearly eight years ago. From my bedroom window, I can just make out the faint outlines of Long's Peak. Our home, though, has given me much more than a sight line toward Rocky Mountain National Park. I am so grateful to my peoples (you know who you are!) for the friendship, love, and good times all of you bring to my life.

Last, but by no means least, I want to thank my wife, Amy Andrews McMaster, as well as our wonderful children, Santiago and Fiona. Completing this book often took me out of their lives when they needed me most. I appreciate their generosity in this regard. But I am even more grateful to them for the love, diversion, and sense of purpose with which they have blessed my life.

◄ INDEX ►

Addison, Frank, 63, 68
Alaska Purchase (1867), 139
Alencaster, Joaquín del Real, 47
American Civic Association, 148
Ammons, Elias, 154
Ancestral Puebloans, 65
Anderson, A. A., 122–124
animals, domesticated: and ecological
    impact, 103–104; in mining, 102; as
    property, 103
Anthropocene, 2, 249, 256
Apaches, 40
Appah, Tommy, 93
Appalachian Mountain Club, 171
Arapahos, 5–7, 41, 44, 51, 54, 68–71, 172
Ashley, William, 49
aspen (tree), 26
automobile tourism, 148, 163, 166,
    170–176. See also Rocky Mountain
    National Park: Fall River Road; Rocky
    Mountain National Park: Trail Ridge
    Road

Baggley, George, 203, 234
Baker, Bruce, 243–244
Baker, William, 99
Bancroft, Hubert Howe, 66–67
Bear Dance, 53
bears, stories about, 113, 115
Beattie, Irwin, 197–198, 200
beaver-meadow complex, 26
beaver pelts. See fur trade
beavers, 12, 26, 49, 132, 216, 223, 230;
    and beaver cycle, 231; ecological

significance of, 230–231; as ecosystem
    engineers, 217–218; and moose, 242;
    perceived overpopulation of, 231
beaver-willow communities: beaver-
    willow crisis, 217, 242–245; beaver-
    willow mutualism, 217, 220–221, 242
Benedict, Audrey DeLella, 10
bighorn sheep. See ungulates
bison. See Nuche: and bison
Black, Ruby (Antwine), 93
boosters, 110–111, 121
Boulder County, 181–182
Bowen Gulch, 97, 230
Breckenridge, 66
Brunot Agreement of 1874, 82
buffalo. See Nuche: and bison
Burnett, Benjamin, 98–99
Burton, Josephine, 127
Byers, William, 66

California Gulch, 66
Campbell Mining District, 97, 99–100
Capotes (Nuche band), 38. See also
    Nuche
Chamberlain, Allen, 171
Cherokees, 65
Cheyennes, 41, 44, 68–71
Chivington, John, 70
Christiansen, Markus, 127, 130
Clear Creek watershed, 66
climate, 40
climate change, 13, 250, 255–256.
    See also Anthropocene; glaciation;
    Pleistocene

Clovis peoples: and climate change, 28; diet, 28; and environmental impact, 28; and social structure, 28

colonialism, 60. *See also* federal government; fur trade; Nuche; Pike's Peak Gold Rush; Spanish Empire

Colorado Mountain Club, 4

Comanches, 40

Conejos Treaty of 1863, 78

conflict zone, 75

Continental Divide, 6

Contor, Roger, 188, 206, 209, 212

Coordinating Commission on National Parks and Forests, 180–181

coyote (animal), 4

Coyote (myth), 4, 52–53; in Arapahoe tradition, 4–7; in Nuche tradition, 5–7

Coyote Creek. *See* Kawuneechee

Coyote Valley. *See* Kawuneechee

Cozens family, 82

Crispin, Tom, 4

crops, 117

Cummings, Alexander, 69, 72, 81

Davies, Benjamin, 72

Demaray, Arthur, 200–201

Denver, 65, 75, 82–83, 171

DeVoto, Bernard, 232

DeWitt, Clinton, 223

Dinosaur National Monument, 232

disease, 42, 52, 60

Dodge, Richard, 51

drought, 40

dude ranches, 177–179, 193–200; appeal to post–World War II families, 196–197; environmental impacts of, 198–199; horses on, 199; meadow cultivation on, 199; and mythic West, 178; and new technology, 200; tourists at, 178; visitor reactions to, 198

Duncan, Clifford, 59

Echo Park Dam, 232

ecology, as emerging science, 225. *See also* trophic cascades: and ecologies of fear

Eifert, Virginia S., 175

1868 Ute Treaty, 79, 81

elk, 10–12: behavior of, 238–239; culling, 231, 246; hides and trade, 44, 49; hunting of, 32, 56–57, 73, 106, 226; impact on riparian ecosystems, 244; impact on willows and beaver, 239; migration of, 236; National Elk Refuge,

224; near extermination and population recovery, 221–222; nuisances posed by, 226, 229; reintroduction of, 222–224; relationships with plant communities, 225, 228; transplants from greater Yellowstone, 224; trap and transplant, 236, 238; Yellowstone herd, 234. *See also* lethal control; ungulates

Elk and Vegetation Management Plan of 2007, 245–247

equestrianism. *See* horses

eradication of apex predators, 220, 225

Estes National Park (proposed), 149, 151

Estes Park, 145–147

Estes Park Improvement and Protective Association, 146

Eutaws. *See* Nuche

Evans, John, 71, 77, 86

fashion, 49

Fauna of the National Parks of the United States (Fauna No. 1), 227–229, 231

federal government: and land ownership in West, 139; and land policies, 140. *See also* Homestead Act of 1862; Indian Wars; National Park Service; Office of Indian Affairs; U.S. Army; U.S. Department of Interior; U.S. Forest Service

fire, 107–108

fisheries restoration, 211–215. *See also* trout

foresters, federal, 140; and "great sponge" forest theory, 141

forests: moderating influences of, 141; public opinion toward federal protection, 142; water quality protection fostered by, 141

Fort Collins Chamber of Commerce, 151

Fort Halleck, 76, 78

Fort Robidoux, 49

Frémont, John C., 51

frontier nostalgia, 195

fur deserts, 49

fur trade: and alcohol, 49; and beavers, 49; and buffalo hides and robes, 47; and intermarriage, 49; and Plains Indians, 50; and Spanish, 46; and traders, 46; and trappers and Kawuneechee ecology, 221

Gachupín, Tomás Vélez, 46
Gadsen Purchase (1854), 139
Gaskill, Lewis, 99
Gaskill (town), 97, 101, 103
glaciation, 23–25
Gold. *See* Pike's Peak Gold Rush
Gold Hill, 66
gold miners, 66; attitudes toward Native
    Americans, 67; beliefs about govern-
    ment policy, 67; environmental impacts
    of, 70; faith in manifest destiny, 66;
    settlements founded by, 70
Grand County, 82
Grand County Board of Commissioners,
    109, 152, 184, 225
Grand County settlers, 86
Grand Ditch, 12, 117, 119–122, 140,
    180, 182–183, 186–193, 213, 248;
    aesthetics, 188–190; boosters of, 125;
    breaches, 189, 191, 213; challenges,
    125; construction of, 119, 122; ecolog-
    ical impacts, 125, 189, 192; greenback
    cutthroat trout, 192; labor, 124–125;
    myths about, 121; real estate, 123; and
    snowmelt, 122; and social progress,
    123; and tourist objections, 190. *See also*
    Johnson, Harvey; Water Supply and
    Storage Company
Grand Lake, 2, 63, 82, 129
Grand Lake Improvement Association,
    168
Grand Lake Mining and Smelting
    Company, 99
Grand River, 2
gray wolves, 26, 165, 168, 220–221,
    224–225, 246–247
Great Exhumation, 23–25
Great Gaskill Marten Massacre,
    113–114
Greeley, Horace, 84
green-world hypothesis, 218
Gregory Gulch, 66
Griswold, Gun, 4
grizzly bears, 26, 58, 144, 168, 224–225

Hanks, Allyn, 203, 233–236
Harbison family, 126, 128, 134
hats, 49
Hatter, Allen, 127
Hatton, J. H., 141
hay meadows, 129–132, 164, 199–200,
    207–208
Hedrick, Charles, 113–114

Hedrick, John H., 105, 126, 130, 132–133,
    136
Hetch Hetchy, 171
historical scale, 1
Holzwarth, John, Jr. (Johnnie), 162, 169,
    177–178, 185, 189, 195, 200, 203–207
Holzwarth, John, Sr. (Papa), 127, 133,
    161–162, 177; and Prohibition, 161–162;
    and taxidermy, 163
Holzwarth, Sophie Lebfromm, 162
Holzwarth family, 161; and dairy, 163;
    and Holzwarth Trout Lodge, 178; and
    Homestead Act, 162; and lumber, 162;
    and Never Summer Ranch, 178; and
    tourism, 163, 177; and trapping, 162
Holzwarth homestead, 129
Homestead Act of 1862, 118; require-
    ments, 128
homesteaders, 118; and agricultural
    ecosystems, 221; crops grown by, 118;
    and economics, 118; environmental
    challenges faced by, 127; fishing
    practices of, 134; food, 135; geographic
    origins of, 126–127; hunting and
    kinship ties of, 134; role in Kawun-
    eechee ecology, 221; possessions of,
    130; relationships to elk, 221; seasonal
    economic adaptations of, 133–134; tree
    cutting by, 221; and wage work,
    135–136; women, 134–135
homesteads: gardens on, 132; home
    construction, 129; livestock, 130;
    structures on, 133; topography of,
    129; water and, 130
Hopis, 70
horses, 36, 42–43; as agents of change
    in indigenous societies, 43; ecological
    niche occupied by, 45; Nuche use of,
    43–45, 54, 63–64, 72, 75; role in Nuche
    dispossession, 83–91
Hotel de Hardscrabble, 129, 164–166;
    as camp, 164; food at, 165; and tourist
    economy, 165
Hot Sulphur Springs, 63, 66, 82
House, Al, 167
Hunt, Alexander, 73

Indian Peaks, 181–182
Indian Wars, 139
irrigation, 118

James, Thomas, 34, 39, 42, 45, 47, 51
Johnson (Canalla), 89

Johnson, Harvey, 185–193, 213
Jones, Jacob, 136
Junction Ranch, 63–64, 82

Kawauneechee (Coyote Valley): aesthetics, 115; ecosystems, 8–11;
environmental changes, 12; geography,
8; geology, 21–23; meaning of name,
4–5; Pleistocene climate change, 26;
Pleistocene ecology, 26; Pleistocene
population, 30; Romanticism, 116;
stakeholder groups, 13
Kiowas, 40

Laramide Orogeny (Laramide Revolution), 22
Lead Mountain Mining District, 97,
101
Leadville National Fish Hatchery, 168
Lechat (Nuche leader), 34–36, 45, 47,
51, 60
Lee, Clarence, 126, 177
Leighou, J. V., 180–181, 183
Leopold, Aldo, 1, 218
Leopold, Starker, 235
Leopold Commission, 235–236
lethal control, of ungulate populations,
222, 227–228, 231–233, 235–236, 245
lethal regulation. *See* lethal control
lodgepole pines, 12, 26, 54–55, 61, 131,
133, 251–254
logging. *See* timber
Long's Peak Inn, 145
Lulu City, 97, 99, 101
lumber. *See* timber

Macy, Abram, 128
maize-based agriculture, 40
market hunters, 105
Marshall, Robert B., 152
Martens. *See* Great Gaskill Marten
Massacre
Mather, Stephen, 167–168, 171, 175
McCook, Edward, 67–69, 73, 76, 79, 83;
attitudes toward Nuche, 68, 71
McFarland, J. Horace, 148–149, 156–157,
170–171
McKinley, Francis, 92
McLaren, Fred, 228–230
Medicine Bow Forest Reserve, 134, 140,
142, 146, 164
Meeker, Nathan, 81, 83–84, 140; as agent
to White River Utes, 84–86, 88;

campaign against Nuche horses, 85–86,
89; and Ute War, 88–91
Mestas (Nuche trader), 47
Middle Park, 28, 31, 49, 54, 63, 66, 78,
81, 222–225
Middle Park and Grand River Mining
and Land Improvement Company, 99
Mills, Enos, 138, 142, 152–154, 164,
170, 180; animus toward U.S. Forest
Service, 146; background and early
career of, 142–144, 156; eccentricities
of, 144; and elk, 222; nature guiding,
145; plan for protecting land near
Estes Park, 146–148; relationship to
John Muir, 142, 144; role in passage
of National Park Service Organic Act
of 1916, 157; work as lecturer and
author, 145; writings on beavers, 218
miners. *See* North Fork Mineral Boom;
Pike's Peak Gold Rush
mining towns: descriptions of, 102–103;
mining claims, 101; population
composition of, 100; real estate market,
101
Mitchell, Benjamin, 136
moose, 12; impacts on beaver and
willow, 243; introduction to Colorado,
239–242
Mormons, 38, 52
mountain lions, stories about, 115
mountain pine beetle *(Dendroctonus
ponderosae)*, 12, 251; and climate,
253–254; consequences for forest
health, 256–257; effect of wildfire,
253–254; life cycle of, 251; lodgepole
pine as food source, 251; western
North American epidemic of 1990s
and 2000s, 251–253
Mountain Tradition peoples, 29; and
climate change, 30; diet of, 31; as
ecological actors, 32; environmental
impact of, 33; impact on ungulates,
29; reactions to climate change, 30;
sacred sites of, 32–33; social and
political life, 31; technology of, 29–30;
and topography, 29; transhumance
rounds, 31–32
Muaches (Nuche band), 38. *See also*
Nuche
Muir, John, 138, 144, 148; influence
on Enos Mills, 144–145
mule deer. *See* ungulates
mythic West, 194, 197

National Park Service, 167; buyout of Coyote Valley lands, 187; fisheries policy, 168–170, 211–215; and management of beetle-killed trees, 12; and management of homesteads, 201–203, 206–209; management of Kawuneechee, 187; and Mission 66, 201, 204, 209, 232–233; and new national parks, 182; and Organic Act of 1916, 157; and park attendance, 171–172; and park rangers in Rocky Mountain National Park, 167; and predator eradication campaigns, 167–168; and restrictions, 167

Native American place names, 4

Natural regulation of ungulate populations, 237–244

Navajos, 70

Never Summer Mountains, 22–23

Never Summer Ranch, 193; sale to National Park Service, 204–205; and tourism, 193–197

Nicholls, Henry, 177

Nicolay, John, 78–79

1916 National Park Service Organic Act, 200–201

North Fork Mineral Boom: and animals, 103; and boosters, 99–102; and doubters, 99; and ecological impact of miners' foodways, 104–106; and economic constraints, 111; environmental impact of, 112; failure of, 111; and fishing, 105; geologic constraints faced by, 112; legacies of, 112–113; mineral deposits, 111; mineral refining, 100; and miners' beliefs, 101; 110; profit, 100; and reliance on outside resources, 109; and town development, 99; and weather, 109, 112

Nuche, 5, 139–140; and accusations of environmental destruction by Anglos, 86–87; and adaptations, 249; American beliefs about, 77; animal skins, 58; and Arapahos, 51; artifacts, 39; baskets, 55; beds, 55; and beef, 80; and bison, 44, 50–51, 71–75; ceramics, 39, 55; continuity with Mountain Tradition, 41, 60; diet, 56; and dispossession, 65, 68, 92; division of labor, 56; dwellings, 54–55; and ecological impact, 61–62; encampments, 54; and enemies, 51; exchange networks, 40; federal government policy toward, 72, 78–80;

and fire, 62, 87–88; fishing, 57; foodways, 56–57; and fur trade, 46–50; and game, 52, 56; and game decline, 72–73; gender, 56; gender and deerskin, 46; Grand River band, 79; hides, 44; "horse property," 93; and horses, 36, 42–45, 81, 85, 93; hunting, 44, 50, 93; and knowledge of landscape, 75–76, 81; and land base, 52; meat processing techniques, 56–57, 59; medicine, 56; and modern stereotypes, 61; political structure, 37–38; possessions, 55; and relationships with Americans, 71; resistance to outsiders, 81–82; response to assaults on enemies, 70–71; seasonal movement, 53; social structure, 39; and Spanish, 41–42; spiritual beliefs, 58–59; survival strategies, 51; tools, 55–56; and trade, 73, 75; transhumance migration cycles, 39, 53, 72–73; travel routes, 54; weapons of, 55–56; White River band, 79, 81; Yamparika band, 79

Office of Indian Affairs, 80

Oñate, Don Juan de, 41

Oregon Treaty (1846), 139

Organic Act of 1916, 157

Osborne, Allan, 172

Ouray (Uncompaghre Nuche leader), 77–78, 89

Ouray Reservation, 92–93

peat fens, 132–133, 192

Phantom Valley Ranch, 19, 203–207

Pike's Peak Gold Rush, 64–65, 117; and animals, 72; gold deposits, 65; and Kawuneechee (Coyote Valley), 81

Pinchot, Gifford, 145–146

pine beetle. *See* mountain pine beetle

Pitkin, Frederick, 88

Platte River watershed, 117

Pleistocene, 2, 23–25, 249

Powell, John Wesley, 52, 57–59

Powell Park, 86

predator eradication, 167–168, 226. *See also* gray wolves; grizzly bears

pristine myth, 61

Pueblo Revolt of 1680, 42

railroads, 82, 110

Riley, Smith, 141, 150–151

roads, 82, 109–110, 112, 147, 170–176;
    building process, 110; ecological
    impact, 110, 173
Rocky Mountain Fur Trade System, 46,
    49. *See also* fur trade
Rocky Mountain National Park, 138;
    automobile tourism in, 170–172;
    backpackers, 209–210; boundaries,
    154, 180; Congressional establishment,
    155; Fall River Road, 172–174;
    Holzwarth homestead and living
    history museum, 206–208; mandates,
    156; and metropolitan growth, 203;
    naming of, 153; Never Summer
    Boundary Extension Act, 183; 1925
    Park Expansion Plan, 181; 1976 *Final
    Master Plan*, 209; and "playground
    ideal," 157; proposals on size, 150;
    reactions to proposed expansion,
    181–182; and regional economy, 170,
    176; road construction in, 170–176;
    tourist-oriented preservation, 158; Trail
    Ridge Road, 174–175, 188; trails,
    209–210; visitation, 194
Rocky Mountain National Park advocates,
    140, 149, 153–154; opinions of U.S.
    Forest Service, 149; "playground" ideal,
    148; vision of park, 149
Rogers, Edmund, 183
Rogers, James Grafton, 4, 148–149, 153,
    156
Rossiter, Raymond, 99
Russell, William Green, 65, 68
Russell Gulch, 66

Sage, Rufus, 49
Sage, Sherman, 4
Sand Creek Massacre (1864), 70
settler colonialism, 69
Seymour, Charles, 127
Shafroth, John, 154
Shipler, Joseph, 98
Smith, Anne, 44, 54
Spanish Empire, 41–42
Stanley, Freelan, 148
Stone, Sam, 129, 132

Tabeguaches. *See* Uncompahgres
Tabernash (Nuche leader), 63, 68,
    81, 89
Taylor, Edward, 2–4, 154
Teller, Henry, 83–84
tepees, 55

Thompson, Charles, 154
Thompson, James, 75, 88
timber, 106–107, 141; and ecological
    impact of logging, 107–108
Toll, Oliver, 4, 22, 54
Toll, Roger, 167, 181
tourism economy, 163–166
trade goods, 49
transportation networks, 82. *See also*
    roads
trappers. *See* fur trade
Treaty of Guadalupe Hidalgo (1848), 52,
    139
Treaty of Middle Park, 79, 81
trophic cascades, 218–220, 244, 246;
    and ecologies of fear, 219–220, 222
trout, 9, 13, 168–170, 211–215; brook,
    168–169, 212–214; Colorado River
    cutthroat, 105, 169–170, 214; cutthroat,
    215, 221; and fisheries restoration,
    211–215; and gene pool, 169, 192,
    214; greenback, 192; and Nuche, 57,
    221; rainbow, 168–169; sport fishing
    and, 211; and stocking, 168–170;
    Yellowstone cutthroat, 211–212

Uintah Reservation, 92-93
Uncompahgres (Nuche band, also known
    as Tabeguaches), 38, 72, 75, 77–78,
    91–92; and life on reservation, 92. *See
    also* Nuche
ungulates, 26, 29–32, 53, 220–221, 224;
    and management of in national parks,
    227–228; and natural regulation policy
    in Rocky Mountain National Park,
    243–245. *See also* elk; moose
U.S. Army, 70, 76
U.S. Civil War, 77
U.S. Department of Interior, 140
U.S. Forest Service, policies of, 141–142
U.S. Geologic Survey, and place
    names, 4
Utahs. *See* Nuche
Ute Reservation, 82
Utes. *See* Nuche
Ute War, 64–65, 81, 88–91, 249

Vaile, Henry, 72–75, 87
Vaughn, Sterling, 188
virgin soil epidemics. *See* disease

Waldron, Wilson, 87
watershed protection, 141

Water Supply and Storage Company (Water Supply): 117, 124, 126, 140, 180, 182–183, 185–193, 213; organization, 119–120; shareholders, 121. *See also* Grand Ditch

Weber, Edward, 99

Wheeler, Herbert, 146, 156

Wheeler, "Squeaky" Bob, 129, 164–166; and wage work, 135–136

White River Agency, 64, 76, 83; and treaty provisions, 83–84

White River Nuche, 85, 93; conflict with Americans in Middle Park, 63

wickiups, 54

wildfire. *See* Nuche: and fire

wildlife eradication, 72. *See also* elk; gray wolves; grizzly bears; predator eradication

willows, 12, 26, 132, 216, 229; and red-napped sapsuckers, 248; threatened by *Cytopora* fungi, 248. *See also* beaver-willow communities

Wilson, Woodrow, 3, 155

Wiminuche (Nuche band), 38. *See also* Nuche

Wirth, Conrad, 232

Wiswall, Harry Bruce, 223

Wolf (myth), 6, 52–53, 85

Wolverine Lode, 99–100

Wright, George, 227

Wynkoop, Edward, 77

Wyoming v. Colorado (1922), 182

Yampa Valley, 82

Yutas. *See* Nuche